D0845185

The Social Milieu
of Alexander Pope

1. Jonathan Richardson, *Alexander Pope, 22 Feb. 1736.* By kind permission of Dr. Dallas Pratt, New York City.

THE
SOCIAL MILIEU
OF
ALEXANDER POPE

LIVES, EXAMPLE AND THE POETIC RESPONSE

HOWARD ERSKINE-HILL

YALE UNIVERSITY PRESS

NEW HAVEN AND LONDON

1975

Published in Great Britain, Europe, and Africa by Yale University
Press, Ltd., London.
Distributed in Latin America by Kaiman & Polon, Inc., New
York City; in India by UBS Publishers' Distributors Pvt., Ltd.,
Delhi; in Japan by John Weatherhill, Inc., Tokyo.

Library of Congress catalog card number: 74-29719
International standard book number: 0 300 01837-1

Designed by John Nicoll and set in Monophoto Ehrhardt

Filmset and printed in Great Britain by
BAS Printers Limited, Wallop, Hampshire

FOR

H.L.E.H.

. . . nous ne croyons pas que la pensée et l'œuvre d'un auteur puissent se comprendre par elles-mêmes en restant sur le plan des écrits et même sur celui des lectures et des influences. La pensée n'est qu'un aspect partiel d'une réalité moins abstraite: l'homme vivant et entier; et celui-ci n'est à son tour qu'un élément de l'ensemble qu'est le groupe social. Une idée, une œuvre ne reçoit sa véritable signification que lorsqu'elle est intégrée à l'ensemble d'une vie et d'un comportement. De plus, il arrive souvent que le comportement qui permet de comprendre l'œuvre n'est pas celui de l'auteur, mais celui d'un groupe social (auquel il peut ne pas appartenir) et notamment, lorsqu'il s'agit d'ouvrages importants, celui d'une classe sociale.

(Lucien Goldmann, *Le Dieu Caché* (1955), Ch. I)

. . . and memory then will trace
Those who no more with living men have place . . .

(George Crabbe, *Posthumous Tales*, VI, ii)

PREFACE

The Social Milieu of Alexander Pope is the first half of a twofold design to explore from different but finally complementary viewpoints the civilization of our English 'Augustan' period. The present study approaches from the fields of social, economic and political history a central life and central series of texts of that time. I hope to develop the second part of the design in a further book, which will approach a wider range of seventeenth and eighteenth-century literature from the field of the history of ideas, the complex and changing concepts of Augustan Rome, and the notions of historical process associated with these.

To the University of Wales, and to Professor George Hibbard, I want to acknowledge with special gratitude two major but dissimilar debts. To Professor Hibbard I owe most that I was able to learn during my period of doctoral research at Nottingham in 1957–60; from those years I trace my particular concern with the social-historical context of eighteenth-century literature, and I am grateful to Professor Hibbard for encouraging me to think that the examination of (for example) estate papers and accounts might be relevant to the task of literary criticism.

To the University of Wales, which appointed me to one of its Senior Fellowships for the year 1964–5, I owe the opportunity to undertake the historical work involved in the present book in a way that (as a participant in the active undergraduate teaching of the Department of English at Swansea) I would otherwise have found impossible. I greatly appreciate this help; certainly not less if the fruits of it have taken long to ripen.

I am grateful to the large number of persons and institutions who have allowed me to study, quote from or refer to manuscript material or paintings in their possession. I wish to thank the Marquess of Anglesey for permission to quote extensively from his family papers at present deposited in the Greater London and Stafford Record Offices, and to refer to documents in his keeping. I especially appreciate the generous and helpful interest he has shown in certain sections of my work. I acknowledge the kind permission of the Marquess of Northampton to quote from the muniments at Castle Ashby; and of the Earl of Verulam for allowing me to quote from the Gorhambury papers in the Hertfordshire Record Office, and to see his portraits and miniatures of the Walter family at Gorhambury. To the Rt. Rev. Dr. Charles-Edwards, Bishop of Worcester 1956–70, and Mrs Charles-Edwards, I am grateful, not only for the opportunity to examine the inscribed books from the libraries of Pope, Ralph Allen and William Warburton, at Hartlebury Castle, Worcester, but also for their generous hospitality on the several occasions when I did so. I am equally grateful to Sir Christopher Medlycott, Bt. for helping me to see several Walter family portraits and related items at Venn House and Sandford Orcas, near Sherborne, and for his generous hospitality. I acknowledge the kind permission of Mr. H. M. C. Allen to quote from the correspondence of Ralph Allen in his possession; and of Miss Fiona Digby to quote from her family papers.

I am grateful for permission to draw upon manuscripts holdings, and for the generous assistance of the staff, at the following repositories: the Bath Municipal Libraries and Victoria Art Gallery; the Birmingham Reference Library; the Bodleian Library; the British Museum Department of Manuscripts; the Buckinghamshire Record Office; the City of London Guildhall Library; the Dorset Record Office; The General Post Office; the Greater London Record Office; the Hereford City Library; the Hertfordshire Record Office, where the County Archivist, Peter Walne was particularly helpful; the Principal Probate Registry, Somerset House; Saint Bartholomew's Hospital; the Somerset Record Office; the Staffordshire Record Office, where the County Archivist, Mr. F. B. Stitt was particularly helpful; The United Society for the Propagation of the Gospel, London; the Victoria and Albert Museum; and the Warwickshire Record Office.

I acknowledge with gratitude the assistance of the staff of the Libraries of the British Museum, the University College, Swansea, and the University of Cambridge; and of the National Portrait Gallery.

Among many who have helped me by information or encouragement are Dr. Sydney Anglo, Mr. J. S. Bull, the late Professor Herbert Davis, Mr. T. L. Ingram, Mr. R. G. Knowles, Dr. Arnold Pacey, Miss E. A. Russ, the late Professor George Sherburn, and the Rt. Hon. Simon Wingfield Digby, M.P. Others have in addition been so generous as to read parts of this book in typescript, and to give me the benefit of their comments. They are Mrs. Annetta Bynum, Mr. G. M. Davies, Professor Maynard Mack (who has shown me generosity beyond my desert), Mr. G. N. Masterman, Dr. and Mrs. Grahame Smith, Mr. Richard Tuck, Miss I. M. Westcott and Professor Charles Wilson. I am deeply grateful for the penetrating and constructive comments of Professor E. P. Thompson. My greatest personal debt is to my old friend Professor George Dekker, who read the whole book in an early and unsightly version, and gave me a great deal of valuable advice; for his patient interest and encouragement over the years I am especially grateful. I also wish to acknowledge several helpful lectures of and discussions with my colleague Dr. Raymond Williams on questions of methodology, from which I have insufficiently profited. Any merit in the present book is in great measure due to those whom I acknowledge here and in subsequent pages; its limitations and mistakes are my own.

Finally, I want to thank Jesus College, Cambridge, and the Cambridge Faculty of English, for grants towards the cost of typing; to express my appreciation of Mrs. Joan Whittow for undertaking this task, and of the Jesus College Office which gave its assistance at the very last stage. I am most grateful for the kind assistance of Mr. Patrick Beaver and Mr. Bill Pollard.

CONTENTS

LIST OF ILLUSTRATIONS

LIST OF ABBREVIATIONS

B.H.	Archives of Saint Bartholomew's Hospital, London.
B.R.L.	Birmingham Reference Library (MSS.)
B.M.	British Museum Department of MSS.
B.M. Add.	British Museum, Department of MSS. (Additional MSS.)
Carswell	John Carswell, *The South Sea Bubble* (London, 1960)
Cobbett	James Cobbett, *Parliamentary History of England* (London, 1806–20) (Numerals refer to column nos. in this work)
Corr.	*The Correspondence of Alexander Pope*, ed. George Sherburn (Oxford, 1956)
Dickson	P. G. M. Dickson, *The Financial Revolution in England* (London, 1967)
D.N.B.	*The Dictionary of National Biography*
D.R.O.	Dorset Record Office
G.E.C.	George Edward Cokayne, *The Complete Peerage . . .*, revised and enlarged edn. by the Hon. Vicary Gibbs and G. H. White (London, 1910–59)
H.R.O.	Hertfordshire Record Office
H.M.C.	Historical Manuscripts Commission
Spence	Joseph Spence, *Observations, Anecdotes and Characters of Books and Men*, ed. J. M. Osborn (Oxford, 1966). (Numerals refer to item nos. in this edition.)
S.R.O.	Staffordshire Record Office
T.E.	*The Twickenham Edition of the Poems of Alexander Pope*, general editor John Butt (London, 1939–67):

vol. i, ed. Emile Audra and Aubrey Williams
vol. ii, ed. Geoffrey Tillotson
vol. iii–i, ed. Maynard Mack
vol. iii–ii, ed. F. W. Bateson
vol. iv, ed. John Butt
vol. v, ed. James Sutherland
vol. vi, ed. Norman Ault and John Butt

vols. vii–x, ed. Maynard Mack, with Norman Callan,
Robert Fagles, William Frost and Douglas M. Knight
vol. xi, ed. Maynard Mack

With the exception of the above, a full reference is given to each work (or repository) on first citation in each chapter, but otherwise in shortened form.

Where a document has originally been dated Old Style, I have referred to the date in Old Style/New Style form.

In quoting from seventeenth and eighteenth-century documents I have attempted to preserve the forms and accidentals exactly, save that superior letters have had to be lowered throughout.

Part One: Introduction

Introduction. Pope: Text and Context

A literary artist, like any other man, lives in a shared world. He has community of knowledge and concern with other members of his society, and some part of his conception of his shared world finds relatively lasting expression in his art. Other parts may not find artistic expression. But this 'world' is never fully shared. It is the sum of all men's partial and often differing conceptions; what is familiar to one man may be unknown to another, and to this rule the artist is no exception. Contemporaries may have known, we may know, what he did not. The historian of an artist and his society may find that, to explore satisfactorily the *object* of the artist's concern—it might be a political or social development, it might be the life of an individual or family—he will need to follow evidence probably or certainly beyond the ken of that artist. Human interest extends from a literary text to the society in which it was written, and, in part, *of* which it was written. Society is not art, nor art more than an aspect of society, yet, at the most basic level of our concern, each offers a pattern of intelligible signs to the historian; a theme in art may be a subject in the social context of that art; and a continuity of concern will make itself felt to all but the most narrowly aesthetic mind. A contextual study of this sort poses special problems of delimitation, for the flow of human interest may wind in endless circles; it offers, as I shall hope to suggest, particular rewards where the intimate understanding of an artist is desired; but, if it is clearly delimited, probably everyone would admit its fascination and importance.

This book is a study of Pope's society, and of the social poetry which, as a member of that society, Pope produced. My approach, while strictly selective, has been conceived in affirmation of the simple idea that the history of a particular span of years is the totality of human experience in that time, and that the corresponding historiography is the balanced factual and critical account of that experience. Traditional 'history'—the political situations and expedients of the past—and 'criticism'—the examination and assessment of works of art— have their place, with other kinds of investigation, in the complex synthesis which is the history of the civilization of an age. I describe the present study as 'strictly selective in approach' because its immediate concern is confined to Pope, certain members of his acquaintance, and certain contemporaries about whom he wrote. It does however move beyond literary criticism and biography, and attempts to display some features of Pope's shared world—political, religious, social, economic—for their own sake, as well as for the light they often throw upon Pope himself. The result is a book which has tried to bring together and synthesize varieties of historical material with literary criticism. A short explanation of why such an approach to Pope appears especially useful will be appropriate.

Literature is at once a social action, a product of society, an imitation of society and a criticism of society. But each of these roles will not be of equal importance in every case. The early Tudor lyric 'Fforget not yett . . .', for example, is more a social action and gesture, and product of a social environment, than it is an imitation or a criticism of it. In the case of Joyce's *Dubliners* the reverse is true. The social poetry of Pope, however, and especially the later epistles and formal satires, fulfil each of these roles equally clearly. The Epistle *To Burlington* is a social act in a sense analogous to that in which the writing of a letter is so; or (more precisely) to the conducting of a conversation, in tones of some intimacy, that is still designed to be overheard and remembered. Like most social actions, it is susceptible to analysis in class terms, since part of its significance consists in its being a familiar address from an ordinary gentleman to a great aristocrat. *To Burlington* may also be seen as a product of those forces, economic, political and social, which brought forth a wealthy and powerful aristocracy, whose members built great houses, transformed their lands, acquired works of art ancient and modern—and had epistles written in praise or censure of what they did. Here the familiar literary roles of displaying and criticizing integrate with those already mentioned. The account of the visit to Timon's Villa is an imitation of social reality in a quite precise sense, yet at the same time an evaluation:

> On painted Cielings you devoutly stare,
> Where sprawl the Saints of Verrio or Laguerre . . .   [ll. 145–6]

and the explicit affirmation of an ideal at the end enforces, retrospectively, the implicit criticism here.

It is in its roles of imitation and criticism that I shall be chiefly concerned with Pope's social poetry in the following pages. And this brings us back at once to the question of text and context. Since literature such as the epistles and formal satires of Pope—like much drama and the novel—seeks to 'mirror' the society which it judges, can there be any literary critical need to look beyond? Will not the texts carry their own evidence of context?

One answer springs from the nature of imitation, and of the metaphor of the mirror applied so often to art in general and satire in particular. Artistic imitation can never be entirely accurate and neutral, or comprehensive, and was never intended to be so in classical or neo-classical literary theory. Even a mirror must be placed, and the act of placing is an act of selection, judgement, and communication. Further, it is true of the novel, more so of a poetic epistle, that this art of communication is in the best sense of the term rhetorical. The writer displays, certainly, but in so doing he also persuades: intensifies or plays down; anticipates, forestalls or heightens response; arouses emotion and lays it to rest; addresses, cajoles, praises and attacks. We can never know the nature of this artistry, or the validity of its judgement, without an independent grasp of that from which its selection has been made. A full understanding of the art of the text necessitates independent knowledge of the context.

There is a further point. The line between the evidence which the literature itself carries, and that to be found only by independent examination of the context, is by no means so easy to draw in practice as in theory. The intimacy of tone and subtle expressiveness of a Pope epistle may make allusion, or assume knowledge, in ways likely to be lost even to the most studious modern reader with his finger in the footnotes. To take an example which I shall develop in a later chapter, Pope's lines on the projector Sir John Blunt, in the Epistle *To Bathurst*, show certain features of language and implication which connect with details given in a footnote by Pope himself. These connections are the clue to the recognition of a moral complexity in Pope's 'attack' on Blunt. For the modern reader, however, it is only when Blunt's career in the political and financial world of his time has been explored that Pope's verse and note become fully meaningful. The apostrophe to Blunt then appears something other than a stock dismissal through irony. The poem had itself been saying something to us which lack of contextual familiarity prevented us from hearing.

Few poets have been more deeply involved in the society of their age and nation than Pope. Perhaps no body of verse in the language expresses such detailed and specific concerns with the people and events of its time as his later epistles and satires. These poems are filled with proper names and allusions. Pope seems to derive from the very acts of naming and allusion a peculiar and various poetic energy which, while certainly communicated to the reader, may yet remain somewhat mysterious. This is not only to be attributed to an initial ignorance of such few salient facts as scholarly editions supply in footnotes and commentary, though fuller information renders sensibly different our experience of the poet's communication with us across the years. It is also the immediate *sense* of Pope's society, as it would once have arisen from casual and confident possession of that network of more or less forgotten fact, which is necessary for a full understanding, though not necessarily an earlier appreciation. The trouble with footnote-information, though helpful, is that it comes to us in fragmented and summary form often quite different, we may suppose, from the artist's or contemporary reader's original experience.

The paradox must therefore be accepted that, if we wish to draw close in understanding to the life and work of a writer such as Pope, we must allow an interest in something more than these. In principle we must be prepared to explore for its own sake the various civilization of which they were only parts. For the literature, like the other arts of an age, is only a special aspect of its total history. If we are fully concerned with literature, and especially with drama, the novel, and social poetry, it will be strange for our engagement to stop short at that point where aesthetic considerations cease to pertain. To perceive the artistic organization of, for example, a novel of Dickens, we must feelingly perceive his concern for the life of his time. The work of art arises from the author's concern, as man and artist, with his shared world. It would be hard to defend if, as students of literature, we could happily trace images and themes through a work of fiction, respond through the character of the writing to the atmosphere of presented scenes and times, deliberate on plausibility of character and situation, yet found our personal engagement fail when its human concerns passed beyond the boundaries of art into social, economic or political history. If our engagement were to fail in this way, we might ask how worthy we were of the authors we had set out to appreciate and understand.

If we wish to approach Pope in a generous historical fashion it may seem that nothing less than a portrait of his society and age will commend itself, partly because only such a study can put us in full communication with his mind and work, partly because the natural, intelligible and satisfying unit of study is not 'the man and his work', but, to borrow the subtitle of Irvin Ehrenpreis's 'biography' of Swift: 'The Man, His Works, and The Age.'[1] Yet this is dauntingly ambitious, and often beyond the scope of even the most rounded and copious biography. Another method may be devised as a means to the same end, as an experimental approach. This is to select particular men who figure significantly in Pope's verse and correspondence; to locate primary sources of information about them, independent, so far as possible, of imaginative literature; and to write their lives briefly in relation to Pope and his work.

Care must be taken, however, in the selection of individuals for study. Since we must hope for them to throw light on Pope and his work, they must either be people he knew well personally, or whom he knew much about, or who made a strong impact on him. The selection will also depend on the kind of question we wish to ask about Pope. If we were chiefly concerned with his literary judgements and values in relation to his age, we might decide to study, perhaps, Roscommon, Gay, Savage, Aaron Hill, Welsted and Cibber. If we were concerned with painting (a concern in no way peripheral to an appreciation of Pope's poetic art) Kneller, Jervas, Jonathan Richardson and Kent might be chosen. In the present study I shall be primarily, though not exclusively, concerned with social, economic and political values, and especially with the use of wealth in relation to public morality. Here a different selection again is required. And in this case, since we wish to learn something about the society of Pope's time, not just his immediate circle with its several unusual and outstanding figures, it is right to choose men of a relatively ordinary kind. We must select people who may, in principle at least, have representative interest. The great figures of Pope's life (Swift, Bolingbroke, Burlington are paramount examples) must feature in any discussion of Pope. They will do

---

[1] Irvin Ehrenpreis, *Swift, The Man, His Works, and The Age* (London, 1962).

so in the following pages.[2] Lesser figures, though neither insignificant in their time nor unimportant to Pope, will serve better in any attempt to reconstruct the milieu in which he moved.

A further step may fairly be taken to secure figures of representative value, and to supply form and clarity to the study. A society may be categorized in various ways, sometimes in its own terms and sometimes in terms totally modern. Since a great part of my concern is to reconstruct a social milieu as it was conceived and felt by some of those who belonged to it, it is necessary to use some of the categories of the society itself. They must be capable of taking us close to individual historical outlooks, though not so much so as to be incapable of comprehending evidence which may lead us beyond the limitations of these. We may thus employ categories of social rank, source of wealth, and political and religious inclination. A well-balanced selection of Pope's contemporaries would thus include a nobleman, a landed gentleman, a merchant or city businessman, and, if possible (the difficulty tells something about the time), a member of the poor. It would include a member of Pope's own Roman Catholic religion, and a dissenter, as well as members of the established church. It would include supporters of the 'Whig' administrations which ruled Britain from 1713 until after Pope's death, but also some who preferred different administrations or the hope of them, older ways, even the exiled dynasty.

It is with these considerations in mind that I have made a selection of Pope's contemporaries to study in relation to his life and social poems. The names have been chosen carefully, and though they could easily, and I think profitably, be added to, they form a pattern of similarity and contrast which tells us something about Pope and something about his time. Their choice has only secondarily been determined by the availability of primary sources; and none has been selected merely because a collection of his letters or papers happens to have survived in some library or county record office. Once the choice was made, however, a wide range of such sources was tapped, and in each case information was forthcoming.

John Caryll (1667–1736), of Ladyholt and West Grinstead in Sussex, chose himself. Pope's longest correspondence was with Caryll; in his earlier life especially he felt great admiration and affection for him; and the Caryll family has a representative value, which it would be hard to secure otherwise so interestingly, in being Roman Catholic and Jacobite. Caryll was in fact a Jacobite peer, though he lived the life of a retired country gentleman. William Digby (1662–1752), fifth Baron Digby of Geashill, may seem a more surprising choice. Pope praises him in one of the few particular allusions of the *Essay on Man*, and also in the 'Epilogue to the Satires', and was a close friend of his son Robert; but the decisive reason for this choice was the interesting and important letter which Pope wrote to Martha Blount, in praise of Digby and

[2] James Lees-Milne has, in *Earls of Creation: Five Great Patrons of Eighteenth-Century Art* (London, 1962), written a study of several of the great architectural noblemen of Pope's acquaintance, in which the relation between short lives and the recurrent presence of Pope is similar to that of the present book.

his country seat at Sherborne.[3] This letter stands out as the affirmation of a major ideal of nobility. Digby was a member of the established church, owning strong connections with the Non-Jurors, and had at least some attachment to the exiled Stuarts though this seems to have dwindled as the years passed by. Ralph Allen (1693–1764), of Prior Park near Bath, himself the subject of a recent biography, has an important place among those whom Pope went out of his way to praise in his poems and letters.[4] Unlike Caryll and Digby, Allen was a self-made man, of humble origin, who made his fortune as an honest projector, and administrator of some genius, ending up as a wealthy landowner and patron. On one occasion, in a letter to a friend, Pope called Allen 'the Most Noble Man of England.'[5] Allen was an ordinary member of the established church, and well affected to the Whig supremacy and the administration of Walpole and his successors, at least during Pope's life. He was an active opponent of Jacobitism. Allen was 'low-born', but Pope would not have come to know him had he not grown at least moderately wealthy. Though the poet is intensely concerned in his social poetry with 'the poor' as such, no poor man figures prominently in the poems and letters. Yet this is not quite true. One man, a gentleman of distinguished family, though poor, retired and sunk in the world, whose life was in many respects that of a yeoman, was given a conspicuous place in Pope's social poetry. This is John Kyrle (1637–1724), 'the Man of Ross'. Like Digby and Allen, Kyrle was a member of the established church. His life was perhaps too humble and retired for the great issues of national politics to touch him deeply; he seems to have welcomed the Restoration, though in the Civil War many of his family were parliamentarian. Kyrle is the earliest of all those studied in this book, and his life is presented first.

Kyrle, Caryll, Digby and Allen were all people whom Pope admired. They may be included among Pope's 'good men' and their lives are partly of interest because they throw light on the positive values which underlie Pope's social attitudes and social poems. But such values are the more readily recognized by contrast with their opposites. Pope's 'good men' must be compared with some of those whom he disapproved and attacked. Peter Walter (1664?–1746), of Stalbridge in Dorset, the attorney and land-steward, was an obvious candidate, if only because he was so repeatedly assailed by Pope, Swift and Fielding, and is the subject of one of Pope's satires.[6] Pope seems not to have known him directly, but that many of Pope's friends had direct dealings with him appears from Walter's letters. Like Allen, Walter was a self-made man, like Allen he soon grew wealthy and purchased an estate, but there the resemblance ends. He was a supporter of Robert Walpole in the Commons, and, in so far as there is evidence of his religion, had perhaps a leaning towards dissent. Walter was a man whose wealth was acquired through land and invested

    [3] *Corr.*, ii, pp. 236–40 (22 June ?1724).
    [4] Benjamin Boyce, *The Benevolent Man: A Life of Ralph Allen of Bath* (Cambridge, Mass., 1967).
    [5] *Corr.*, iv, pp. 221–2 (Pope to Fortescue, 23 Jan. 1739/40).
    [6] 'The Second Satire of Dr. John Donne . . . Versifyed'; T.E., iv, pp. 129–45.

in land. Allen grew wealthy in an entirely different way; and both Caryll and
Digby, though their inherited wealth was in land chiefly, were prepared to
consider other forms of investment. In Sir John Blunt (1667–1733), however,
we have a man for whom the acquisition of landed wealth seems only to have
been a move in the game of financial manipulation; indeed he was a manipulator
of credit rather than a dealer in wealth in any solid form. A man of the City,
self-made like Allen and Walter, he rose to a peak of celebration and notoriety
in 1720 as the chief author of the South-Sea Scheme which seemed first so
extravagant a success, and was afterwards so dire a failure. As in the case of
Walter, Pope knew about Blunt indirectly through a number of close friends.
He has a prominent place in the Epistle *To Bathurst*, where Pope also noted,
correctly, that Blunt was 'a Dissenter of the most religious deportment.'[7]
Blunt had no constant political stance; at different points in his career he threw
in his lot with Tories, Whigs, and with an alliance of Tories, Old Whigs and
Jacobites. Each of these six contemporaries evokes a different aspect of Pope's
outlook. The span covered by their lives, taken chronologically, stretches for
over a century, from the Civil War to the administration of the Elder Pitt,
and one or other of them was involved in most of the major changes and
events which took place in England during that time.

The mention of change—economic, social, political—suggests a further way
in which these six lives may be seen. They may (I believe) comprise a balanced
selection of evidence as to the nature of late seventeenth and early eighteenth-
century society, segments of a notional whole, but when approached more
closely it is rather the sense of movement, of living through change, of lives as
projects in an ever-incomplete process, which they most strongly convey. To
ask what it was like to live in certain parts of eighteenth-century society is to
own a concern with this sense of movement, and for this reason I have ventured
to adopt a narrative form in Chapters I–VII, rather than assemble the social
evidence as merely the static-seeming objects of modern analysis.

If, for the moment, we take the text of Pope's epistles and satires as our
starting-point, there are five ways in which we may fairly be concerned with
the society of which they speak. We may first consider the function in a single
poem of the evidence of its society which that poem displays. Here, though the
poem makes reference beyond itself, it is in practice treated by the reader as
an autonomous world, allowed to verify its own judgements. Example supports
precept and judgement to form a fictional 'truth' which is also the pattern of
art. Thus we may compare John Kyrle's life of charity, as portrayed in *To
Bathurst*, with the numerous examples of the abuse of wealth in that poem,
drawing conclusions as to Pope's society, his opinion of it, and the degree to
which these have been successfully asserted by the formal structure of the
epistle in an act of literary communication. Secondly, we may look at the social
context of the poems for a fuller realization of their meaning. Such a realization,
we may think, would have come spontaneously to Pope's contemporary reader,
as a conscious member of that social fabric about which the modern reader

[7] *To Bathurst*, l. 135n.; T.E., iii–ii, p. 104.

must take steps to inform himself. Thus a study of the events leading to the South-Sea Bubble disaster has the effect of displaying as a coherent series numerous allusions in the Epistle *To Bathurst* which might otherwise have seemed isolated thrusts, of showing how deeply Pope is concerned here with the financial revolution of his time, and of suggesting a new historical model for the portrait of Sir Balaam with which this poem ends. Thirdly, we can explore the social context of these poems for verification of statements which the poems make, where these are of an historical and factual kind. Thus Pope's claim that John Kyrle was a notable peacemaker in legal disputes can be substantiated by surviving documents.[8] Or again, in 'The Second Satire of Dr. Donne', Pope levels the accusation of sharp practice in the drawing up of legal documents (part of the earlier poet's portrait of the probably fictional lawyer Coscus) at a living contemporary: Peter Walter. It might be thought that Pope was more concerned here with his imitation of Donne than with offering contemporary and factual truths to the reader, but there is evidence that Walter was untrustworthy in precisely this respect.[9] On the other hand, it does not appear possible to substantiate Pope's assertion that Walter was tried and barely acquitted for forgery in 1737; this was perhaps a piece of rumour-mongering on the poet's part.[10]

Fourthly, we may explore the context of these poems for evidence which they do not display, but which it is certain or probable that the poet knew. In his earliest and most impressionable years, Pope certainly learned of the chequered and rather heroic history of the Caryll family during the last two decades of the seventeenth century. This history connects with the sentiments Pope expressed in an epitaph, originally upon Caryll's uncle the Jacobite Secretary of State, and in letters to Caryll at the time of the 1715 Jacobite Rebellion. The experience of the Carylls gave immediate human point to a number of general ideals, such as commitment to a principle at the expense of one's private interests, loyalty to one side without being narrowly partisan, resignation in politics and religion, all of which flow into Pope's later poetry. Or again, we know that, shortly before writing the letter in praise of Digby's life at Sherborne, Pope saw Nost's monument, and John Hough's inscription, to the third Earl of Bristol in Sherborne Abbey.[11] That the values there expressed, in stone and word, influenced Pope's praise of the country house ideal in his letter is extremely probable, while the letter anticipates Pope's praise of the country house ideal in more general terms in the later poetry. Contextual information of this kind is not carried in the poems; it cannot be said to reveal their meaning more fully, or verify the claims they make. But it has strong biographical interest, and is certainly connected with the poems in the matrix of Pope's experience. It is this fourth category of contextual information, also, which approximates to that area of experience from which a poem, as a work of art, is a significant selection. We may need to see what

   [8] See Ch. I below.
   [9] See Ch. IV below. Pope imitated Donne's ll. 97–8 in ll. 99–100; T.E., iv, pp. 140–41.
   [10] 'Epilogue to the Satires:' Dialogue II, l. 57n.; T.E., iv, p. 315.
   [11] See n.3 above, and Ch. V below.

the poet might have included but did not, for a fuller understanding of the poetic process. Pope chose not to mention, when he wrote about Sir John Blunt in *To Bathurst*, that Blunt had once been closely associated with the Tory administration of 1711–13, though this may be thought to have had some effect on Pope's presentation. We may postulate both personal and artistic reasons for this exclusion, and such reasons are, in principle, of critical as well as biographical relevance. Again, what Pope chose to stress when he named Allen in the 'Epilogue to the Satires', was his 'low' or 'humble' origin, and his habit of unostentatious generosity.[12] Pope might have mentioned the stately public mansion which Allen was building, and the public nature of his hospitality. Something is to be learned from information of this kind.

In each of these four categories of information, the area of exploration has not extended beyond the knowledge, or probable knowledge, of the author himself. The fifth and final category is of information of which, for one reason or another, the author was not or could not be aware. Pope was probably unaware of the parliamentarian sympathies of the family of the Man of Ross in the Civil War. He was probably unaware of the sardonic wit which Peter Walter often showed in his private correspondence with Lord Uxbridge, and stressed only the more solemn public manner. Obviously he was unaware (though he would have been highly gratified if he could have known) that Allen was ultimately to become an important supporter of the most distinguished of the 'boy patriots', William Pitt. Matters of this kind have intrinsic interest, and may fairly be included in a study of men whose lives are in many respects relevant to Pope and his writings. Indeed it is this final category of information that most fully challenges the reader's capacity for serious engagement with Pope's milieu for its own sake. Little sense of the lived context of Pope's work could be gained by focusing only on what is immediately relevant to the poetry. The light must be cast more widely, for it is this which leads to that broader study of the civilization of an age in which criticism of Pope's art asks to be finally subsumed. Accordingly, part of the material presented in the following pages is of this kind.

In this survey of the different categories of contextual information, we have moved outwards from the texts themselves to their shared world, for this seemed the readiest way to explain the relationships involved. In the following pages, however, the reverse procedure will be adopted. Short lives of each of the six chosen contemporaries of Pope will first be given, showing at which points they contact the life and work of the poet. The lives follow one another in approximately chronological order, opening with Kyrle and ending with Allen, but with some further arrangement to secure contrast and point. The six lives provide, in ways intimated above, a context for reading Pope's later social poems. The later section of the study then turns to the poetry, and traces some of the dominant concerns of the lives through into Pope's art. The poems are thus discussed in the light of the lives, and of such literary background as bears upon the themes in question. Thus the first chapter of the later section,

[12] 'Epilogue to the Satires:' Dialogue I, ll. 135–6; T.E., iv, p. 308.

'The Betrayal of Society', isolates the qualities in the lives of Walter and Blunt to which Pope was most hostile, and, under the subtitles of 'The Theme of False Stewardship' and 'The Theme of Corruption', displays the importance of these in a wide range of Pope's later poems. The next chapter, 'The Country House Ideal', takes one of Pope's chief reasons for admiring Caryll, Digby, Allen, and, in a special sense, Kyrle, and attempts to show how this ideal, arising in Pope's mind from a conjunction of literary tradition and social reality, manifests itself in his own art, and is central to his outlook. The final chapter, 'Imperial Works', forms an epilogue. Here the country house ideal is seen as extended into a more comprehensive, Roman, ideal of civilization itself. This ideal, with its architectural metaphor, has its roots in classical antiquity, and yet is Pope's most comprehensive summation of such positive example as he found in his own society; it is precisely this ranging from a concern with particular and often everyday detail to the most comprehensive and ideal conception, which is the habit of mind in Pope that the present approach abundantly reveals. I hope in the final three chapters of the book to display in Pope a powerful and fundamentally searching art: greater and more comprehensive than the particular social concerns which have contributed to it, just as, for the historian in the widest sense, this art contributes to and is finally subsumed in the civilization of its age.

Part Two: Lives

I. 'Private Country Gentleman'[1]: John Kyrle Esq. (1637–1724), the Man of Ross

1. CIVIL WAR AND RESTORATION

ON 25 May 1660 Charles II, his kingdoms restored to him, landed at Dover and proceeded through shouting multitudes to his capital where, as Evelyn records, he was greeted with a triumph of above twenty thousand horse and foot,

> brandishing their swords and shouting with Unexpressible joy: The wayes straw'd with flowers, the bells ringing, the streetes hung with Tapissry, fountaines running with wine: the Major, Aldermen, all the Companies, in their liver[ie]s, Chaines of Gold, & banners; Lords & nobles, Cloth of Silver, gold & vellvet everybody clad in; the windows & balconies all set with Ladyes, Trumpets, Trumpets, Musick & [myriads] of people flocking . . . I stood in the Strand, & beheld it, & blessed God. And all this was done without one drop of bloud, & by that very army which rebell'd against him: but it was the Lord's doing, *et mirabile in oculus nostris*: for such a Restauration was never seene in the mention of any history, antient or modern . . .[2]

Public celebration spread throughout England, to every provincial city and every country town; in the Herefordshire market-town of Ross,

> Upon Wednesday, being the happy day of His Majestie's birth, as well his and the Common Prayer Book's restoration, the most and most considerable persons in Ross thought it not enough to celebrate the day with praise and prayer, as well as sermon, but to express their inward joy of heart the better, they caused a face of wood to be cut, which being dressed with a long mantle and a cape, with a *solemn league and covenant* upon his breast, was carried on a pole by a chimney-sweeper (instead of a hangman) dressed in his holyday apparel, that is, as black as he could be; two of the same quality carried up his train, and in this triumphant manner after evening prayer he was solemnly carried quite through the town, the drummer

---

[1] The title is taken from one of Pope's early MS. notes on Kyrle; see E. R. Wasserman, ed. *Pope's Epistle to Bathurst: A Critical Reading with an Edition of the Manuscripts* (Baltimore, 1960) p. 67.

[2] *The Diary of John Evelyn*, ed. E. S. de Beer (Oxford, 1955), iii, p. 246 (29 May 1660).

2. Artist unknown, *John Kyrle*, reproduced in T. D. Fosbroke, *The Wye Tour* ... (1818).

and guard of musqueteers besides the pikemen attending him, till at last he was brought to the market-place, fixed in the ground, the covenant having the inscription—

> 'Who set three kingdoms in a flame,
> Tis just, should perish by the same,'

and so burned to ashes with acclamations of great joy not easily to be paralleled . . . and all this to show their affection to His Majesty and the Ecclesiastical Government, under which they and their ancestors lived so happily, to God's glory and their own comfort.[3]

Evelyn's account conveys the sense of a noble scene, and a miraculous providence, but when we turn from the metropolitan to the provincial celebrations it is hard not to detect something primitive in the way the loyal townspeople expressed their 'inward joy'. John Kyrle, the son of a junior branch of an old-established Herefordshire family, is likely to have witnessed one or other of these celebrations; he cannot have done so without feeling uneasiness as well as joy at the Restoration, for his family had played at best an ambiguous part in the Civil War in Herefordshire and the West.[4]

Herefordshire had been a predominantly loyal county. At the outbreak of the Civil War John, Viscount Scudamore, its only nobleman, had headed the Royalist interest with popular support. His one powerful opponent was the far-seeing Puritan knight Sir Robert Harley, who had already fortified his house at Brampton Bryan before the hostilities began. Harley was backed by other Herefordshire gentlemen: Sir Richard Hopton, Sir John Kyrle of Much Marcle, his kinsman Kyrle of Walford, and Sir Edward Powell of Pengethly.[5] After Harley much the most interesting and certainly the most enigmatic of these is Robert Kyrle of Walford, first cousin of the John Kyrle who is the subject of this chapter. Robert Kyrle had followed the military profession early: at the outbreak of the Civil War, when he was only twenty four, he had already by his own account served with 'the *Swede* in Germany, and the States in *Holland*.' Arriving home, he enlisted with the Parliamentary troops in Stamford's regiment, encouraged no doubt by his kinsman. According to his own later statement he was swayed by the grievances of his countrymen against the crown, as he remembered them before he went abroad, but was less familiar with more recent events. In the first year of hostilities things went badly for the Parliamentary forces in the south-west. The activities of Stamford's regiment, including Captain Robert Kyrle, were much complained of in Herefordshire, but these were of minor importance compared with the fall

---

[3] John Duncomb, *The History of Hereford* (Hereford, 1804), contd. by W. H. Cooke, iii (London, 1882), pp. 107–8 (quoting *Mercurius Publicus*, 6 June 1660).

[4] Kyrle is likely to have been in London (where he had been enrolled as a student at the Middle Temple in 1657) or Ross (where he is stated to have retired 'after leaving university' and 'at the Restoration'); *Alumni Oxonienses*, ii, p. 867; D.N.B., xxxi, p. 262; Cooke, op. cit., p. 109.

[5] J. and J. W. Webb, *Memorials of the Civil war . . . as it Affected Herefordshire* (London, 1879), i, p. 23.

of Bristol to the King.[6] At a time when it looked as if all that part of England were secure for the Royalists, Charles I summoned his parliamentary Convention to meet in Oxford. Among those anxious but unable to attend the Convention, in January 1643, was Walter Kyrle, barrister-at-law, M.P. for Leominster in the Long Parliament, the uncle of Robert Kyrle and father of John Kyrle, 'the Man of Ross'.[7] There is no evidence for thinking that Walter Kyrle was an ardent Royalist. His withdrawal from the Parliament at Westminster and submission (though absent) to the Convention may have been no more than a precautionary measure. Whatever was the case he was not the only member of his family to have a wary eye on the King's success in the south-west. By March of the same year Robert Kyrle, probably in all sincerity, came to think he had chosen the wrong side. He managed to obtain a pardon from King Charles at Oxford, and wrote to a Parliament friend at Windsor to justify his desertion. He declared that he had not been convinced by that spirit pretended to on the Parliamentary side 'of meeknesse and peace' but had found instead 'fury and madnesse'; their pretensions of principle: 'Religion, safety of the King, Liberty and Propriety' merely hid the reality: 'Atheisme, Anarchy, arbytrary government and confusion.' By contrast the 'discipline, unanimity, and exact obedience' of 'His Majesties Army' had impressed him deeply, and

> to conclude, what *English* Gentleman that ever heard of the antient honour of this Kingdome ... can tamely see our courage (terrible sometime to forraigne Nations) basely degenerate into a rebellion against our naturall Prince, to whom malice it selfe can object no crime ... and since it cannot touch His Person, quarrels at His Crowne: you see him powerful at the head of His Army, and may see him glorious in his throne of Peace, you ought not to doubt his justice, (and, if you will) you may (as I have done) obtaine his mercy.[8]

However Robert Kyrle's motives for turning Royalist were mixed, the strength of the King's claims and the fairness of his prospects at this time, make themselves felt in this letter. Thus for a time the Kyrles were evenly divided: the Much Marcle branch for Parliament, the Walford branch for the King. Then, in 1644, when the Royalists were less secure in possession of the south-west, Robert Kyrle, with considerable skill and self-command, betrayed the Royalist garrison of Monmouth to the Parliamentarians, thus not only turning coat a second time, but also rendering himself *persona grata* once more with the side which he had originally espoused. This choice, in the short term, proved the right one, but it must have looked very different in 1660. John Kyrle, who cannot have been ignorant of his family history, may have felt some remorse on behalf of his relatives, and some resolution to be constant in his own loyalties, as he watched the celebrations.

[6] Ibid., pp. 311–12.

[7] *Alumni Oxonienses*, ii, p. 867; Cobbett, ii, 609, iii, 220. For a Kyrle genealogy, see C. J. Robinson, *History of the Mansions and Manors of Herefordshire* (London, 1873), pp. 280–1.

[8] Webb, op. cit., ii, pp. 350–3. See pp. 157, 161, 230–1, 34, 96, 103, 238–9 for a fuller account of Robert Kyrle's part in the Civil War.

He was then twenty three years old, having been born on 22 May 1637 at the White House in the village of Dymock in Gloucestershire, a property brought to Walter Kryle, probably for life only, by his wife, daughter of John Mallet of Berkeley.[9] Walter, a younger son of a family of lesser gentry, had little land of his own. He is said to have built in 1620 the house in the Market Place of Ross in which his son was to live most of his life; certainly he is referred to as 'of Ross' in the record of his admission as barrister at the Middle Temple in 1625. But this was a small property indeed, and John, his eldest son, was clearly brought up for a professional career. Like his father and cousin he was sent to Oxford, where he matriculated on 20 July 1654, presenting to his College of Balliol a silver tankard engraved with the arms of the College and his family 'ex dono Johannis Kyrle de Ross in agro Herefordiensi' to mark the occasion.[10] Like his father he did not graduate, but proceeded in 1657 to study at the Middle Temple.[11] Yet he did not make a profession of the law, as it was the clear intention of his family he should. He is said to have returned to Herefordshire at the Restoration, and possibly he did, but the first clear evidence of his residence and activities in Ross is a deed of 27 Sept. 1666 between himself and Sir William Powell of Pengethly.[12] This deed shows that Kyrle had recently purchased from Sir William the 'Messuage and diverse parcells of land meadow ground and pasture' in Ross called Cleeve-field Bank (of which more later), and shows also that he had close and complex relations, *vis-à-vis* property, with the Powells of Pengethly, who it will be remembered had sided with Parliament in the Civil War. From this time on a succession of deeds, as well as the much later accounts of his life, show that John Kyrle was living in Ross, in the ordinary timber-frame house in the market-place which he had inherited from his father.[13] From his house he could see the new Market Hall which between 1660 and 1674 was being built in the centre of the town at the expense of Frances, Duchess of Somerset, whose family held the lordship of the manor of Ross.[14] In the gable at one end was set a bust of Charles II, invisible from Kyrle's windows. In the light of Kyrle's family history in the Civil War, the report is convincing that Kyrle, complaining that he could not see the bust from his house, caused to be set in the wall of the Market House opposite his windows a monogram composed of the letters F and C interwoven with a heart, signifying 'Faith to Charles from the heart.'[15] It was not only a public gesture which seems to have expressed his convictions, but one calculated to remind himself and others of his re-

[9] D.N.B., xxxi, p. 262; Cooke, op. cit. p. 109; Robinson, op. cit., pp. 280–1.
[10] D.N.B. loc. cit.; Cooke, op. cit., pp. 109, 138. The tankard is preserved at Balliol College.
[11] *Alumni Oxonienses*, loc. cit.
[12] Hereford City Library, Hopton Collection (Deeds), 77.
[13] Robinson, op. cit., p. 244.
[14] Cooke, op. cit., pp. 114, 105–6.
[15] T. D. Fosbroke, *The Wye Tour* (Ross, 1837), 'An Account of Ross', p. 15; S. C. Hall, *A Pilgrimage to the Tomb of John Kyrle* (Ross, 1850), pp. 19–20; the editor of the *Ross Gazette* ('Mr. Stratford' according to H. C. Money-Kyrle, in Compton Reade, ed. *Memorials of Old Herefordshire* (London, 1904), p. 235), *The Wye Tour . . . to which is added A Memoir of John Kyrle* (Ross, 1885), p. 24. The Market House, bust, and monogram opposite Kyrle's house, may still be seen.

jection of the part played by his family during the Civil War. But history was kinder to Kyrle than it had been to his father and cousin, and than it would be, as we shall see, to John Caryll and William Digby; it put him to no severe test. For him twenty eight years of Stuart rule were to pass peacefully by, living as he did far from the tension and crises of the capital. There is no evidence that the year 1688 caused him a crisis of conscience, and when in 1695 the tenor bell, which he was giving to Ross church, was cast at Gloucester, he attended with 'his old silver tankard, which after drinking "Church and King"'—as he might have done in Charles's days—'he threw in and had cast with the bell.'[16] The change from Charles to James, and James to William, seems to have made little difference to his sentiments, and the succession of different sovereigns' names at the heads of the deeds he signed continued through his long life, with no hint of dissatisfaction on his part. Such, perhaps, was one of the blessings of a retired and unambitious life.

More unexpected, in the circumstances, than Kyrle's loyalist resolutions, is his rejection of the kind of career planned for him by his family and which seems to have become common in its two preceding generations. Kyrle had not been sent to Balliol College and the Middle Temple to settle down at Ross in his later twenties and live in the market-place on his very modest income; this showed neither the professional perseverance and ability of his father in becoming a barrister and a Member of Parliament, nor the bold enterprise of his cousin in going soldiering on the Continent after leaving Oxford. John Kyrle's instincts were no doubt those of the wealthy landed gentleman, expected and ready to settle down at his country seat and look after his estates, yet the property he had to fulfil these instincts was little more than that of a substantial yeoman: a small house, suitable perhaps for a modestly prosperous merchant; a tract of woodland in the village of his birth at Dymock; and a few pieces of ground around Ross.[17] And indeed, in many ways, Kyrle led a yeoman's life. One of the first accounts of him, after Pope's own enquiries and portrait in the Epistle *To Bathurst*, noted that 'He was . . . a tall thin Man; sensible and well bred; and went so very plain in his Dress, that when he work'd in the fields with his own Labourers, (which he frequently did) he was not distinguished from them by anything more than a certain Dignity in his Air and Countenance . . .'[18] and one who, as a boy, had known Kyrle in his last years, described how 'With a spade on his shoulder, and a glass bottle of liquor in his hand, he used to walk from his house . . ., to his fields, and back again, several times every day, and was always assisted by two or three, and sometimes more workmen, according as circumstances

[16] Hall, op. cit., p. 20.

[17] It is hard to establish exactly what Kyrle inherited from his father (d. 1650) and mother (d. 1662) apart from the house. The wood at Dymock is likely to have been left him by his mother, if not by his father, since she was heir to her father who was of the parish of Berkeley (Robinson, op. cit., pp. 280–1). Fosbroke, op. cit., p. 4, mentions ground in Ross.

[18] Joseph Spence, *Anecdotes, Observations and Characters of Books and Men*, ed. S. W. Singer (London, 1820), pp. 437–8 (Duck to Spence, 1 Jan. 1751). The letters about Kyrle are not included in J. M. Osborn's modern edition of the *Anecdotes*.

required . . .'[19] Yet in his early days at least he cannot have been rustic in any limited sense; he did not decide in favour of a rustic life because he had never known anything different, but must have chosen it with deliberation when other scenes and ways of life were fresh in his mind. English society was mobile, and inevitably more people moved down from the higher to the lower ranks than the other way round.[20] Kyrle is interesting because of the striking and apparently conscious change in his life, and also because, as we see from the first of the two quotations above, he retained the awareness and manner of being a gentleman, even in his confined circumstances and yeoman-like employment. This, as I shall suggest, may have been of particular human significance to Pope when he so markedly singled Kyrle out for the most central and positive 'example' of his most carefully constructed social poem.

2. LAW AND BENEVOLENCE

A difficulty in writing about John Kyrle is to bring together reliably the large body of interesting report and legend, some of which is dubious and all of which must be treated with caution, and the smaller body of more or less discrete but certain information which may be derived from the surviving deeds to which he was a party or set his signature. One respect in which this can be done concerns Kyrle's reputation as an arbiter in disputes. Pope was to write of him in *To Bathurst*:

> Is there a variance? enter but his door,
> Balk'd are the Courts, and contest is no more.
> Despairing Quacks with curses fled the place,
> And vile Attornies, now an useless race.   [ll. 271-4][21]

Thomas Hearne, enquiring independently a year after the publication of Pope's poem, elicited the information that 'When any litigious suits fell out, he would always stop them, and prevent people's going to law. They would, when differences happened, say . . . go to "the man of Ross", and he will decide the matter.'[22] R. Wheeler, writing on 25 Feb. 1748 in answer to enquiries from Joseph Spence, gives the same picture.[23] It is probable that Kyrle first acquired this reputation by helping to settle a dispute 'between the Town and fforeign of Ross Touching the Inequallity of their Taxes' in the year 1674. Several accounts of Kyrle mention this achievement, which is confirmed by a document in the Hereford City Library.[24] On 22 Sept. 1673 three justices of the peace referred the dispute to four negotiators (two for each contending

---

[19] Charles Heath, *The Excursion Down the Wye* (Monmouth, 1826), np. (account given c. 1796 by William Dobbs, aged 84, who was twelve on Kyrle's death in 1724. Heath seems first to have issued his collections on the Wye area in 1791 — see Preface. The account of Dobbs was afterwards quoted in Fosbroke, op. cit.

[20] Cf. Peter Laslett, *The World We Have Lost* (London, 1965), pp. 35-6.

[21] The fullest commentary on Pope's lines on Kyrle, which the present account is much indebted to, is that of F. W. Bateson in T.E., iii-ii, pp. 113-16.

[22] *Reliquiae Hearniae*, ed. Philip Bliss (London, 1869), iii, p. 95 (9 April 1733).

[23] Spence, *Anecdotes*, ed. S. W. Singer, p. 424.

[24] Eg. Fosbroke, op. cit., p. 13; Hereford City Library, L.C. (Deeds), 908.

interest) with the proviso that 'in Case they should faile to Compose the same thereby that then the said Difference Should be determined by . . . John Kyrle as Umpire . . .' They did fail to reach a composition, and the matter was settled by Kryle. The formula by which he compounded the difference is unimportant, but it is important to understand that the people with the most vital interest in the settlement of this dispute were not the representatives of the Town or Foreign of Ross as such, but the poor of both, whose subsistence depended almost entirely on these taxes which financed the Poor-Rate. Kyrle's 'award' of 1674 provides in detail for the fair and efficient distribution of the taxes for the future, and stresses at every point the welfare of the poor '. . . that the Money raised by the Assessment as Aforesaid shall be distributed to the Poor Indifferently, as they shall have need . . .' That Kyrle was proud of this settlement is suggested by the grand flourish with which the document of award begins: 'To all Christian People to whom this Present Writing shall come I John Kyrle of Rosse in the County of Hereford Gent. send Greeting in the Lord God Everlasting.' Another document with which he was concerned, a lease regulating the use of the Ross Market House in 1690, is similarly meticulous in guarding against any neglect of the interests of the poor.[25]

Kyrle's arbitration of the taxation dispute no doubt prevented the two parties from contending in a lawsuit expensive for them and grievous to the poor. But for the most part the surviving legal documents which concern Kyrle show him helping others to use rather than avoid legal processes. Of the fourteen deeds of Kyrle which I have been able to examine, only three concern his private interests.[26] In all the rest he is evidently included in one of the litigating parties as an overseer and guarantor of the agreement; sometimes he is specifically a trustee.[27] It is clear from this that Kyrle was able to profit from his years at the Middle Temple in advising his fellow townspeople about their practical affairs and in acquiring a reputation as a man knowledgeable in the law. The fact that Kyrle was a man of law in no professional sense, and was far from a 'vile Attorney', such as Peter Walter, who would profit from other people's disputes, no doubt helped to enhance this reputation. And from the reputation must have sprung the well-authenticated practice by his neighbours and fellow townspeople of bringing their disputes to him to settle. Whether it also accounts for his being appointed Sheriff for the County of Hereford, in 1683, is doubtful, since apparently five members of his family, including his grandfather and his uncle, had held this office since the reign of Elizabeth.[28]

Pope not only praised Kyrle for being an arbiter of disputes, but also for his generosity to the poor—

[25] Hereford City Library, L.C. (Deeds), No. 10,718 (2 Aug. 1690).

[26] Hereford City Library, Hopton Collection (Deeds), 77 (1666); L.C. (Deeds), 4164 (1677); B.M. Add. Charters, 13610 (1721). (The final figures, in brackets, indicate the year of the document.)

[27] Hereford City Library, L.C. (Deeds), 7498, (1703); 7499 (1703); 7071 (1716); 929.2 (Rudhall and Westfaling Papers), Item 34 (1708).

[28] Duncomb, op. cit., i, pp. 147–8.

> Behold the Market-place with poor o'erspread!
> The Man of Ross divides the weekly bread:
> He feeds yon Alms-house, neat, but void of state . . .
>
> [*To Bathurst*, ll. 263–5, final version]

That he should have cared for the poor is entirely credible from a perusal of the deeds mentioned above, but Pope's lines are particular. No doubt they refer to Kyrle's own weekly hospitality, communicated to Joseph Spence in 1751: 'He kept two public days in a Week; the Market Day, and Sunday. On the former, the Neighbouring Gentlemen and Farmers dined with him . . . On Sunday he feasted the poor people of the Parish at his House; and not only so, but would often send them home loaded with broken meat and jugs of beer.'[29] Yet this account applies better to Pope's third line than the first two (Rudhall's Almshouse in Ross stood 'close by Mr. Kyrle's garden door'), and it was perhaps to an even more public act, in the Market Place, that Pope chiefly referred:

> Ross was formerly a considerable corn-market; and the tolls of all corn brought to the market, had, on some pious occasion, been given by one of the Bishops, when Lord, to the use of the poor. This was a long while continued by the succeeding Lords. Mr. Kyrle last received such toll, 'having it ground, and having the bread sometimes made at his own house, and baked in his own oven.' This done it was taken every Saturday to the steps in front of the market-house, and distributed by him . . . Tradition reports, in homely language, that 'it would have done one's heart good to see how cheerful the old gentleman looked,' while engaged in distributing the bread. Thus, for a series of years was divided 'the weekly bread;' but on some questions arising between the Townsmen and the Lord, wherein they claimed . . . this concession as matter of perpetual right, the Lord refused so to allow it; and Mr. Kyrle himself was fixed upon by both parties as arbitrator, who honourably making his decision, in favour of the Lord's ownership, the gift was discontinued.[30]

This late, but full and particular account of the weekly alms-giving is a much better explanation of Pope's lines than that given Spence; yet it is not clear why Kyrle, who was far from being the lord of the manor, came to receive the toll. It has been suggested that he acted as almoner for the lord of the manor, and the passage perhaps implies that this duty was discharged in turn by the citizens of Ross.[31] It seems clear that this charity was not entirely at Kyrle's own personal charge, whatever Pope may have thought. Kyrle's contribution, characteristic of his provident and thoughtful ways, was to grind the corn and bake the bread at his own expense, instead of merely selling the corn for the poor's benefit.

---

[29] Spence, *Anecdotes*, ed. S. W. Singer, p. 438 (Duck to Spence, 1 Jan. 1751).

[30] Fosbroke, op. cit., pp. 10–11.

[31] R. Chambers. *The Book of Days: A Miscellany of Popular Antiquities* . . . (London, 1864), ii, p. 557.

The life Kyrle chose to lead enabled him to be an understanding patron and companion of workmen, and it is evident that he had a special regard for those who were old or in difficulties. He indulged his 'incorrigible passion for planting', on his small estate, by employing 'very old Men, such whose Age or infirmities rendered them incapable of doing such very hard labour, as the Farmers required their Servants to do. With these old Men he would frequently work with a spade himself; pay them amply for their Labour; and often feed them at his own Table.'[32] 'He used to send many old and infirm poor persons of Ross into the woods and fields, to pick up self-sown oaks, ashes, &c. to embelish the hedge-rows of his walks and estate.'[33] Financial hardship at any age was something Kyrle tried to mitigate, and it seems tenants and workmen of other masters sometimes brought their problems to him. This is shown in the first of the few of his letters which have survived:

> Ross, this 8th of November, 1703
>
> Good Sir,
>
> When I writ to you last I defer'd my giving you an account of your tenant Thomas Hopkins; since w'ch time his daughter call'd upon me every Thursday, and told me that her father was busie a sowing, but if I would have him come hither any day on purpose he would come, but his sowing being over, he was with me on Thursday last. He sed he was very sensible of his owing you a good deal of rent; but ever since the cheapness of corn, he began to be behind with Mr. Rogers. He shewed me an acquittance for paying lately at Bristow for his use 40l.; also he shew'd me a harsh letter writ to him for more: but he sed that Mr. Rogers had not don anything unjust in ye least: This I mention, tho' I know it is nothing to you; but as to your concern, he sed he will be sure by Christmas to clear with you last Lady-Day's rent, and last Michaelmas rent before next Lady-Day. The first I believe he will do, but I fear he will not be punctual to the latter . . .

The homely discursive tone expresses a steady, unflustered concern for the tenant as a person, which Kyrle is rather conscious that his correspondent will not share ('This I mention, tho' I know it is nothing to you . . .') and he is wisely anxious that Hopkins should not make things worse for himself by making unrealistic promises. Kyrle does not appeal to his correspondent for forebearance, but the picture of Hopkins which the letter gives is of a man doing his best under difficulties, and whom it would be pointless to press to greater effort. The correspondent, Mr. Walwyn of Longworth, could draw his own conclusion.

I shall quote the letter to the end because of the authentic sense it conveys of Kyrle's everyday concerns:

> . . . Wee did talk of moving the stocks in the nursery, and with them to make two small orchards in two places standing most convenient. He is

---

[32] Spence, *Anecdotes*, ed. S. W. Singer, p. 438 (Duck to Spence, 1 Jan. 1751).
[33] *The Gentleman's Magazine*, 1786, lvi–ii, p. 1026.

to inquire if there are any workmen in ye neighbourhood that are expert
in planting and give me an account thereof on Thursday next; If there are
none such, then I intend to take some from hence that know very well how
to digg and set trees.

I lately spoak w'th Mr. Roberts, who sees that your fine will be perfected by ye end of this term, and then he intends to wait upon you with
all yo'r writings. I thought to have seen you before this, and I lately resolved
to be at Longworth on Friday next, but something falls out yt. prevents;
and now I think to be with you on Saturday next in ye evening, if ye weather
proves favourable, but of that I am not certain; for our maid Francis lyes
very ill and 'tis fear'd will not recover.

With my service to yr brother and all ye ladies.

I rest

Your friend and servant,

John Kyrle.[34]

The letter is typical. Two of Kyrle's recurrent interests, planting and the law,
are lightly touched on here, preserved as it were accidentally in the everyday
discourse of a letter which has chanced to survive; so is his solicitude for a
sick servant. Such ordinary impressions as these went to the making of a
reputation which eventually reached Pope's ears and became a part of his
work.

3. GOOD HUSBANDRY

In February 1706 a report reached Kyrle that a gentleman of his acquaintance,
George Scudamore of Blackbrook, Monmouthshire, something of an early
industrialist as well as the possessor of an estate, considered himself to have
been maligned by him. The old gentleman wrote in some confusion to Scudamore to defend himself, and in so doing produced a letter which reveals much
that was closest to his heart:

Sir,

I lately understood that you were inform'd that I did speake scurrilous
words reflecting on you, at which I was very much surprised, knowing
that twas much against my thoughts and inclination so to doe. I could not
imagin from whence such report should proceed; at length I call'd to mind
that some gentlemen dining with me (amongst other discourse) it was
talk't of some that had good estates and did not make use of them; and I
remember I sed, that I knew no difference between a man of an estate
that still made it his business to be richer and richer, or a man of a smaller
estate and made use of it, or words to this purpose; and I remember we had
afterwards some occasions of speaking of you, but cannot say, or think that
this discourse was applied to you; but take it that it was, I am sure I speak
no hurt, for I think I should do very ill to speak against one that did not

[34] John Kyrle to J. Walwyn of Longworth, 8 Nov. 1703; *The Gentleman's Magazine*, 1828,
xcviii-2, p. 196–7.

deserve it of me, especially against yourself, from whom I have received kindnesses; and then again, if I should be so base as to raile at you undeservedly behind your back, certainly I had been a mad man so to doe in presence of a person that I very well knew was like to be neare related to you . . .

If Merchant Pye had been alive and I had said so much of him, he had but laught at it, and me, for talking so prodigally, in running down good husbandry, which he lov'd; for he often sed, that he would have every one that sold his estate after to be hang'd; therefore pray do not harbour any thing against me on this account, for on my salvation there is nothing in it, being I did alwaies desire appear

Your Friend, and humble Servant,
John Kyrle.[35]

Ross this 7th of February 1705 [O.S.].

What emerges even more clearly from this letter than Kyrle's desire not to be thought guilty of 'scurrilous words' is the importance with which he regarded the proper handling of an estate. The letter rambles, is not entirely consistent (since it is not clear that 'good husbandry' is the same thing as getting 'richer and richer'), and the force of his final 'therefore' is very uncertain, but his fundamental affirmation is clear. An estate should not be regarded primarily as a capital asset for increasing one's wealth, but as something which has been granted for *use*—perhaps for the benefit of the community as well as the owner. And the use of an estate demands 'good husbandry', in order that the most can be made of it. Kyrle possibly agreed with the violent sentiments of Merchant Pye on those who sold their estates. Pye had been a Barbados merchant, and resembled Scudamore of Blackbrook in deriving income from sources other than his lands, which is perhaps why Kyrle mentions him. We may speculate as to what lay behind Pye's remark. It is likely that he considered land the most secure form of wealth, in the first place; and since there is difference between land and an estate, it is likely that he also thought there were human responsibilities consequent upon the possession of an estate. Whether Kyrle too held such opinions can best be judged from a consideration of the 'husbandry' with which he treated his own small holdings of land, and with which he encouraged his fellow-townsmen to treat the environs of Ross.

In 1733 Hearne accepted that Kyrle's estate 'was worth five hundred pounds per annum, and no more' and was informed a year later that 'he had a wood, which perhaps once in about fifteen years might bring him in between a 1000 and 1500 lbs.'[36] Spence was told, in 1748, that Kyrle's income 'was no more than 600£ a year. 200 of it lay about Ross.'[37] Thus Pope's dramatic revelation, in his Epistle *To Bathurst*, that Kyrle had no more than 'five hundred pounds

---

[35] Heath, op. cit. np. There is a MS. copy of this letter in the British Museum, Add. 9828, f. 28.

[36] *Reliquiae Hearniae*, iii, pp. 95, 131.

[37] Spence, *Anecdotes*, ed. S. W. Singer, p. 425.

a year' was probably substantially correct. If so, Kyrle had £50 more than the average annual income of the Esquires of England, as calculated by Gregory King for 1688. Kyrle's will mentions freehold lands 'in the town and parish of Ross; and also in the several parishes of Bridstow, Walford, and elsewhere, in the said county of Hereford; and also in the several parishes of Dymock and Berkley . . . in the County of Gloucester'; it refers also to copyhold lands and premises in the manor of Ross Foreign.[38] These were the source of Kyrle's income. It is clear that his land, freehold and copyhold, was very scattered, and that there would have been no possibility of joining it into a continuous estate. Kyrle's good husbandry consisted in great measure of the planting and nurturing of trees, shown by the rather categorical instructions of his will:

> And in regard thereto I have improved my estates by planting fruit and other trees, which are as well ornamented [sic] as well as beneficial to the same, I do hereby order, direct and desire that no wilful waste or destruction shall be committed thereon by defacing or cutting down timber trees, before they come to their perfection or otherwise; the same having been planted by my great care and industry, for the improvement of the sd premises.
>
> And I do hereby also order, direct and desire that the coppice wood called *Dymokes Wood* shall not at any time hereafter be fallen under sixteen years' growth, that being the most proper and advantageous time for cutting thereof . . .[39]

Trees were a capital asset and direct source of livelihood for Kyrle; his concern for them was far from being wholly aesthetic. Yet he was concerned with this too: '. . . as well ornamented as . . . beneficial' are his words. In planting was to be found that identity of usefulness and beauty, which Horace had recommended in poetry, and which Pope and the Earl of Burlington were to make the cardinal principle of their philosophy of architecture and landscape gardening.

It is clear that Kyrle had the enthusiasms of a landscape gardener. While he had neither means nor land to create large-scale effects for the gratification of his eye alone, he was able, by a careful use of certain of his small pieces of land, to contribute to a major landscape effect. We have already noticed his purchase in 1666 of the 'meadow ground and pasture' called Cleevefield Bank.[40] This land started a little south-west of Ross Church (which stands at the edge of the highest part of the town) and stretched 'for nearly a mile along the brow of land commanding so many and so changing views'.[41] Half way along the land mounted to 'a rocky eminence, partially clothed with underwood'.[42] The bank commands a fine view over the plain below Ross, through the midst of which runs the Wye which, as Wheeler beautifully des-

[38] Gregory King, *Natural and Political Observations . . . on the State . . . of England* (1697), in *Two Tracts*, ed. G. E. Barnett (Baltimore, 1936), p. 31. Cooke, op. cit., pp. 134–5.
[39] Ibid., p. 136.
[40] See n. 12 above.
[41] Hall, op. cit., p. 24.
[42] Heath, op. cit., np.

cribed it to Spence, 'seems in no hurry to leave the Country, but, like a Hare thats unwilling to leave her habitation, makes a hundred turns and doubles.'[43] Through this land Kyrle constructed a path from which the view might be enjoyed, and along the path planted trees and placed seats.[44] Though the land was in itself so limited, the view it commanded was not. Equally the trees he planted there formed a major element in the prospect of the town and its environs from the plain and river which his land overlooked. As with his philanthropy, so with his landscape gardening, Kyrle created much out of little. The factual reference behind Pope's grand line

> Who hung with woods yon mountains sultry brow?
>
> [*To Bathurst*, l. 253]

is to Kyrle's planting activities on Cleeve-field Bank.[45] The plain, like the hill, received his attention also. A part of the prospect from Cleeve-field Bank was the road and bridge over the Wye which connected Ross with Hereford and Monmouth. On the Ross side of the bridge the ground and road were low-lying and were often rendered impassable by floods. 'Accordingly, Mr. Kyrle, (whose mind seemed ever awake to promote the public interest) procured a subscription, and accomplished the purpose, by building a noble Stone Causeway, so that the road was kept constantly open, except in cases of very extraordinary *freshes* . . .'[46] 'It is certain', says another writer, 'that the recently levelled causeway leading to Wilton bridge was built through the exertions of Mr. Kyrle, who procured large contributions, and subscribed himself amply for that generous purpose; and that the late "shady rows" of elms on each side were planted with his own hands,'[47] and Wheeler, writing to Spence, noted that Kyrle substantially contributed to the 'long handsome Causeway which leads to the Town . . . with the stately Avenues of Elms planted by it.'[48] This improvement was both useful and handsome. Pope referred to it and to Cleeve-field Bank in his couplet:

> Whose Cause-way parts the vale with shady rows?
>
> Whose Seats the weary Traveller repose?
>
> [*To Bathurst*, ll. 259–60]

Cleeve-field Bank was presumably laid out and planted early in Kyrle's residence at Ross; the building and planting of the causeway must have been comparatively early too, if the elms grew into shady rows in time for Pope to hear about them.

Kyrle was already fifty six, however, when the opportunity occurred for his best piece of 'good husbandry'. In 1692 the Dowager Duchess of Somerset

---

[43] Spence, *Anecdotes*, ed. S. W. Singer, p. 424.

[44] Heath, op. cit., np.; Fosbroke, op. cit., p. 9.

[45] Heath, op. cit., np.; Fosbroke, op. cit., pp. 8–9. Pope's peculiar poetic blend of fact and panegyric, in the portrait of Kyrle and elsewhere, is valuably discussed in Rachel Trickett, *The Honest Muse: A Study in Augustan Verse* (Oxford, 1967), pp. 1–3, and Ch. VI.

[46] Heath, op. cit., np.

[47] Fosbroke, op. cit., p. 9.

[48] Spence, *Anecdotes*, ed. S. W. Singer, pp. 424–5.

died, and the lordship of the manor of Ross passed to Thomas Thynne, Viscount Weymouth.[49] On 1 Oct. 1693 Kyrle procured a copyhold lease from Lord Weymouth, for £5 per annum, of the six or so acres of land which separated Ross Churchyard from his freehold property of Cleeve-field Bank. The lease was for five hundred years.[50] The coincidence of dates suggests that Kyrle may have had some difficulty in obtaining a lease from the Duchess of Somerset. In May 1696 Kyrle granted a sub-lease to the proprietor of the Pounds Inn, which stood on the copyhold property, and to which the land was a valuable amenity, for a period just short of that in which Kyrle's heir or representative was due to render the property back to the lord of the manor. In this document Kyrle recites his original intention in procuring the lease from Lord Weymouth, and states that he

> still did intend and design at his own costs, to set out the parcel of land (called Bishop's Court,) into walks, and to plant rows of trees, and to raise fine grass plots therein, and ornaments as he should devise, to make the same *a public and free walking place for the inhabitants of Ross and all other persons who should resort thither for their walking and diversion* . . .

The sub-lease was granted (including grazing rights on the land) in return for a rent of £5 per annum, but reserved to Kyrle 'full liberty and power to accomplish and perfect his designs', and

> free liberty, power, and authority, for every person or inhabitant of Ross, and all other persons whatsoever, from time to time, and at all times during the term, to go into and have free ingress and egress to and from and in the said piece of land . . . as well for their walking and diversion as also for the whitening and drying of linen clothes, upon the grass plots and hedges there, without the leave or licence, or of paying or rendering any recompence or reward whatsoever.

The sub-lessee was precluded from hindering or spoiling 'the prospect and the pleasantness thereof' and bound to keep the walls in repair.[51] We may infer from this document that Kyrle had encountered opposition to his design from the keeper of the Pounds Inn, but had managed to surmount it by making a concession which at the same time established the sub-lessee as an effective trustee for his new 'public and free walking place'.

All was now ready for Kyrle to go ahead with his plan. The land was to be levelled, surrounded by a stone wall with gateways, and in the centre there was to be a fountain. It is probable that Kyrle was his own architect for this work; Wheeler reported to Spence that 'Tho' he was passionately fond of Architecture, yet he was contented to live in an Old House' and that though he was normally early to bed, yet

[49] Cooke, op. cit., pp. 105–6.

[50] Hall, op. cit., p. 24. This work contains the fullest account of Kyrle's design in leasing the Prospect, and quotes from the relevant deeds which seem, since the lawsuit about the Prospect in 1887, to have disappeared.

[51] Ibid., pp. 29–32.

friends, who knew his Passion, enter'd upon the subject of Building, when they had a mind to have an hour or two extraordinary with him. I've heard, to encourage a Gentleman who wanted a better House, he wou'd offer to advance a moderate Sum of Money, provided that he shou'd plan and supervise the Building. I'm told his taste was often gratify'd without any expence . . .[52]

Only the southern half of the enclosed area, since called The Prospect, survives today. Nevertheless the original Prospect can be reconstructed to a degree of probability. There were three gateways, in the centres of the north, south and east walls, the west wall overlooking the steep drop down to the plain and the Wye. The east and south gateways remain, and are in different styles: the east, which was the main entrance, opening from the Churchyard, composed of piers upholding big vases, supported from left and right by volutes.[53] The south gate stands 'very dignified, like some College gate at Oxford, with its Corinthian pilasters, its pediment, and its cypher and date.'[54] It is probable that a gateway in similar style faced it from the north wall, thus completing the symmetry of the Prospect. In the centre of the west wall, facing the main entrance, was originally a recess which contained a sundial with Kyrle's name and arms carved on the plate.[55] In the centre of the Prospect there was an oval basin, paved at the bottom with square stones, in the middle of which stood a fountain in the form of a figure, through which the water was thrown up. This water was pumped up from the river Wye below by means of an engine, passed through the sandstone rock of the Prospect in pipes, was thrown to 'an amazing height' in the fountain, and then conveyed by underground pipes to cocks in the streets of the town, thus giving Ross its first water-supply.[56] The pumping machinery must have been a water-engine (using the current of the river to turn a wheel) such as the engineer George Sorocold had designed for several English cities between 1692 and 1696.[57] The basic principle was not new (one had been designed for use in London in 1581) and the Herefordshire gentleman Thomas Baskerville described, c. 1673, a water engine at Worcester which sounds very similar to Kyrle's: 'a waterwork, which [by] the stream of the river, without help of horses, having a wheel which gives motion to suckers and forcers, it pumps the water so high into a leaden cistern that it serves any part of the city.'[58] It is probable that Kyrle saw such an engine operating in London or in Worcester, and realized its potentialities for Ross. It may be seen that Pope's very dramatic line:

From the dry rock who bade the waters flow?

[*To Bathurst*, l. 254]

[52] Spence, *Anecdotes*, ed. S. W. Singer, pp. 423-4.
[53] Hall, op. cit., p. 25; and see Nikolaus Pevsner, *The Buildings of England: Herefordshire* (Harmondsworth, 1963), p. 279.
[54] Pevsner, op. cit., p. 279.
[55] Hall, op. cit., p. 25.
[56] Heath, op. cit. 'The Prospect', np.; Fosbroke, op. cit., p. 8; Hall, op. cit., p. 27.
[57] See F. W. Robins, *The Story of Water-Supply* (Oxford, 1946), pp. 164-5.
[58] Robins, p. 163; H.M.C. 29 (Portland), ii, p. 291 (for the date of the account see p. 259).

with its powerful allusion to Moses striking the rock,[59] has also an extremely precise factual reference. The only other feature of the Prospect not so far mentioned is a brass plate set in the north wall, in the north-west corner, which set out a table of equivalent distances by which someone who had walked so many times round the Prospect might gauge how far he had walked, and how this compared with known local distances such as Ross Church to Western Church, Brampton Church, etc. It was inscribed with a Latin motto: 'Trahit sua quemque voluptas' and the date: 1700.[60]

The gates also bore the date 1700, and it is probable that by the turn of the century John Kyrle had completed his work on the Ross Prospect. With a small, but well-chosen, piece of ground he had once again created a major piece of landscape-gardening. This time it cannot have been cheap. Kyrle regained his £5 per annum rent through his sub-lease, and a subscription was raised to meet the cost of the waterworks.[61] Nevertheless he must have had to contribute substantially to the subscription to get it started, and the fine architecture of the gateways (and probably the fountain) must have been expensive in time as well as money to a man of his small means. But his achievement was a fine one. The splendid view had always been there, but by his lease and his architecture Kyrle dedicated it with goodwill, dignity and grace to the *public*: 'inhabitants of Ross and all other persons'. The river Wye had always been there, but now its waters were used to provide power, a beautiful spectacle, and a fundamental amenity, again for the welfare of the public. And in the service of the public Kyrle's conception had a certain dignity and magnificence. Furthermore the execution was adequate to the conception; the south gate shows no trace of the rustic or amateur, which would hardly have been surprising in the circumstances; mass, form and decoration are all well judged.[62] Only the table of equivalent distances seems to have been quaint and clumsy, but even this betrays part of Kyrle's inner purpose. He was, as Pope saw, concerned with achieving the great through the small; he could not walk, as he might have liked, from Ross Church to Western Church on his own land, but he and others poorer than himself could walk an equivalent distance, before an extensive and magnificent view, on land which through him had become that of the public. In this achievement Kyrle was not modest and self-effacing. His name and arms adorned the sundial opposite the chief entrance to the Prospect, his cypher the pediment of the south and north gates. As he made clear in his will, he desired that his name should be perpetuated.[63]

Two further details must be added to this picture of Kyrle's activities in Ross. The first Pope makes no reference to but it would certainly have aroused his interest. In the garden behind his timber-frame house in the Market

[59] See Wasserman, op. cit., p. 42.

[60] Hall, op. cit., p. 26; Heath, op. cit. 'The Prospect', np.

[61] Fosbroke, op. cit., p. 8; Hall, op. cit., p. 27.

[62] See Pevsner, op. cit., p. 279.

[63] Hall, op. cit., p. 25; and see the surviving South Gate. For the will, see Cooke, op. cit., p. 135 (it states that if Kyrle's lands are inherited by a female line, the heir shall take the surname of Kyrle).

Place Kyrle sometimes occupied himself with decoration on the smallest scale: a winding path to a summer house is crossed by three little grotto arches; this was very early for such garden embellishments. The second detail is one fraught with symbolic implication which Pope was not slow to exploit by another of his resonant lines in Kyrle's portrait in the Epistle *To Bathurst*. In 1721, three years before Kyrle's death, it became evident that the spire of Ross Church badly needed repair; by his motion a parish meeting was convened which resolved to take down and rebuild some forty eight feet of the spire. Once again Kyrle contributed a substantial sum towards this work, which he is also said to have inspected every day.[64] Once again Pope's line suggests precise practical knowledge. A correspondent of Hearne in 1733 declared that Pope was mistaken in thinking Kyrle 'the founder' of the church and spire of Ross,[65] but what Pope actually said:

Who taught that heav'n-directed spire to rise?   [l. 261]

would have been a pointless circumlocution had he meant that Kyrle built the spire. It is beautifully apt for what Kyrle actually did: to take down and rebuild a spire which already existed. Kyrle's motives were no doubt mainly pious, but it is worth noticing that the view of Ross from Wilton Bridge and the Wye, including his planting and improvements on Cleeve-field Bank and the Prospect, is dominated by the church spire: the centre and culmination of the scene. Religious and aesthetic motives probably blended in his mind.

From the way in which Kyrle used his land, and from his other activities in Ross, we may infer what he had in mind when, at that dinner at his house, he grew warm on the subject of estates and gave offence to George Scudamore of Blackbrook. He believed that the latent value of an estate should be exploited to its utmost for the public benefit and the maintenance and fame of the owner. If this is not precisely what Merchant Pye had meant by 'good husbandry' the phrase nevertheless describes very well the nature of Kyrle's life, his treatment of his property, and his attitude to the public.

There can be no doubt that Kyrle was loved and esteemed at Ross for his good husbandry, but not everyone thought well of him. On 18 April 1734 Mr. Matthew Gibson, the incumbent of Abbey Dore in Herefordshire, paid a call on Thomas Hearne. Asked if he knew Kyrle, Gibson said he did, and that his wife was Kyrle's niece. 'I told him,' noted Hearne,

the said *man of Ross* was an extraordinary charitable generous man, and did much good. He said he did do a great deal of good, but that 'twas all out of vanity and ostentation, being the vainest man living, and that he always hated his relations, and would never look upon, or do anything for them, tho' many of them were very poor.[66]

[64] Pevsner, op. cit., p. 281. The garden may still be seen. For the spire see Fosbroke, op. cit., pp. 9–10; and Cooke, op. cit., p. 109, quoting the Parish Register (now in the Hereford City Library) for 1721, which reads: 'This Year the Spire was rebuilt, (i:e) abt. 16 yards of it. And also three of ye. Pinacles.'

[65] *Reliquiae Hearniae*, iii, p. 131.

[66] Ibid., pp. 131–2.

Doubtless Kyrle was proud of his works and reputation, and we have already noticed his name and arms on the architecture of the Prospect. It would not be surprising if the poorer members of his family resented his gifts to the public, though they too might benefit from them. That Kyrle always *hated* his relations is an interesting charge. It is no doubt exaggerated, but it cannot but call to mind his marked departure from family expectations at the beginning of the Restoration, and perhaps suggests a continuing failure to see eye to eye with them politically. It is hard to believe he refused to help them, however, and there is one piece of evidence which calls in doubt Gibson's testimony. On 11 Feb. 1712 Kyrle wrote to Harley, the Lord Treasurer (with whose family the Kyrles had been in political alliance during the Civil War) to beg the place of postmaster at Hereford for a relative whom he specifically mentioned to be the nephew of Colonel Kyrle. This relative, described as a person in bad circumstances from the decay of trade, but civil, and conforming to the established Church, was probably Vandevort Kyrle, whom John Kyrle named in his will.[67] But perhaps Hearne himself had the best answer to Mr. Gibson:

> I know not what credit to give to Mr. Gibson in that account, especially since this same Gibson hath more than once, in my presence, spoke inveterately against that good honest man Dr. Adam Ottley, late bp. of St. David's. Besides, this Gibson is a crazed man, and withall stingy, tho' he be rich, and hath no child by his wife.[68]

4. KYRLE AND POPE

John Kyrle was not only 'a *daily* attendant at church' ('at the chiming of the bells, all business ceased with him . . .') and a strong supporter of 'Church and King': that 'Ecclesiastical Government' under which the people of Ross 'and their ancestors lived so happily, to God's glory and their own comfort,' but all the actions of his life have an almost early Christian ring. He cared for the poor, fed the hungry, healed the sick, used his talents and his lands to the full, and gave to the public rather than to his family. And just as the spire of Ross Church, pointing heavenwards, was the culminating point in the prospect of Ross which he helped to create by his labours on Cleeve-field Bank, the Wilton Bridge Causeway and the Prospect itself, so all Kyrle's life may be seen as a single act of worship. The nature of his Christian inspiration and emotion is well conveyed by an episode which, though it has almost the feel of folklore, is particular and likely to be authentic. The old custom of perambulating the parish boundaries, on Holy Thursday and at other times of the year, was traditionally practised in Ross. The parish priest in his surplice, with a number of followers often including children, would move from one point of demarcation to another on the parish boundary, and at each point a passage from the Gospel would be read aloud. Such a demarcation point, between the parishes of Ross and Weston, was a 'large and handsome' oak

---

[67] H.M.C. 29 (Portland), v, p. 143. The father of this relative, according to the letter, was the youngest brother of Colonel Kyrle. See Robinson, op. cit., pp. 280-1.

[68] *Reliquiae Hearniae*, iii, p. 132.

tree, known as the gospel oak,

which grew over a spring, in the bottom of a little meadow, called 'the Flaxridge.' . . . at this spring, and beneath this oak, rested Mr. Kyrle, with the Rev. Thomas Rosse, then curate of Ross and the parishioners (including boys of the blue-coat school,) in perambulation on the 31st of May, 1709.

Mr. Rosse being vested, the company reverently uncovered as he unclasped the sacred volume, and, where the book chanced to open, he began to read. The tradition of that interesting moment is preserved which infers the genuine piety of 'The Man of Ross'. He stood near to the minister, and as the reading proceeded, was observed raising his hat to his face to conceal *his tears*! The portion of scripture was nearly the whole of the 4th chapter according to St. John; and the scenery seemed to associate with the subject: —our Lord and the woman of Samaria.[69]

The passage which most associates with the scenery, as they stood by the spring in Flaxridge Meadow, concerns Jacob's well near the city of Sychar:

There cometh a woman of Samaria to draw water: Jesus saith unto her, Give me to drink . . .
Then saith the woman of Samaria unto him, How is it that thou, being a Jew, askest drink of me, which am a woman of Samaria? . . .
Jesus answered and said unto her, If thou knewest the gift of God, and who it is that saith it to thee, Give me to drink; thou wouldst have asked of him, and he would have given thee living water . . . whosoever drinketh of . . . the water that I shall give him shall be in him a well of water springing up into everlasting life.[70]

When the reading was finished, the party settled down to eat.

The procession had provisions in a basket, and bottles of cider; but Mr. Kyrle dipped a wooden can in the well, and drank of the spring. One of the churchwardens, (a Mr. Maddocks) expressed a fear that Mr. Kyrle might take *cold*. '*No*' replied the good old man, '*what we have just been listening to, has made my heart warm!*'[71]

The episode of the Woman of Samaria is almost an acted parable, designed to drive home the reality of spiritual sustenance and inspiration. Later in the chapter (verses 32, 35) Christ says: 'I have meat to eat that ye know not of . . . Lift up your eyes and look on the fields; for they are white already to harvest.' By refusing the drink the party had brought with them, and drinking instead from the spring, Kyrle symbolically acted out and applied the parable. He

[69] Fosbroke, op. cit., pp. 34–5: 'There is,' he notes, 'an original memorandum of this perambulation extant, among the parish papers at Ross, having the signatures of Mr. Rosse, Mr. Kyrle, the churchwardens, and others present.' (p. 34). The memorandum does not appear to have survived, but the Parish Register confirms that Thomas Rosse was curate in 1709.

[70] John 4: 7–11, 13–14.

[71] Fosbroke, op. cit., p. 35.

affirmed his choice of 'living water', of a Christian inspiration within him, 'steady as a water in a well, to a poise, to a pane,' constantly replenished.[72] Report of this episode may or may not have come to the ears of Pope, but Pope grasped the central truth which it expresses, that Kyrle's life was a 'living example' of Christianity.[73]

Kyrle died on 20 Nov. 1724, aged eighty seven, and his soul, if he were not deceived in his faith, was 'made a partaker of those heavenly mansions which [Christ] has prepared for his elect before the beginning of the world'—a hope which Kyrle expressed in these words in his will.[74] His body lay in state in his house for twelve days; then 'he was borne to the grave by his workmen with usual attendants, male and female mourners, and amidst the whole population of the parish of Ross.'[75] 'No monument, inscription, stone,' as Pope's poem correctly bore witness, marked the vault in Ross Church until 1750, except that his initials were carved on the adjoining wall.[76]

This was the life of John Kyrle, the Man of Ross. While it is in many ways a remarkable life, there is nothing about it that would have seemed brilliant, dramatic or striking to a society which increasingly looked to the capital for the most compelling human achievements and events of the time: London from the restoration of Charles II to the coming of the Hanoverians. Kyrle's life was unashamedly provincial; he might have been a man of the City but chose instead that the significance of his life should be in the country, in the market town where most of his small property lay. The surrounding neighbourhood gave him his 'title' of the Man of Ross, and his fame spread in Herefordshire, and the adjoining counties.[77] But how did Pope come to hear about him, and why did he attach so much importance to this example? Before publication of Pope's two letters to Jacob Tonson Senior, in *The Gentleman's Magazine* of 1836, local writers about Ross used to assume a personal acquaintance between Kyrle and Pope. Charles Heath heard it said that Pope, taken ill while staying in the neighbourhood, came to Ross for the benefit of the air, and received the friendly attentions of Kyrle.[78] T. D. Fosbroke was categorically informed that

> Pope used to visit a Roman Catholic family, then living at Old Over ross, in the parish of Ross: he was thus in the way of correct information, as to the character and acts of Mr. Kyrle. Possibly too the old gentleman himself might have been a neighbourly visitor, or at the same house; for it is certain, that he was very adverse to bell-ringing and bonfires on the fifth of November.[79]

[72] G. M. Hopkins, 'The Wreck of the Deutschland', stanza 4.
[73] *Corr.*, iii, p. 316 (Pope to Caryll, 27 Sept. 1732).
[74] Ross Parish Register, 20 Nov. 1724; Cooke, op. cit., p. 134.
[75] Fosbroke, op. cit., pp. 14–15.
[76] Ibid., p. 14.
[77] Regarding the title: 'Man of Ross,' see Cooke, op. cit., p. 110, Heath, op. cit., np. and Pope's note: 'a name given by way of Eminence' (Wasserman, op. cit., p. 67).
[78] Heath, op. cit., np.
[79] Fosbroke, op. cit., p. 7.

There was a Roman Catholic family at Over Ross, the Vaughans, one of whom was suddenly put into the commission of the peace in 1687, when James II created many J.P.s of his own religion.[80] Subsequently they fell into difficulties (common enough for Catholics at this time) and between 1694 and 1703 John Kyrle stood in trust for several substantial sums owing to John and Mary Vaughan and their children, connected with the sale of their property in Over Ross. By 1703, John Vaughan is referred to as 'late of Over Rosse, now of Hundsome.'[81] These references sketch what must have been the fortune of many of the less wealthy Catholic gentry in the reigns of James II and William III. There is thus some slight substance in Fosbroke's information, and it is worth knowing that Kyrle befriended Roman Catholics, but I have been able to find no connection between Pope and the Vaughans of Over Ross. The publication of Pope's two letters to Tonson about Kyrle seemed (deceptively) to put an end to speculation of this kind, for in the first of these Pope was found to have written:

> You live not far from *Ross*. I desire you to get me an Exact information of the *Man of Ross*, what was his Xtian name & Surname? what year he dyed, & about what age? and to transcribe his Epitaph, if he has one. And any Particulars you can procure about him. I intend to make him an Example in a Poem of mine.[82]

That was on 14 Nov. 1731. On 7 June 1732 Pope thanked Tonson for sending him 'so many particulars of the Man of Ross' and remarked: 'You know, few of these particulars can be made to shine in verse, but I have selected the most affecting, and have added 2 or 3 which I learnd fro' other hands.'[83] These letters not only ruled out the possibility that Pope had been acquainted with Kyrle, but seemed to confirm what Hearne had noted (but not published) in 1734: 'Mr. Pope had the main of his information about Mr. Kirle . . . from Jacob Tonson, the bookseller . . .'[84] But the matter is not so simple, for Pope would hardly have decided to make Kyrle so important an example in his poem, having heard only a *little* about him. However much Tonson told him (his letter has not survived) Pope must originally have had 'the main of his information' from another source. This is confirmed by an earlier letter of Pope, not published until 1956. Writing on 8 Sept. 1731 to Hugh Bethel about 'the Moral Book' which was to be his Epistle *To Bathurst*, Pope declared:

> I have been so pleasd, when I meet with a Good Example or character (as it is a Curiosity now) that I have sent Express Enquiries after the Particulars to be Exact in the celebration of it and with great contentment find, that

---

[80] Cooke, op. cit., p. 108.
[81] Hereford City Library, L.C. (Deeds), 7465 (1694); 7498 (1703); 7499 (1703). The last of these records John Vaughan's move from Ross to Huntsome.
[82] *Corr.*, iii, p. 244.
[83] Ibid., p. 290.
[84] *Reliquiae Hearniae*, iii, p. 131.

what I writ of the Good Works of the Man of Ross, is to a Tittle true. I
think you saw those Verses—[85]

Thus Pope had not only heard about Kyrle's good works, and checked up
on them, before writing to Tonson, but had also drafted the passage on Kyrle
and shown it to Bethel. Pope's purpose in writing to Tonson must have been
to confirm his information by another source, and make doubly sure of its
authenticity by pretending to know little or nothing already. Since it was rare
indeed for any gentleman *not* to have an epitaph, Pope's request that Tonson
should 'transcribe his Epitaph, *if he has one*' (my italics) now suggests that
Pope knew perfectly well he had not, and the reference to '2 or 3 particulars
fro' other hands' is revealed as a genteel equivocation for the fact that Pope
already knew more about Kyrle than Tonson had told him. It is also possible,
as Sherburn suggests, that Pope was using Tonson to create interest in his
poem and its portrait of the Man of Ross prior to publication.[86] Pope's knowledge of Kyrle can be followed one definite stage further back. In the first
week of May 1730 Joseph Spence made a memorandum concerning a draft
poem by Pope on the subject of Job:

> . . . Sir Balaam: The Man of Ross: The standing jest of Heaven. And sure
> the Gods and we are of a mind. The man possesd of debts & taxes clear,
> children and wife—five hundred pound a year (public buildings, alms
> houses, walks, road; The Man of Ross divides the weekly bread; public
> table twice a week for strangers etc.)—Will give what we desire; fire, meat
> and drink. What more? meat, drink, & fire.[87]

This note is of great interest. It shows that Pope knew a number of the salient
facts about Kyrle before the date of Spence's entry; it almost certainly shows
what particulars first impressed Pope in what he heard about him: his single
state, his small income, his public works and his open hospitality; most important of all it suggests how central Pope's idea of the Man of Ross was to
the whole design of the poem in which Pope was to place him. For although at
the stage of this memorandum the Epistle *To Bathurst* had not emerged into
separation from the wider moral scheme ('Mr. Pope says he foresees already
[it] will take up at least a thousand verses') Kyrle's example is here seen in
close connection with other dominant examples and conceptions of the
completed Epistle.[88] The fundamental contrast between Sir Balaam and the
Man of Ross is here suggested: the one putting his trust in chance and the
world, through pride, to end in violence, disease and death; the other accepting
a lowly station with humility to lead a life entirely outgoing and creative.
Balaam and Kyrle mark the two moral and religious extremes of the poem,
the positive example being placed significantly at the centre, the negative at

[85] *Corr.*, iii, p. 227.
[86] Ibid., p. 290.
[87] Spence, 316.
[88] Spence, 293.

the end, as the poem curves downwards into darkness; these two extremes help Pope to answer the opening dilemma of the poem: is man merely 'the standing jest of Heav'n' [l. 4] or something more? This phrase too occurs in Spence's note. So does the line in which Pope was to express the only legitimate expectations man may have of wealth: 'Meat, Cloaths, and Fire.' [l. 82] The line does not occur close to Kyrle's portrait in the completed epistle, and it is interesting that the modest mean by which Pope was to expose the extremes of extravagance and avarice was originally connected in his mind with Kyrle's contentment at a life of relative simplicity. Spence's memorandum shows that Kyrle was behind the scenes of much of the Epistle *To Bathurst* when he did not actually hold the stage.

Sometime before May 1730 Pope heard a good deal about the Man of Ross. His picture of the man and of the place may have built up gradually with different details from different sources. He had several friends who may have told him about Kyrle. Robert Harley, the Earl of Oxford, whose family as we have seen had been acquainted with the Kyrles in the past, lived at his Hereford-shire seat after his fall from power, where Pope sent him his Epistle *To Robert Earl of Oxford* in Autumn 1721.[89] The Man of Ross had corresponded with him on at least one occasion.[90] Oxford's son Edward Harley was long a friend of Pope; he may have told him about Kyrle. Another Herefordshire acquain-tance was Lady Scudamore, the cousin of his friend Robert Digby.[91] Pope twice spoke of visiting Lady Scudamore at her house at Holme Lacy, not far from Ross, and may possibly have done so. Again Lord Bathurst, with his estate at Cirencester in neighbouring Gloucestershire, may have heard of Kyrle and mentioned him to Pope.[92] That Pope should have made him an important example in a poem addressed to Lord Bathurst would have been the more appropriate in this case. It would obviously be appropriate that praise of Kyrle should be prefaced, in the poem, by praise of two of the great nobles of his area, who were also probably sources of information about him. Certainly Lord Bathurst would have been interested in Kyrle's landscaping achievements: the walk, the causeway and the Prospect. If Pope never himself visited Ross (it cannot be proved and equally cannot be ruled out) he must have had an in-formant with a very good visual memory, for Pope presents Kyrle essentially through *scenes*, and in the first place through the view of Ross from the west. This is particularly striking if we look at the earliest surviving MS. version of the passage. This is how it ran:

[89] *Corr.*, ii, pp. 90–91.

[90] H.M.C. 29 (Portland), v, p. 143.

[91] *Corr.*, i, p. 473 (Pope to Robert Digby, 31 March 1718. For Robert Digby, see Ch. V below.)

[92] *Corr.*, ii, p. 240 (Pope to Robert Digby, 27 June ?1724): 'I hope one day to try if she [Lady Scudamore] lives as well as you do . . .'; also ii, p. 314 (Pope to Robert Digby, 12 Aug. ?1725). Bathurst is the source suggested by Cooke, Duncomb's *History of Hereford*, iii, p. 110; that he was the chief source is suggested by his intention to 'survey & criticise' Herefordshire around Holme Lacy (*Corr.*, ii, pp. 304–6 (Robert Digby to Pope, 2 July 1725)). It is curious to note that one Mary Pope, of Twickenham, spinster, leased property in Ross in 1728; Hereford City Library, L.C. (Deeds), 1020.

> Round the white Town on yonder Sunny brow,
> Who hung the Woods, and bad the Waters flow?
> Not to the Skies in useless columns tost,
> Or in vast Sheets magnificently lost,
> But clear and artless, pouring thro' the Plain
> Health to the Sick, and Solace to the Swain?
> Whose Seats the weary Wanderer repose?
> Whose Trees divide the Vale in equal rows?
> Who rais'd that Almshouse, neat, but void of State,
> Where Age & Want sit smiling at the Gate?
> Who taught yon Heav'n-directed Spire to rise?[93]

The first line, with the word 'yonder', establishes the poet and reader in a specific imagined relation to the town; Pope is pointing it out from a distance; it is part of a wider landscape. From the imagined vantage-point the trees which Kyrle had planted at the highest part of the town are visible, so is the spire of the church rising from their midst, so is the river Wye, so are the rows of elms which divide the plain along the Causeway from Wilton Bridge. It was on 'yonder Sunny brow' that Kyrle had placed his seats, and to the top of this eminence that he had raised water from the Wye for the benefit of the town. This is an actual view of Ross: that from the Hereford and Monmouth road across the plain immediately to the west of the town. Only the almshouse could have played no part in the actual scene, and it is significant that this detail was subsequently shifted to a later point in the passage, where we have 'moved into' the town itself. It is worth comparing an ordinary prose description of Ross from the west.

> On a rocky eminence overlooking the Wye stands the town of Ross. Nothing can be more picturesque than its position: it is seen to most advantage from the Hereford road. The Church stands upon an elevated ridge of rock; and the town occupies the rising ground; while behind are wood-crowned hills, as grand in their character and as beautiful as many more celebrated continental scenes . . .[94]

Even the phrase 'white Town' is likely to be descriptively accurate, for though it also suggests a kind of brightness and innocence appropriate to Pope's purpose in the passage, most of the buildings would have been white-washed timber-frame houses like Kyrle's own. Artists reproducing this view a century or so later depicted it as a white town and even the stone-built church tower and spire as light-coloured in the sunlight.[95] It is fairly hard to credit that Pope had not, however briefly, witnessed this scene.

---

[93] Wasserman, op. cit., p. 65.

[94] Hall, op. cit., p. 1.

[95] See, eg. C. Radclyffe's lithograph, coloured by hand, c. 1840, in the Hereford City Museum. Except for the Royal Hotel, built in 1837 on the north part of Kyrle's Prospect, there had been no substantial changes in the town since the time of Pope. It is worth noting that the modern practice of pitching black the timber parts of timber-frame houses had not then begun; such timber weathered to a silver-grey. For the appearance of Ross Church, see the unsigned lithograph, dated 1832, in the Hereford City Museum.

By the same token, however, it does not seem likely that Pope ever entered
the town of Ross itself and saw Kyrle's Prospect. Here Pope seems to have
been working from particulars of information only and to have just grasped
that Kyrle's waterwork was primarily useful rather than ornamental. Had he
visited the Prospect itself he would have realized that the water was raised in
(strictly speaking) a 'useless column' before being conveyed into the streets.[96]
Other particulars were corrected, sharpened or altered between this draft of
the Kyrle passage and the final version. 'Rais'd that Almshouse' was corrected
to 'feeds . . .' no doubt as a result of his enquiries; 'Whose Trees divide . . .'
was sharpened and concentrated to: 'Whose Causeway parts the vale with
shady rows' and 'vast Sheets' was improved to the religiously suggestive
'proud falls'. In the first line quoted, 'Town' was first altered to 'Church'
(perhaps because Kyrle's elms surrounded the church not the town) and
'sunny' to 'airy'; in later MS. drafts and the final version Pope decided in
favour of a less particular but grander effect: 'Who hung with woods yon
mountain's sultry brow' which suggests the conversion of dryness to fertility
and life, and, as we have seen, created in the line following a similar effect and
a more precise factual reference at the same time. From the command:
'Behold the Market-place . . .' onwards the scene has changed. The distant
prospect of Ross has been left behind, and we are in the town itself. Here
the visual quality of the first half of the Kyrle passage is largely absent, despite
Pope's formal intention conveyed in the words 'Behold' and 'yon'; this part
of the passage could easily have been written from information alone. There
have been fewer corrections and changes in the manuscripts here; Pope seems
to have said what he wanted early and stuck to it, improving only minor points
of expression. The one material addition was anticipated in a marginal note
by Pope on the earliest manuscript: 'Trustee for Children'. This, in the next
draft, became:

> Him portion'd maids, apprentic'd orphans blest,
> The young who labour, and the old who rest: [ll. 267–8][97]

which is kept in all the later versions of the poem.

The three manuscripts of the Kyrle passage in the Epistle *To Bathurst* are
the final evidence we have for answering the question: when and in what
way did John Kyrle come into Pope's ken? In this discussion of Kyrle I hope
also to have contributed towards some answers to the further and more important question: why did Kyrle, a person whom Pope never met, mean so
much to the poet? This problem I shall pursue in the third section of this
book, drawing upon the information set out above in the process. Meanwhile
it is appropriate to end this chapter with Pope's somewhat public-sounding
declaration to Tonson of his 'honest purpose of setting up his fame, as an
example to greater and wealthyer men, how they ought to use their fortunes':

---

[96] Pope's lines are also off-target, in that he seems to have thought the water poured through
the plain *after* being raised through the rock.

[97] Wasserman, op. cit., pp. 65, 93.

My motive for singling out this man, was twofold: first to distinguish real and solid worth from showish or plausible expence, and virtue fro' vanity: and secondly, to humble the pride of greater men, by an opposition of one so obscure and so distant from the sphere of publick glory, this proud town. To send you any of the particular verses will be much to the prejudice of the whole; which if it has any beauty, derives it from the manner in which it is *placed*, and the *contrast* (as the painters call it) in which it stands, with the pompous figures of famous, or rich, or high-born men.[98]

[98] *Corr.*, iii, p. 290 (7 June 1732).

II. 'A Principle Profest': John Caryll, second Baron Caryll of Durford (1667–1736) (i)[1]

1. THE PLEA OF THE ROMAN CATHOLIC

No one who reads through the Caryll papers in the British Museum can fail to be struck by the strong sense of identity possessed by this family. Their correspondents felt it too, and phrases such as 'the worthy family', 'all the noble family' occur again and again at the end of letters dealing with personal, financial and religious affairs.[2] The picture of himself entertained by John Caryll, the friend with whom Pope conducted his longest correspondence, was one in which his uncle, Lord Caryll, the Jacobite Secretary of State, had a prominent place; and this in its turn explains why one of Pope's earliest and most elaborate epitaphs, from which the title of this chapter is taken, was for this man, whom the poet never met.[3] My account of John Caryll must keep in sight the recent fortune of his family as a whole; and it must begin with the subject of Pope's epitaph, the man who brought this fortune to its brief and fatal zenith, and whose career casts light on the rest of his family as far as to the third generation. The history of the Carylls in the seventeenth and eighteenth centuries is not, however, like the life of 'the Man of Ross', a body of information which throws light directly on a particular major poem. Rather it is relevant to an understanding of Pope in the context of his age in a less obvious but deeper and more comprehensive way, which bears upon his whole stance as man and artist in relation to the state.

John Caryll, later Lord Caryll and the uncle of Pope's friend of the same name, came of a Sussex landed family, whose chief characteristic was its loyalty to the Roman Catholic religion in a Protestant England. His father, indeed, was arrested at the fall of Arundel Castle to the Parliamentarians in the Civil War, and there followed two painful years in which he was obliged to pay a

---

[1] This is a Jacobite title; see The Marquis of Ruvigny and Raineval, *The Jacobite Peerage* (London, 1904), pp. 26–7. Reference to the Carylls can be confusing, since so many were called John. Of the John Carylls in this and the next chapter, I have (*where context does not make identification clear*) designated John Caryll, the uncle of Pope's friend, as 'Lord Caryll'; Pope's friend as 'John Caryll'; the eldest son of Pope's friend as 'Caryll the younger'; the cousin of Pope's friend as 'Caryll the Usher'; and the grandson of Pope's friend as 'John Baptist Caryll'.

[2] Eg. B.M. Add. 28228, f. 172; f. 320; *Corr.*, iii, p. 316.

[3] 'Epitaph. On John Lord Caryll'; T.E., vi, p. 81; *Corr.*, i, p. 133. The title of this chapter is taken from l. 3.

fine of £2980 to Parliament, and in which he 'resolved to reconcile himself to the Protestant religion.'[4] But by the Restoration he had repented of this; from henceforth the Carylls were steadfastly faithful to Roman Catholicism.[5]

His son, John Caryll, born about 1626, was probably educated at St. Omer; by the age of twenty three he was so much a master of the manners of a small Italian court that the Dowager Duchess of Parma was moved to write two affable and complimentary letters to his parents, at the end of his time 'au service du Duc mon fils'.[6] He married Margaret Drummond, daughter of Sir Maurice Drummond, who had been a page at the courts of James and Charles I.[7] Nothing further is heard of Margaret Drummond, apart from her death in 1667, nor did John Caryll have children. His upbringing and marriage suggest that the Carylls hoped their heir might serve the monarch in some personal capacity, perhaps provide welcome contact at court during times likely to be difficult for Papists. The defeat of Charles I ended their hopes; nothing is known of Caryll's activities during the Interregnum; by the Restoration he was already thirty five. His father still lived, and Caryll seems to have devoted himself to religious and political controversy, and to poetry. There survives in the Caryll papers an eloquent treatise from his hand: 'Not Guilty, or the Plea of the Roman Catholick in England'. It is likely to have been written early in the Restoration, when there was much debate as to whether some of the anti-Catholic laws might not be repealed. In this work Caryll stresses the sufferings of English Catholics in support of Charles I, and boldly declares, at the end, that their religion does not exempt them from but strongly enjoins, loyalty and obedience to the sovereign.[8] So, as we shall see, were the Non-Juror friends of William Digby to argue, on the departure into exile of the Catholic James II. Caryll wrote also for the stage: a tragedy entitled *The English Princess; Or, The Death of Richard III* (1666), which had some success in the theatre with Betterton as Richard ('A most sad, melancholy play, and pretty good, but nothing eminent in it . . .' was Pepys' comment, when he saw it on 6 March 1667); and, very much better, *Sir Salamon Single: or The Cautious Coxcombe* (1671), whose light, terse English is due to Caryll, but the conception and design to Molière.[9]

The year 1679 put an end to a relatively undistinguished period of Caryll's life. In 1678 the five Popish Lords (Stafford, Powis, Arundell, Bellasyse and Petre) had been arrested, on the accusation of Titus Oates, for alleged complicity in the Popish Plot; they were committed to the Tower on 28 October, the Commons resolved to impeach them, and on 3 Dec. the Middlesex Grand Jury found them guilty. Sometime in 1679 Caryll published a poem entitled

---

[4] H. D. Gordon, *The History of Harting . . .* (London, 1877), p. 82.

[5] Henry Foley, ed. *Record of the English Province of the Society of Jesus*, iii (London, 1878), pp. 535–6; Max de Trenqualéon, *West-Grinstead et les Carylls* (Paris, London, 1893), i, p. 434. And see B.M. Add. 28250, f. 175 (Indenture of 1671).

[6] B.M. Add. 28226, f. 2 (16 Sept. 1648).

[7] Foley, op. cit., iii, [facing] p. 534.

[8] The treatise is to be found in B.M. Add. 28252, ff. 140–8.

[9] William Van Lennep, Emmett L. Avery and Arthur H. Scouten, ed. *The London Stage*, Part I (Carbondale, Illinois, 1965), i, pp. 104, 190.

Naboth's Vineyard: Or, The Innocent Traytor: Copied from the Original of Holy Scripture, in Heroick Verse, a work which commented on the Plot, and the unjust arrest, trial, and condemnation of the Catholic Lords. Late in 1679 Caryll himself was arrested and committed to the Tower. One can only wonder whether the publication of his poem was the real cause of the obviously trumped-up accusation against him. It can have carried little conviction for on 22 May 1680, as Luttrell records, 'Sir Henry Tichburn, Mr. Roper, and Mr. Caryll, prisoners in the Tower, were brought to the kings bench bar on their writs of habeus corpus, and their being but a single witnesse against them as to the plott, they were bailed.'[10] We must look more closely at Caryll's part in these events. His poem, *Naboth's Vineyard*, and especially its subtitle: *The Innocent Traytor*, shows the continuity of his thought about the situation of the English Catholics with his treatise 'Not Guilty'. In the poem, however, at least some individuals are reflected upon, though the biblical parallel does not work efficiently. Achab the king must be Charles if anyone; Malchus is certainly Oates; Arod the judge is Sir William Scroggs, the Lord Chief Justice, and at that time a well known scorner of Catholics.[11] Jesebel the queen, however, an important character in the poem, cannot surely be Catherine of Braganza, herself a Catholic. This is a poem of unjust trial and condemnation; the portrait of Naboth clearly alludes to one, perhaps more than one, of the Catholic Lords found guilty on 3 Dec. 1678. The importance of the vineyard itself in the chosen fable of Caryll's poem suggests he had William Howard, Viscount Stafford (1614–80), particularly in mind, for Stafford, in 1664, had unsuccessfully petitioned Charles to restore to his wife the Earldom of Stafford, and other dignities, lost to her family on the attainting of her ancestor Edward, Duke of Buckingham.[12] On the other hand, Caryll's Naboth had distinguished himself by military service to his monarch, and here perhaps Arundell of Wardour betters fits the part.[13] Caryll must have been acquainted with his kinsman, Lord Petre, and his neighbour, Lord Arundell; probably he knew all five of the accused lords. Probably the Naboth of his poem is a composite figure.

The importance of this poem is twofold. First, as a poem in 'Heroick Verse', employing a biblical fable to comment upon individuals and situation of the Popish Plot, it must have suggested to Dryden most compellingly what *he* might do with the same idea.[14] *Naboth's Vineyard* (1679) and *Absalom and Achitophel* (1681) work from similar conceptions, but while Caryll's execution of his idea is poor, Dryden's, in its handling of personality, of the time, of the biblical parallel, in its poetic richness and energy, shaped a masterpiece. It should be added, considering the relationship between Caryll and Dryden,

[10] Narcissus Luttrell, *A Brief Historical Relation of State Affairs* ... (Oxford, 1857), i, p. 45.
[11] D.N.B., li, pp. 127–8; Sir Walter Scott, ed. *The Works of John Dryden* (London, 1808), ix, pp. 198–9.
[12] G.E.C., xii, Part i, pp. 190–1; Scott, ed. cit., ix, pp. 198–9.
[13] G.E.C., i, p. 264.
[14] The relation between *Naboth's Vineyard* and *Absalom and Achitophel* is discussed by Ian Jack, *Augustan Satire* ... (Oxford, 1952; rev. ed. 1961), pp. 55 and 74 n.1; and James Kinsley, ed. *The Poems of John Dryden* (Oxford, 1958), iv. p. 1878.

that though *Naboth's Vineyard* says nothing of Shaftesbury, the heroic villain of Dryden's poem, Caryll had written about him as early as 1678 in his poem 'The Hypocrite', published in the fourth part of Dryden's Miscellany:

> His body thus and soul together vie
> In Vice's empire for the sov'reignty.
> In Ulcers that, this does abound in sin,
> Lazar without, and Lucifer within . . .   [ll. 60–3][15]

Such representations of Shaftesbury were not unusual but these lines show Caryll and Dryden close in their conception of the man. The second point about *Naboth's Vineyard* is that Caryll's portrait of innocence unjustly arraigned comes most to life when it is informed by something in the poet's own family experience: the life of the country gentleman:

> In the first Rank of *Levites Arod* stood,
> Court-favour plac'd him there, not Worth, or Blood.
> *Naboth* amongst the Tribes the foremost Place
> Did with his Riches, Birth, and Vertue grace:
> A Man, whose Wealth was the Poor's common stock;
> The Hungry found their Market in his Flock:
> His Justice made all Law-contentions cease;
> He was his Neighbours safeguard, and their Peace.
> The Rich by him were in due bounds contain'd;
> The Poor, if strong, imploy'd; if weak, maintain'd.
> Well had he serv'd his Country, and his King . . .[16]

These lines express the country house ideal of John Caryll. It is interesting that Pope's lines on the Man of Ross, in *To Bathurst*, should be reminiscent of them.[17] Of the Catholic Lords alluded to in Caryll's poem, Stafford was beheaded on 23 Dec. 1680 (thus far had the portrait of Naboth been prophetic), Petre, Caryll's kinsman, died in the Tower in 1683/4, Arundell, Powis and Bellasyse were released in 1685. Caryll himself was discharged on 22 May 1683.[18]

In the same year reappeared *Ovid's Epistles, Translated by Several Hands* (1680), with a Preface and two poems by Dryden, and one poem by Caryll. It is probable that Caryll was by now, if not earlier, acquainted with Dryden. The inference is strengthened by the inclusion of another poem by Caryll in the *Miscellany Poems . . . by the Most Eminent Hands* (1684) a collection which also contained *Absalom and Achitophel*, *The Medal*, and *Mac Flecknoe*. Caryll's contribution is a translation of Virgil's First Eclogue; his notes explain

---

[15] *Poems on Affairs of State*, general editor G. de F. Lord, ii, ed. E. F. Mengel, Jr. (New Haven, 1965), pp. 104–6.

[16] *Naboth's Vineyard* . . . (London, 1679), p. 11 (v. 12). This passage is not included in the folio first edition of the poem reprinted in *Poems on Affairs of State*, ii, pp. 83–99 (the only text the editor consulted), but is in the quarto first edition. It is referred to by Scott, ed. cit. ix, pp. 198–9.

[17] ll. 249–74; T.E., iii–ii, pp. 113–16.

[18] G.E.C., x, p. 508; Luttrell, op. cit., p. 259.

it in almost entirely political terms, and it is perhaps because the original spoke so home to Caryll on the subjects of civil discord and exile (pressing preoccupations indeed for Catholic gentry in Restoration England) that his poem is not unsuccessful.

> We leave our home, and (once) our pleasant fields,
> The native swain to rude intruders yields; . .

> Ah! must I never more my country see,
> But in strange lands an endless exile be?
> Is my eternal banishment decreed,
> From my poor cottage rear'd with turf and reed?
> Must impious soldiers all these grounds possess . . .?[19]

It is a measure of the Eclogue's relevance to the times that it was to turn out so prophetic for Caryll. Only five years later, faced by exile himself, he might indeed have echoed Meliboeus' lament with literal truth to his own situation.

2. MR. SECRETARY CARYLL

While these events were taking place in the greater world, the Caryll family had in modest ways been pursuing its fortune. Sometime before 1667 John Caryll's younger brother Richard acquired from his cousin Phillippa, Lady Morley, the estate of West Grinstead in Sussex.[20] It was probably here, on Dec. 1667, that John Caryll the friend of Pope was born.[21] The first reference in the Caryll papers to the young heir of the family is in his uncle's accounts for October 1680: 'sent to little Mr. John Caryll a ginny'.[22] While little Mr. Caryll was growing up, the family was building itself a new seat at Ladyholt, to empark which they divested of its lands their old manor house at Harting.[23] Pope was often to stay at this new house, and its name occurs frequently in his correspondence. Ladyholt seems to have been completed by 7 Jan. 1680, when the 'new erected Mansion house' was leased to Edward Roper by Richard Caryll, on behalf of 'John Caryll of Holt'.[24] Ladyholt cannot be associated with the work of any well-known architect, and was probably designed by a master-builder. In the latter half of the eighteenth century it was dismantled, and the only surviving evidence of its appearance is in a sketch of its front elevation and ground-plan by John Baptist Caryll, the grandson of Pope's friend.[25] From this drawing it appears that Ladyholt resembled the style of

[19] *Ovid's Epistles Translated by Several Hands*, 3rd. edn. (London, 1683), pp. 291–2; *The First Part of Miscellany Poems . . . Publish'd by Mr. Dryden* (London, 1684; 4th. edn. 1716), pp. 315–19.

[20] D. G. C. Elwes and C. J. Robinson, *A History of the Castles, Mansions, and Manors of West Sussex* (London, 1876), p. 107.

[21] D.N.B., ix, p. 255; De Trenqualéon, op. cit., ii, Plate II.

[22] B.M. Add. 28240, f. 97.

[23] Gordon, op. cit., p. 122.

[24] B.M. Add. 28250, ff. 86–7.

[25] B.M. Add. 28250, f. 563. The sketch must be interpreted with care, since it includes some (relatively recognizable) proposed extensions.

builder-designed country house exemplified by Peter Mills's Thorpe Hall
(1653–6). Like Thorpe Hall, Ladyholt had a symmetrical front composed of
two ranges of seven windows and one (the ground floor) of six, a central door-
way, and a hipped roof with dormer windows and tall chimneys. Unlike
Thorpe, Ladyholt appears to have had a central hall; and it differed also from
Thorpe in an apparent absence of classical detail, in its failure to give special
emphasis to one principal story, and in its unusual stepped roof-line—which
may in itself suggest that the two ends of the house, as shown in the elevation,
were later additions.[26]

The building of Ladyholt must mean that the Carylls enjoyed moderate
prosperity during the Restoration. Yet the fortunes of Catholics were vulnerable. It is not surprising that in 1684, we find Caryll, recently freed from
suspicion with the end of the Popish Plot, engaged in negotiations for investment in the Hotel de Ville in Paris: 'the best security for English Catholicks'
as he was later to put it. His aim, as stated after his death by Lewis Innes, was
'in case upon any account his heir should happen to lose what he had in
England, ther should be still for him a provision in France, at least such as
might give him bread.' A great part of the Caryll fortunes and an even greater
part of the correspondence, in the years to follow, was to be bound up with
the rents of the Hotel de Ville.[27]

With the accession of James II, however, more than modest prosperity
seemed within reach. Those persecuted with James during the Popish Plot
now had strong credentials; for the first time for years it looked as though the
Catholic gentry might enjoy court favour and office. Almost immediately
Caryll, now sixty, was sent to Rome on a mission from King James to the
Pope. He was to beg a bishopric *in partibus* for England for Dr. Leyburn, and
a cardinal's hat for Prince Rinaldo d'Este, the queen's uncle. This, according
to Dicconson's *Life of James II*, based on James's own memoirs, Caryll
'perform'd with great fidelitie, privacy and success, which made it of little
expense to the King, and no dissatisfaction to the people . . .'; for though the
Pope refused the second request, fearing that Rinaldo d'Este favoured the
French interest, 'Mr. Caryll finding wher the shoo pinched, made a con-
ditional proposal, not doubting but what it would be approved of by the
King his master, Whether upon the Prince D'Estés engagement, not to concern himself with any intrest but that of England, the Pope would agree to it,
which his Holyness . . . promised he would . . .'[28] This diplomatically won
concession was thrown away by the ensuing ill-advised and ostentatious mission
of Lord Castlemain to the Pope.[29] Caryll was supplanted, and was back in
England before the end of 1685, where another form of preferment awaited
him.

[26] John Summerson, *Architecture in Britain, 1530–1830* (Harmondsworth, 1952; revised and
enlarged edn. 1963), pp. 96–7.
[27] B.M. Add. 28250, ff. 95–6; 28226, f. 130.
[28] *The Life of King James II . . . Collected Out of Memoirs Writ of His Own Hand*, ed. J. S.
Clarke (London, 1816), ii, pp. 75–6; cf. James Macpherson, ed. *Original Papers Containing the
Secret History of Great Britain . . .* (London, 1775), i, p. 148 (Extract I).
[29] *The Life of King James II . . .*, ii, pp. 77–9.

This was the appointment of Secretary and Master of Requests to Queen
Mary. It is possible that Caryll owed this preferment, as also his having been
chosen for the mission to Rome, to his kinsman Father Petre who had influence at James's court. His youthful service at the court of Parma may also
have been drawn to the attention of the young queen from neighbouring
Modena. Caryll may have hesitated before accepting the post; he wrote on
5 Nov. to his friend the Cardinal of Norfolk, at Rome, to ask for his advice,
but by the 27 Nov. had accepted the appointment, before receiving Norfolk's
letter of strong encouragement, dated 22 Dec. 1685.[30] This was to prove a
significant step in the history of the Caryll family, for it was to add to the
political and religious loyalty, that Caryll must (despite *Naboth's Vineyard*)
have felt towards the Stuarts, a strong personal bond between himself and his
mistress, for which he was ultimately to accept exile. In the meantime he
devoted himself to serving the queen, and his surviving correspondence from
the next three years consists almost entirely of drafts of royal letters. Yet there
was family news. On 2 Jan. 1686 'little Mr. Caryll', his nephew, now eighteen,
married Elizabeth Harrington of Ore Place in Sussex.[31] In 1687 several
Justices of the Peace were 'turned out, & papists put into commission instead,
as Mr. Caryll & others'; Luttrell's reference is in fact to Richard Caryll whom
we find writing to his brother, in May probably of the same year, to ask for
advice on the recent act of parliament concerning the poor.[32] Gradually, in
these few personal letters, the trend of national events makes itself felt. On
23 June his sister Mary, foundress and Abbess of the Convent of English
Benedictines at Dunkirk, sent him a joyful letter:

> to congratulate with yu in perticuler, that the Queen your Mrs. draws soe
> neere her time and I place soe great a confidence in the prayers of the iust
> that in spight of the Divell and all your protestant presbiterians her Majesty
> will be preserved by the Ally powre, and make us all happy very shortly in
> a Prince of Walles . . .[33]

Mary Caryll's loyalty to her family, her religion, and to the House of Stuart,
shines out from adversity in many a subsequent letter, but we never find her
again in this mood of confidence. The 'Allmighty powre' did indeed provide
the longed-for Catholic heir, but He had not given James the wisdom to
hold his throne. What must have seemed to Catholic gentry a providential
opportunity to serve their prince and pursue their fortunes was slipping from
their grasp for lack of a competent monarch. The next surviving letter to
Caryll, now a Privy Councillor,[34] has an ominous ring; the news of William's
invasion had come home to the court, and Caryll wrote to his Harting neighbour
Lord Grey, an erstwhile supporter of Monmouth, appealing to him to rally
behind James. Perhaps this was not so desperate as it sounds; the Carylls and

[30] De Trenqualéon, op. cit., ii, pp. 24–8; B.M. Add. 28226, f. 11.
[31] Ibid., ii, Plate II.
[32] Luttrell, op. cit., i, pp. 391–2; B.M. Add. 28226, ff. 90–1.
[33] B.M. Add. 28226, f. 112; Foley, op. cit., iii, p. 540.
[34] G. A. Ellis, ed. *The Ellis Correspondence* (London, 1829), ii, p. 32.

the Greys were good neighbours despite their contrary religious and political creeds, and the well-meaning Secretary may have seen the crisis as a chance for Grey to show his loyalty to the side which he, Caryll, was almost obliged to believe would prevail. But Grey was a different kind of political animal; he feigned 'crafty sick', pleading a recent fall from his horse, which made it impossible for him to show his loyalty and zeal for the service of his Majesty.[35]

A month later Queen Mary and the young prince made their escape to France, Caryll making the necessary arrangements with the Comte de Lauzun.[36] Historians of the Caryll family agree that he followed James into exile in 1688, though no evidence has survived to show precisely when he did so, or whether, as seems possible, he actually accompanied the queen to France.[37] A Jacobite document of 1702 (Thomas Sheridan's 'An Historical Account of Some Remarkable Matters . . .') implies that Caryll was at the court of St. Germains in 1689, and states that he was there in 1690, on James's return from his unsuccessful Irish campaign.[38] Caryll is here spoken of as preparing a draft of a manifesto to be issued by James, which suggests that he was now, officially or unofficially, more than just Secretary to the Queen. Other references in Sheridan confirm Ruvigny's suggestion that Caryll was probably Acting-, or possibly Under-, Secretary of State at the court of St. Germains from 1690.[39] We first hear from Caryll himself, after the Revolution, in a letter of 2 Aug. 1690 to Bishop Ellis at Rome. He expresses hopes of 'the people of England's coming to their senses . . . because they now begin more than ever to smart for their folly . . . the nature of the disease will require much purging and blooding . . .'[40] In the summer of 1694 the Duke of Melfort was dismissed from his post as one of James's Secretaries of State, and Caryll was appointed in his place.[41] Much of his correspondence was now taken up with the complicated diplomacy between James and the Vatican, but on 14 July he wrote to his bailiff at Ladyholt about the upkeep of the new mansion, then being rented to his brother and his nephew. The 'lead about the cornish' must be 'new cast, & new layd', he wrote, 'for the doing whereof I fear you can hardly rely upon any Country Workman, but must be forced to gett a Plummer from London.'[42] Perhaps he still hoped for a new Restoration in his lifetime, and the chance to see Ladyholt once more—on 6 Sept., writing to Bishop Ellis, he considered that Louis XIV could only bring the war to a speedy end by a bold attack on Britain, which would not only serve his interest but 'complete the glory of his reign' by restoring the right, 'towards which', he adds with interesting asperity, 'I doubt not but that we shall have the good wishes, prayers

[35] B.M. Add. 28226, f. 71 (Caryll to Grey, 10 Nov. 1688).

[36] John Lingard, *The History of England . . .* (London, 1854–5), x, p. 177.

[37] B.M. Add. 28240, f. 193 (a draft petition to George I for the reversal of John Caryll's outlawry) states that Lord Caryll was outlawed for High Treason, having remained in France 'where he went with the late Queen.'

[38] H.M.C. 56 (Stuart), vi, pp. 53, 56.

[39] Ibid., pp. 66–7.

[40] Ibid., i, pp. 78–9.

[41] Ibid., p. 87 (Melfort to Bishop Ellis, 7 June 1694; p. 88 (Caryll to Ellis, 28 June 1694).

[42] B.M. Add. 28250, ff. 118–25 (12 Nov. 1688); 28226, f. 97.

and benedictions of his Holiness and everything but his money.'[43] Two
months later he was more pessimistic:

> All the world over, I am afraid, we shall find but few just and religious to
> that degree, as not to think the particular concern of England a lawful
> sacrifice to the peace of Europe, so that we may very well say *Nolite confidere
> in principalibus, etc.* But, since the discerner of hearts knows his Majesty's
> intentions to be as right as his cause is just, we have that Providence to rely
> upon which still governs the world *en dernier ressort*, and in whose hands
> the wisest heads and strongest arms are no more than the chisel and the
> mallet in the hands of the workman.[44]

It is *en dernier ressort* that men turn to the cold comfort of ultimate providence, but Caryll seems by this time to have reconciled himself to his personal
fate within the larger pattern of events which only God could alter. In a letter
to his brother Richard, on 17 Nov. 1694, he expresses a resignation which,
far from being bitter or stoical, draws comfort from the prospect of new
life, the assurance of a landed family's continuity, and a certain reverence
for the past. It is a letter which expresses much of Caryll's class and time.

> As for my self, considering my age, & the prospect of affaires, I can intertain
> no reasonable hopes of outliving the bad times, & consequently of seeing
> my friends again at home . . . All our ioy and confort heer is in our Nursery,
> which is as thriving & promising as can be wisht; & the pleasure of it is to
> me like that which you take in the young trees planted at La. H, which
> probably your sone & g. children may see come to perfection. I am very
> glad my Neveu takes so much delight in planting; t'is not only a cheap, &
> therefor suitable to our condition, but allso a Royall divertisment, for our
> great man heer, besides what he is in other things, is the greatest planter in
> the world of trees; they may be reckond by hundred thousands that are of
> his owne plantation, & ther hardly passeth a day when the season is proper,
> that he does not worke at it himself. Pray lett the pond in the Harehurst
> be repaird in the manner you mention, & to have it substantially done I
> shall not think the charge by you propos'd too much. I am extremely glad
> that my sister is thoroughly reconciled to La. Ho. upon so good a motive,
> as her inioying better health then formerly; since Hartg. is like to be the
> Mansion of the family heerafter, I would not have it want any thing for
> health and convenience, that so the owners of it may love home, wherby
> Estates & familys are best preserved. I can not think the old house will be
> much lived in, but yet I would not have it drop down in my time for old
> acquaintance sake, so that I would have it kept well couer'd; but for Ladyholt
> I would have nothing left undone for the keeping it in good and perfect
> repaire, . . . I hope my Neece is, or will be quickly well deliver'd of her
> 7th. Child; ther can never be too many of so good a breed . . .[45]

[43] H.M.C. 56 (Stuart), i, pp. 91–2.
[44] Ibid., pp. 94–5 (Caryll to Ellis, 13 Dec. 1694).
[45] B.M. Add. 28226, ff. 99–100.

This is in no sense a doctrinal or philosophical letter. Caryll writes as things come into his mind, and the letter is scattered with practical instructions and comments on mundane matters. Yet there is unconsciously assumed a sense of correspondence and harmony; his mind moves naturally from the royal children at St. Germains, to the young trees at Ladyholt, to the heir of his own family in England, and to the planting activities of Louis XIV, the greatest monarch of Western Europe. The activities of the king and the country gentleman are seen to be analogous ('A Manor *is a* Kingdom *in Miniature*', as one eighteenth-century writer put it)[46] and to be in harmony with that natural growth which promises a longer continuity and stronger hope than can be encompassed in the span of a lifetime. Caryll's awareness of a living tradition and continuity prompts his instructions about the old house at Harting, and the more so those about the new, for this is a letter which looks primarily to the future. After disappointments, persecutions, the final strong hopes and then tragedy of 'endless exile', Caryll expresses in this letter a sense of ultimate assurance and harmony.

3. FRANCE AND ENGLAND

Caryll was able to display this 'singulier calme d'esprit' (as the French historian of his family calls it) because his brother and nephew were in secure possession of the family estates in Sussex.[47] This security was procured, however, through the good offices of his master King James and the generosity of William of Orange; Luttrell speaks of 'Mr. Carryls estate in Sussex . . . which his majestie permitted him to enjoy tho beyond sea' and it appears that this permission was granted by William at the special request of James—probably very soon after the latter's arrival in France.[48] The security was thus by no means absolute, and the more prominent Caryll became in the hostile designs of the court of St. Germains the more vulnerable would his family in England be. Of the two parties which contended for influence at the Jacobite court, Caryll seems to have belonged to the more moderate one, sometimes known as the Compounders. These were willing that James should accept certain conditions for his restoration, and that he should proclaim a general pardon. The fact that Caryll was made Secretary of State with Lord Middleton, on the dismissal in 1694 of the extremist Melfort, suggests Caryll's political alignment, as his discreet execution of his mission to Rome in 1685 suggests a moderate character.[49] The point is clinched, however, by an exchange between Caryll and Thomas Sheridan in 1697. Sheridan had drawn up a statement of the sufferings of the catholic clergy in Ireland which he submitted to James:

> . . . his Majesty approved of it, but told him he would not trust his own judgment, but shew it to the Queen and Mr. Carryll. The next day Mr.

---

[46] *The Compleat English Copyholder: Or, A Guide to Lords of Manors . . . By A Gentleman of the Inner Temple* (London, 1735), i, Preface.

[47] De Trenqualéon, op. cit., ii, p. 44.

[48] Luttrell, op. cit., iv, p. 62 (23 May 1696); D.N.B., ix, p. 255; Gordon, op. cit., p. 108.

[49] Macpherson, op. cit., i, pp. 494–5. Cf. W. S. Churchill, *Marlborough, His Life and Times* (London, 1933–8), i, pp. 437–8.

Carryll sent for Sheridan and told him what was affirmed in it, that the true reason of the loss of the Crown was his being of the Roman Catholic religion, must be left out, Sheridan said he knew no other cause that could be assigned; yes, answered Mr. Carryll, the breaking of the laws. Sheridan replied the King had broken none . . . Well, says Mr. Carryll, notwithstanding all you say, this clause I have razed must be left out, it can do no good . . .[50]

Pope was well-informed to a degree when he wrote in his Epitaph on Caryll:

> Honour unchang'd; a Principle profest;
> Fix'd to one side, but mod'rate to the rest;   [ll. 3–4]

Yet the moderate had written of 'purging and blooding' Britain and, even after his letter to his brother of Nov. 1694, had looked to Louis for 'a vigorous attempt on England.'[51] Two had already been made, Beachy Head and La Hogue; now, in 1695, with Caryll Joint Secretary of State, another was in preparation. Once more Louis was willing to send an army to England, a fleet and transports were once more available, were assembling at Calais, and might set out on the fulfilment of one wise condition of Louis: that James's supporters in England should rise first. The Duke of Berwick, James's natural son, was despatched to England to discuss the matter with influential Jacobites. In Feb. 1696 James prepared a proclamation of general pardon, beginning: 'Whereas it has now pleased the Divine Providence to furnish us with means and enable us to enter again into possession of our kingdoms . . .' and promising a free parliament; after which he travelled to the coast in readiness to cross with the troops.[52] Seldom had Jacobite hopes run higher in either kingdom. But within this design there was another more secret, and perhaps more foolish: the plot to assassinate William of Orange. It is perhaps impossible to know precisely how far this plot was commissioned by James and his Secretaries. Such a design seems contrary to the known characters of Middleton and Caryll, and to the Compounder spirit which manifested itself in James's 1696 proclamation. It is less irreconcilable with the character of James in his last years, and possibly he gave instructions to Sir George Berkeley of which the Secretaries knew nothing. Caryll may have given money to Berkeley for his English expedition, as was reported in England, and yet been innocent of his actual mission. But when all is said and done, the plot has surely to be seen in the wider context of the 1696 invasion plan. While the court of St. Germains believed that England was currently in a fermentation of discontent, it must still have feared what the Duke of Berwick discovered in the winter of 1695–6: that the Jacobites of England would not rise unless the army of Louis invaded first. In this exasperatingly nicely balanced situation, the assassination of the usurper might well have been thought sufficient to trigger off a rising of discontented English who would then acclaim their

---

[50] H.M.C. 56 (Stuart), vi, p. 74.
[51] Ibid., i, p. 95 (Caryll to Ellis, 13 Dec. 1694).
[52] Ibid., i, pp. 110–12 (quotation from p. 110).

rightful king, as he set sail with French troops for his native land. One cannot confidently say that even the 'Honour unchang'd' of Caryll, if he saw Berkeley's mission in this light, would not have connived at the scheme. If he did, Caryll must have know that he was risking the life and fortune of his family in England.[53]

And in England, superficially, it might have seemed that the court of St. Germains was right. These were still very much the 'middle years' about which Keith Feiling has written so compellingly:

> ... the times were hard, and conspiracy had much to nourish it. Steenkirk, Landen, Beachy Head, and the Smyrna fleet; taxes, even the hated excise, which hit the smaller country gentry; Dutch favourites, Dutch guards, Dutch generals, a Dutch policy ... English blood poured out like water in Flanders ... As the clouds gathered over the *de facto* Government, as the wonderful tidings percolated to Saint-Germain that Marlborough was remorseful, or that Halifax had budged, the Jacobites in London grew bolder and more insolent. They thronged the coffee-houses and haunted the lobby, cocked their hats in the Queen's face, and boasted of what the spring would bring: one of them fastened a legend on the gate of Whitehall itself:

> > Molly, do not cry,
> > Daddy will be here presently.

> Nightly you might hear their rousing chorus:

> > For we shall see the King again,
> > Not as he was on Salisbury Plain,
> > But with a far more faithful train.[54]

In the midst of such an atmosphere the conspiracy broke, information was carried to William, and several of the conspirators were arrested. News from Flanders of the French naval and military preparations followed, and fifty men-of-war under Russel stood over to France and drove the opposing fleet into harbour. James lingered at the coast some days before writing to Caryll that: 'I see no manner of reason for my staying here any longer, now that the world must find the decent is layd a side for the present';[55] Middleton and Caryll besought the French government not to abandon the invasion, but the design was broken. The English Jacobites were not ready to rise on their own, as Berwick had accurately reported, and the news of an unsuccessful plot to assassinate William, and the consequent arrests, can only have made them more cautious still.

Lord Cutts, one of William's most successful generals, was present at the

[53] A full narrative of the Assassination Plot, based on the chief primary sources, is to be found in Lord Macaulay, *The History of England From the Accession of James II*, ed. C. H. Firth (London, 1913–15), v, pp. 2584–616.

[54] Keith Feiling, *A History of the Tory Party, 1640–1714* (Oxford, 1924), pp. 303–5.

[55] Gilbert Burnet, *History of His Own Time*, ed. M. J. Routh, 2nd. edn. (London, 1833), iv, p. 303. For James's letter to Lord Caryll about abandoning the invasion, see B.M. Add. 28224, f. 15 (29 April 1696).

first interview between William and Prendergrass, the most reliable of their informants about the plot.[56] Whether Caryll's name was mentioned at that interview we cannot know, but it is probable for on 30 April 1696 Luttrell had got the news that 'His majestie has given the estate of Mr. Carryl of Sussex, being near 2000l. per ann., to the lord Cutts.'[57] Caryll's name was now widely connected with the assassination plot, and on the 23 May Luttrell noted that 'On Monday the Lord Cutts goes to take possession of Mr. Carryl's estate in Sussex', which William had allowed him to keep, ''till 'twas discovered he gave sir George Barclay 800. to buy horses, arms, &c., to assassinate him, &c.'[58] John Caryll, now a father of six children, was arrested on 28 March and imprisoned for fourteen days in Chichester Gaol.[59] On his release he must have discussed expedients for saving the family estates with his father, and perhaps with his 'powerful neighbour' Lord Grey at Up Park, since an 'Inquisition for upon ye Outlawry of Jo: Caryll, Esq., who is said to be Outlawd on Monday next after ye Purification of ye Blessed Virgin Mary 1695 [O.S.]' had already been completed. This showed Caryll's estates in Sussex to have been worth an annual rental of £2,155.11.2.—rather more than Luttrell's report of its value—and also adds that for the previous six years John Caryll the younger 'was bayliff to his Uncle' in France.[60] Caryll cannot have heard about William's grant of Ladyholt to Lord Cutts long after the well-informed Luttrell, and must soon have decided to attempt a bargain with the 'impious soldier' who now held his uncle's inheritance. For even in this desperate situation the provident Carylls had one strong card to play; as a correspondent of the family pointed out to Richard Caryll on 2 May 1696 with a certain bitter triumph, the uncle had only a life interest in his Sussex estates, which were entailed in the family by deed of 1652. Thus the outlawry of his uncle only enabled William to grant to Lord Cutts 'a bare possession for ye life of a person allready above ye Comon Age of Man' of the Sussex estates.[61]

In these circumstances perhaps Lord Cutts would be ready to sell this life interest to a member of the family guiltless of complicity in the plot. Before negotiations could be opened, however, John Caryll was once more thrown into prison, where despite rumours of early release he remained, this time in Horsham gaol, until 16 July.[62] When he was freed the second time (presumably nothing could be fastened on him with regard to the plot), Caryll probably found Lord Cutts in possession of Ladyholt. Within less than a year, however, a bargain had been reached. In the words of John Caryll's own personal memorandum: 'Lord Cutts to have in all £6,060. May 13, 97. paid him . . . [£]2000 . . . and 2 mortgages for ye remg. 4,000'. Of this £2000, £1,100 was Caryll's own, £100 was the payment of an outstanding debt to

[56] Ibid., iv, pp. 304–5.
[57] Luttrell, op. cit., iv, p. 51.
[58] Ibid., p. 62.
[59] Foley, op. cit., iii, p. 537.
[60] B.M. Add. 28250, f. 145.
[61] B.M. Add. 28227, f. 11. And see 28250, ff. 34 et seq. and 154.
[62] B.M. Add. 28227, ff. 10, 15; 19.

his uncle, but the remaining £800 had to be borrowed.[63] The remaining £4,000 had still to be paid to Lord Cutts in May 1697. This was done by the raising of two mortgages on the estates, and of additional loans. The mortgages were paid off by 18 May 1699. However Ladyholt, 'like to be the Mansion of the family hereafter', was regained, and John Caryll spent a further £1.2.0 that the bell-ringers of Harting church might help celebrate his bargain.[64]

The family was fortunate to survive so well, on this occasion, the unsuccessful designs of the court of St. Germains. True, it had to buy back its own, but £6,060 for (as it proved in the event) fifteen years' life interest in a £2,000 per annum estate was a good bargain. The £1,100 mentioned in the memorandum seems in fact to have been money belonging to the elder John Caryll in his nephew's hands; the former contributed a mortgage for another £1,000; the sale of timber brought in another £1,200; the remaining £2,700 had to be charged on the estate.[65] The stigma of outlawry now lay upon both uncle and nephew, but it does not seem to have prevented the latter from living quietly on his estate, while the former, cut off from his English sources of income, was probably not dependent on the impoverished court of St. Germains, owing to his investments in the Hotel de Ville.[66] Lord Caryll, indeed, seems to have relinquished the post of Secretary of State on the failure of the 1696 designs, but he is referred to as 'Secretary Caryl' on 23 April 1698, and as 'Minister and Secretary of State of the King of Great Britain' on 30 April 1699.[67] For both personal and practical reasons, Caryll had become indispensable to the exiled royal family, and Mary of Modena might well have referred to her friends, 'at the head of wich without wronging any, i putt Mr. Secretary Caryll'.[68]

A letter which well displays Caryll's relationship with James and Mary, and also the wealth of his family at this time, was written to his sister Mary, Abbess of Dunkirk;

the older I grow the more busines is layd upon me, which, thô it agrees as litle with my lazy temper, as it does with my Age, yet I know not how to decline in the circumstances I am in. The duty we owe to our [Prince or] Parent, is indispensable, so that what they comand (in things not unlawfull) we must take to be the will of God; to which motive ther is allso added this satisfaction that my service is not ill accepted: for to say the truth, my Master & Mistris want such servants at present, as can serve them without wages. I beleeve it is in my power to have a title of honour conferrd upon me, which as to my owne particular, I should not accept of, for it would be only an increase of Enuy & expense to me, without adding any advantage and privilege to me more then what I allredy injoy. Nothing therfor would

---

[63] Ibid., 28250, ff. 149, 154. See also De Trenqualéon, op. cit., ii, p. 57.
[64] B.M. Add. 28250, f. 149; Gordon, op. cit., p. 112.
[65] B.M. Add. 28227, f. 492.
[66] Ibid. 28250, ff. 95–6.
[67] H.M.C. 56 (Stuart), i, pp. 130–8.
[68] B.M. Add. 28224, f. 21 (5 June 1696).

move me to it, but the benefite of my Family: But whether it would be a
benefite or no, is the question; ffor unlesse ther be Estate enough conveniently to support the title, the necessary increase of expense in the way
of living will be rather a ruine then an advantage to the ffamily. Lesse then
3500lb a year to go along with the title can not support it; If therfor my
brother's & my Nephew's Estate alltogether can make up 1500lb a yeer,
I shall leave 2000lb a year good rent to make up the above mentioned summe;
Unlesse all this can be done, I shall intertain no thoughts of the matter . . .
nothing is so wretched as beggerly honour.[69]

Caryll was a faithful servant to his exiled prince; history had cast him in the
role of a second Hyde, and he determined to play out his part. He held to the
doctrine of Passive Obedience, as the letter shows, in a form similar to that
held by William Digby, but, in its rejection of obedience to unlawful commands,
arguably less extreme than that of Digby's Anglican mentor, John Kettlewell.[70]
There is something blunt and admirable about Caryll's service to his 'Master
& Mistris . . . without wages' and about his contempt (which coming from
the court of St. Germains carries much conviction) for 'beggerly honour'.
Yet he must have wanted the honour for his family, if only the estate were
'answerable therunto', and his brother and nephew must have reassured him
in the end, despite the debts they had incurred to Lord Cutts. By 29 Jan.
1698–9 he had become John, first Baron Caryll of Durford, and as a witness
to King James's will on that date signed himself simply 'Dunford'.[71]

4. LETTERS AND LIFE:

Like his uncle, John Caryll cherished an interest in literature. Educated in
France, he is likely to have been encouraged in a concern for polite learning
also by his uncle, who perhaps brought him up to London during King James's
reign and introduced him to eminent acquaintances such as Dryden. Caryll's
correspondence with several distinguished men of letters, during the last years
of the seventeenth century, suggests this. On 10 June 1694, for example, the
Franciscan philosopher Antoine Le Grand, who had sought to synthesise
with scholasticism the thought of Descartes, wrote to thank Caryll for a
present in return for a copy of his *Entire Body of Philosophy, according to the
Principles of R. Des Cartes* 'having before been Enform'd that you did not
dislike the Latin Edition': an English translation which had appeared that
year.[72] On 21 July 1698 Dryden himself wrote to Caryll to thank him for a
gift and an invitation:

'Tis the part of an honest Man to be as good as his Word, butt you have
been better: I expected but halfe of what I had, and that halfe, not halfe
so Good. Your Veneson had three of the best Qualities; for it was both

---

[69] Ibid. 28226, f. 103 (15 July ?1695). Gregory King calculated the average annual income of the
Temporal Lords of England as £2,800 for the year 1688 (ed. cit., p. 31).
[70] See Ch. V, Section 1.
[71] H.M.C. 56 (Stuart), ii, p. 515.
[72] B.M. Add. 28618, ff. 89; 84.

fatt, large & sweet. To add to this you have been pleased to invite me to Lady holt, and if I could promise my Self a year's Life, I might hope to be happy in so sweet a Place, & in the Enjoyment of your good Company. How God will dispose of me, I know not: but I am apt to flatter my Self with the thoughts of itt, because I very much desire itt, And am Sir with all manner of Acknowledgement . . . John Dryden.[73]

This letter shows that Dryden and Caryll were already acquainted, and leaves us with the possibility that the poet visited Ladyholt. It also shows a generous concern in Caryll to help the old poet, a Catholic now like himself, who had fallen on hard times. Two years later, Sir Roger L'Estrange was another of Caryll's correspondents. Caryll had consulted him about his own English version of the (in fact apocryphal) *Memoirs* of St. Evrémond—himself an earlier correspondent of the Caryll family.[74] L'Estrange refers to the commission on 26 Aug. 1700; again three days later ('no man living hath a greater reverence for your Name and Character than my self'), and in a number of subsequent letters. On 12 Sept. he sees the hand of Caryll behind an anonymous 'Glorious present of Partridges', a week later he is obliged to break it to his friend that 'these Memoires are not in my opinion worthy of Mr. Caryll's Pen' and on 28 Sept. he expands his point:

As to the memorialls (in the Originall I mean) they are undubtedly *Diverting*, as you say, & in the same measure *Instructive*: but the Humour and Phansy, runs a little too much methinks upon the same Biasses that is to say Knight-Errantry & Love; and then the Morall, in conformity to the air of the novell, must be the same over againe to; which signifyes little more in plain English [than] *This comes of Whoring* . . .

These doubts, however, 'are all discharg'd under your own hand, when you declare that *you never design'd to affix your Name* to the Translation.'[75] On 23 Nov. he writes to Caryll to thank him for a subscription to his *Josephus*, and still has misgivings about the *Memoirs*, wishing Caryll would agree to remodel his Preface to the work.[76] L'Estrange seems to assume publication, but the project must have been dropped in the end. Another literary veteran of the Restoration to write to Caryll was Wycherley. On 17 May 1704 he thanks Caryll for an invitation to his house, and would be 'as proud of the honour of your Conversation as I should be pleasd, and instructed by it . . . no man who has been longer acquainted with you than me, has better opinion of your Moralls, or judgement, and humanity, than, Dear Sir, . . .' and he encloses

---

[73] Ibid. 28618, f. 84; printed in C. E. Ward, ed. *The Letters of John Dryden* (Durham, North Carolina, 1942), p. 100.
[74] B.M. Add. 28618, f. 84.
[75] Ibid. 28618, f. 87; 28237, ff. 6, 8; 28618, f. 88. See 28237, ff. 1–16. The twelve letters from L'Estrange in the Caryll papers are referred to only cursorily by George Kitchin, *Sir Roger L'Estrange* . . . (London, 1913), p. 391n.
[76] B.M. Add. 28618, f. 89.

his 'damnd Book' as a 'Scurvy present'.[77] In this letter Wycherley seems
likely to accept Caryll's invitation. It is interesting, as will appear, that the
date of Pope's first letter to Wycherley is 26 Dec. of the same year, and that
in this letter Pope speaks of having but recently met the dramatist.

It has hitherto been assumed that Pope became acquainted with John
Caryll shortly before his first letter to him, on 31 July 1710, opening as it
does with the phrase 'After the kind permission you gave me to write to you
. . .' Yet the same letter speaks of Caryll's 'having treated me so often in a
style of compliment' and on 25 Jan. 1711 Pope refers to a stay at Caryll's
house 'a year ago'.[78] The discovery in the Caryll papers of early drafts of
three poems by Pope, dated 1703, now suggests that Pope was friendly with
the Caryll family by that date if not earlier.[79] No doubt, as Sherburn says,
the acquaintance grew through Caryll's relative and Pope's neighbour at
Binfield, Anthony Englefield, after the Popes had moved into Windsor Forest
in 1700. It is clear that in getting to know Caryll Pope was not only making
friends with a man who took a civil and sincere interest in poetry and letters
(and who was into the bargain of the same faith as Pope and his family); he
was also making contact with the world of Restoration writing through a
person who enjoyed the friendly respect of men such as Dryden, L'Estrange,
Wycherley and Betterton. It is likely to have been through Caryll, rather than
Sir William Trumbull as Sherburn suggests, that Pope met Wycherley, and
perhaps the Carylls with their strong Tory and loyalist background were more
likely to introduce Pope to this world than was Trumbull; the Jacobite Secretary
of State at St. Germains could through his nephew give as strong an introduction as the retired Whig Secretary of State in Windsor Forest.[80] Yet why
has no letter of Pope to Caryll between 1703 and 1710 come to light? Common-
place letters may of course have passed between them and been destroyed;
it might not have occurred to Caryll, at this early stage, to keep Pope's letters
for posterity. But there is perhaps a better reason for the absence of correspondence during this period. The Carylls were inevitably a family under
suspicion. What made John Caryll a candidate for imprisonment in 1696 made
him a dangerous person for a humble papist family with little influence and
only modest wealth to correspond with. Dryden was an old man and a respected public figure; Wycherley and L'Estrange were not Catholics; but the
Popes had to be careful. No correspondence between Pope and any Catholic
acquaintance has survived from before 1709.

While Caryll, in his unaffected and unpatronising manner, was fulfilling
the aristocratic role of patron of letters, he, Lord Caryll, and other members
of the hard-pressed family, continued the struggle to maintain themselves and
their traditions in a hostile world. Lord Caryll was now an outlaw, their estates

[77] Ibid. 28618, f. 85.
[78] Corr., i, pp. 93, 114.
[79] Howard Erskine-Hill, 'Alexander Pope at Fifteen: A New Manuscript', Review of English
Studies, N.S., xvii, No. 67 (Aug. 1966), pp. 268–77. See also Pope to Caryll, 2 June 1733 (Corr.,
iii, p. 373), where Pope speaks of having experienced his friend's humanity 'near thirty years'.
[80] George Sherburn, The Early Career of Alexander Pope (Oxford, 1934), p. 48.

like those of other Catholics were double-taxed,[81] and were in addition burdened with mortgages as a result of the bargain with Lord Cutts. Communication between England and France was dangerous and difficult; letters were
liable to be opened, and it was necessary to sign with a false name and insert
anti-Jacobite sentiments, to be on the safe side.[82] However the Peace of Ryswick,
in Oct. 1697, made some difference; within the next year or two John Caryll
crossed to France to see his uncle, and Abbess Mary Caryll was able to comment
in a letter to her brother:

> I like very well of his caution in makeing soe quick a dispatch of his iourny,
> before he be mist out of the Kingdom, espetially now the government is soe
> peevish on that point, I am a litle curious to inquire how you find affaires
> as to your owne estate, and whether my Nephu thrives in the world, ther
> is many Children to provide for . . .[83]

It may have been on this or an earlier journey that Caryll brought his eldest
son over to France to be educated under the care of his uncle. In a letter of
uncertain date, perhaps early in 1699, Lord Caryll wrote to his nephew about
the boy, commenting on his good health, backwardness in languages, and
pleasant disposition.[84] He alludes to the funds he will leave him on his death,
which together with a marriage portion, should set the young man 'well forth
in the World'. Stating himself to be 'quite in the dark' as to 'the Incumbrance
which lyes upon the Estate', he warns against indiscriminate selling of timber;
enough must be left for repairs to the farms, and 'As to the cutting down
Ashe aboue the hill, I would not willingly have anything done that might
deface the beauty of the seat, Wood being the cheifest ornament of it . . .'[85]

Since there was no danger that mail between Dunkirk and St. Germains
would be tampered with, the letters between Mary Caryll and Lord Caryll
during the first decade of the eighteenth century most clearly reflect the state
of their family and its hopes. On Dec. 1699, after a visit to France by her
husband, Mrs. Caryll has written how they are 'even transported with ioy
att the account he has given her and my Brother of the great improvment of
his Son by your conduct and tender care . . .' but on 25 Jan. 1700 Mary
Caryll is sorry to hear that the progress of 'our litle young Heyre' is disappointing: 'I am sencible paines must be taken with him, and alsoe incourrag'd
being soe very backward in his booke when he came over . . .'[86] In May 1701
occurred the death of Richard Caryll, 'soe well beloved in the Neighbourhood',

[81] For the situation of English Roman Catholics in the earlier eighteenth century, see Richard
Burn, *The Justice of the Peace and Parish Officer* (London, 1755), ii, pp. 273–92. Pope's most public
statement of the situation occurs in his imitation of the second epistle of the second book of Horace,
ll. 52–67; T.E., iv, pp. 168–9, l. 60n.

[82] Lord Caryll signed himself Jo: Southwell, and this pseudonym was used by other members
and friends of the family.

[83] B.M. Add. 28226, f. 113.

[84] Ibid. 28226, f. 93. The letter has been endorsed 19 Nov. 1689, but this cannot be right. 1699
is the most likely.

[85] Ibid. 28226, f. 93.

[86] Ibid. 28226, ff. 111, 120.

and John Caryll succeeded to his father's house and estates at West Grinstead.[87] As the letters continue shortage of money becomes a more and more pressing problem; a niece's annuity at the convent has not been paid and there is a dispute about the responsibility; the convent is poor and Mary Caryll has to anticipate her own annuity to buy corn; she sends her brother a pound of 'tobacka', for business at court is 'cross and Shagrine' to him and he has not written for a long time. On 5 Nov. 1706 'our young Nephu' has returned to England; Mary Caryll supposes 'his hault at London is now at an end, & wish[es] his congratulations were soe in the Country . . . which I feare may expose him to unnecessary expences.'[88] The expenses of educating the numerous Caryll children are now a recurring theme; the same letter begs help for four of the children of Philip, another nephew of Lord Caryll, and on 17 Nov. Lord Caryll replies with asperity:

> . . . I will perform all that I promised concerning [Catherine Caryll] in a former letter of mine to you, where you will find I told you only this, that if she made her profession with you I would for her portion settle upon the monastery a perpetual rent of three hundred livres a year . . . I much wonder how good mother feteplace at Leer should come to fancy that I had settled 300 pounds upon each of Phill's two younger daughters . . . however to the end that these two girles may have christian breeding, if you know any monastery, be it English, Dutch or Wallon that will receive them & keep them both in all things for five hundred livres a year, I will be contented to pay that pension for them but I will be at no other charge about them . . . What you write to me concerning Phill's son to have him placed amongst the Garde-marines seemes to me a litle extraordinary, for what figure do you think an unbred whelp without fashion or language would make amongst these young french sparks? In short I will not allow him a penny towards his maintenance unless it be at St. Omers, or in some College where he may be bred a Christian . . .[89]

Lord Caryll might well regret his earlier remark: 'ther can never be too many of so good a breed' when natural breeding entailed 'christian breeding' at such troublesome expense. John Caryll's family caused anxiety too: the 'young Heyre' arrived home but Mary Caryll can

> never think of this young man without a sigh, that you have sent him soe farr from under your protection, and I phantsy that very thought will much abate the pleasure in seeing him at home, espetially his father, my thoughts tell me; what can be learnt in that miserable wicked country, more then Idleness, and pleasure, for I doe not think his father is in a con-dition to make any advantagious propositions, for England is soe drain'd by these Warrs, and still Catholic's goo by the worst . . . but you may iustly reproach me . . . my intention being only that our fammilly may

[87] Ibid. 28226, f. 117; Foley, op. cit., iii, [facing] p. 534.
[88] Ibid. 28226, ff. 121–4.
[89] Ibid. 28226, ff. 125–6.

propogat Religion and be servisable to theyre King, as theyre Antiosters [ancestors] have bin; witnes your self that has lived this eighteen years in Banishment for theyr servis.[90]

The question of marriage for John Caryll the younger, alluded to here for the first time, will be an abiding theme in the correspondence for the next few years; at the moment the prospects were not good, for a successful match depended on the prosperity of both sets of parents. Enclosing a letter from Mrs. John Caryll to Lord Caryll, the Abbess comments gloomily:

I suppose this is from your Niece: and yours I feare is of the same stile, for she gives me such a dismaile account of her affairs I could half wish I might not pertake, of the recitall of theyre miserys, since tis not in my powre to doe more than pray for them . . .

Richard Caryll had left his son debts, there were other expensive domestic problems, John Caryll's health was affected by his worries; the truth is they have not 'bine used to Crosses' but 'one thing I take as a mark of his honesty, his paying soe constantly for all his Children both heere, St. Omers, and at Liedg; and this iustice will procure him blessings heere after.'[91] Writing to her brother for Christmas 1707 the Abbess reports that 'our Nephu is in a great push of wants . . .' but she hears 'a very good Caracter given of the young squire of Lady Holt.'[92] On 13 July 1708 there is news of an unexpected holiday for John Caryll, an English pilgrimage: '. . . it seemes the Duke of Norfolk had ingaged Sr Edmund Southcote and my Nephu, to make this progress wth him, the first place was St. Winefrid's well, and the pleasur is, that iournay will be without any charg to them, I hope it may do our Nephu a pleasure . . .'[93]

Meanwhile in the greater world of Europe a new series of events had transformed the precarious peace. In 1700 Charles II of Spain had died leaving his huge, largely defenceless empire to a grandson of Louis XIV, who accepted the will. In September 1701 a Treaty of Grand Alliance against him was signed by the Allies, and in the same month, on the death of Lord Caryll's master James II, his son James was proclaimed in France as King of Great Britain. He was recognised by Louis, who thus broke the Treaty of Ryswick. This chivalrous and costly gesture overjoyed the Jacobites, and made England enter the new war with France with added resolution. On 8 March 1702 occurred the death of William of Orange, but the war was not suffered to flag on this account. In August 1704 Marlborough won his great battle at Blenheim, and there commenced that series of victories which must have progressively dispirited the dwindling and impoverished court at St. Germains and the supporters of the exiled Stuarts in England. Week by week the Jacobite correspondence went on, painfully gathering in the shreds and rags of political

[90] Ibid. 28226, f. 127 (soon after 17 Nov. 1706).
[91] Ibid. 28226, f. 128 (23 Feb. 1705/6).
[92] Ibid. 28226, f. 134 (23 Dec. 1707).
[93] Ibid. 28226, f. 135 (13 July 1708).

hope, always looking for favourable signs from Marlborough and Godolphin, and when such a sign was thought to have been received, suspecting it (dutifully) before eagerly pursuing it. Like the repeated playing of the same record, Lord Caryll's code letters went out to the Jacobite agents, as the war continued:

> What you tell me of your acquaintance Mr. Goulston [Godolphin], that he appears out of humour . . . does not much surprise me . . . I am only sorry this sourness of humour will make him unfit to be applied to in your cousin Wisely's [the pretender's] affair, at least at present; and as for Mr. Armsworth [Marlborough], I believe he has so much business of his own upon his hands, that notwithstanding all former engagements, he will hardly have the leisure, perhaps not the will, to mind old promises.[94]

On 1 Jan. 1710, when France was still staggering from the blow of Malplaquet, the Abbess Mary Caryll wrote to her brother:

> I neuer gave the wishes of a happy yeare to you, and all the other frends, with a heavier heart in my life, but that it may be accompanyed with submission to God's will, to you as will as my self, and that you may live to see peace and better days is my present to you, with my earnest prayers for your preservation this insueing yeare, and as many more as God pleases.
>
> Pray Deare Brother lett me coniure you once more to lay my profound respects and duty to her Ma'tys feet, with the ioy it gives her Ma'tys subjects, her health is soe well restored, as I am lately inform'd, ther is very few howrs in the day, her Ma'ty is not in my thoughts, for thô' I dispaire of this yeares peace, yett not att all disponding of our Kings restoration, and I hope not farr off; and this is the faith, that raises our drooping hearts.[95]

The letter seems to express the end of an era of Jacobitism. Both Mary Caryll and Lord Caryll were octogenarians; they could remember the Civil War, the execution of Charles I, Cromwell and the Restoration. When a Stuart king had once again gone into exile, their loyalty had still sustained him in misfortune. It is impressive, in Mary Caryll's letter, how the very recognition of misfortune and an apparently hostile providence brings forth a brave hope: the ashes glow into flame at the end. But their lives were done. Lord Caryll died on 4 Sept. 1711, and eleven months later, on 8 August 1712, Mary Caryll herself.[96]

5. 'THE BEST MAN IN ENGLAND'

John Caryll was forty three when Pope's formal correspondence with him began. He had a family of ten children, four sons and six daughters. His eldest son, John, had, as we have seen, been educated at Lord Caryll's expense near St. Germains; he was now twenty three and had been back in England four years. The next son, Richard, had been educated at St. Omer and was to

[94] Macpherson, op. cit., ii, pp. 84–5 (20 March 1706/7).
[95] B.M. Add. 28226, f. 138.
[96] D.N.B., ix, p. 255; De Trenqualéon, op. cit., ii, p. 123.

enter the Society of Jesus in September 1711. The next two sons, Edward and Henry, were also educated in France, but not for the priesthood; Edward eventually returned to England to marry and settle down on a small estate, while Henry, who died in 1726 at the age of twenty four, was page to the Duke of Lorraine, the exiled King of Poland. All John Caryll's daughters were educated abroad in Roman Catholic convents; of these only Catherine, the second eldest, failed to become a nun. Elizabeth, and Anne were professed nuns of the Holy Sepulchre at Liège, while Fanny died there during her noviciate. Mary and Arabella were professed nuns of the Dames Benedictines at Dunkirk, which their great aunt Mary Caryll had founded and of which she had been abbess forty nine years.[97] The Caryll procedure for the disposal of a large family is clear. Greatest care was taken with the eldest son, for he was the heir and, all being well, would bring a good portion to the family on marriage. University, parliament, the established church, army and navy were debarred to Catholics in England, but another son could be given to the Catholic priest- hood. Minor places at the courts of Catholic monarchs might be sought for younger sons, as they were in the first place for both Edward and Henry. Daughters, it seems, were of small importance in the family's development. Caryll could not afford portions for his daughters to marry; money had to be found for their 'christian breeding' at convents, but the portions they brought with them to the convents in which they were professed were smaller than if they had married anyone but Christ; their livelihood was bought cheap. Only two of John Caryll's children did not fall in with such plans: Edward and Catherine. Edward did not wish to be a priest, and the court of St. Germains was too poor to be able to find him a place as a page; Catherine did not profess, but neither did she marry; she lived a single lady until her death in 1759.[98] In this way John Caryll's children fulfilled the family aim 'to propagat Religion and be servisable to theyre King'. No word was spoken of trade, though in prosperous Elizabethan days Sir Edward Caryll had married a merchant's daughter.

The state of John Caryll's affairs in 1710 may be seen from a letter on the subject to Lord Caryll. Mary Caryll's messages concerning her nephew's difficulties must have alarmed the old gentleman; the matter came to a head during the protracted negotiations for a wife for John Caryll the younger, and Lewis Innes the historian, Principal of the Scots College at Paris and Almoner to the Queen Regent at St. Germains, wrote

That my Lord did not think your present condition would allow you to make such settlements as would be required upon such a portion as you expect: That of late he had severall tymes told me he wished you sold some parcell of lands to clear the rest, & that you lived for some tyme more privatly to avoid the expense of housekeeping which he thought the ressort of freinds augmented beyond what you could now bear.

[97] De Trenqualéon, loc. cit.
[98] B.M. Add. 28227, ff. 73, 118; Ruvigny, op. cit., pp. 27–9.

Innes, whose considerable diplomatic gifts were currently being devoted to finding a wife for the Caryll heir, represented to the old man the danger that 'a change in your [i.e. John Caryll's] way of living' might well 'frighten' away 'any tollerable match' but failed to convince. He thus advised John Caryll to state his situation to his uncle, and if anything make it seem a little better than it really was.[99] Thus John Caryll wrote his

> account of the present state of my affairs, which I will faithfully include under two heads, one shewing how I came to be in Debt and the other what means I thank God I have still in my hands for cleering myself one time or other.
>
> As to the first, [Caryll recites the details of the bargain with Lord Cutts]. After that, to skreen it better from Double taxes, Worledge, a Protestant attorney, was putt in by my father to receive the rents of itt [the estate]; butt before I could gett him to deliver up his Acts. he was run 1100 and odd pounds in our Debt . . . The next thing that followed was an expensive Lawsuit with ye Parson, which there was no avoyding off, and then itt cost me fourteen hdd. and fifty pounds to take a new lease of the tythes. Sometime after I gave 2,400 ll. for Mr. Brining's share of Winchelsea; which I bought purely because I knew it to be very improveable Estate . . .

He next cites his expenses in educating his children; and moves on to the provision of annuities:

> I have been liable to pay £100 a year in annuity to my wives Relations, and fifty pounds to Mr. Inborô', nor did any of them drop till abt. two years since . . . I also paid some years £50 p. ann. to my cousin Cope by your direction till such a time as she marryed . . . great part of the Estate has been all along double tax'd.
>
> Having now laid before your Lordship the occasions of my Debts, give me leave to observe to you the course I may take to clear 'em. [I purchased] halfe ye tythe[s] of Hart[ing,] for we have now the moiety also which before was in ye Ford family, . . . and I think I shall have very ill Luck if we get not Portion enough with a wife for my son to goe clear [of] our Debts besides my Lord I have a great deal of Timber upon my Estate . . .
>
> If I have not alreddy tyr'd yr Lordship with so long a detail of matters, give me leave to add a word or two more—that I need not goe about to vindicate myself from any assertion of Extravagance, &c., for nobody can accuse me of Gaming or any other Unjustifiable expences: the only [one] I have been att that has not been precisely necessary has been horse and hounds . . . I ever design'd so soon as I had settle'd my son, to live beyond sea for some years to save for younger Children, and in ye mean time you may please to observe that I have constantly resided near halfe ye. year att

[99] Ibid. 28227, f. 84.

Grinsted as a cheaper place, of less Ressort and thinner Neighbourhood than Ladyholt.[100]

This was the wordly situation of John Caryll in 1710. To Lord Caryll, who discussed every article of the letter with his friend Innes, it gave 'full satisfaction'—Innes had never seen him 'in better humour'.[101]

The death of Lord Caryll and the final 'settlement' of John Caryll's son occurred in the same year. In a will made in 1707 John Caryll the younger was made the heir of the old Secretary, whose estate consisted almost entirely of the principal and interest of his investments in the Hotel de Ville: 'the best security for English Catholicks'. A memorandum of John Caryll the younger, from this year, shows that Lord Caryll's contracts on the Hotel de Ville were estimated to bring in 12,960.10.00. livres per annum, out of which however the legatee was responsible for paying many annuities, amounting to some 2,850 livres per annum (the greater part to institutions such as the Scots College, the lesser to dependent nephews and nieces). This left 'coming in cleer' 10,110.10.00. livres per annum: the fulfilment of Lord Caryll's promise to leave £2,000 per annum 'good rent' to maintain the 'title of honour' conferred upon the family by the late King James.[102]

Negotiations for the marriage of John Caryll the younger had been in full swing since 1709. Approaches were made among the English Catholics in France, as well as at home, and Lewis Innes was active on Caryll's behalf. No state negotiation could have been carried out with more solemnity and *finesse*. First an unlikely and ambitious match was mooted, in order to see how far Lord Caryll would contribute to the settlement if the incentive were there. Then an approach was made to the three daughters of Sir Robert Throgmorten, through their aunt ('a woman of great piety and good sense'); the hazards of a stammer, an incidence of King's Evil, a suspected inclination to be a nun, were all deliberated upon; a grave but obscure warning was given against the Newbourgh family; there was a taint of madness in the Touchburns; Lord Arundell's daughter had a portion of £10,000. All collapsed when the favoured Throgmorten daughter decided she *did* want to be a nun. Finally John Caryll arranged a marriage with Mary Mackenzie, only daughter of Kenneth Mackenzie, Fourth Earl and First Marquis of Seaforth: a noble but impoverished Jacobite family, of whom Innes wrote: 'I should be sorry you trusted to her brother's Estate for security of her portion.' Precautions were duly taken, and it is probable that Caryll got the 'very moderate' portion of £7,000 which he was demanding.[103] Such was the background to that gay

---

[100] Ibid. 28227, ff. 492–3; cf. ff. 494–5. For general comments on the situation of landed papist families, see G. E. Mingay, *English Landed Society in the Eighteenth Century* (London, 1963), pp.41–2, 132.

[101] Ibid. 28227, f. 88.

[102] Ibid. 28227, f. 116. See also 28244, ff. 156–7.

[103] Ibid. 28227, ff. 72, 74, 76, 84, 86, 88, 97, 124. This marriage settlement, with its stipulation that £10,000 be provided for any two eldest children of the match other than the heir, was an ultimate cause of the last Caryll's financial downfall in 1758; *Private Acts* 32 George II, 1758–9, No. 37.

occasion in 1712 on which Pope planned to accompany the young bride and bridegroom from London to Ladyholt.[104]

From 1710 to John Caryll's death in 1736 Pope's letters form an important part of the family correspondence. The first surviving letters between them are not, as I have suggested, likely to be the first letters of all, but they are certainly the opening of what must at first have been intended a formal, literary correspondence; Pope's manner in the earliest letters is consciously witty and essayistic, and from what one can gather Caryll's answers were the same.[105] Gradually Pope's ritual protestations of frankness and spontaneity ('You see, sir, with what freedom I write or rather talk upon paper to you') become true, and thereafter plain communication becomes a mode to which each regularly resorts. Yet the essay style of letter, a work of art of its kind, must have delighted those to whom it was addressed, and Pope continued to write them to Caryll from time to time; his letter of 14 Aug. 1713 is a good example. As early as 18 June 1711, however, a pressing concern arose, which was also a matter of principle, and temporarily banished from the correspondence the element of leisured display. This concern was the hostile comment aroused among certain of Pope's fellow-Catholics by his lines from *An Essay on Criticism*:

(Thus *Wit*, like *Faith*, by each Man is apply'd
To *one small Sect*, and All are *damn'd beside*.)   [ll. 396–7]

I don't mean to recapitulate the well-known and spirited defence of himself against religious bigotry which Pope made to Caryll; but rather it is important to suggest that this introduces what is, in different forms and contexts, an abiding theme of the poet in the first ten years of his correspondence with Caryll, and one of the first importance for his development as a satirical poet. This is the theme of partisanship and principle: the need to rise above narrow-minded party-spirit, bigotry whether religious or political, and yet have the firmness of mature thought and fundamental conviction. Pope did not wish to be a fanatic; neither did he wish to turn aimlessly in the winds of changing times and opinions. The whole issue must have arisen from Pope's acute awareness of civil and religious conflict and of the fact that, whether he liked it or not, he had been born and 'bred a papist, when one is obnoxious to four parts in five as being so too much, and to the fifth part as being so too little'. No choice could deliver him from this conflict; he had to find ways of living with it, of putting down roots which would go deeper than superficial allegiance, at the same time as growing above it to an impartiality and freedom which would come not from deserting an inherited situation but from accepting and transcending it. 'I am ambitious of nothing but the good opinion of all good men of all sides, for I know that one virtue of a free spirit is more worth than all the virtues put together of all the narrow-souled people in the world', he wrote to Caryll.[106] Hence Pope's praise of Erasmus, in *An Essay on Criticism*

---

[104] *Corr.*, i, pp. 144–5.
[105] Ibid., pp. 113–15.
[106] Ibid., pp, 220–1 (1 May 1714).

and in the letters to Caryll, for in religious controversy Erasmus had held to one side and yet seen it critically, had attacked its abuses, and yet remained loyal to the Roman Catholic Church.[107] And hence Pope's epitaph for Lord Caryll, whom he never met:

> A manly Form; a bold, yet modest mind;
> Sincere, tho' prudent; constant, yet resign'd;
> Honour unchang'd, a Principle profest;
> Fix'd to one side, but mod'rate to the rest:
> An honest Courtier, and a Patriot too;
> Just to his Prince, and to his Country true:
> All these were join'd in one, yet failed to save
> The Wise, the Learn'd, the Virtuous, and the Brave;   [ll. 1–8]

From what has gone before it is clear how appropriate an epitaph for Lord Caryll this was; we recognize in these lines the man who contended in the court of St. Germains that James II had lost his throne through 'the breaking of the laws' but who yet held that 'The duty we owe our Prince or Parent, is indispensable, so that what they command (in things not unlawfull) we must take to be the will of God.'[108] It is evident that Pope must often have discussed with his friend John Caryll the decisions and fortunes of the Jacobite Secretary of State. When Pope confessed to Swift that he was 'of the religion of Erasmus a Catholick' and when he praised Lord Caryll for being 'Fix'd to one side, but mod'rate to the rest' he was among other things exploring his own situation, in relation to the religion in which he had been born, and to the family of fellow-Catholics he knew best. This does, I think, go some way to explaining how Pope can, in his *Imitations of Horace*, convert Erasmus into his *aurea mediocritas* ('Like good *Erasmus* in an honest Mean') and yet, in the best sense, be so magnificently partisan as he is in some of the major epistles of that group.[109]

Neither Lord Caryll nor John Caryll can ever have reflected upon the fortunes of their family without a painful awareness of the trials and dangers of religious and political conflict. It is there in 'Not Guilty: or the Plea of the Roman Catholick in England', in *Naboth's Vineyard*, in the imitation of Virgil's First Eclogue, and in the letters of both men. Conflict among Catholics they knew too, only too well: in England and in St. Germains how the excesses of some brought trouble to the rest. In a smaller context Pope was learning the same from Catholic reactions to his *Essay on Criticism*. It is not surprising that when a conflict broke out which *might* be healed by personal intervention and wit: the quarrel between the two hitherto friendly Catholic families, the Petres and the Fermors, John Caryll, who had close relations with each, appealed to his talented Catholic friend Pope 'to laugh them together again'.[110]

[107] Ibid., pp. 117–19, 126–8 (18 June and 19 July 1711).
[108] B.M. Add. 28226, f. 103.
[109] *To Fortescue*, l. 66; this poem illustrates the point particularly well.
[110] Spence, 104.

Nor is it surprising, in these circumstances, that the first line of *The Rape of the Lock* echoes Lord Caryll's rendering of a key-line of Virgil's First Eclogue:

What dire effects from civil Discord flow![111]

The complimentary allusion, which would be recognized by John Caryll, makes the shortly following line: '—This Verse to *Caryll*, Muse! is due' more widely suggestive, and (to the dedicatee and some others) brought the troubled history of the Caryll family during the previous thirty years, through Virgil, into the heroic reference of Pope's poem. The greater discords no few men could heal, and were the proper subject of tragedy and epic; but this conflict appeared local enough and foolish enough to bear hope of reconciliation by being placed, through the agency of a comic work of art, in a wider context of human values and endeavour. And it is possible that the poem, pleading as it does for reconciliation and harmony, was intended to have a bearing upon affairs of state, and 'civil Discord' itself, the microcosm passing judgement on the macrocosm. It seems highly improbable that the incident which the poem purports to describe actually took place at the royal palace of Hampton Court; but Pope, by setting it there, has been able to sketch in, albeit with the eye of comedy, the wider and more remote realm of 'Great Anna' and 'Foreign Tyrants', as well as the smaller and more immediate one of 'Nymphs at home'. All this Caryll, whom Pope later described as 'so many years one of my best critics, as well as one of my best friends', must have seen; an intelligent understanding of Dryden and Boileau would be enough to suggest the possibilities of the situation.[112] Caryll's unaffected interest in Pope's work, and his true sense of its value, may be seen from a letter of Caryll to Pope very shortly after the publication of *The Rape of the Lock* in May 1712:

> I hope your health permitted you to execute your design of giving us an imitation of *Pollio*, I am satisfy'd 'twill be doubly *Divine* and I shall long to see it. I ever thought church-musick the most ravishing of all harmonious compositions, and must also believe sacred subjects, well handled, the most inspiring of all Poetry.
>
> But where hangs the *Lock* now? (tho' I know that rather than draw any just reflection upon your self, of the least shadow of ill-nature, you would freely have suprest one of the best of Poems.) I hear no more of it—will it come out in *Lintot's* Miscellany or not?[113]

Civil discord impinged upon Pope and Caryll in a more formidable way soon after the appearance of the longer version of *The Rape of the Lock* in May 1714. A fortnight after Anne's death Pope wrote to Caryll, with dissembled anxiety, 'I thank God ... I am below all the accidents of state-changes by my circumstances, and above them by any philosophy ... I am sure, if all Whigs and all Tories had the spirit of one Roman Catholic that I

---

[111] *The First Part of Miscellany Poems ... Publish'd by Mr. Dryden*, ed. cit., p. 318.
[112] *Corr.*, ii, p. 140.
[113] *Corr.*, i, p. 142.

know, it would be well for all Roman Catholics . . . The greatest fear I have under the circumstances of a poor papist is the loss of my poor horse . . .'[114] On 6 Sept. 1715 the Earl of Mar proclaimed the Pretender at Braemar, and the Jacobite Rebellion had begun. In the Autumn John Caryll's son and his young wife returned to England from Paris, where they had been attending to their affairs. Their return seems to suggest innocence of Jacobite designs; France would have been a safer place for them at such a time. Yet Lady Mary Caryll's own brother, the Earl of Seaforth, was, somewhat hesitantly, in arms for the Jacobite cause. On 13 Oct. Catherine Petre, the young widow of the Baron in the *Rape of the Lock*, told Caryll she could not 'but be in some concerne for Lady Mary, who I fancy is under some apprehensions for her Brother . . .'[115] By November the rebellion had spread to Northumberland, and Pope's Catholic friend Edward Blount, no Jacobite, wrote: 'What a dismal scene has there been open'd in the North? what ruin have those unfortunate rash gentlemen drawn upon themselves and their miserable followers, and per-chance upon many others too, who upon no account would be their followers?' and went on to commend Pomponius Atticus.[116] On 24 Nov. the English Jacobites surrendered at Preston, and in Scotland the Battle of Sheriffmuir, though militarily indecisive, proved a strategic defeat for Mar. The tide of events was now running clearly one way; as Edward Blount had predicted the Jacobites achieved only the bringing of hard times to English Catholics. John Caryll's estates were remote from any area of England where Jacobite strategy had planned a rising; he remained quiet, and must have fervently hoped that the Jacobites would either be swiftly and conspicuously successful, or so ineffective that they constituted no threat to the Hanoverian government, and thus provoke no persecution of Catholics. He was disappointed in both wishes. Probably in December 1715 Pope, sensing a danger to Caryll and to a lesser extent himself, was moved to express his loyalty to his friend:

> It is an old thing to tell you how much I love you, and all that's yours; how entirely my own heart makes all your interests mine; and how sensible a stroke to it everything must be, which affects your quiet, or happiness in any kind. Perhaps accident, or distance, or private cares, or public calamities . . . may prevent the usual frequency of our expressions of that friendship, which I'm sure to carry with me to my grave . . . I beg you at all times, to believe me as zealous to continue our friendship, as I was the first moment I began it: . . . it shall never suffer any abatement by any intervals of absence or fortune . . .[117]

Pope's friendship with Caryll was to undergo some coolness in the coming years; it is creditable that the poet should have chosen to acknowledge it so warmly, in a letter, when the connection could be a serious embarrassment to him. The heavens did not fall, in the next few months, but life promised to

[114] Ibid., p. 241.
[115] B.M. Add. 28227, f. 259.
[116] *Corr.*, i, p. 320 (11 Nov. 1715).
[117] Ibid., p. 323.

be hard indeed for land-owning Catholics. On 5 Jan. 1715/16 Caryll's cousin Eyre, who was a lawyer, wrote from London to answer a question concerning the commission of Justices of the Peace 'to Administer the Oaths' to suspected persons:

> And since appearance and Refusall, and Not appearance Equally Encourages a Conviction, so as to make a Retourn of it in the Courts above, I see no way to Escape their Entring down your Refusall And to Return it . . . If it be put realy and strictly In Execution and Double Taxes There will be no living for poor papists And I can not think It will goe to the Extremity with those who live peaceably and quietly, but if it shoulde be, the onley way to secure our Estates Is, to make it lyable to the payment of just debts, and that being . . . a precedent and prior Charge, no subsequent forfeiture Can take place of it— This is for those who are but tennants for life:—but those that have the Inheritance, they may take up Money upon their Estate's . . .[118]

Such were the preoccupations and fears of Catholics at this time, and perhaps nothing could better explain the decision of Pope and his parents to sell their house at Binfield, and place themselves under the protection of the protestant Earl of Burlington, at Chiswick. Shortly before their removal Pope wrote again to Caryll:

> Such a man as I know you are, has no need of being spirited up into honour . . . 'Tis enough to do and suffer what we ought; and men should know that the noble power of suffering bravely is as far above that of enterprising greatly, as an unblemished conscience and inflexible resolution are above an accidental flow of spirits or a sudden tide of blood. If the whole religious business of mankind, be included in resignation to our Maker, and charity to our fellow creatures; there are now some people, who give us the opportunity of affording as bright an example in practising the one, as themselves have given an infamous instance of the violation of the other . . . The misfortunes of private families, the misunderstandings [of people] whom distresses make suspicious, the coldness of relations whom change of religion may disunite, or the necessities of half-ruined estates render unkind to each other,—these at least may be softened some degree, by . . . humanity . . .
>
> I write this from Windsor Forest, of which I am come to take my last look and leave of. We here bid our papist-neighbours adieu, much as those who go to be hanged do their fellow-prisoners, who are condemned to follow 'em a few weeks after . . .
>
> Perhaps now I have learnt so far as—Nos dulcia linquimus arva, the next day may be—Nos patriam fugimus.[119]

[118] B.M. Add. 28227, ff. 279–80.
[119] Corr., i, pp. 335–7 (20 March 1715/16).

Numerous Catholic letters spoke of resignation at this time; it was in this political and religious situation that Pope feelingly learnt the meaning of the concept (so crucial for his *Essay on Man*), and dramatised it by yet another reference to the First Eclogue of Virgil: he has learnt how to leave his pleasant fields, and may yet learn how to fly his native land.[120] Life and art seem to weave themselves here into a single tapestry.

In these scenes John Caryll figured for Pope not only as the generous and unaffected critic and friend which the correspondence shows him to have been, but as a man who could (as in their reading at least of Lord Caryll's life) maintain a principle without being 'narrow-souled', be loyal yet not narrowly partisan; who sought to heal discord where he could, and, where he could not, bore misfortune with a bravery of resignation which yet implied no trace of moral neutrality. These were some of the reasons why Pope called John Caryll 'the best man in England'.[121]

---

[120] Ibid., p. 338 (Edward Blount to Pope, 24 March 1715/16).
[121] Ibid., p. 512 (Pope to Martha and Teresa Blount, 17 Sept. 1718).

III. 'A Principle Profest': John Caryll, second Baron Caryll of Durford (ii)

1. 'A LITTLE COMMONWEALTH'

ANOTHER reason for Pope's admiration was that Caryll was a remarkably family-spirited man. The struggle of the Carylls to maintain themselves as a family in troubled times has been demonstrated and would be well known to Pope. When Caryll's son and daughter-in-law returned to England in the Autumn of 1715, Pope made him, characteristically, a compliment both Scriptural and Augustan:

> ... I should see you in all the shining circumstances of a *pater familias*, upon the recovery of almost all that is dear to you. Jacob that recovered his son Joseph from the land of Egypt might give one some idea of you. Pray own the truth, did not you begin to *prophesy* when you saw 'em all about you like the old patriarch? Had you no delightful prospects in your mind of the *nati natorum, et qui nascentur ab illis*?[1]

Caryll is dramatised as both Jacob and Aeneas. Other friends of the Carylls were impressed by their apparent family happiness and harmony, and the impression was not superficial. But, inevitably, the truth was less simple and less perfect. One is startled, in reading through the family collection of manuscript poems and transcripts, to come upon a poem which can only have applied to themselves:

> Three Generations have We known;
> From Bad to Worse They all have grown.
> The First had honor, Worth and Parts,
> Which gain'd him Male & Female Hearts;
> Yett Rebell hangs upon his Name,
> Which stain'd the Lustre of his Fame.
> The next a Man well bred and Civill,
> Butt Lew'd and Vicious as the D---ll.
> The last an Ill-bred Marry'd-Boy,
> Horses and Doggs are all his Joy:
> Nor could he on Companions hitt

[1] *Corr.*, i, p. 317. *Aeneid*, iii, 98.

More for his Sence and Moralls fitt!
Yett Bles'd he is with Such a Wife,
As well deserves a better Life:
That's all the hopes We can pretend
Why Heaven, att last, the Breed may mend.[2]

The first generation refers to Lord Caryll; even if by extension 'Rebell' were held to 'stain' his nephew's honour, the outlawry was lifted in 1724, before the nephew's grandson was near old enough to marry. The next generation must therefore refer to John Caryll, Pope's friend, and the last to John Caryll the younger (who was undoubtedly a keen huntsman) and his wife Lady Mary. The poem must have been written between the date of his marriage in 1712 and his death from smallpox in 1718.[3] The picture of John Caryll and his son given here is unlike any other reference to them I have found; this and the hand in which the poem is written persuades me it is possibly the work of John Caryll himself. It is improbable that so strong an attack on so otherwise well-loved a head of family would have been written and preserved by any other of its members.[4] It must certainly have been written by a member of the family in a mood of unusual pessimism, when premonitions of family decay were strong in the writer's mind.

Such premonitions might easily have arisen from a consideration of the Shipley branch of the family. Conditions for Catholic gentry were so hard that a very little extravagance, mismanagement and bad luck might bring a modest estate into debt. Philip Caryll, John Caryll's first cousin, seems to have had little sense of responsibility; it was provision for his children that Lord Caryll and Abbess Mary Caryll had had such sharp exchanges about before 1711, and in January 1712 he seems to have been attempting to induce his invalid son, still in his minority, to agree to break the entail on the estate, in order to raise money.[5] This son, in July 1716 wrote to John Caryll the younger asking for help ('My father abandons me . . .') and followed it up by a piteous letter three months later:

. . . my distemper came on me last night about one of the clock as it does very often of latter days, and had I not a man to attend me in those occasions I should be found perhaps choked or smothered in my bed in the morning, this I feare must be my fate, if my Father failes to doe what he is obliged, as to the past arreares and future payment of my allowance [to] prevent it,

[2] B.M. Add. 28253, f. 22.

[3] For Pope's letter on his death, see Corr., i, 474 (Pope to Caryll, 1 May 1718).

[4] John Caryll certainly wrote verse (see Section 2 below; and Corr., i, p. 113). For evidence supporting this view of his eldest son, see B.M. Add. 28237, ff. 62–4. The alternative and less plausible reading would be to identify John Caryll with the first generation, and conclude that 'Rebell' still hung on his name after the lifting of the outlawry in 1724. The middle generation would then be John Caryll the younger (who is, however, unlikely to have been so harshly attacked after his death in 1718) and the last John Baptist Caryll, though neither he nor his wife fit the description.

[5] B.M. Add. 28227, f. 322; 28228, ff. 247–50.

Dr. Cousin, for gods sake . . . acquit yourself thereby of what is incumbent upon you . . .[6]

Little else is known about this unfortunate young man, who is said to have died young as a monk at Douai.[7] Philip Caryll, his father, was, in 1723, an informer to the Government concerning the Atterbury Plot, attempting to prove the complicity of Atterbury with Sir Henry Goring, a neighbour of John Caryll, and known Jacobite conspirator. His motive may have been partly financial; he was in money trouble again in May 1724, and in 1727 alarmed his brother by selling yet more of the family land without consulting him. This is the background to the sad affair of Philip Caryll's sister, Mrs. Anne Cope, with which Pope was to be so concerned.[8] John Caryll must often have considered this situation, felt: there but for the grace of God go I, and wondered how long the grace could last. In addition, he and his son, as the head and only prosperous, landed members of the family, were constantly being asked for help by poor relatives and dependents. When Pope praised Caryll as a patriarch and Philip Caryll told him, as he often did, that the continuance of the family depended on him, their meaning was partly a very material one.

Pope's concern with the situation of Mrs. Cope shows that he saw Caryll's patriarchal role as one which might be of real use to remote members of the family who were in need. Anne Cope, from whom in 1711 Pope heard 'more wit and sense in two hours, than almost all her sex ever spoke in their whole lives', was deserted by her husband, but responded to her misfortune with a brave spirit. She made two voyages to Port Mahon, where Captain Cope was stationed and had entered into a bigamous marriage, though it is not clear whether she was originally activated by love or a resolve to wrest from him a means of subsistence.[9] Something about her reminded Caryll of Pope's *Elegy to the Memory of an Unfortunate Lady*: 'Butt pray in your next', he wrote to Pope in July 1717,

tell me who was the Unfortunate Lady you addresse a Copy of Verses to. I think you once gave me her history, butt tis now quite outt of my head. Butt now I have named such a person Mrs. Cope occurs to my mind. I have comply'd with her Desires, tho' I thinke a Second Voyage to such a Rascall is the most preposterous thing imaginable butt *mulierem fortem quis inveniet!*[10]

and indeed her misfortune seems to have been partly what prompted Pope, with 'every incentive to write an obituary elegy, except that of an actual bereavement', to conceive his poem.[11] Certainly Pope was aroused to a strong emotional concern, which expressed itself through practical and financial help over a period of more than ten years. The tone of Caryll's remarks in the above

[6] Ibid. 28227, ff. 322; 329–30 (from which the letter, dated 29 Oct. 1716, is quoted).

[7] Foley, op. cit., iii, p. 534.

[8] *Journals of the House of Lords*, xxii, p. 155; B.M. Add. 28228, ff. 142–6; 247.

[9] *Corr.*, i, p. 129; T.E., ii, p. 353.

[10] *Corr.*, i, pp. 416–17.

[11] T.E., ii, p. 253.

letter are interesting; they have the genial loftiness of the great nobleman, but at the same time his compliance with her wishes almost certainly meant financial aid for her 'Second Voyage'. In a letter perhaps written in November 1718 Pope is helping Mrs. Cope take legal measures against her husband, to 'bring him to some composition', and asks for Caryll's support; in October of 1720 she is once again staying with Caryll, and Pope complains he has not been told.[12] Five years later, it appears that Pope is devoting the proceeds of those subscriptions to his *Odyssey* translation, procured by Caryll, to Mrs. Cope.[13] She was practically destitute; there was talk of her going into a convent, but this too would have cost money, and the Caryll estates and investments were already heavily burdened with annuities owed to the religious houses in which numerous daughters of the family had been professed. From 1725 on Pope gives Caryll more and more unmistakable hints (though he is delicacy itself at first) that Mrs. Cope should be an object of charity to the head of her family. It is clear, however, that it was once again Philip Caryll, the head of the Shipley branch, who was evading his responsibilities. Thus Pope wrote to Caryll in January 1725/6:

> I had three days since a long letter from poor Mrs. Cope from Bar-sur-Aube en Champagne, where she tells me she has stayed several months in hopes of her brother's coming there (as he gave her assurance) to live together, but she knows no more of him yet than the first day she arrived, nor hears when, or how, he can assist her, insomuch that the little money I sent her half a year since, was actually all gone then and she really wanted bread when I remitted her a little more this Christmasse . . . I wish you could remit her something . . .[14]

Caryll replied he had already done so.[15] In a letter which he published in all his collections, Pope sought to raise her spirits; his manner of bantering flattery accords uneasily with the wretched circumstances of what Mrs. Cope had called her 'Vagabond Life' until the end when his emotion finds almost poetic form:

> . . . even in a Monastery your devotions cannot carry you so far toward the next world as to make This lose the sight of you, but you'll be like a Star, that while it is fix'd to Heaven shines over all the Earth.
>
> Wheresoever Providence shall dispose of the most valuable thing I know, I shall ever follow you with my sincerest wishes, and my best thoughts will be perpetually waiting upon you, when you never hear of me or them. Your own guardian Angels cannot be more constant, nor more silent. I beg you will never cease to think me your friend . . .[16]

[12] *Corr.*, i, p. 522; ii, p. 58.
[13] *Corr.*, ii, p. 299.
[14] Ibid., p. 361.
[15] Ibid., p. 367.
[16] Ibid., p. 368. Sherburn (p. 367, n. 2) designates this letter 'to Mrs. Weston, Mrs. Cope, or some other worthy but hitherto unappreciated lady . . .' but the opening reference to her brother identifies her pretty certainly as Mrs. Cope.

Providence had a final cruelty in store for Mrs. Cope. In May 1727 Pope wrote
to tell Caryll she had developed 'a cancer in her breast' and stress that she
was now 'a greater object of charity than other people': he bluntly hopes that
Caryll will 'add something to her relief'.[17] Pope's pleas for help were seconded,
at the end of that year, by John Caryll, sometime Gentleman Usher at the
Court of St. Germains, and younger brother of Philip Caryll. He reported that
his sister had been operated on, had bravely borne the operation, 'one of the
most terrible of the kind', and asked that Caryll should send money since he
had 'drain'd myself to the last penny for her'. Again, Caryll responded to the
appeal, for the next letter from Caryll the Usher thanks him for his gift of
£25 and reports that Philip Caryll has ignored all requests for help: '. . . as
he has never had much regard for his own children 'tis not to be wonder'd
at if he does nothing for his sister, You know the gentleman as well as any
body . . .'[18] Mrs. Cope died on 12 May 1728.[19]

Both Pope and Caryll the Usher were well-acquainted with the defects of
Philip Caryll who, though in financial difficulties, was all this time corresponding about the letting of his English properties with Caryll himself. In
default of assistance from Philip, both turned naturally to the head of the
family, whom they also assumed to be in comfortable circumstances. Both
of them now gave Caryll their assessment of his conduct, Caryll the Usher in
guarded though finally telling terms, Pope more bluntly. Caryll the Usher
wrote first:

> I . . . am very sensible of your good intentions as well as your deeds in
> relation to my deceased sister, You did more for her in her illness than any
> one of her kindred or friends as she herself said not long before she died—and
> if you did not do more, you had (without doubt) good reasons for it. The world
> judge by the superficies of things without seeing the bottom, and reason
> according to their own imaginations, They think you ought to be very rich
> because you have a good estate which you have allways managed well, and
> that if there were debts upon it, the portion you had by your son's Marriage
> was sufficient to clear it, that you have not married your daughter, that you
> had a considerable wind-fall by the death of your Brother, that your expences
> —are diminisht by the death of your son Harry, that you never was extrava-
> gant in your housekeeping or equipage, that you never was a gamester, and
> consequently that you must be in good circumstances . . .

but, he continues, to judge by appearances is often wrong.[20] Pope evidently
composed a letter of rebuke to Caryll, decided not to send it, then, pressed by
Caryll himself to declare his resentment, admitted:

> The truth is what you guess: I could not much esteem your conduct, to an
> object of misery so near you as Mrs. Cope; and I have often hinted it to your

[17] Ibid., p. 434.
[18] B.M. Add. 28228, ff. 259–60, 266.
[19] Ibid. 28228, ff. 275, 277.
[20] Ibid. 28228, f. 277 (8 June 1728).

self. The truth is I cannot yet esteem it, for any reason I am able to see. But this I promise, I fully acquit you as far as your own mind acquits you: I have now no farther cause; for the unhappy lady gives me now no farther pain. She is no longer an object either of yours or of my compassion . . .[21]

The first letter is both fair and adroit. It acknowledges all Caryll did (the extent of which Pope did not know when *he* wrote) and concedes that there may have been good reasons why he did not do more. But it is clear Caryll the Usher had expected Caryll to do more, and the long catalogue of why Caryll seemed in comfortable circumstances may be construed as a rebuke. It is a diplomatic letter, and one should remember that the Usher himself was poor, and could not afford to offend the head of his family. That Pope's rebuke assumes a different tone comes partly from the fact that Caryll had told him to speak out, partly (as subsequent correspondence reveals) from his ignorance of the extent of Caryll's assistance—and partly from his own greater financial independence. But each takes for granted that a particular responsibility lies with the head of the family in respect of (not necessarily especially close) kinship and conspicuous need.

Pope was reconciled with Caryll on the latter's assurance, not just that he had helped Mrs. Cope, which the poet knew, but that he had been sending her £20 a year.[22] Caryll may well not have chosen to tell Pope all he was doing in this family affair. But before Pope is condemned for not trusting the friend whose goodness he had so often praised, it should be noted that Caryll the Usher, who knew the full extent of Caryll's help, could still write to him: '. . . if you did not do more, you had (without doubt) good reasons for it.' In truth, 'the best man in England' had not quite come up to scratch in this case; Pope's picture was not entirely false, but there were reasons for this. The demands upon Caryll's charity were clearly numerous, more so than if he had not been a Roman Catholic, and this point he seems earlier to have put to Pope, when the latter replied that Mrs. Cope was 'a greater object of charity than other people'. Furthermore, Caryll the Usher was right when he implied that Caryll might be in less good circumstances than he seemed. From this time on, several items in the family correspondence suggest that Caryll was again in financial difficulty.[23] He was not entirely able to sustain the idealized patriarchal role in which Pope had portrayed him in earlier and more enthusiastic letters. It is perhaps because Pope felt so strong a need to find in his society the embodiments of his deepest ideals that he allowed himself to be so sharply censorious about one of his oldest and best friends. It is interesting that a rather similar estrangement, sharp but temporary, was to occur between Pope and Ralph Allen, a man on whom the poet was to lavish, not without justification, much the same kind of praise for his public, patriarchal role, that he had bestowed on Caryll. In both cases the source of the estrangement was the lack of due consideration by the other man for a woman whom Pope con-

[21] *Corr.*, iii, p. 13 (3 Feb. 1728/9).
[22] Ibid., p. 18.
[23] B.M. Add. 28228, ff. 409, 414; 28229, f. 16.

sidered to be helpless or vulnerable, and to whom (in the case of Allen, Martha Blount) Pope was deeply attached. In both cases there was some substantial evidence on Pope's side, and in both cases Pope allowed himself to become reconciled when the difference was afterwards thoroughly talked over.

The poet too was a part of the 'little Commonwealth' of Caryll's concern, which thus extended beyond the widest circle of his kinship. As there was a valued place for the poet in the society of the seventeenth-century country house poem, so Pope was in the circle of Caryll's benevolence, and was constantly being invited to stay with him at Ladyholt or West Grinstead. The relationship between nobleman or great landowner and poet was in many ways a subtle one, as may be seen from Pope's connections with men such as Burlington and Bathurst, as well as with a Jacobite peer such as Caryll. Social intercourse was on terms of strict equality and familiar friendship, but it was still understood that the more powerful man would use his wealth and influence on the poet's behalf. Caryll, whom Pope called in 1722 'for so many years one of my best critics, as well as one of my best friends', showed a keen and constant interest in Pope's work for its own sake, but also exerted himself to help the writer in practical ways. In the first place, Caryll wrote verses himself, and exchanged them with Pope. He prompted the writing of *The Rape of the Lock*, which showed considerable literary culture and imagination, however obvious the suggestion may seem in the hindsight of literary history. Pope sought his judgement, not just in compliment, but in important specific cases: the comparison of his *Windsor Forest* with Tickell's poem *On the Prospect of Peace*; different imitations of Adrian's *Animula vagula, blandula*; different poetic descriptions of winter; above all he was to seek Caryll's literary and Christian response to *An Essay on Man* before the latter knew the identity of the author.[24] In the second place, Caryll exerted all his family influence to further the success of Pope's literary activities, and especially the poet's most ambitious and daunting project: the translation of Homer. It was doubtless not lost on Caryll, a practical man, that the success of the Homer project might go far to ensuring Pope's lasting financial independence. The poet spoke of Caryll's efforts with total frankness and trust:

> . . . I am sure in my dependence on the utmost of your interest . . . I hope, by the assistance of such solicitours as Mr. Caryll, to make Homer's works of more value and benefit to me than ever they were to himself . . . While I am engaged in the fight, I find you are concerned how I shall be paid, and are soliciting with all your might that I may not have the ill fate of many discarded generals, to be first envied and maligned, then perhaps praised, and lastly neglected.[25]

The utmost of Caryll's interest produced the sum of forty guineas, twenty subscriptions to the *Iliad* translation. In the letter in which Pope thanks Caryll for this effort, the play of his fancy suggests interesting analogues to

[24] *Corr.*, i, pp. 157, 178–9, 166–8; iii, pp. 354, 390, 403.
[25] *Corr.*, i, pp. 204, 207, 220.

the social relation between the two men. 'I begin to look upon myself', wrote Pope in June 1714, 'to have a title to you by long possession, like some of those old servants and tenants who expect your kindness on no other account than because you have long been good to them.' But he goes on to add: 'I protest I am sorry you are not a first minister; for I am satisfied if you were, my fortune were made . . .'[26] Pope's fancy runs up and down an implied social scale as it explores the nature of the relationship; in the analogy of the country house society Pope is like the tenant or servant to his lord; if, as could still be argued in the eighteenth century, that society was like a kingdom in miniature, then Caryll, as first minister, was playing the Maecenas to Pope's Horace. In each case it is the house and estate which is the foundation of the analogy, and these were also important to Pope in *fact*. It appears that the first volume of the *Iliad* translation was finally revised at Ladyholt, where (as Pope told Caryll in anticipation), 'I shall have a peculiar advantage, from a daily conversation and consultation with so good a critick and friend as yourself.'[27]

The efforts of the Caryll family on Pope's behalf resulted in two of the earliest comments on his work by distinguished Britons abroad, both at the Scots College in Paris. Robert Gordon, the biblical scholar, writing hastily to Caryll's eldest son on financial affairs, added, on 17 April 1717:

> I am sorry your friend Pope should be so much criticized, here appears the most Satyrical peace [sic] in English that was ever heard off against his Homer, that he does not so much as understand the Greek, that he does not take the sense of the author, on the Contrary that he speaks non sense, &c but men of judgment looks upon this as most malicious, and that they do Pope abundance of injustice, he being a man of extraordinary parts, and absolutely the best Poet in England.[28]

This pleasing judgement would not perhaps have given Pope more satisfaction than the verdict of Lewis Innes, Principal of the Scots College, distinguished historian (with his brother Thomas Innes) of Scottish antiquities, and an influential figure at the Jacobite court. Thanking the young Caryll for a gift of books (including Pope's *Works*) to the library of the College, Innes wrote in Aug. 1717:

> Mr. Pope's works are indeed charming, & shews him to be a great Master in Poetry. I have seen a Critick upon Mr. Pope's Homer which in most things appeares to be equally unreasonable & unmannerly: if the author of this critick had as much iudgement as he has of spite and passion, the critick might serve for an Eloge to Mr. Pope's performance, since nothing but such impertinent trifles could be objected against it.[29]

[26] Ibid., p. 232.
[27] Ibid., p. 267.
[28] B.M. Add. 28227, f. 362. The 'Satyrical peace' is hard to identify, but may be one of those described in J. V. Guerinot, *Pamphlet Attacks on Alexander Pope, 1711–44* (London, 1969), pp. 38–40, 47–8.
[29] Ibid. 28227, f. 386.

The approbation of these two distinguished scholars, at a relatively early stage of Pope's career, is of interest. If, however, both correspondents are also anxious to say something which they knew would please the heir of the important Jacobite family they both served, this only confirms how clearly Pope had been brought within the 'little Commonwealth' of the family's practical concern.

Pope was himself concerned with a wider aspect still of Caryll's benevolence. In a letter to him at Christmas 1717 Pope praises him for the upkeep at West Grinstead of traditional housekeeping:

> As for good works they are things I dare not name, either to those that do them, or to those that do not. The first are too modest, and the latter too selfish, to bear the mention of things which are become either too old fashioned, or too private, to constitute any part of the vanity or reputation of the present age. However, it were to be wished people would now and then look upon good works, as they do upon old wardrobes, merely in case any of them should come into use again . . .
>
> I am strongly inclined to think there are at this very day at Grinsted, certain antique charities and obsolete devotions yet in being: that a thing call'd Christian cheerfullness, ([not] incompatible with Christmass pies and plum-broth) whereof frequent is the mention in old sermons and almanacs, is really kept alive and in practice at the said place: That feeding the hungry, and giving alms to the poor, do yet make a part of good housekeeping in a latitude not more remote from London than forty miles; and lastly that prayers and roast beef, do actually make some folks as happy, as a whore and a bottle.[30]

We must be careful to note the shades of Pope's irony in this letter. It seems to be true that housekeeping—in the sense of public hospitality to visitors, neighbours, tenantry and poor—was on the decline by the early eighteenth century, and Pope's language ('antique charities and obsolete devotions') recognizes this. Also, the phrase 'prayers and roast beef' is so blandly bucolic that it is hard not to see Pope indulging in the faintest of quizzical ironies at Caryll's old-fashioned hospitality. But the irony is chiefly rhetorical; its main purpose is to show that an obvious, not a merely antiquated, duty is beginning to be neglected, but that Caryll is not guilty of this neglect. The simile of the wardrobes comes from Donne's discussion of the decline of housekeeping, in his *Satyre II*; the same rhetorical irony is to be found there. In this letter, therefore, Pope praises Caryll for a generosity which extends beyond his own family to the surrounding community.

How far did Caryll deserve this praise? Despite the bulk of surviving family accounts it is not easy to know whether Caryll practised housekeeping in the sense defined. Yet there is some fragmentary evidence to suggest that he did, and also that his family were generous landlords despite their difficulties. As the previous head of the family, Lord Caryll must have influenced him, and there can be no doubt what *his* ideal had been, expressed in Naboth:

[30] *Corr.*, i, p. 457.

> A Man, whose Wealth was the Poor's common stock . . .
> He was his Neighbours safeguard, and their Peace.[31]

In Lord Caryll's Harting Rent Roll for 1682 an item occurs: 'Rents forborn in Charity . . . £2.2.4'; since these accounts, as they have survived, are neither complete nor systematic, there may have often been rents forborne in charity. In the accounts for the year 1707 (when John Caryll himself was in charge of the estates) there is one: 'of the Severall poor People who were partakers of my Masrs. Charity of Beef given them against Xmasse' at Horsham. On this occasion 80 stones of beef were shared between upwards of 62 people: 3 to 7 stones per family depending on the size. In 1709 80 stone was again given, in 1710 only 66. Despite the absence of further reference in the accounts, this practice is likely to have continued as Caryll grew more prosperous (1710 was the year in which Lord Caryll was pressing him to retrench). Pope's references to feeding the hungry, to prayers and roast beef, are thus likely to be accurate.[32] Lord Caryll's wish, in 1710, that his nephew should live more privately and avoid the expense of 'housekeeping' does much to confirm Pope's picture, and that this housekeeping meant public hospitality is suggested by John Caryll's self-justifying statement that he always spent part of the year at Grinstead as a place 'of less ressort and thinner neighbourhood than Lady Holt'. If Caryll had given up housekeeping in the old sense this distinction would have had no relevance. In 1716 John Caryll the younger, having been accused of hunting without permission on a neighbour's land, asserted that '. . . my father who has none of ye least Royalltys in this Country never refuses any Gent. coming in Person upon it [to hunt], nor was he yett ever refused the same priviledge by any . . .'[33] which again suggests an open attitude to the surrounding country. The actual hospitality of Caryll's great houses to the poor is not likely to appear in the accounts since it would be largely in kind, and never represent a cash transaction. Even here there is some retrospective evidence. Caryll hospitality seems to have been remembered among poor people in Harting as late as the nineteenth century: 'When the Carylls were at Lady Holt there was an archway . . . for the servants and travellers; and there was always a large cask of beer in this passage with a chain on it and a *harn* [horn]: every one that went there had to help themselves, and then he [the horn] was filled again . . .'[34] Finally, it is relevant to notice the nature of the celebrations which took place for the coming of age of the last Caryll (grandson of Pope's friend) in January 1738, two years after the old man's death. It is unlikely (despite the final sentence) that there had not been some tradition to make the following festivities expected:

> . . . I may say I believe you are the best belov'd by all sorts of people, from the highest to ye Lowest of any man in the Country. yesterday I intertain'd the farmers & their wives, with some others of the neighbours, we were

[31] See n. 20 above.
[32] B.M. Add. 28244, f. 26.
[33] Ibid. 28237, f. 64.
[34] Gordon, op. cit., p. 205.

three and twenty at my table . . . they dance'd & drunk till two in the morning . . . to-morrow I have all the work men of all sorts, & My Brother's servants with ours, who are to have a ball alsoe, they dine in their hall, & afterwards are to dance & play in the drying room & new infirmiry . . . on Munday I am to have the trades people, with their wives, & all the Second rate Gentry in the Neighbourhood, . . . & then I think we may rest till you come home; for I'me sure ther never was such true merryment in this Country before . . .[35]

So wrote Lady Mary Caryll to her son. These instances do not prove that John Caryll maintained traditional housekeeping, but they strongly suggest it, and make Pope's letter to Caryll at Christmas 1717 more than empty compliment.

The 'little Commonwealth' of which Caryll was the centre comprised his own family, the country adjacent to his estates, and the Catholic families with whom he was related or friendly. He was also, as we have seen a patron of letters, and in the best sense: he had a generous, unaffected interest in literature. Thus Pope too was in a sense a member of the commonwealth, and benefited materially from it. Not that Caryll could afford to dispense large sums. Rather he introduced the young Pope to other writers of his acquaintance, such as Wycherley and Steele, and later helped him at the most crucial point of his literary career.

When, in a letter to Caryll in June 1718, Pope applied the phrase 'a little Commonwealth' to the 'family nowadays' he was doing so in a negative sense: 'a little Commonwealth of malignants, where each has a paltry, separate interest from the other. The son wishes the death of the father, the younger brother of the elder, the elder grudges the portions of the sisters; and when any of them marry, then rise new interests and new divisions in *sæcula sæculorum*.' The political overtones of the compliment, as Caryll would perhaps appreciate, align the *true* family with loyalty to an exiled monarch. Pope goes on to say that 'It would be no ill praise of your family to say it is the most unlike a family in the world', thus suggesting that Caryll's family resembled a little commonwealth in a positive sense, which recognizes it as mediating between the personal and the public. Some of the ways in which Pope found that the Carylls fulfilled this ideal, or in which he expected them to do so though they did not, have now been seen.[36]

2. 'SO HARD . . . MY FATE'

The high point of Pope's relation with Caryll, at least from the poet's point of view, is marked by the letters of 1715–16, and the subsequent 'country house' praise of Caryll's life at West Grinstead and Ladyholt. Increasingly, after this, it seems always to have been Caryll who took the initiative, asked Pope to visit him, requested the latest publications and literary news, protested at the other's long silences, and long absence from his houses. Pope

[35] B.M. Add. 28229, f. 187.
[36] *Corr.*, i, 475–6.

assumed a defensive manner, clearly not wishing to spend so much time with Caryll as he had once done, yet unwilling to offend or hurt someone to whom he was bound by old friendship and obligation, as well as by a common network of papist acquaintance. Caryll was, for example, the godfather of Martha Blount, and, even had he wished, Pope could not easily have dropped the one without the other.[37] So he protested his extreme business and, later, the precariousness of his mother's health: both with perfect truth, but still managed to visit many of his other friends and see Caryll only when the latter came to Twickenham or London.

If the love of literature was one of the dominant features of Caryll's life, family and financial misfortunes were still, as they had always been, his chief care. And in 1718 we may see, with the advantage of hindsight, a train of events developing which was to lead, some sixty years later, to the selling of the Caryll lands, the pulling down of Ladyholt, and the extinction of the family and its Jacobite title. On Palm Sunday, 1718, Caryll's son and heir, with whom six years earlier Pope had had sufficient intimacy to request his help in amatory affairs, died of smallpox.[38] Caryll recorded the event piteously in his diary: 'April 6, Being Palm Sunday My Dear Son (never to be forgotten) dyed of ye small Pox. Sweet Jesus grant me resignation, and to him eternall rest.[39]

Pope, knowing his bereaved friend well enough, wrote 'sincerely and tenderly': ''Tis impossible for me to say anything to you, which your own sense and your own religious thoughts have not already suggested in your comfort. Those are the strong supports that still must maintain you . . .'[40] The heir was now John Baptist Caryll, the infant grandson of Pope's friend. He was the direct heir of the Caryll investments in the Hotel de Ville, and his mother, not Caryll himself, was his guardian.[41] John Baptist Caryll was brought up, under the care of his mother, even more exclusively in Paris than his father. He was a young man by the time he settled down on his Sussex estates, and probably had little enough grasp of the economic realities of being an eighteenth-century landowner.

In addition, the Paris investments which had been so providently made, so long ago, as 'the best security for English Catholicks', were, at the end of the second decade of the eighteenth century, running into trouble. How could the family have anticipated the brilliant, but in practice disastrous, innovations in France of the economist John Law? Robert Gordon, writing to Caryll on 6 July 1718, sounded an ominous note: 'It's very hard to take measures against the unaccountable proceedings of this Countrey they heighten and diminish the money when they please, and their proceedings very Secret.'[42] Just over

[37] Ibid., pp. 414, 411.
[38] Victoria and Albert Museum, 48. g. 4/19#446 (Forster); (Pope to John Caryll the younger, 1 March 1712/13). I owe my knowledge of this letter to the generosity of Professor Maynard Mack, of Yale University.
[39] B.M. Add. 28241, f. 102.
[40] Corr., i, p. 474.
[41] B.M. Add. 28227, ff. 445–6, 448.
[42] Ibid. 28227, f. 455.

a year later Alexander Smith, Gordon's successor in looking after the Caryll investments in Paris, wrote in breathless haste to Lady Mary:

> . . . the King is to pay all the debts of the crown, and reimburse the perpetual rents on the Hotel de Ville. those who have not a mind to take up their principal will get contracts, only at three p cent upon the Compagnie des Indes . . . Yr Lap will no doubt have heard of the wonderful progress that Company has made of late . . . I heartily wish the Family had had something in it at first.[43]

In September that year Lady Mary was faced with the decision whether to realize the capital, or invest it in the Compagnie des Indes at 3%.[44] But in the event shareholders were not allowed to withdraw money from the Hotel de Ville, and in June 1720 Lewis Innes wrote to announce the creation of 'new rents' at $2\frac{1}{2}$%—'tho the rente be small, yet the security be good . . .'[45] Next the rate fell and Innes's considered advice was now to invest in 'the Clergy of France' since it was more secure to deal with a 'substantial Corporation, than with the King'—and the Clergy proposed to pay 3%.[46] But even this proved impossible, since the original investments were so clogged with entails and substitutions.[47] Much of the financial security of the Carylls was lost to them with the failure of John Law. In Jan. 1724/5 Lord Caryll's original capital, as it stood at his death, was bringing in little more than half the original interest.[48] In addition Lady Mary had, like thousands of others, been speculating in the French stocks. Innes's wry comment sums the situation up:

> . . . as to the money your Lap putt into our Stocks here, I never knew anything till of late that all was past remedy, & I own I should never have advised it had I known in due time. But at present the Actions are fallen so very low that nothing can be done to any purpos. Upon the new form they have put the Company since Mr. Law's retreat, many think the actions will yet rise, but they can never rise so high but that your Lap will be a great loser.[49]

Thousands lost their fortunes in the Bubbles of the Mississippi and South Sea Companies, but the prospect of successful speculation was perhaps an especially potent and fatal temptation to British papists or Jacobites, living beyond their means with estates double-taxed, or in jeopardy, or forfeited. Whether Caryll knew of Lady Mary's losses in the Mississippi when, in May 1720, he showed a marked interest in Pope's and Martha Blount's South Sea investments is uncertain, but the point he evidently put to the poet must have been what many families in his position were thinking: hitherto he had

---

[43] Ibid. 28228, f. 19 (30 Aug. 1719).
[44] Ibid. 28228, f. 22 (Lewis Innes to Lady Mary Caryll, 9 Sept. 1719).
[45] Ibid. 28228, f. 42.
[46] Ibid. 28228, ff. 64–5.
[47] Ibid. 28228, f. 67.
[48] Ibid. 28228, f. 168.
[49] Ibid. 28228, f. 86.

always been on the losing side; now perhaps he could win.[50] Pope carried out
a commission for him to Secretary Craggs soon after, and this may have been
an investment in South Sea stocks, which Craggs was then so busily helping
to promote. Perhaps Caryll knew what he was doing, for Pope's next remark
to him on this subject was that 'Your doctrine of *selling out* was certainly the
most true and important doctrine in the world . . .'[51] Unlike some other
members of his family, Caryll emerged unscathed from that mad period of
speculation in Britain and France[52]—an economic, political and social phenomenon which we shall explore more fully in the life of Sir John Blunt. Caryll
may not have sought to invest in South Sea stocks, but, as Pope seems to have
recognized in a tone of rallying reproof, the 'Best Man in England' was certainly not psychologically or morally above the idea of playing the stocks to
his advantage.[53] In the circumstances it is easy to see why.

Good news came for Caryll at the end of 1724. William Pulteney had been
able to assist him in bringing about the reversal of Lord Caryll's outlawry.
This stigma, which the family had borne since the days of the Assassination
Plot against William III, involved Caryll himself, and in one of his notes to
Pulteney he refers to 'the affaire of my Outtlawry'.[54] A good deal of patience,
and at least some influence and money, were evidently necessary to bring
about the desired end, but on 31 Oct. 1724 the Warrant for Reversal was issued,
and on 24 Nov. 1724 Nathaniel Pigott, the Roman Catholic lawyer much
concerned with Caryll's affairs, wrote to congratulate him on its accomplish-
ment.[55]

Perhaps this prompted Caryll to review his life. Perhaps, as he looked over
the accounts of his estates, or drafted letters on business affairs, he often did
so; certainly those parts of the accounts which are in his hand often contain
memoranda and diary entries. And it is in a volume of the family accounts,
rather than the separate collection of manuscript poems, that we see Caryll
sum up his own life in verse:

1724

A Serious Thought of my own Concern, in Rhyme,

Born in an Isle (so hard has been my Fate!)
Where Rich I never dar'd to be nor Great

[50] *Corr.*, ii, p. 43.

[51] Ibid., p. 53 (Pope to Caryll, 19 Sept. 1720). But Craggs seems to have been too busy to respond (p. 57). This suggestion is not incompatible with that of Sherburn, that Caryll wished to sell
Craggs some land.

[52] On 14 Jan. 1723/4, Alexander Smith informed Lady Mary Caryll that the Paris investments
had been taxed by mistake, because the name of John Caryll had been observed 'deeply concern'd
in the Stocks' (B.M. Add. 28228, f. 130). He had pointed out that this was neither her son, nor
father-in-law, nor necessarily even a relation. It was in fact almost certainly John Caryll the Usher
(*Corr.*, iii, p. 18).

[53] *Corr.*, ii, p. 43 (Pope to Caryll, *c.* 1 May 1720).

[54] B.M. Add. 28240, ff. 193, 195.

[55] Ibid. 36125, ff. 192, 206 (the Warrants); 28228, f. 159 (Pigot's letter). See De Trenqualéon,
op. cit., ii, p. 190–1.

Yett *Sixty years of Life I have* neerly run
Submitting still to see my self Undon!
But my Good God into my Lott has cast
Joys more refin'd & of Sublimer Taste.
He blest me first in those that gave me Birth
(A pair more Worthy never breath'd on Earth.)
Next in a Wife (the Patern of her State)
That well deserves a more deserving Mate;
Then with such Children from her Vertuous Womb,
As nere cause Grief butt when lay'd in their Tomb.
Blest farther yett by an United Stock
The fairest Yeild of Great Mackenzy's Flock.
And thence an offspring that such Charmes display,
As speak the Gloryes of a future Day.
Whilst Grand-Sire pleasd, exults with Joy to see
His youth renew'd in a third Progeny.

Then Gracious God, Lett me still grateful prove
For all these Tokens of thy wondrous Love.
And thy great Mercyes lett me still adore:
Since Heaven is All that I can wish for more.[56]

The poem is an exercise in piety, a conscious self-dedication to the ideal of gratitude and love for God. It is not a cold exercise—the precisely used hyperbole at the end comes over with convincing emotion—but as so often when people count their blessings the sense of disappointment remains strong. The first four lines of the poem are perhaps the most memorable. What is interesting is not so much their recognition of material difficulty and personal misfortune, but the way they reveal disappointed ambition—'Rich I never dar'd to be nor Great'. In education, and in political background, Caryll was so much more than a plain country gentleman. His uncle had been the indispensable minister to a prince, though at an exiled court, and it is likely Caryll considered that this would have been his own proper level in the state, had the history of Britain gone another way. It is notable that the phrase 'Gloryes of a future Day', where Caryll speaks of the promise of his grandson, has a wholly secular sense. It is interesting, also, that during his visit to France in 1725 Caryll was a figure of sufficient importance or influence to attend at the French court and, as Pope put it with scandalised sarcasm, 'run about with a king of sixteen': the young Louis XV.[57] Greatness and glory for Caryll, it may be thought, pertained particularly to princes and courts. In France his concept of nobility would have been in place; as a papist in the Britain of Sir

[56] B.M. Add. 28240, f. 218r. The MS. shows the process of composition. Several corrections have been made (and are embodied here), but Caryll never found a version of the words italicised in l. 3 which pleased him. The poem is found under the year 1724 in the accounts, and there are accounts on the verso. It may be noted that l. 10 confirms the more violent judgement of l. 8 of 'Three Generations have We known', as interpreted above.

[57] *Corr.*, ii, p. 341 (Pope to Caryll, 23 Nov. 1725).

Robert Walpole he could only ignore his title, read *The Craftsman*,[58] and improve his estates for the sake of his heir. The tone of his feelings concerning political and family circumstance, at a more everyday level than that of his poem, may be gauged from a letter to Lady Mary on 3 June 1726:

> The best peice of Newes I've heard a great while is that concerning my Lord your Brother's Pardon: to which I hope our Gracious King will add a competent Substance or else 'tis not worth acceptance since he is outt of harm's Way . . .
> Be pleased to tell Dear Boy [John Baptist Caryll], that I am improving this place for him as fast as I can; trusting in God that he will Enjoy itt many many Yeare after I am under Ground.[59]

3. 'Suspicion and Coldness'

There was one further way by which Caryll might connect himself with greatness. That was through his early recognition and encouragement of, and continuing friendship with, the man whom Robert Gordon had described in 1717 as 'absolutely the best Poet in England': Alexander Pope. Caryll's name already stood at the opening of *The Rape of the Lock*, but he longed for converse and correspondence with Pope, for knowledge of his projects, of the authorship of new works, and of all the political and literary ephemera of the day. For Caryll the literary world, with his old friend and one-time *protégé* Pope at its centre, was one of absorbing interest. He was repeatedly mortified that Pope did not write to him frequently, and that the poet had not visited Ladyholt since (as it would appear from the correspondence) 1717, or even 1714.[60] In fact at least eighteen, perhaps twenty one, years elapsed before Pope again visited the country seat of his old friend.[61] The few surviving letters of Caryll to Pope are couched in a confident and genial manner, but it is evident from the other side of the correspondence that he repeatedly charged Pope with neglect, and that he felt something like jealousy towards the other gentle or noble acquaintance whom Pope seemed to visit so frequently. On one occasion Pope remarked that he might the more readily visit Caryll at West Grinstead since Sir John Evelyn, apparently a casual acquaintance, lived on the route. This was tactless; Caryll protested, and Pope attempted to smooth it over. Nine months later Caryll reverted to what he had certainly received as a slight, and prompted Pope to defend himself:

> I hope . . . I shall always live in such a manner and such a constant tenour, agreeable to my oldest professions (both of veracity and principle) as you shall never be ashamed of me . . .

---

[58] B.M. Add. 28618, ff. 115–17 (Pulteney to Caryll, 6 June, 30 Sept., 6 Oct. 1731).

[59] Ibid. 28228, f. 96. 'My Lord your Brother' is the Marquis of Seaforth, who had borne arms on behalf of the Jacobite claimant in the 1715 Rebellion. In the circumstances Caryll asks rather a lot of 'our Gracious King' (George II).

[60] The last certain date seems to be 1714 (*Corr.*, i, p. 267 n.1), though Pope's letter to Caryll on 6 Oct. 1717 (*Corr.*, i, pp. 242–3) suggests he seriously intended a visit that winter.

[61] *Corr.*, iii, pp. 384, 387 (Pope to Caryll, 4 and 24 Sept. 1733).

Of late your letters pique me: they are writ in a style of suspicion and
coldness, as if you doubted my inclinations to hear from you or see you.
You remind me *that Sir John Evelyn's stands as much in my Way to your
house as ever* . . . that you have a much stronger and older title to me and
my projects is a truth you ought not to contest: indeed you ought not . . .
Dear sir, believe me truly yours, and think well of me, that is . . . charitably,
forgivingly and kindly . . .[62]

If we ask what the friendship of Pope meant to Caryll the answer is clear
though complex. Caryll prized the friendship through a genuine love of
literature; because, as the above letter concedes, he had an old and strong
title to the gratitude of the man who was now the most celebrated poet in
England; because Pope seemed so much at the centre of the literary, social
and political life of his time whereas Caryll felt something of an exile within
his own land; and, almost certainly because this celebrated poet remained a
co-religionist. Pope's letter shows the nature of Caryll's (at this time) bitter
suspicion. Pope now had more to give Caryll (as it might have seemed) than
Caryll had to give him: would the poet, now so busy, so courted by the rich,
intelligent and famous of the land, increasingly ignore a man who was no longer
of use to him? And could this personal neglect have a wider social and doctrinal
significance? Was Pope becoming embarrassed by his Roman Catholic
connections; was it not extremely likely that his friends would try to persuade
him to embrace the established church, and quite possible that Pope would
adopt a course of action so much in his interest?

For some years such suspicions may have been laid to rest by Pope's re-
sponding letters with their mixture of practical explanation, loyal acknowledgement, and hint of apology. But the coolness between Pope and Caryll concerning
the affair of Mrs. Cope revived, early in 1729, the other causes of the sense of
grievance in Caryll's mind. He wrote another of his cold, hurt and forthright
letters to Pope, and had it out with him on several scores. It was now Pope's
failure as a correspondent that perhaps most pained him; but Pope seized on
this complaint and turned it to his own advantage:

Now for the interruption of our correspondence; I am sorry you seem
to put the test of my friendship upon that issue of my writing as formerly,
because it is what I am disqualified from towards all my other acquaintance,
with whom I hold no such correspondence. I'll name you a few obstacles
which I can't surmount: want of health, want of time, want of eyes, and one
yet stronger than all . . . I dare not while there are Curlls in the world. . . .
I've small reason to indulge correspondences . . . unless my friends would
do (as indeed some have been prevailed upon, and as you know I have for
many years desired you would do) send me back those forfeitures of my
discretion, commit to my justice what I trusted only to their indulgence,
and return me at the year's end those trifling letters, which can be to them
but a day's amusement, but to me may prove a discredit to posterity.[63]

[62] *Corr.*, ii, p. 112 (Pope to Caryll, 7 April 1722); p. 78.
[63] *Corr.*, iii, pp. 13–14 (Pope to Caryll, 3 Feb. 1728/9).

Pope had indeed several times requested Caryll to return his letters; this was
not an attempt to recall the evidence particularly of a Roman Catholic friendship, since Pope was to make similar efforts to persuade, for example, Swift;
but it may be imagined how the sensitive Caryll took the request.[64] Pope's
letters, which Caryll had evidently kept with care since their deliberate
'correspondence' had begun in 1710, were, apart from their personal and
literary interest, the tangible record of that old and strong title Caryll had to
Pope and his projects. Was the recall of these letters to be a part of that gradual
casting off by Pope of his original Catholic connection which Caryll had already
reason to suspect? Perhaps Caryll felt some scepticism as to whether the long
arm of Edmund Curll could reach as easily to his personal papers at Ladyholt
as it had to the saleable property of a surviving mistress of Henry Cromwell.
On the other hand Pope *had* suffered from the pirated publication of some of
his private letters, and was evidently now making the return of those he had
written to Caryll a condition of continuing their correspondence. It was a
matter which Caryll, uniquely among Pope's acquaintance, took so seriously
that he decided on a very discreet compromise: the autograph letters he would
indeed return to Pope, but not before his daughter Catherine had made
transcripts; and transcripts would also be made of Pope's future letters to
Caryll. It seems certain that Pope was kept in ignorance of this arrangement.[65]
Caryll's purpose was to preserve for posterity, and in the first place the posterity
of his family, the authentic record of his long connection with Pope. His
device served his purpose well, for at least part of his suspicions were justified.
Pope often told Caryll that he moved very little among Catholic society, and
he did not wish his continuing connections with it to be a conspicuous part of
the public picture men had of him. When, after Caryll's death, the authorized
edition of Pope's letters appeared, many of the letters to Caryll were printed
as having been written to others. Edward Blount of Blagdon, not Caryll,
there emerges as Pope's chief Catholic correspondent. We owe it to Caryll's
amour propre that the picture of Pope's life that we now have is substantially
different from that which Pope chose to give to the world in the mid-1730s.

   To ask why Pope wished, at least in public, to play down his connection
with Caryll is to ask the larger question: what did Caryll's friendship mean

[64] Pope first asked Caryll to return his letters on 19 Nov. 1712 (*Corr.*, i, p. 156; see also ii, pp.
449, 419.
[65] Sherburn assumed, from Pope's words on receiving back his letters: 'I thank you too for your
friendly care about 'em, which I discover from your enclosure that covers 'em' (*Corr.*, iii, p. 31)
that Caryll told Pope that transcripts had been made. This is very unlikely. The retention of the
transcripts defeated Pope's purpose, and had he been told he would surely have protested to Caryll.
Again, even after Caryll's death in 1736, Pope would surely have hesitated to publish a collection
in which many letters to Caryll were reassigned to other correspondents, had he realized that
transcripts were in the hands of surviving members of the family. Caryll's widow, and Catharine
Caryll, the amanuensis, both survived Caryll's death, as Pope could not fail to know. The words
to which Sherburn draws attention seem to refer only to the way in which the letters had been
preserved (an orderly system of endorsement), such as Caryll had evidently mentioned to Pope as
early as 1727: 'For the letters, I am obliged to the care you have taken, in the endorsement and
order you mention: however, I beg once more to see them' (Pope to Caryll, 1726–7); *Corr.* ii,
p. 423.

to Pope, in the last ten years of Caryll's life? Was he (as Caryll seems to have feared) the exasperating old friend who traded too much on the early encouragement and assistance he had given the poet; who was a less interesting companion than Bolingbroke, Burlington and Bathurst; and whose pattern of life, which Pope had often idealized, seemed now more limited and ordinary than it had once done? Did Pope find Caryll's papist piety oppressive because he wished to forget his own Roman Catholic origins? Did he find Caryll's Jacobite connections politically embarrassing?[66] There is, I think, a degree of truth in all these suppositions; to try to assess the precise degree is to ascertain a fine balance in Pope's character between opposing tendencies and interests. Let us consider the more personal questions first.

These concern Caryll's later conduct. Here two points were crucial in influencing Pope's view: firstly, Caryll's candid statement to Pope of what he had done for Mrs. Cope; and secondly Caryll's anxiety to help his godchild Martha Blount in her family troubles. Pope and Caryll had it out over the affair of Mrs. Cope during a visit the older man paid to Twickenham in the Spring of 1729. The two men evidently achieved a midway between plain speech and friendliness. Afterwards Pope wrote to Caryll in a tone very different from his protestingly polite and defensive manner:

> I protest I never twice in my life have found my own sincerity succeed so well; and I beg your pardon for doubting, but I was not without some doubt of it, herein. I am now glad you questioned, glad I disguised nothing, glad we were both in the right, nay not sorry if I was a little otherwise since it has occasioned the knowledge of that dependence which I ought and am to have on your friendship and temper . . .
>
> Adieu, till I hear from you. Be assured, dear sir, I am at all times, glad to do so; and will at some times tell you so; but if not so frequently as I really wish, impute it charitably. Forgot you never can be, esteemed you ever will be, and loved and wished well you ever must be, by Dear sir, your affectionate obliged Friend and servant. A : P :[67]

Any falling away on Caryll's part from Pope's patriarchal ideal (and if Caryll's conduct in the Cope affair was generous it was hardly glorious) has been made good here by the candour and goodwill of a successful personal encounter, in the light of which Pope appreciated what Caryll *had* done, and judged this by a perhaps more realistic standard than before. But more than this emerges from the letter. The closing words ('Forgot you never can be . . .') show that Pope had apprehended Caryll's deepest personal concern in their relationship; it was not after all so much a question of repaying old obligations as of meeting a present need. To this recognition Pope was able to make a generous response.

The unhappy situation of Martha Blount was a recurring topic in the later correspondence of Pope and Caryll. She was in the desperately vulnerable

---

[66] Pope to Caryll, 13 Nov. 1729 (*Corr.*, iii, p. 70, n. 2) probably indicates Caryll's continuing involvement in Jacobite correspondence.

[67] *Corr.*, iii, pp. 35–6 (Pope to Caryll, 30 May 1729).

position of an unmarried woman moving in 'good society', unable to rely on
the regular payment of her annuity by an apparently irresponsible brother,
unable to rely on any regular moral support from her mother or sister, the
latter of whom was involved in a relationship which was considered scandalous
and flagrant.[68] Because of Martha Blount's own loyalty to her family, little
could be done to assist her, or not at least, in any simple practical way. In
encouraging Caryll to invite Martha Blount on her own to Ladyholt, Pope
remarked: 'Your part is good and generous; but in truth that's all. I expect
little success . . .'; but it seems to have been Caryll's urgent wish to help in
some way, which powerfully renewed Pope's esteem.[69] Together they pursued
a common aim which Pope expressed to Caryll thus: '. . . if she could be
drawn from them [ie. her mother and sister], it would be one of the most
virtuous deeds, and to the most deserving person, you ever could do.'[70] Caryll's
generous goodwill was confirmed to Pope when, soon after, Martha Blount
showed him the letter she had received from her godfather: '. . . it gives me
a full view of your worth and I will say no more on that side . . .' Pope later
wrote to Caryll.[71]

But Caryll was prepared to go further to relieve Marth Blount's plight and
Pope's grave concern. Martha Blount was someone with whom Pope had
preserved a long and constant friendship. Caryll probably appreciated that
Pope's feeling for her constituted one of the deepest loyalties of his life—a
point which will emerge clearly in Chapter VII. Frequently a matchmaker and
family diplomatist, Caryll now conceived the possibility that Pope and Martha
Blount might marry. It was not a wild idea. If Pope had long lived single,
this was chiefly due to his 'crazy constitution' and often invalid state. But
(setting aside epistolary infatuations such as that with Lady Mary Wortley
Montagu) we know that Pope had not been uninterested in women in his
youth—as Caryll may perhaps have had confirmed from his eldest son.[72]
Perhaps little sexual ardour could now be expected. Yet Pope might well be
ready to exchange his single condition for the companionship and practical
care of a woman for whom he had so long cherished affection. Martha Blount,
for her part, might be prepared to espouse the bent and fragile figure of Pope
in view of their long mutual regard, and to envisage a match that was by strict
social standards somewhat beneath her if her husband were to be Britain's
most celebrated poet. As for the rest of the Blount family, Caryll's assumption
seems to have been that Martha's brother could provide neither dowry nor
objection. Caryll himself was willing to supply a dowry. An attractive feature
of the idea for him was that two Roman Catholics might thus be brought
together in marriage, and Pope acquire a practising papist wife. It was, for
Caryll, perhaps a minor aspect of the proposal that it would liberate Martha
Blount from all her troubles, but it was undoubtedly these, together with

---

[68] Ibid., pp. 38–9, 40–2 (Pope to Caryll, 8 and 20 July 1729).
[69] Ibid., p. 45 (12 Aug. 1729).
[70] Ibid., p. 61 (19 Oct. 1729).
[71] Ibid., p. 75 (20 Nov. 1729).
[72] See n. 38 above.

Pope's concern, which prompted Caryll's suggestion in the first place, and this brought him further credit in Pope's eyes.

Yet the poet's response was in the negative:

> ... I have no tie to your God-daughter but a good opinion, which has grown into a friendship with experience that she deserved it. Upon my word, were it otherwise I would not conceal it from you, especially after the proofs you have given how generously you would act in her favour; and I farther hope, if it were more than I tell you that actuated me in that regard, that it would be only a spur to you, to animate, not a let to retard your design. But truth is truth. you will never see me change my condition any more than my religion, because I think them both best for me.[73]

It will be appreciated that the moralistic tone in this passage—'friendship with experience that she deserved it'—was exactly the right tribute to pay Martha Blount, at a time when association with her sister brought her under a cloud of moral suspicion.

In personal ways, Caryll proved himself eager and able to act positively where Pope felt this was needed; this, in his very last years of their friendship, seems to have outweighed his sense that Caryll invoked too often his old and strong title to the poet's intimacy. But there was no resumption of Pope's once frequent visits to Caryll in Sussex; Pope was to see Ladyholt only once again before his death. Since Pope's personal esteem for Caryll had, by the 1730s, risen to something like its old level, it is likely that religious and political factors have a bearing on the relationship.

4. RELIGIOUS AND POLITICAL TENSIONS

A consideration of the friendship of Pope and Caryll confronts us with that most striking paradox of Pope's life: the fact that he never disavowed the Roman Catholic church, which it would have been in his worldly interest to do, while at the same time he wished to play down, what he could never forget or evade: his papist origins and connections. From the early days of the correspondence, Caryll had been one of those who conveyed to Pope contemporary Roman Catholic judgements that some parts of his writings were strictly heterodox. Pope never attributed this judgement to Caryll himself, or to his eldest son, though the poet's letters to them in his own justification may imply that he recognized some need to convince them of his case. To the 'mistaken zeal' which objected to the 'simile of wit and faith' in *An Essay on Criticism*, and to the 'ignorance' which might object to the line in the same poem in vindication of Erasmus: 'The *Glory* of the Priesthood, and the *Shame*!' (l. 694), Pope responded with his concept of 'a true Catholic' whose character, in his own time, he plainly judged by 'so great a light of our Church', Erasmus himself.[74] Pope vehemently rejected those Roman Catholics who

[73] *Corr.*, iii, p. 75.
[74] *Corr.*, i, pp. 117–19 (Pope to Caryll, 18 June 1711).

could acknowledge no fault in their church, and he disapproved all views concerning the 'errors' of other Christians, within or without that church, which might weaken 'the charity of mankind, the very greatest bond in which we are engaged by God to one another as Christians.'[75] In these terms, Pope professed himself to be 'an unbigoted Roman Catholic'. The immediate source of the bigotry which Pope attacked would appear to have been the French seminary of St. Omer (where, Pope charged, 'they do not learn the English grammar'); and in a burst of impatient frankness to Caryll the younger, 8 Nov. 1712, he declared that the enemies to his writings were: 'first, priests; secondly, women, who are the fools of priests; and thirdly, beaus and fops, who are the fools of women.'[76]

Pope's defence of his religious position through appeal to the example of Erasmus was not a manoeuvre he employed only in defending his position to other papists; 'Yet am I of the Religion of Erasmus, a Catholick' was an affirmation he made to Swift as late as 1729, while twelve years earlier he had explained his views to Francis Atterbury in the following way: 'I am not a Papist, for I renounce the temporal invasions of the Papal power, and detest their arrogated authority over Princes, and States. I am a Catholick, in the strictest sense of the word ... the things I have always wished to see are not a Roman Catholick, or a French Catholick, or a Spanish Catholick, but a true Catholick ...'[77] From these statements, and especially the last, it is clear that Pope had doctrinal as well as personal and family reasons for not embracing the Church of England; it is clear, equally, that his 'true Catholicism', with its latitudinarian tone, was at the opposite extreme from Jesuit Roman Catholicism, and from Counter-Reformation Roman Catholicism generally. It is in the letter to Atterbury that we can see in Pope the careful student of Donne's *Pseudo-Martyr*.[78] Pope had evolved for himself a brand of doctrine which would almost certainly have provoked more acrimony from Roman Catholics than from Protestants; for the former the temptation to convert or recall this apparently evasive 'true Catholic' to 'orthodoxy' must have been overwhelming, and his position more exasperating than that of the plain Protestant. Caryll was no bigot, but he took serious note of the zealous orthodoxy of others, and was in frequent contact with British Roman Catholics overseas. His second son, Richard, was educated at St. Omer, and became a priest in the Jesuit order on 7 Sept. 1711. It is probable that he was at Ladyholt during the Summer when Pope was writing to Caryll about *An Essay on Criticism*; he seems to have acted as Caryll's chaplain there on several occasions, and Pope was certainly acquainted with him.[79] It is probable that Pope's

[75] Ibid., pp. 126–7 (Pope to Caryll, 19 July 1711).

[76] Ibid., p. 127 (Pope to Caryll 19 July 1711); p. 151.

[77] *Corr.*, iii, p. 81 (Pope to Swift, 28 Nov. 1729); i, p. 454 (Pope to Atterbury, 20 Nov. 1717).

[78] Pope possessed a copy of Donne's *Pseudo-Martyr* (1610), and made his own index in it (Geoffrey Keynes, *A Bibliography of the Works of John Donne* (London, 1914; 3rd. edn. 1958), p. 7). In this work it was Donne's purpose to argue that Roman Catholics might take the Oath of Allegiance to Protestant princes.

[79] Foley, op. cit., iii, p. 538. He was professed at Watton, and had perhaps recently returned to England from St. Omer. For Pope's knowledge of him, see *Corr.*, ii, p. 112 and i, p. 164.

reluctance to visit Ladyholt arose from the pious importunities to which he would be peculiarly subject in an orthodox and practising Roman Catholic household. That, for the greater period of their friendship, Pope held Caryll himself in high esteem, and would thus be reluctant to hurt his feelings, only made the circumstances more delicate. This was not a reason Pope could give Caryll for his long neglect of Ladyholt, but it seems likely that it lay behind the not wholly adequate reasons which he did give. And if there is any truth at all in the claim that Pope made to Caryll: that his 'own acquaintance . . . [had] happened not to run much in a Catholic channel', this might be accounted for in the same way.[80]

The strength of Pope's position, however, lay in his constancy. When Pope affirmed his hope, in answer to Caryll's suspicions, that '. . . I shall always live in such a manner and such a constant tenour, agreeable to my oldest professions (both of veracity and principle) as you shall never be ashamed of me, as you have been of some others of our acquaintances, whose miserable defection from their principles renders [them] so contemptible . . .',[81] he is likely to have been affirming, among other things, that he would not reject the church to which they both belonged. His views as a Roman Catholic might be unusual, but he had the merit of suffering the same disabilities as other Roman Catholics in eighteenth-century Britain, and could hardly be accused of accommodating doctrine to self-interest. For Pope, the realization of the ideal of being 'Fixed to one side, but mod'rate to the rest' was to embrace the penalties of Roman Catholicism, and thereby guarantee, to both papist and Protestant, the loyalty and integrity of his stand as 'an unbigoted Roman Catholic', a 'true Catholick', one who looked to the bonds between Christians in the spirit of the 'charity of mankind'. This was, in itself, a complex enough personal and intellectual position to build a life on, but Pope exploited it to the utmost by his decisions as an artist, specifically in the writing of the 'Universal Prayer' and *An Essay on Man*. It was probably Pope's desire to remain true to professed principle and yet enlarge his art through a free-ranging and open outlook, which prompted him to make a special point of seeking Caryll's view of *An Essay on Man*. It was published anonymously, and was a sufficiently new departure in Pope's work, for the authorship to go at first unrecognized, even by Caryll. If Caryll did not disapprove, indeed if he could discern and approve in it at least an orthodox Christian tendency, then Pope might indeed feel that he had managed to preserve the two essential sides to the paradox of his religious position. Pope is quite aware of the risks of what he has written, and clearly nudges Caryll towards the conclusion he hopes he will take:

> The town is now very full of a new poem intitled *an Essay on Man*, attributed, I think with reason, to a divine. It has merit in my opinion but not so much as they give it; at least it is incorrect and has some inaccuracies

---

[80] *Corr.*, iii, p. 154 (2 Dec. 1730). One cannot help feeling that this claim is disingenuous, though Pope may have tried to limit the extent of his Catholic acquaintance.

[81] *Corr.*, ii, p. 112 (2 April 1722).

in the expressions; one or two of an unhappy kind, for they may cause the author's sense to be turned, contrary to what I think his intention a little unorthodoxically. Nothing is so plain as that he quits his proper subject, *this present world*, to insert his belief of *a future state* and yet there is an *If* instead of a *Since* that would overthrow his meaning and at the end he uses the Words *God*, the *Soul* of the *World*, which at first glance may be taken for heathenism, while his whole paragraph proves him quite Christian in his system, from *Man* up to *Seraphim*. I want to know your opinion of it after twice or thrice reading. I give you my thoughts very candidly of it, tho' I find there is a sort of faction to set up the author and his piece in opposition to me and my little things . . .[82]

Within twelve days Caryll replied, but his view was perhaps cautious and qualified since Pope expressed neither agreement nor disagreement in return.[83] His reaction as next commented on by Pope was simple and positive: why did the poem say nothing about Jesus Christ? Because, Pope replied, this would be incongruous with the 'confined and strictly philosophical subject' but the author might 'magnify the Christian doctrine' as the perfection of morality.[84] Pope returned to 'the author''s defence in the New Year of 1734, asserting that he

shews himself a Christian at last in the assertion, that all *Earthly Happiness* as well as *Future Felicity* depends upon the doctrine of the gospel, love of God and man, and that the whole aim of our being is to attain happiness here, and hereafter by the practice of universal charity to man, and entire resignation to God. More *particular* than this he could not be . . .[85]

Perhaps Pope's line of argument—that the poem was consistent with Christian doctrine, and as close to a statement of it as its general and philosophical nature would permit—began to seem persuasive to Caryll; certainly he began to have a shrewd idea of the author's identity; and Pope finally obtained the approval he had been seeking, though perhaps too mingled in personal tribute to be exactly what he desired.

Your candid opinion not only on the *Essay on Man*, but its author pleases me truly. I think verily that he is as honest and religious a man as myself, and one that never will forfeit justly, your kind character of him. It is not directly owned, and I do assure you never was, whilst you were kept in ignorance of it.[86]

At all events Pope had fended off Caryll's possible disapproval.[87] And his

---

[82] *Corr.*, iii, p. 354 (8 March 1732/3). Pope does not usually ask Caryll's opinion so specifically, when sending copies of his latest works.

[83] Ibid., p. 358 (Pope to Caryll, 20 March 1732/3).

[84] Ibid., p. 390 (20 Oct. 1733).

[85] Ibid., p. 400 (Pope to Caryll, 1 Jan. 1733/4).

[86] Ibid., p. 403 (Pope to Caryll, 28 Feb. 1733/34).

[87] Cf. the Roman Catholic reactions recorded in Spence, 305–6.

judgement had been of value, as a touchstone and standard, on a uniquely important occasion in Pope's poetic career.

The Caryll family's Jacobite connections were a perhaps less important factor in Pope's later relationship with Caryll. Since those years when, as Pope was to put it in 1736,

> Hopes after Hopes of pious Papists fail'd,
> While mighty WILLIAM's thundring Arm prevail'd
> [*Imitations of Horace*, Ep. II. ii. ll. 62–3]

there had been two occasions when Pope expressed extreme political anxiety, even disaffection, with regard to the government of Britain; and these must be distinguished from his association with Bolingbroke's campaign of opposition to Walpole. The first of these occasions was after the 1715 Jacobite Rebellion when Pope and his family moved from Windsor Forest to Chiswick. Then, as we have seen, Pope had professed his love to Caryll, lest 'accident, or distance, or private cares, or public calamities . . . may prevent the usual frequency of our expressions of that friendship . . .' and had written: 'We here bid our papist-neighbours adieu . . . Perhaps I have now learnt so far as—Nos dulcia linquimus arva, the next may be—Nos patriam fugimus.'[88] The second occasion was the imprisonment in the Tower of Francis Atterbury, on a charge involving Jacobite conspiracy. This crisis, every stage of which, as we shall see in Chapter V, Pope was in a position to follow in detail, impelled him in two directions: towards an impulsive affirmation, but also towards caution; and his hints at the possibility of exile were a good deal more plain. Indeed, on 20 April 1723, he had written to Atterbury in the following surprising terms:

> I fear there will be no way left me to tell you this great truth, that I remember you, that I love you, that I am grateful to you, that I intirely esteem and value you, but that one which I will find, even though it were death to correspond with you. A way which needs no open warrant to authorize it, or secret conveyance to secure it; which no Bills can preclude, nor any Kings prevent . . .
>
> I am tenderly sensible of the wish you express, that no part of misfortune may pursue me; But God knows how short a time we may be suffered, or we may desire to be suffered, to live in this Country. I am every day less and less fond of it, and begin seriously to consider a friend in exile, a friend in death, one gone before, where I am not unwilling, nor unprepared to follow after . . .[89]

Pope wrote this brave and rather desperate letter under the stress of friendship, and in the prospect of further anti-Catholic legislation.[90] There is no tendency to principled Jacobitism here, familiar with varieties of Jacobite outlook

---

[88] *Corr.*, i, pp. 336–7.
[89] *Corr.*, ii, pp. 166–7.
[90] Cf. *Corr.*, ii, p. 171 (Pope to Caryll, 17 May 1723); T.E., iv, p. 168–9, n. 60 (5).

though he must certainly have been from many of his acquaintance, and cognizant of Atterbury's Jacobite correspondence though he conceivably was. And on the other hand there are several, if sometimes politic, statements that he was not ill-disposed on dynastic or religious grounds towards the Hanoverian establishment:

> I am a Catholick, in the strictest sense of the word. If I was born under an absolute Prince, I would be a quiet subject; but I thank God I was not. I have a due sense of the excellence of the British constitution. . . .
> [I have wished to see] . . . not a King of Whigs, or a King of Tories, but a King of England. Which God of his mercy grant his present Majesty may be . . .[91] [Pope to Atterbury, Nov. 1717]

> I resolve to take any opportunity of declaring (even upon Oath) how different I am from what a reputed Papist is . . . that *if to be a Papist be to profess & hold many such Tenets of faith as are ascribed to Papists, I am not a Papist. And if to be a Papist, be to hold any that are averse to, or destructive of, the present Government, King, or Constitution; I am no Papist.*[92] [Pope to Viscount Harcourt, May 1723, regarding his testimony on Atterbury's behalf before the House of Lords]

> And yet you know I am no enemy to the present constitution . . .[93] [Pope to Swift, Nov. 1729]

The probably correct view that Pope was no Jacobite finds its chief support in these statements, though on one occasion he sought to advance a specifically Jacobite interest with Robert Walpole himself.[94] It may be inferred from these statements that Pope was sometimes prepared to take considerable political risks in order to assert his personal loyalty to a friend, but that he was acutely aware that a 'reputed papist' was a potential rebel, and that it was therefore necessary for him to exercise caution in general. The Atterbury affair probably shook him a good deal. He was clearly aware of the Caryll family's association with the Jacobite movement,[95] and it is a fair inference that political caution was a further reason why Pope did not frequently visit Caryll at Ladyholt after the early years, and why, personal differences apart, he was willing to keep this 'ancient friendship' from becoming too conspicuous an intimacy.

[91] *Corr.*, i, p. 454.
[92] *Corr.*, ii, pp. 171–2.
[93] *Corr.*, iii, 81.
[94] Spence, ii, p. 615.
[95] The greatest danger of association with the Carylls might have seemed to arise from their marriage-alliance with the Seaforth family. The Pretender still considered the Marquis of Seaforth (the brother-in-law of Caryll's eldest son) a loyal supporter in 1725 (B.M. Stowe MSS. 186, f. 82), and while Seaforth's feelings may in fact have been lukewarm and ambiguous, he had notoriety in Britain as a Jacobite (B.M. Add. 28251, ff. 48–9). It may be relevant to note that the name of 'Lord Caryll' occurs in a list of English Jacobites drawn up by exiled activists in 1743 (G. H. Jones, *The Mainstream of English Jacobitism* (Cambridge, Mass. 1954), p. 223) though such memorials were often characterized by false optimism.

5. THE LAST YEARS

All these factors, practical, personal, ethical, religious and political, governed Pope's relation with Caryll in the later years of the latter's life. It is significant, and much to the credit of both men, that the friendship remained so warm. The outward testimony of this lies, not so much in the exchanges between the two over *An Essay on Man* or other matters of common interest, but in the fact that Pope paid one more visit to Caryll at Ladyholt before his old friend died. It followed soon after the death of Pope's mother, who had so long been a reason, perhaps even longer an excuse, for Pope's not visiting Caryll. Pope wrote of this event to Caryll in a strain of such candour that it is hard to doubt that the death indeed threw him into a state of increased affection for and dependence upon that 'friend's humanity now experienced near thirty years'[96]:

> I found you too true a prophet; but God's will be done ... I'm really more troubled than I would own ... not to seem a better man than I am, my attendance upon her living was not virtue, but only duty, and my Melancholy for her dead, is not virtue but weakness ...
>
> To see you at Ladyholt was the first thought I had upon this event ...[97]

Two months later Pope was able to accept Caryll's renewed invitation: 'Few words are best: you shall be troubled with me whenever you will ... I write this in haste, or if I did not, could not pretend to express the joy it will be to me to see you in your domestic light, with all about you to whom I wish so well.'[98]

Some of the subjects which Pope and Caryll discussed, during the fortnight's visit to Ladyholt were Caryll's late neighbour Richard Norton, who had bequeathed his estate to the poor; Pope's character of the Duke of Wharton, in the Epistle *To Cobham*, which Caryll thought 'too hard' and which seems to have been altered accordingly; and it was on this occasion that Caryll expressed the view that the author of *An Essay on Man* should 'mention our Saviour directly'. It is probable that other, more political, topics also had a place in their conversation, for in the chief follow-up letter to the visit, Pope paid Caryll a very unusual courtesy: 'My sincere services attend your Countess', he wrote, 'I mean not your countess in gallantry, your neighbour's wife, but your true Countess, your own.'[99] This pointed reference to Caryll's Jacobite title may have arisen from some discussion of that alternative political and social order (the realization of which after 1688 was never likely though never impossible) in which Caryll would have 'dar'd' to be 'Great'. Caryll's ambition had been sacrificed to the principle of fidelity to his religion and (perhaps less clearly) to the exiled dynasty. In remembering and using the title conferred on Caryll's family by an exiled, *de jure*, Roman Catholic monarch, Pope, in a passing courtesy, recognized the true desert of a fidelity which the

---

[96] *Corr.*, iii, p. 373 (Pope to Caryll, 28 May 1733).
[97] Ibid., p. 375 (Pope to Caryll, 25 June 1733).
[98] Ibid., p. 383.
[99] Ibid., pp. 390–1 (23 Oct. 1733).

world would not reward. The virtue of constancy seems to have been what Pope finally most appreciated in Caryll, and most wished to display to him; many phrases in the correspondence bear witness to this: 'I need not tell you the old title and long right you have to claim in me . . .', 'I really am in an ancient & settled respect for you and yours', '. . . you have a much stronger and much older title to me . . .', 'the kind token of ancient friendship . . .', and the last words of the final letter which Pope wrote to Caryll, on 17 July 1735, affirms, as it were symbolically, that ideal of constancy which, despite vicissitudes, had been a striking feature of their long acquaintance: 'Believe me, therefore, unalterably, what I always was, Dear sir, Your most affectionate faithful friend and humble servant . . .'.[100]

Fidelity to a principle professed, despite the consequences in the realm of practical life, was perhaps the most significant value which Pope learnt from his friendship with Caryll. Indeed for Pope it was the fidelity itself, rather than what was (for the Carylls) its *object*, that assumed the quality of an absolute value, and afforded him, combined with other experience and transmuted into his art, a poetic stance satisfying at once the need of his variable and open temperament for continuity and tradition, and of his passionate independence for intransigent individualism:

> Yes, the last Pen for Freedom let me draw,
> When Truth stands trembling on the edge of Law:
> Here, Last of *Britons*! let your Names be read;
> Are none, none living? let me praise the Dead . . .
>
> ['Epilogue to the Satires, Dialogue II', ll. 248–51]

Yet the other essential side of the paradox which Pope learned, among other ways, through his acquaintance with Caryll was that commitment to a principle, and to one side, must be complemented by a generous and open attitude to people of other persuasions ('. . . While you believe me what I profess as to Religion,' he told Caryll in 1714, 'I can bear any thing the bigotted may say . . .').[101] Thus 'Fix'd to one side, but mod'rate to the rest' was a line which not only described Lord Caryll, and indeed his nephew, but expressed for Pope a fundamental human standard, which he did not always manage to live up to, but which was always relevant to his decisions as man and artist.

It is in one respect possible to be more specific about what Pope took from the Carylls and other families like them. It seems possible that the whole significance of Jacobitism for Pope has been insufficiently considered. The simple question: was Pope a Jacobite—which I have tried to answer—is by no means the only one that arises, and it fails to recognize the very fluid political situation as many saw it. If Pope decided that he was no Jacobite, it is unlikely to have been an easy and obvious decision: what was the effect on his outlook of the awareness of numerous people, some of them close and

---

[100] *Corr.*, ii, pp. 72–3, 78, 112, 418; iii, p. 474.
[101] *Corr.*, i, p. 238.

admired friends, who despite a lukewarm allegiance to the Hanoverians held
that beyond the changing of administrations, the joining up or dividing of
factions, there was a further and more radical alternative for the ruling of
Britain: the restoration of the *de jure* monarch? The point is not so much
that a Stuart restoration would, if achieved, have made a large difference to
Britain; it may seem likely that it would not. It is rather that, whereas for the
convinced Whig the Hanoverian monarch was in a final sense the king, for a
family such as the Carylls he was no more than the prince who happened to
be occupying the throne. Whether or not they were ready to take up arms for
'James III', the greater availability for them of an attitude of critical detachment from the whole political establishment of the time is clear, and emerges
as a distinctive tone even in professions of loyalty or gratitude to the *de facto*
monarch. 'The best peice of Newes I've heard . . . is that concerning my
Lord your Brother's Pardon: to which I hope our Gracious King will add a
competent Substance or else 'tis not worth acceptance . . .' (Caryll to Lady
Mary, 3 June 1726); 'Not a King of Whigs, or a King of Tories, . . . but a
King of England. Which God of his mercy grant his present Majesty may
be . . .' (Pope to Atterbury, Nov. 1717)—the sense of ironic reserve in these
statements is palpable. There was, among many Roman Catholic and Jacobite
families in the earlier eighteenth century, an ambience of at least passive disaffection towards the Hanoverian line and its ministries, and it must seem
very likely that this, together with his involvement in the Tory campaign
against Walpole, contributed to Pope's own evolution of something still
comparatively new in English literature: a poetry of political opposition. It
seems probable that Pope's early society contributed to the kind of total
political attack which the poet produced in his last years:

> Can the light packhorse, or the heavy steer,
> The sowzing Prelate, or the sweating Peer,
> Drag out with all its dirt and all its weight,
> The lumb'ring carriage of thy broken State?

Pope rhetorically asked of Britain in 'One Thousand Seven Hundred and
Forty: A Poem',

> Alas! the people curse, the carman swears,
> The drivers quarrel, and the master stares.   [ll. 69–74]

John Caryll died intestate at Ladyholt in April 1736, in his sixty ninth year.[102]
The friends and advisors of Lady Mary Caryll, and her son, now the new
head of the family, judged that the situation warranted instant and ruthless

[102] The precise date is given by *The Gentleman's Magazine* (vi, p. 823) as 18 April, and a letter
to Lady Mary Caryll, 19 April 1736 (B.M. Add. 28229, ff. 76–7) already alludes to the circumstances of the recent death. Of the last two letters to Caryll preserved in the family papers, one
(from Samuel Berry, 2 Feb. 1735/6) was to thank him for a gift of £20 to the poor; and the other
(from Elizabeth Bowes, 17 Feb. 1735/6) to congratulate him on the 'Jubilee' of his fifty years of
marriage; B.M. Add. 28229, ff. 73, 75.

precautions. A Caveat was entered in the Doctor's Commons 'against ye Widows taking Administration until an Inventory is made & security is given' and the correspondent who reported this move remarked candidly enough: 'I do not matter how others may take it providing Master's interest is safe (I should now say, my Lord's).'[103] At Ladyholt, it was reported, 'all are in great confusion' and Lewis Innes, writing to John Baptist Caryll over a year later, noted that the latter had found the estate 'in great disorder'.[104]

No letters of condolence on the death of Caryll are to be found in the surviving correspondence. Many must have been written to his widow, and it is inconceivable that these did not include one from Pope. It is likely that they (perhaps with other letters of special personal concern) were not left in the family papers at Ladyholt, but taken by Caryll's widow to West Grinstead, where she and her daughter Catherine lived until her death in 1754.[105]

The history of the last John Caryll is interesting here only as epilogue. For thirty years all the economic ills endemic in the family ravaged his fortune, the annuities and portions which it was his responsibility to pay to the numerous unmarried ladies of the family fell into arrears, his two sisters finally taking their case to law, and for a time Caryll appears to have been liable to arrest for debt. In 1744 the West Grinstead estate may have been sold (though old Mrs. Caryll, the wife of Pope's friend, continued to live there until her death); nine years later his mother-in-law, Lady Molyneux, wrote from Lancashire to say she was resisting arrest for debt, and to appeal to him to 'hasten the sale of ye estate'.[106] At last an Act of Parliament was obtained to reverse the entail on the main Caryll estates, and the means by which these had been preserved for the family in 1696 was thus abandoned. Caryll's wife died in 1760, he had no children, and of all that numerous family there was by 1767 no heir to the estates, the title, or the debts. In that year Ladyholt itself was sold, and soon after pulled down.[107] But Caryll had nearly twenty more years to live, and was not quite without resource. He seems to have emerged financially comfortable, for a time, from the sale of his estates, and there was a cause for him to serve on the continent that was not yet quite dead. Caryll had played no part in the Jacobite rebellion of 1745, though his name occurs on a list compiled in 1743 of English Jacobites prepared to rise for the House of Stuart,[108] and Charles Edward had accorded him a gracious interview at Gravelines in 1744.[109] In 1768 Caryll joined 'Charles III' in Italy, is said to have arranged his marriage to Princess Louisa of Stolberg, and to have acted as his Secretary of State until 1777.[110] Later still he remarried and lived at

[103] B.M. Add. 28229, ff. 76–7 (19 April 1736).

[104] Ibid. 28229, f. 114.

[105] The date of her death, at West Grinstead, is established by B.M. Add. 28231, f. 216. De Trenqualéon states it correctly (op. cit., ii, Table 2) and Ruvigny, who has it as 1723 (op. cit., pp. 27–8), is wrong.

[106] B.M. Add. 28231, f. 156 (26 Oct. 1753).

[107] Private Acts 32 George II, 1758–9, No. 37, pp. 1–20; Gordon, op. cit., p. 201–2.

[108] See n. 95 above.

[109] B.M. Add. 28230, f. 245.

[110] Ruvigny, op. cit., pp. 29, 215.

Maisons-sur-Seine near Paris. He retired finally to Dunkirk where he died on 7 March 1788 in poverty and distress.[111]

To read through the Caryll Papers as they have survived is to see a remarkable anatomy of the life and concerns of an eighteenth-century landed family. The deeds, the accounts, the correspondence, the learned and pious treatises, the poems, obscurely intimate some relation between material interests and moral, political, and religious principle which remains nearly always elusive. The impression that the dominant collective concern is with land, influence, wealth, and the continuation of the family and its honours is almost overwhelming, yet from time to time, in one or another person, Abbess Mary Caryll in a letter, John Caryll in a poem, a stronger spirit finds expression, and for a moment all the effort seems to be dedicated to some ideal (to 'propogat Religion and be servisable to theyre King'). Often, no doubt, the ideal only rationalized what material interest prompted, yet, either through convinced idealism, obstinacy, or sheer collective conservatism, even the most feckless of the family continued to adhere to the Roman faith, and thus contributed to their material downfall. Lord Caryll showed a double and more self-sacrificing fidelity when he followed James II into exile, though he must have hoped for glory and gain in a second Restoration. Principle and ambition, both on a petty and a great level, run side by side, sometimes joining, sometimes one controlling the other: a constantly changing pattern. And perhaps the nature of their ambition was as harmful to them as their principle, for as one watches the process by which, over a century, this huge family disposed of itself in the roles of landed gentry, priests, gentleman-ushers at minor or exiled courts, nuns, and spinsters, one cannot help remembering that in Elizabethan times much of the Caryll fortune was, in all probability, founded on iron-mining,[112] and that in those days marriage into families of wealthy merchants was not unthinkable.

---

[111] Ibid., p. 29; Foley, op. cit., iii, p. 537. See B.M. Add. 34635, ff. 58, 108, 151, for a correspondence, c. 1780, between John Baptist Caryll and Henry, Cardinal of York. In the last letter, Caryll offers his further service to the Pretender.

[112] Irene Hernaman, 'The Carylls of West Sussex,' Sussex County Magazine, ii (1928), p. 305. An instructive comparison is between the Carylls and another old Sussex family of similar status, the Ashburnhams (see G. E. Mingay, op. cit., pp. 61–7). The Ashburnhams increased their wealth and power, unhampered by Catholic disabilities, because their chief ambition seems to have been to develop their estates.

IV. 'Dexterous Attorney': Peter Walter Esq. of Stalbridge (1664?–1746)

1. THE MAN AND HIS WORK

SOON after 22 March 1690, William Baron Paget of Beaudesert, British ambassador to the court of Vienna, and soon to perform valuable service to William III by making peace between the Holy Roman and Ottoman empires, thus releasing the Emperor's forces to help William against France in the West, set down a hasty memorandum of 'Persons I am to write to'. The list includes 'Mr. H. Paget,' his son, and one 'Peter Walter'.[1] These two men, casually associated here, were through business and personal ties to be closely connected throughout their lives, as the correspondence of Walter shows. Walter was at this time an obscure person compared with 'Harry Paget', the Tory-inclined heir of the Whig Lord Paget of Beaudesert, but he was to become familiar with the most powerful nobility of the land, and was to win the distinction of being violently attacked by Pope, Swift, Fielding and other satirists; by Pope in his social poetry on no less than ten separate occasions.[2] What kind of life was this obscure man to lead which would warrant the favour

---

[1] B.M. Add. 8880, f. 16.

[2] Pope's references to Walter in the poems are as follows: *To Bathurst*, ll. 20, 125–8 (T.E., iii–ii, pp. 85, 102); *Imitations of Horace*, Sat. II. i, ll. 3, 40; Sat. II. ii, l. 168; 'The Second Satire of Dr. John Donne,' ll. 35–124; Ep. II. i, l. 197; 'Epilogue to the Satires', I, ll. 121; II, ll. 57–61; *1740. A Poem*, ll. 25–6 (T.E., iv, pp. 5, 9, 69, 137–45, 211, 307, 315–16, 333). Note also the curious epigram in T.E., vi, 348, which might refer to Walter. Swift's chief references to Walter are: *The Answer of William Pulteney to Sir Robert Walpole* (1730), *Miscellaneous and Autobiographical Pieces*, ed. Herbert Davis (Oxford, 1962), p. 117; and 'To Mr. Gay on his being Steward to the Duke of Queensberry', ll. 101–30; *Poems*, ed. Harold Williams (Oxford, 1937), ii, p. 530. Fielding portrayed Walter in the character of Peter Pounce, in *The History of . . . Joseph Andrews* (see especially Bk. I, Ch. x and Bk. III, Ch. xiii; ed. M. B. Battestin (Oxford, 1967), pp. 47, 274–6) and in *The History of . . . Jonathan Wild*, Ch. VII; and as 'Mynheer Petrus Gualterus', a lately deceased natural philosopher, whose remarkable 'Observations and Experiments upon the Terrestrial Chrysipus or Guinea' he published as *Philosophical Transactions for the year 1742–3*; *The Complete Works of Henry Fielding*, ed. W. E. Henley (London, 1903; reprinted 1967), xv, pp. 61–74. (For Fielding and Walter, see W. L. Cross, *The History of Henry Fielding* (New Haven, 1918), i, 176, 241; B. M. Jones, *Henry Fielding: Novelist and Magistrate* (London, 1933), pp. 84–5, 107; and F. Holmes Dudden, *Henry Fielding: His Life and Times* (Oxford, 1952), pp. 160–2. An example of straightforward aristocratic satire upon Walter is Sir Charles Hanbury William's 'Peter & My Lord Quidam', *Works* (London, 1822), i, p. 37.

3. Artist unknown, miniature of *Peter Walter*, from the Gorhambury
Collection by kind permission of The Earl of Verulam.

of so many wealthy nobles, and provoke the wrath of so many illustrious writers? An account of his life must seek to answer this question.

At this time Walter was Lord Paget's steward, and for the moment it was his master and Henry Paget who were dissatisfied with him. On 13 Jan. 1692/3 Lord Paget wrote to his son expressing surprise '... to hear Peter Walter should make any, ye. least, difficulty to pay you ye. hundred Ginneys I ordered for Monsr Blancard, there is difference betwixt giving Mony to any body yt. asks it in my name, and paying you what I give you order to receive from him ...'[3]

Two months later Lord Paget wrote to Walter himself; his letter is full of the mundane cares that a landed aristocrat, serving his country abroad, had from time to time to attend to, and tells us something also about Walter's job:

> ... the last post brought yours ye. 23d. feby., wch. tells mee, three hundred pounds due to my Br Tho: Pagett is payd, I hear it willingly tho ... [he] ... says he hears nothing from you about it; My Son ... [had] ... orders some time since to receive from you one hundred Guinneys to be employed according to my direction but seeing tis not delivered yet you are to forbear paying it now ... I wish I had your last years accounts, wch might, my thinks, have been sent, before now, by Post; according to ye. appointment you must have received, long since, from mee; ye leases may also be sent by post; for by any other way they will lie too long upon ye way; if the tenants will not alow anything for The despatch of their leases after agreement, ye charge must be considered in ye agreement for ye future ... I desire you to return mee upon the receipt of ys. one thousand pounds payable to ... my Marchant in Amsterdam; if you can have it at 35 Dutch shillings and a half, or 36, The change will be good.[4]

When in 1698 Lord Paget was appointed ambassador to the Sublime Porte, Walter made his practical contribution to the flamboyance of diplomatic show; and advised Henry Paget how to proceed about the bills of exchange to meet his master's considerable expenses in travelling in properly prestigious style from Vienna to Constantinople.[5] The picture of Walter that emerges from these letters is of a man evidently officious, probably self-willed in the handling of his master's affairs, but indispensable. Lord Paget's tone of clear annoyance in the first letter has changed in the second to one of muted irritation; all three letters show that Walter was secure in a position of responsibility and much relied upon. They also show what was to be the fundamental stuff of Walter's career: lands, leases, accounts, bills of exchange; now and throughout his life, though on an impressively increasing scale, he was to be a man of business in the wealth which derives from land.

It is thus at least partly in terms of such business that the human significance of Walter's career must be presented. His parentage, place of birth, and

---

[3] B.M. Add. 8880, ff. 66–7.
[4] Ibid. f. 76 (30 March 1692).
[5] Ibid. f. 93 (19 June 1698).

education remain obscure; since he practised as an attorney he probably
received legal training by apprenticeship, but of this too nothing is known;[6]
it is in the context of business that the first references to him are to be found.
In a draft Court Book for the Paget manors of West Drayton, Harmondsworth
and Iver, in Middlesex, Peter Walter, gentleman, deputy steward of the
manor, is recorded as having held the manorial court at Harmondsworth on
3 Dec. 1687, and seems to have entered Lord Paget's service in 1686 at the
age of twenty two.[7] From April 1693 he held courts as deputy steward or
steward for all three manors. As steward he held all three manorial courts at
least until April 1699, when this particular record comes to an end.[8] Fuller
information about Walter's work at this time comes from another document:
'An Account of the Estate of the Right Honourable William Lord Pagett in
the Countys of Stafford, Derby and Warwick in the Receipt of Mr. Peter
Walter. (1689–1702).[9] This shows that he was paid a salary of £50.0.0. a
year, plus his travelling expenses, for his services to Lord Paget, but that his
first four years' salary and expenses were not paid until 1689.[10] In return for
this Walter supervised and recorded all payments and receipts, including the
Government's contribution to his master's diplomatic expenses which came
to £25,001.7.2. for the period 1689–99.[11] The more everyday receipts included
the 'Profitts' of the manorial courts, fines upon leases, rents, money from the
sale of timber, 'arrears in the hands of several Bailiffs', and the interest upon
loans made by Lord Paget to various people.[12]

Ordinary payments in a typical year (1694) comprised:

Allowances to the bailiffs . . . . £591.11.3.
Taxes and payments to Marlow tenants . . . .   71.19.6.
Payments of interest money . . . . 298.14.0.
Payment of annuities and rents . . . . 773. 9.0.
Payments to tradesmen . . . . 793.16.7.
Fees and gratuities in the Secretary's Office, Treasury and
    Exchequer . . . .   89.14.6.

[6] For the unregulated state of the profession of attorney in the seventeenth and early eighteenth
centuries, see Robert Robson, *The Attorney in Eighteenth-Century England* (Cambridge, 1959),
pp. 5–20. Recorded enrolment by oath, after examination, was not obligatory before 1730 (pp.
11–12). It is worth noting, in view of Walter's later notoriety, that of all professions at this time
that of attorney was most predictably subject to contempt and attack (pp. 18–19).

[7] Greater London Record Office (Middlesex Records), ACC. 446/M20. Walter's accounts for
Lord Paget's estates record his being paid four years' salary in 1689 (Staffordshire Record Office,
D(w) 1734/3/1/16, p. 38). For Walter's age, see *The Gentleman's Magazine*, xvi (1746), p. 45,
which states him to have been 82 on his death that year (1746). For a brief modern summary of
his career, see The History of Parliament: Romney Sedgwick, ed. *The Commons, 1715–54* (London,
1970), ii, p. 517.

[8] Greater London Record Office (Middlesex Records), ACC. 446/M20. See ACC. 446/EF/8/2–8
(1722–8) for Walter's subsequent stewardship of these manors.

[9] S.R.O., D(w) 1734/3/1/16.

[10] Ibid. p. 38 et seq. His expenses usually came to about £5 a year.

[11] Ibid. pp. 21–2.

[12] These include Viscount Shannon (ibid. p. 28), Lord Paulett (pp. 27–8) and Sir Richard
Newman (p. 28 et seq.).

Accidental payments (including remittances to Lord Paget
  abroad, and Walter's salary and expenses) .... 1897.14.8.

'Totall of the discharge in 1694 .... £4516.19.6.'

It is worth noticing, in view of Walter's later reputation, that the interest
money referred to above included the payment of £21.14.0. to himself, on a
loan of £362.0.0. by him to Lord Paget in 1690; it was probably paid off in
1697. Fielding was strictly accurate when, in *Joseph Andrews*, he depicted
Walter as lending money at interest 'even to his own Master and Mistress'.[13]
Two other items of payment are of interest in these accounts. In 1692 Walter,
at Lord Paget's direction, 'Paid the Widow Northcott for an Herriott, seized
on her husband's death more then was due' £3.0.0., which may suggest that
Walter was keener at getting money out of the tenants than Lord Paget always
approved.[14] In 1695 he paid out £100.0.0. towards Henry Paget's election
expenses as one of the knights of Stafford.[15]

Walter was not just an accountant in the narrow sense of the term. He was
concerned with improving resources and making production more efficient,
as well as with recording existing income and expenditure. In a proposition,
in his own hand, to the town of Burton, concerning the division of its common
lands, in August 1694, much emphasis is laid on improving the navigability
of the Trent. Because

> ... the Wealth & Honr: of all Cittyes, Townes, and Societyes of men, doo
> very much depend upon and follow the publicke trades, Manufactures,
> and imploymts. of the Nation, ffor Want of wch: ye. sayd Towne [Burton]
> is very much ruined decayed in its buildings, and the Inhabitants in generall,
> much impoverished, And because the River Trent (wch. soo conveniently
> waites upon the said Towne) by its being made a Navigable River, may
> and without doubt will much advance ye. designes ... of Trade, within
> yr. Townshipp ...[16]

he recommends the prosecution of the design. A part of the proceeds of the
enclosure was therefore to be devoted to this project, which may perhaps be
connected with one 'for bringing to Burton the iron Trade' mentioned in a
letter of Walter some thirty years later.[17] The present proposition, framed by
Walter and approved by Lord Paget and his son, may be genuine in its concern
for the public good; the enclosure provided, though perhaps obligatorily,
that 'some convenient part or parts of the sayd Common, be sett out for the
use of ye. poore, to be held by them as their Common right, or the profitts
thereof to be applyed to the poorest Housekeepers ...'[18]

---

[13] Ibid. pp. 57 et seq., 65. *Joseph Andrews*, Bk. I, Ch. x; ed. cit. p. 47.
[14] Ibid. p. 50.
[15] Ibid. p. 61.
[16] S.R.O., D(w) 1734/2/5/1s.
[17] S.R.O., D 603, Walter to the Earl of Uxbridge, 11 Sept. 1725.
[18] Ibid. D(w) 1734/2/5/1s.

In the efficient running of existing industry Walter was highly successful.
In 1696 the proceeds of the 'Coale Mines' on Lord Paget's estate of Beaudesert
had sunk from £400 *p.a.* to £330 upon which 'Mr. Walter took the Coale
Mines into his own Mannagement'. The proceeds then went up as follows:

$$
\begin{array}{r}
1697 \ldots\ldots\ldots £510.\ 0.\ 7. \\
1698 \ldots\ldots\ldots £393.\ 7.\ 7. \\
1699 \ldots\ldots\ldots £397.14.10. \\
1700 \ldots\ldots\ldots £422.12.\ 6. \\
1701 \ldots\ldots\ldots £436.12.\ 5. \\
1702 \ldots\ldots\ldots £478.\ 2.\ 1.
\end{array}
$$

making a total of £2638.10.0. for the period of six years.[19] It is hardly surprising
that those who employed Walter were prepared to put up with a degree of
officiousness, and that, when he served Lord Paget so well, many other members
of the nobility were ready to employ him.

A long letter from Walter to Lord Paget, on 20 Aug. 1702, the last year for
which his accounts for the Paget estates have survived, displays the care with
which he went into any proposed purchase by his master, and assessed realities
of fact and figure. He surveys, at Beaudesert, two little farms which, 'by
reason of their neareness to the House are necessary purchases for your Lordshipp . . .' One 'is now Lett att 40 l. p anno, but it is too deare, and by some
encouragements to the Tennant att the time of his entry, was strayned upp
to that Rent, on purpose to give a rule to the Sale of it, and will not in the
opinion of men of better understanding than I am, Lett upon the square for
more than 35 l. p anno.' Later in the letter he notes that '. . . some of the
Gentlm of the Countrey, and some of the Townes: people and better sort of
Tennants att Burton, have usually had Venison given to them at this Season
of the Yeare, a Brace or Leash of Bucks att the most have usually payd all the
compliments . . . I would not venture to doe it without orders . . .' Finally
he expresses his relief that Lord Paget is not to visit Beaudesert at present:

> . . . ffor here would have been all the confusion immaginable, unless a
> Long preparation had been made for your [?] Reception and the enter-
> tainment of those that would have resorted hither; If youre Lordshipp
> had come downe you would have been mett att Your entrance into the
> County, by not less (as I am informed) then 500 persons, and the Bayliffs
> and Alderman of Lichfield had resolved to entertaine your Lordshipp there
> . . . These ceremonyes I Know are not new to your Lordshipp, & haveing
> upon many occasions received much higher distinctions of Honr., but
> these are the best this Countrey affords, and the people that pay them,
> expect to bee requited for them, according to the manner practised here.[20]

With an air of disapproval, Walter here reminds Lord Paget of his obligations
as a great landed aristocrat.

[19] Ibid D(w) 1734/3/1/16, pp. 3–4.
[20] Ibid. D 603, Walter to Lord Paget, 20 Aug. 1702.

2. FAMILY POLITICS

By the beginning of the eighteenth century Walter had himself become a man of property. Indeed he computed his fortune in 1700 as £13,357.0.0.,[21] which shows he was earning a great deal more than his salary from Lord Paget. A deed of 6 Sept. 1694, to which Walter was a party, refers to him as 'of the parish of Saint Margarett Westminster'; so does the first of a series of leases to him of lands at Ewarne Minster in Dorset, in 1698.[22] A letter of 7 April 1706 is addressed to him 'at his house in St. Margaretts Church Yard Westminster'; and it is a reasonable inference that this house was acquired as early as 1694.[23] By 1706 a great purchase had been made; Walter had become the owner of Stalbridge Park in Dorset. Exactly when Walter acquired this property is hard to tell. It appears to have been sold to Lord Paget by Francis Boyle, Viscount Shannon, through his son the Hon. Robert Boyle, sometime before 1699. In January of that year Walter surveyed it for Lord Paget and valued it at £4720.0.0.[24] A sketch of a coat-of-arms for Walter, recently hanging in the manor house of Sandford Orcas (near Stalbridge) in Dorset, is endorsed: 'The Family arms of Peter Walter of Stalbridge in Dorsetshire The motto to which is *Deus providebit* 1700 A.D.'[25] If this evidence is reliable, Walter must have bought the estate from Lord Paget in 1699 or 1700, and the survey would probably be related to the sale. Walter surveyed the estate again in 1705; here it is referred to specifically as his property.[26] From now on, though not every stage can be traced, Walter's career was a steady accumulation of landed property, chiefly in Dorset, Somerset and Wiltshire, until he might well have said, in ostentatious modesty as Fielding presents him: '"I thank God I have a little, . . . with which I am content, and envy no Man: I have a little, Mr. *Adams*, with which I do as much good as I can."'[27] To enter into the details of this accumulation is unnecessary, but we must not forget, as we consider other aspects of his personality and career, the constant steady acquisition of property in the background of his other activities.

Though no accounts of Walter for the Paget estates after 1702 appear to have survived, it is clear from his later correspondence that he continued to oversee their management, and to visit them regularly, to the last years of his life. At the same time a variety of business was coming his way; in 1706 he was involved in timber valuations on the Dunton estate of the Hampdon

[21] Hertfordshire Record Office (Gorhambury MSS.), IX.C.136, p. 33. This is Walter's personal account book.

[22] Greater London Record Office (Middlesex Records), ACC. 446/ED 363; J. N. Dalton, ed. *The Manuscripts of St. George's Chapel, Windsor Castle* (Windsor, 1957), LXVI, p. 388.

[23] Buckinghamshire Record Office, D/MH 39 (J. Welch to Walter).

[24] S.R.O., D 603, Walter to Lord Paget, 20 June, 1699. Francis Boyle died in 1699 (G.E.C. vol. xi, pp. 655–6).

[25] Kindly shown me in 1965 by Sir Christopher Medlycott, Bt., then owner of Sandford Orcas, whose family is descended from Jane Walter (1710–1801), a grandchild of Peter Walter. See *Miscellanea Genealogica et Heraldica*, ed. J. J. Howard, New Series, vol. ii (London, 1877), pp. 3–11.

[26] H.R.O. (Gorhambury MSS.), XI. 38.

[27] *Joseph Andrews*, Bk. III, Ch. XIII, ed. cit., p. 274.

family; in 1711 his Dorset neighbour William, Lord Digby put into his hands his defence against Sir Nathaniel Napier; in 1712 Charles, Lord Halifax, reposing 'especiall Trust & Confidence in the Ability Care ffidelity and Circumspection of Peter Walter Gent:' appointed him his deputy as steward of the royal honour and manor of Hampton Court, '. . . hereby Giving Granting & Assigning unto the said Peter Walter the said Wages or Fee of £6.13.4. per Ann. to me Granted for the Execucon of the said Office . . . together with all other ffees Wages rewards Profitts Advantages and Emoluments whatsoever to the said Office belonging . . .'[28] Walter held courts for this manor regularly until his death.

Possibly the most powerful noble family served by Walter was that of the Dukes of Newcastle: the Holles and Pelham family. His early involvement with their affairs is of interest because, in the opinion of some at least, his behaviour was both skilful and suspect. Walter was acquainted, as early as 1703, with John Holles, Duke of Newcastle, who died in 1711 leaving an only daughter, Henrietta, with a dowry of £20,000. Thomas Pelham-Holles (formerly Pelham) now inherited the lands but not the titles of the late Duke. In 1713 Henrietta, whose mother had been a daughter and coheir of the last Duke of Newcastle of the old Cavendish line, married Edward, Lord Harley, eldest son of Robert Harley the Lord High Treasurer, and since 1711 Earl of Oxford.[29] This elaborate pattern of relationships was of significance to Walter, as indeed it was to those who composed it, owing to the all-important question of money: an expensive lawsuit depended between Pelham-Holles (created Baron Pelham of Laughton in 1712) and Lord Harley, concerning the last Duke of Newcastle's will and the Cavendish Estate. In such cases it was often more profitable to each side to compound than to press the lawsuit to a conclusion. Thus on 8 Oct. 1713 the Earl of Oxford wrote to Henry Paget, now Lord Paget since the death of his father earlier in the year, and spoke of 'Inclinations to Peace'; on the 10th. Lord Paget wrote to Mr. Naylor, one of the intermediaries, passing on the news of an 'Inclination to end that dispute in a more amicable way' and offering his services to compound the difference.[30] On the 14th. Lord Pelham wrote to thank Lord Paget for his services in passing on communications from the Earl of Oxford and Mr. Naylor, and on 3 Nov. a proposal to treat for terms was made to Lord Oxford.[31] At this point it emerges that Walter has been playing a part in the solemn diplomacy, for on 4 Dec. he writes to Lord Pelham to press for a decision:

> . . . it will become requisite for your Lōshipp to determine your self upon this Single quesõn *vid* Whether you will yeild that my Lord paget name a

[28] For the Dunton business, see Buckinghamshire Record Office, D/MH 39, 35, 39/5, 35/3, 39/6, 39/8. For the Digby-Napier lawsuit, see Dorset Record Office, KG 2732–4, 2746A, 2752. Greater London Record Office (Middlesex Records), ACC 634/70, ff. 12–13.

[29] S.R.O., D 603, Walter to Lord Paget, 28 Aug. 1703. G.E.C. vol. x, p. 264. For an illuminating discussion of Walter's role in the Newcastle finances, see Ray A. Kelch, *Newcastle, A Duke Without Money: Thomas Pelham-Holles, 1693–1768* (London, 1974).

[30] B.M. Add. 33064, ff. 9–12.

[31] Ibid. 33064, ff. 13, 16, 17.

man of probity to forme a Scheme of accomodation, by which neither side is to be bound, unless they thinke fitt, or intirely breake off the Treaty . . . this queõn needs noe great deliberation . . .[32]

Clearly Lord Paget and Walter had together been working for an accommodation; and they were to have some success, for on the 8 Dec. terms were put to the Earl of Oxford, and Lord Cowper was named as the 'man of probity'.[33]

Far from being brought to a speedy conclusion, however, the affair now extends and ramifies, with Walter (as assured in dealing with the great nobility of the land as in managing Lord Paget's coal mine) in the midst of the negotiations. The motive-force behind this dispute was Lord Pelham's shortage of funds. On 30 July 1715 the matter was still dragging on, and Dr. Bowers, his old tutor, who had just been consulting with Walter, wrote beseeching his master to give his mind to business, and attend to his friends when they told him he was on the brink of ruin.[34] But Lord Pelham, who had been created Duke of Newcastle earlier this year, now turned his attention to another way of getting money, and we hear for the first time of a marriage treaty between himself and Henrietta, first daughter and coheir of Francis, second Earl of Godolphin, by Henrietta, later *suo jure* Duchess of Marlborough.[35] Politically and financially this was a great match, but Newcastle had to reckon with the Duke and Duchess of Marlborough themselves, the young lady's formidable grandparents, as well as with her ailing and hostile mother. Sir John Vanbrugh, the dramatist and architect, whom Newcastle had been employing as an intermediary between himself and the Marlboroughs, wrote to him on 10 Nov. 1716, of 'this Abominable Woman' (the Duchess of Marlborough) but hastened to add that this opinion did not 'lessen my regard to my Lord Duke, nor good Opinion of his Grand Daughter, who I do not think has one grain of this Wicked Woman's Temper in her; if I did, I wou'd not advise you to take her . . .'[36] On the 15th. he wrote again, to complain how 'my Lady Dutchess has treated me, both in respect to your Grace's concern, and that of Blenh.' and how she has 'employ'd Mr. Walters to you' about the marriage treaty. He proceeds:

I don't at all believe however, she's Indifferent in the Matter, for she is not a Fool, tho' she's a —— Worse thing. But, as in all her other Traffick, so in a Husband for her Grand Daughter, she would fain have him good, and Cheap: and she certainly fancys she can wheedle Peter Walters to play a cunning Knaves part, and bring her business About with you, alone, without meddleing much with your Friends & Relations . . .[37]

---

[32] Ibid. 33064, f. 27.
[33] Ibid. 33064, ff. 29–33.
[34] Ibid. 33064, ff. 81–2.
[35] Ibid. f. 110; G.E.C., ix, pp. 530–1.
[36] *The Complete Works of Sir John Vanbrugh*, ed. Bonamy Dobrée and Geoffrey Webb (London, 1927–8), iv, p. 86.
[37] Ibid., pp. 86–7. For Walter's part in these negotiations, see also pp. 83–4. Kelch, op. cit., p. 45, considers that the Duchess turned to Walter when financial issues came to the fore.

Walter, the great duchess's potential 'cunning Knave', wrote two days later
to Newcastle to discuss both the marriage treaty and the negotiations with the
Harleys.[38] He writes again on the 24th. to say that 'this matter is not to be
further treated about till the Dutchess comes to Towne ... and that Sr.
John who was once thought a necessary instrument is now become the very
reverse . . .'[39] This perhaps fulfils Vanbrugh's prediction; certainly the two
'instruments', Vanbrugh and Walter, are trying to exclude one another from
the negotiations. Walter seems to have won his way to the vital centre for
three days later Vanbrugh reports that the 'Great Lady' will soon 'begin to
Say something directly to Walters'.[40] On 2 April 1717 the marriage took
place, and we must assume Walter to have been well rewarded for the part he
had played in bringing it about.[41]

Meanwhile the treaty with the Harleys dragged on uncompleted, and the
Duke of Newcastle continued to be hard up. On 30 Oct. 1717 Dr. Bowers
wrote once more to ask him to face the facts; even £10,000 would not make
him easy for half a year. He advised 'immediate retrenchment' and further
efforts at 'getting your due from Lord H., or at least such security for it, as
may enable you to raise money on yt. security. This I hope your Grace will
mention to Mr. Walter when he comes to Town, who is a proper person to
influence them, if he will heartily engage in it.'[42] Walter did engage in it, and
ten months later the renewed negotiations had come to a climax, with Walter
and Bowers in a flurry of activity and consultation. Bowers writes to the
Duke to say he has visited Mr. Walter's chambers last night, attended him at
his house today; their demands are to be put in writing, and Walter will
show them to Lord and Lady Harley this evening; he will then communicate
their reply. If the Harleys consent to these terms, 'it will be, as Mr. Walter
says £4000 advantage to you more than those were yt. we first gave in.' Mr.
Walter advises the Duke to sign the agreement if Lord and Lady Harley agree.[43]
Walter, in fact, appears producer, stage-manager and prompter rolled in one.
It remained for the plot to resolve. It burst like a bubble. In an undated
answer ('Thursday Noon') to a letter from Bowers which has not survived,
the Duke finds himself back where he started, and a very dubious light is cast
on Walter:

> as to Mr Walters surprise relating to ye. Harleys I have nothing to say,
> only yt. 'tis plain He has been deeply engaged in their Interests these
> seven years, & therefore I shall have little regard to what he says upon ys.
> subject, & I am apt to think had My own scheme been followed, it had
> brought them to reason long before this. For My Part I always desire to
> fight My own Battles, & therefore I shall not trust Mr Walters & ye. Vanes.

[38] B.M. Add. 33064, f. 116.
[39] Ibid. 33064, f. 120.
[40] *The Complete Works of . . . Vanbrugh*, ed. cit., iv, p. 88.
[41] G.E.C. vol. ix, p. 531. Walter was a trustee for the payment of an annuity from the Duke to
his new wife; Kelch, op. cit., p. 47.
[42] B.M. Add. 33064, ff. 131–2.
[43] Ibid. 33064, ff. 150–1 (26 July 1718).

Positive I am in bringing My Bill in Chancery . . . Dear Dr. once resolve to trust nobody but yr. own Eyes.[44]

How should one describe Walter's part in these seven years of largely futile negotiation? He may genuinely have hoped for a compromise, he may personally have preferred one side to the other, but his rule of thumb was quite probably to maximize his own profit by keeping both parties in hope as long as he could. This is what Pope was to say, in blunter terms, fifteen years later:

> For you he sweats and labours at the Laws,
> Takes God to witness he affects your Cause,
> And lyes to every Lord in every thing . . .
> ['The Second Satire of Dr. *John Donne*', ll. 75–7]

But this is not quite the whole story; it is time to disclose not Walter's final but his original move. On 19 July 1711 Robert Monckton wrote to the Earl of Oxford about the then projected marriage between Lord Harley and the Newcastle heiress, and concluded by mentioning the late Duke of Newcastle's will: 'You may see a copy . . . which we despatched by the last post to Harry Paget. Jessop says it is very unadvisedly drawn and leaves great blots to be hit by the heir-at-law. By the hand it is of Peter Walter's doing.'[45]

The very will, over which there had been seven years of profitable negotiation to Walter, had actually been drawn up by Walter, and in such a way as to leave it open to dispute by Pelham-Holles, the heir-at-law. This may of course have been incompetence, but that would not be in character, and it is hard to dismiss the possibility that Walter was happy to create a situation in which he would be well placed to serve either or both of two powerful noble families.

3. PARLIAMENTARY POLITICS

Whatever the truth of the matter, Walter continued to serve the Duke of Newcastle. He was one of the trustees under a provision of the final Newcastle-Harley settlement, achieved by Private Act of Parliament in 1719; while a letter of 10 Aug. 1723, in which Walter's usual assurance has changed to faint servility, begs the Duke not to be angry with him if he is unable 'to Hold the Audit att Nottingham as usual', for he has been ill of 'a constant ffeaver' and treated by the fashionable and expensive Dr. Meade.[46] In November 1723 the Duke requested Walter to survey his whole financial situation, especially his household expenditure, and advise him how best to reduce his indebtedness; on 12 March 1724/5 he was to present his accounts. This was a considerable trust and responsibility, one reward for which may have been his appointment

---

[44] Ibid. 33064, f. 152. (It does *not* seem possible that this replies to ff. 150–1, Bowers's previous surviving letter to the Duke.)

[45] H.M.C. 29 (Portland), v, pp. 53–4. Kelch, op. cit., p. 70. Kelch also notes, p. 29, that Walter, as one of the late Duke's men of business (Jessop was the other) was himself a beneficiary of this will to the tune of £1,000.

[46] Kelch, op. cit., pp. 53, 67; B.M. Add. 33064, f. 230.

as Clerk of the Peace for Middlesex, on 26 March 1724.[47] As the *Custos Rotulorum* for the County was Newcastle, this rather lucrative place must have been secured through his patronage. This important connection with Newcastle continued; Walter was his steward, not just in the ordinary sense, but as a trusted expert on the whole elaborate pattern of Newcastle's debts and expenses, of which he made periodic assessments. Not only did he himself lend the Duke large sums at interest, but, in 1728, refused to arrange a further loan, until Newcastle could bring his affairs into better order. As late as 1740, six years before Walter's death, the assiduous man of business wrote to the Duke to ask if he would join with his relative Vane in barring the entail of the Newcastle estates.[48] There are two reasons why Newcastle (despite his recurrent disappointments in Walter) was reluctant to dispense with his services. The first is Walter's evident efficiency in the overseeing of estates, in the collection of the income they produced, and in advising on the service and reduction of large-scale debt. The Duke lived on a grand scale, ran a huge system of political patronage, and was seriously in debt. It was imperative for him to get the maximum from his estates, and bring his affairs under control. The second reason is more directly political: Walter had himself been an M.P. since 1715, representing Bridport in Dorset.[49] That the office of Clerk of Peace for Middlesex was conferred on Walter by Newcastle, not only as a reward for services rendered, but to secure his adhesion to the Government and Sir Robert Walpole, seems extremely likely. The fact that Walter had not held office as Deputy Clerk for Middlesex or Westminster before his appointment makes this conjecture the more probable. This complex situation goes some way to explain the paradox, noted by Pope some years later, of Walter being at once distrusted yet found indispensable.

What was the nature of Walter's political attitudes and alignment? He appears to have been a completely self-made man, and we certainly have no evidence of the kind of family background or possessions which would, as was the case with the Carylls, carry with them an inheritance of political loyalty or obligation. We first find him in the service of a powerful Whig nobleman, William Lord Paget, but it is noteworthy that William's son Henry, with whom Walter kept up a life-long intimacy, albeit based on the discussion of business, was a man of Tory loyalties, and indeed was one of those through whom the Earl of Oxford gained control of the House of Lords in 1712 by making peers.[50] Again, Newcastle's assertion that Walter was 'deeply engaged' in the interests of Oxford and his family would suggest if anything a Tory inclination. But these considerations are slight. The first clear evidence of the colour of Walter's politics is his vote in the Commons in the Septennial Bill debate in 1716. The lists of those who spoke and voted for and against

[47] Kelch, op. cit., pp. 55–8; B.M. Add. 33064, f. 230, ff. 249–50; Greater London Record Office (Middlesex Records), MJ/SBB. 819/45. Also MJ/OC. 2/107d. For the nature of this office, see Sir Edgar Stephens, *The Clerks of the Counties 1360–1960* (London, 1961), pp. 30–44.

[48] B.M. Add. 33065, f. 395 (11 March 1740/1).

[49] Cobbett, vii, 33.

[50] G.E.C., x, p. 286.

this important Bill show that the issue divided Whig from Tory pretty clearly, and that all those who had formed the opposition to the Harley-St. John administration of Queen Anne's last years, and who were most unequivocally for the Hanoverian Succession, were the champions of the Bill. Its purpose was to lend stability to the new succession and it was to be defended by Walpole as a corner-stone of his administration and policy. Newcastle spoke for the Bill in the Lords; Peter Walter was among the majority for it in the Commons.[51]

In the same year a motion was passed in the Commons to bring in a bill 'to strengthen the Protestant Interest' by removing some of the distinctions between churchmen and dissenters. The new king was anxious to reward a section of his subjects which had always been zealous for the Hanoverian Succession, but was informed by his ministers that the Test Act at least would have to stand. There remained the Occasional Conformity and Schism Acts, which had been passed in the last years of Anne. A bill to modify these two acts in the dissenters' favour was thus, in 1718, narrowly passed in the Lords, and in January 1719 hotly debated in the Commons. The lists of those for and against this bill do not reveal so central and clear a division as those for the Septennial Bill; it seems to have been a more extreme Whig measure, and it is interesting to note that Robert and Horatio Walpole, stronger supporters of the new dynasty than friends of dissent, voted against the bill. Walter is to be found among the majority in favour.[52] From these two votes it appears that Walter was a Whig, and it is not surprising to find him referred to, in the election of 1722, as the government candidate elected for Bridport.[53]

Walter's vote for the Protestant Interest Bill prompts one to consider the nature of his religious convictions, and their relation to his political alignment. It is perhaps significant in itself that in the large surviving body of MS. evidence on Walter so little throws any light on his religion. The long sequence of letters to Henry Paget (created Earl of Uxbridge Oct. 1714), which extends from 1723 to 1738/9,[54] is a personal as well as a business correspondence, yet it contains only the faintest clues. We must infer either that religion was for Walter a private affair, or that it was not an obvious subject to mention when writing to his old patron and friend the Earl of Uxbridge. Yet there is some evidence. On 9 Oct. 1723, an indenture was signed between him and 'Henry Rutter, Clerke' and six other inhabitants of Stalbridge, in which he leased 'All that Barne or Building with the appurtenances thereof . . . in the Towne of Stalbridge . . . now used for a Meeting House or Place of Religious Worship . . .' to Rutter and the others for a term of 99 years, in consideration of the sum of £4.0.0. and for the annual rent of 'One Pepper Corne'. The lease makes it clear that it was to replace an earlier one, by which Walter had rented the meeting house to one Richard Snooke of Stalbridge in 1712. Henry Rutter had been Presbyterian minister in Stalbridge since 1700. A year after the signing of this lease a certificate was brought to the Bridport Quarter Sessions

[51] Cobbett, vii, 300–1, 372.
[52] Ibid., 292, 567–81, 587.
[53] H.M.C. 19 (Towneshend), p. 137.
[54] S.R.O., D 603.

'of a new erected House, called a Meeting house, situated in Stalbridge . . .
designed to be set apart for the worship of God by a Congregation of Dissenting
Protestants called Presbiterians . . .'[55] It would seem that the new lease had
been negotiated so that the meeting house might be rebuilt. The interest of
this lease is that a man like Walter, who usually lost no opportunity of making
money, should grant it at a peppercorn rent. It suggests either that he may
himself have been a Presbyterian, or that at least he had sympathy with them.
This accords with his vote for the Protestant Interest Bill which, in itself,
might have been construed as a purely political act.

This impression of Walter's religious position must be qualified by one or
two of his comments in letters to the Earl of Uxbridge. On 24 Aug. 1724,
Walter writes:

> I was yesterday att Burton Church to say my prayers, and to hear mr:
> Harris the Curate there preach, I had besides another reason for my going
> thither, which was to observe how conveniently the Church contayned the
> Congregation, after the great Outcry that had been made, that it was too
> Little . . . the Church was hardly halfe fill'd thô the Congregation was
> more numerous than usual . . . [there has been] an unequall distribution
> or Allotment of the Seats . . . But if all th: Complaynants were not obstinate
> ffools they might relieve themselves . . . [and] by sitting in the empty
> Seates, which noobody will gainsay, Have the principall places in the
> Synagogue . . .[56]

It is clear from this passage what was Walter's stronger motive in attending
a parish church; it was not to say his prayers and hear the curate. It is also
interesting to notice his attitude of contemptuous detachment towards those
whom he admits have been denied their proper rights at public worship. The
same detachment, expressed this time in highly effective ridicule, emerges
from a letter Walter wrote from Kenilworth Castle on 12 Aug. 1725. It is
one of the finest passages in his letters.

> Here has been an Horse Race next doore to mee, but my curiosity did not
> invite mee to it, However the fame of it has reached my Ears, and I am told
> that the Horse of a Low Church parson, by name Thorpe, Has shamefully
> beaten the Horse of an High Church Lord, by title Craven, and that
> abundance of money has been Lost by the High, to the Low Church Xtins,
> the odds Layd being seaven to one, which still shows that those Low
> puritanicall fellows are the greater picke pockitts of the two, an accident
> has befallen a young man, of what faith or persuasion I cannot Learn, in
> this nonsensicall assembly of people, for not contented, with the good
> Liquors the Towne of Warwicke afforded him, Hee by mistake road into
> ye Avon, and was Drowned, together with his silver spurrs and many other
> implements of Gentility about him . . .[57]

[55] Dorset C.R.O., 796. W. Densham and J. Ogle, *The Story of the Congregational Churches of
Dorset* (Bournemouth, [1889]), pp. 278–83.
[56] S.R.O., D 603, Walter to Uxbridge, 24 Aug. 1724.
[57] Ibid., Walter to Uxbridge, 12 Aug. 1725.

If Walter's attitude seems here to be: 'A plague on both your houses!' it must be remembered that it is to High and Low Church in 'nonsensicall assembly'. Walter's detachment has in itself something of the 'puritanicall' about it, while from a man who prided himself on his ability to amass wealth the comment on 'those Low puritanicall fellows' may be thought to possess intentional irony. It is possible that what we have here is a little joke at the writer's own expense, which was also in his eyes a compliment. In both the passages quoted Walter's chief concern has been practical. It is fair to conclude that his outlook was materialistic rather than spiritual, but that he had a strong enough leaning towards the dissenters to make him treat them generously in Stalbridge when he might have made them pay. There is no evidence of any gift by Walter to his parish church at Stalbridge, but he was to be buried there, as his will was to instruct, 'very privately in a Vault in Some Sort already made in the Isle belonging to my Mansion House . . .'[58] These details are in keeping with the impression we have already gained; so also, perhaps, is the motto in his proposed coat of arms: '*Deus providebit*'; that a man who laboured so tirelessly as Walter to amass a huge fortune, the annual increase of which he recorded meticulously every year in his notebook, should choose a motto such as this unmistakably recalls the type of puritan business-man familiar from the pages of *Religion and the Rise of Capitalism*.[59]

Clearly such a man would find his natural place, in the parliament of his time, not with Jacobite, Tory or even Whig opposition, but with Walpole and the Government. Walter was a steady supporter of the administration, and an alert follower of political events (in which he was often involved) even after he ceased to be an M.P. in 1735, at the age of seventy one. In August 1727, when preparations for the new election were afoot, he comments on a political setback suffered by the son of the Earl of Uxbridge, and makes some sardonic remarks about electioneering:

> I am sorry, very sorry indeed, for my my Lord Pagetts disappointment in the County of Middx, it is too Late to joyne in opinion with my Lady, that hee would have succeeded better here [presumably Staffordshire as the letter is written from Beaudesert], ffor althô his voteing in parliament, was not quite agreeable to the Whiggs, Yet in opposition to the other side, they would have been for him, and the interest of the House of Blythfield is soo much declyned, that when the Masr of that House sent his Agents about to make an interest for him, they were Scouted and ridiculed, and asked if they had brought with them the Key of the small Beere Cellar, soo soon, and by such little instances of scantyness, is an antient family interest Lost, and brought to nothing.[60]

Walter himself may have encountered problems in this election, for he rejoined parliament representing not Bridport, as before, but the Cinque Port of

---

[58] H.R.O. (Gorhambury MSS.), IX. C. 9a, f. 1.
[59] R. H. Tawney, *Religion and the Rise of Capitalism* (London, 1926), Ch. IV, Section iii.
[60] S.R.O., D 603, Walter to Uxbridge, 29 Aug. 1727.

Winchelsea.[61] In April 1729 Walpole was obliged by the Court, much against his own judgement, to bring in a bill granting to the king an alleged arrear in the Civil List of £115,000. It met with much opposition, especially in the Lords; in the Commons Walter voted as usual with the Government.[62] On 16 Jan. 1732/3, Walter reports to Uxbridge that 'The Project of Excise, notwithstanding all the clamour that has been made against it, is resolved upon, and will be pursued to Effect'.[63] Two months later, on 14 March, the Excise Scheme came up for debate in the Commons, an occasion which both government and opposition realized was to be a crucial trial of strength in the House, and an event of more widespread concern in the country than had occurred in parliament for a decade. Once more Walter's vote was with the Government, contributing to what was this time an empty parliamentary victory for Walpole.[64] On 12 Jan. 1733/4 Walter writes to the Earl of Uxbridge to brief him on the management of a petition for damages to be submitted to the House of Lords. His instructions show his thorough knowledge of procedure and tactics: those who are to testify at the Bar of the Lords are to 'bee such, as can speake to the greatest distance of time, and behave, with as little bashfulness and concerne as may bee.'[65] In 1734, also, he voted with the Government against the repeal of the Septennial Act.[66] Walter's consistent support of Walpole, held firm no doubt by Newcastle and the Clerkship of the Peace for Middlesex, was probably also confirmed by personal acquaintance with 'the great man', as Walpole was everywhere familiarly though not necessarily affectionately called. On 13 April 1734 Walpole obliged Walter to put certain propositions to the Earl of Uxbridge, which the latter in his reply to Walter seems to have repudiated with force. Walter, in an embarrassing situation, explains himself as follows:

> Your Lordshipps observatōns upon my Last Lre are soo just and reasonable, that noo Lawyer or prudent man, could excell them . . . and indeed, if your Lordshipp had showed an inclination to have closed in the propositions therein made, and referred it to my owne opinion, I should have beene of opinion against it. ffrom what I have now sayd, I am not insensible, that I have given you a faire opportunity to ask mee the reason why I wrote about it, To this I answere that the great man compelled mee to it, and I could not by any meanes resist his commands, att the same time resolveing, not to prostitute my fidelity to your Lordshipp . . .[67]

This letter nicely conveys the personal balance between commitment and independence which Walter managed to maintain in a difficult and, for a

[61] Cobbett, viii, 625. He had planned to stand for Dorset in Walpole's interest, it seems (H.M.C. 29 (Portland), vol. vii, pp. 405–6).

[62] Cobbett, viii, 705.

[63] S.R.O., D 603, Walter to Uxbridge, 16 Jan. 1732/3.

[64] Cobbett, viii, 1311.

[65] S.R.O., D 603, Walter to Uxbridge, 12 Jan. 1733/4.

[66] Cobbett, ix, 482.

[67] S.R.O., D 603, Walter to Uxbridge, 13 April 1734.

man who served so many different members of the nobility, probably common predicament.

Walter ceased to be an M.P. in 1735. But he evidently continued to follow parliamentary affairs and the fortune of Walpole's administration with unabated interest. On 24 Feb. 1738/9, he writes Lord Uxbridge a letter full of parliamentary news and requests, and with a real sense of the excitement of an important occasion; the debate in the Commons on the merchants' complaints about the Spanish depredations (another crisis for Walpole) had, he reports, 'an almost Excise Attendance'.[68] His grandson, elected M.P. for Shaftesbury in 1741, was to continue the family tradition of loyalty to Walpole, yet the grandfather was to see the fall of 'the great man' before he died.[69]

4. THE SATIRISTS' PETER WALTER

On 12 Oct. 1727, at the end of a letter to Pope, Swift casually commented that he would lose 'two or three hundred pounds rather than plague my self with accompts: so that I am very well qualified to be a Lord, and put into Peter Walter's hands.'[70] This seems to be the first notice that any of that formidable group of satirical writers, in their hawk-like surveying of the contemporary scene, gave to the now wealthy, influential, and indispensable man of business; and lord of the manor of Stalbridge. The immediate cause of Swift's remark, as John Butt observes, is likely to have been an experience of Pope's and Swift's mutual friend, Viscount Bolingbroke. The Earl of Essex was engaged to be married to the sister of the Duke of Bedford, but her family refused to let the match take place until Bolingbroke had undertaken to extricate Essex 'out of Peter Walter's hands', and Essex 'promised to have done with Peter Walters'.[71] It is significant that the information quoted is from a source independent of Pope, Swift, or any of their friends. It is less important to know the full story than to notice that it turns on Walter's already possessing a dubious reputation in the way he served his noble clients. It is also clear from these comments that Walter's money-lending activities, which we noticed when as early as 1690 he was lending money at interest to Lord Paget, and when subsequently he lent to Newcastle, had continued and probably increased.[72] Other evidences of the suspicion with which Walter was often regarded are to be found at this time.[73] At any rate the attack upon Walter was now on; in 1730 appeared Swift's *Answer of William Pulteney to Sir Robert Walpole*, in 1733 Pope's Epistle *To Bathurst*, and the first two imitations of Horace, in 1735 the extended portrait of Walter in his new version of Donne's *Satyre II*, and Swift's poem 'To Mr. Gay', and in 1737 Pope's Epistle *To Augustus*. In all these works Walter was attacked by name.

[68] Ibid., Walter to Uxbridge, 24 Feb. 1738/9.
[69] B.M. Add. 32695, f. 205 (Peter Walter the younger to the Duke of Newcastle, 6 Oct. 1740). Cobbett, xii, 199.
[70] *Corr.*, ii, p. 452.
[71] T.E., iv, p. 392.
[72] See n. 13 above.
[73] H.M.C. 29 (Portland), vii, p. 414.

They were followed up in 1738 by the two dialogues of Pope's 'Epilogue to the Satires', by *Joseph Andrews* in 1742, and by Hanbury Williams's 'Peter and My Lord Quidam' in 1743.[74] It was the wealthy and conspicuously successful Walter of the later years (the 1720s and 1730s) which prompted the satirists' attack. His great wealth, great parsimony, and confident self-righteous manner, together with his political alliances, made him an obvious target. Since the bulk of Walter's correspondence with the Earl of Uxbridge is co-extensive with this period, it will be useful to look further into these letters, not this time for evidence of his political and religious position, but rather of his attitude to the noblemen he served, to the tenants and labourers whose work he surveyed, to money, and to the law. For these were matters with which the satirists were concerned.

In 1720 Peter Walter was fifty six years old. He had owned his manor and estate of Stalbridge for twenty years. In this year, according to the account book in which he recorded his wealth and annual profit, he was worth £88,548. His expenditure for the year had been £824, and the net gain £6,153.[75] His annual gain in the previous ten years had varied between £3,023 and £11,141, this last figure being exceptionally high. His expenditure for the same period varied between £333 and £824, the lower figures being generally the earlier ones.[76] He had accumulated above fifty-four thousand pounds in these ten years, as compared with some twenty thousand in the previous ten, and some one thousand nine hundred in the decade before that.[77]

> 'Sir,' [said Parson] *Adams*, 'I have heard some aver you are not worth less than twenty thousand Pounds.' At which Peter frowned. 'Nay, Sir,' said *Adams*, 'you ask me only the Opinion of others . . .' 'However, Mr. *Adams*,' said he . . . 'I would not sell them all I am worth for double that Sum; and as to what you believe, or they believe, I care not a Fig, no not a Fart. I am not poor because you think me so . . .'

Thus Fielding. And we may well ask, with Parson Adams, '". . . can it be credible that in your short time you should have amassed such a heap of Treasure . . .?"'[78] Without jumping to the conclusion clearly implied by Fielding ('"Where could I possibly, without I had stole it, acquire such a Treasure?"'), we have to ask how Walter was making his fortune. He was doing so in four main ways. First, from the rents of his estates. Secondly, from his professional practice as a Westminster attorney. Thirdly, from his work as land-steward to a large number of the wealthiest and most important nobility of the land. Fourthly from the interest from loans and investments. To these one must add such offices as Deputy Steward of Hampton Court and Clerk of the Peace for Middlesex. And one must consider his industry and his parsimony, which his enemies all admitted and exploited in their

---

[74] These literary references are set out fully in n. 2 above.
[75] H.R.O. (Gorhambury MSS.), IX. C. 136, p. 73.
[76] Ibid. pp. 53–73.
[77] Ibid. pp. 33–73, 13–33.
[78] *Joseph Andrews*, Bk. III, Ch. XIII; ed. cit., pp. 275–6.

attack. Whether Walter was indeed the kind of man to make dishonest or illegal profits may be decided in due course.

Much the most prominent of his activities was his work as a land steward. In the late Summer of every year Walter set out upon a tour of inspection of all the estates, whose owners he served in this capacity, to hold the audit, collect rents, renew leases, inspect books, and to cast a sharp eye on the general condition of the land, the people and their work. His itinerary for 1724 shows him on the move from country house to country house from 1 August to 25 October. His journey included over thirty different estates, though some of his own are numbered among these.[79] Walter's letters to Uxbridge seem most often to have been written on these tours of duty, and for this reason we must be wary of the impression we get that his work as land steward was the most important. His legal and political business may well have occupied a greater part of his year.

On these tours of inspection Walter often met the owners of the estates where he held audit; his letters frequently record the way they treated him and his own reaction. Sometimes his vanity was flattered by a hospitable reception: 'Lord Cornbury and Lord Boyle, emulated their goodness towards mee, and were alwayes with mee, They showed mee every thing they could thinke of, and entertayned mee in a very sumptuous manner, and wee drank your Lordshipps Health agen and agen, they in Oxford wine, and I in Oxford Ale . . .'[80]

He was particularly gratified when great nobles or ladies put their coach at his disposal, and made a point of telling Uxbridge when this happened. On 22 July 1729, 'The Dutchess of Newcastle sent her Coach & six to carrie me to Claremont to Bed. ffryday I dined att Oatelands, and had the conveniency and Grace of the Countess of Lincolns Coach and six to fetch mee and carrie mee backe againe.'[81] A lavish reception did not necessarily satisfy him however; his pride demanded informality and cordiality while, judging from some of his letters, he kept up a certain austerity and reserve. Thus he can note: 'I Dyned Thursday with the Lord of the Mannor of Walton in a disagreeable manner, being received by him as a Stranger, and in Sumptuous [sic] manner.'[82] His ready contempt, which we have already observed, could be called forth by the most illustrious company:

Saturday with a Groom & pad I went to my Lord Shannons & dyned with him, and the same day the Duke of Newcastle mr. pelham his Brother and Duke Disne dyned att Worcester park with the Duke of Grafton in Company with the Earl of Burlington, where they were all of them detestably drunke with sweet punch, and next day very deservedly Sicke, However they recovered towards the Evening, and wee were very merry when our business was over, of which wee did more in this Hott Headed way in one

[79] S.R.O., D 603, 'Mr. Walter's Route. 1724.'
[80] Ibid., Walter to Uxbridge, 7 Aug. 1725.
[81] Ibid., Walter to Uxbridge, 22 July 1729.
[82] Ibid.

Houre, than wee could have donne otherwise in one day. All this noo otherwise concerning your Lordshipp than to answer you and make you Laugh . . .[83]

Peter Walter's attitude to the aristocracy was in fact twofold; he had the pride and sensitivity of a self-made man, but also the detachment. Many of his clients who had inherited, took for granted and were losing, what he had laboured for and was amassing through profitable loans to them in their difficulties, must have seemed men of a very different kind from himself. At the same time his own importance, affluence and success could only be realized and measured against that hierarchically conceived society of which the aristocracy was still the topmost rank in power and importance. Hence the satisfaction with which Walter regarded the very good terms he did business on with the nobility. His relation with the Earl of Uxbridge was not wholly typical, by virtue of their long acquaintance. Walter's attitude here varies between obviously sincere affection and gratitude to 'my best of Masr.s that dwells att Drayton, in my County of Middx', with special appreciation of the 'wise and well guarded plenty' and 'good Humour' he enjoyed there, to injured reproof and proud rebuke: 'I will allow my selfe after fforty yeares experience to bee a very ignorant Steward,' he sardonically remarks on one occasion, and on another opens his letter in high dudgeon in the following way:

If your Lordshipp, contrary to your good Sense, and Christian clemency, should deale with mee after the Example of the Ottoman Judicature, which, as I have been inform'd, is to condemne, or to acquit, according to Success, I am in more danger now, of the Sabre or ye. Silken String, than I have ever been, since I have had the Honr. of acting under your Lordshipp or your Noble father, without relaxing from, or deviating out of my Duty in the strictest sense imaginable.[84]

Good relations between Walter and Uxbridge were never long in re-asserting themselves. There seems to have been special loyalty here, and when Peter Walter the grandson was faced, less than ten years after his grandfather's death, with the probable failure of the male line of the Walters, and took the remarkable step of leaving the family estates and wealth to the heirs of the Pagets, he was probably acting in a way of which the original Peter Walter would have approved.[85]

The passage last quoted from Walter's correspondence was prompted by a rebuke from the Earl almost certainly directed against Walter's insistence upon the poverty of some of the tenants at Burton, the difficulty he had in collecting due rents, and in negotiating new leases. It is a curious fact that

[83] Ibid.

[84] Ibid., Walter to Uxbridge, 7 Aug. 1725, 23 Dec. 1732, 26 Aug. 1732.

[85] Established by the Interrogatory, c. 1769?, in the possession of the Marquess of Anglesey, which recites parts of the wills of Peter Walter senior and junior, and which was drawn up to find out whether Henry and Nicholas Bayly, heirs of the Paget family, might raise credit on their expectations under Peter Walter the younger's will. See also G.E.C., i, p. 138; and The Marquess of Anglesey, One-Leg: The Life and Letters of Henry William Paget (London, 1961), pp. 20, 346.

Walter's most common remark about tenants and labouring poor is that they are in a sad condition and can ill afford to pay their rents. In 1725 he reported that 'the Tennants wring their hands, from the generall Calamityes of the Yeare', in 1729 that 'the poverty of the people . . . is a Complaint by noo . . . meanes groundless'; in 1730 he points out Lord Uxbridge's comparative 'prosperityes' as against 'other peoples adversityes' (ie. landlords whose tenants are even more in arrears) and in 1731, in the same connection, he ominously remarks: '. . . what will become of the Landlords a Little time will Show.'[86] The gloomy tale continues, and on 19 Aug. 1732 Walter paints a picture likely to arouse both apprehension and anger in the hearts of absentee landlords: the corn crops are good, there is no shortage of grass or hay, but money is so scarce that there is 'no visible prospect to put the Tennants in a better condition than they are, and indeed they are in generall brought soo feeble that the Least blast of winde will blow them downe never to rise againe.' 'This is not your Lordshipps Case alone', Walter assures Lord Uxbridge, but every landlord must be ready to accept unpaid arrears, and not demand the annual value of their estates 'as they stand on their Rentalls'.[87] It was this letter that provoked the rebuke from Uxbridge which drew from Walter his protesting allusion to the 'Ottoman Judicature'. The kind of suspicion which may have lurked at the back of Uxbridge's mind was to be bluntly expressed by Swift, three years later, when he published his poem on stewardship, *To Mr. Gay* . . ., in which Walter was prominently attacked.

> The Tenants poor, the Hardness of the Times,
> Are ill excuses for a Servant's Crimes: [ll. 67–8]

But Walter persisted in his gloomy accounts, and on 16 Sept. 1734 even included his own manor of Stalbridge in the depressing picture:

> In this Countrey, the generall Language of the Tennants! is, Desolatõn and destructõn, and noo money for the Landlords, and the calamity indeed is soo great, and soo universall, that I am almost persuaded, to abate five shillings in the pound to every one of my Tennants. This is a certaine & undeniable truth which you are now told . . .[88]

These repeated statements of the poverty of the working people may possibly, as Swift's couplet suggests, have been made to cover up some systematic cheating of Walter's clients, which no doubt could have been done. Yet it is unlikely that Walter would want to cheat Uxbridge, to whom so many of these protestations were made. It is more probable that Walter knew what he was talking about, and wrote simply to convey his own businessman's austere and realistic assessment of the situation to a landlord who would otherwise have blamed him for the poor returns. Walter's sympathies are with the landlords,

[86] S.R.O., D 603, Walter to Uxbridge, 21 Aug. 1725, 4 Sept. 1729, 29 Aug. 1730, 3 June 1731.
[87] Ibid., Walter to Uxbridge, 19 Aug. 1732. Cf. Charles Wilson, *England's Apprenticeship 1603–1763* (London, 1965), pp. 243–6, for a discussion of the agricultural depression of the period 1720–50.
[88] Ibid., Walter to Uxbridge, 16 Sept. 1734.

and he rarely suggests or asks for any practical measures to *help* the tenants in their difficulties. The one word 'almost', in the last quotation, is significant, in view of the strong language with which the passage begins.

Walter's general lack of humanity towards working people is well demonstrated by his lack of a sense of proportion in a letter to the Earl of Uxbridge, on 31 July 1723 about a tenant who had been caught poaching fish. The pretentious generality of its opening is extraordinary:

> All government from a King to the Masr. of a family depends upon Subordination, and if nothing else was to bee considered upon the Subject of your Lre. that alone should not bee disregarded, If inferiour men should bee permitted to trample upon Superiour ones, wee should soon fall into Confusion, But to come to the point, the man that has wrongfully taken the ffish, is guilty of a breach as well of the common Law as the Statute Law, ffor hee may not onely bee punished by actōn of Trespass, but alsoe before a Justice of the peace, and the Offender being poore, I think the Latter punishment should be attempted against him, and hee may bee arrested afterwards if it shall bee thought fitt . . .[89]

The opening statement is almost identical with that traditional defence of a cosmological, theological or social *status quo*, theodicy, which Pope was to deploy with such poetic brilliance, less than ten years later, in his *Essay on Man*.[90] That it should be so disproportionately evoked here shows Walter's strength of feeling against such moderation or mercy as had apparently been proposed by Lord Uxbridge. Did it occur to Walter how easily it could have been used against his own rise to affluence and the rank of landed gentleman? Did his rigidity and severity spring from his uneasy self-awareness as a newcomer to the ranks of the 'Superiour'? The legal cat-and-mouse game with the poacher that he proposes (all the easier, 'the Offender being poore') is, to say the least, unpleasant, and suggests that the satirically exaggerated sentiments on the distresses of the poor, which Fielding put into the mouth of Peter Pounce, were not unwarranted.[91] However, this is not quite the whole story; a man is usually more complex than a satirist's representation of him. Thus when a contractor who had engaged to repair a lock at Burton for £250 found that, through no fault of his own, the cost would be no less than £350 unless Lord Uxbridge would allow him free timber to finish the job, Walter warmly took his part, and begged that Lord Uxbridge should give him what he asked. 'I am thoroughly satisfyed', he wrote, 'that Harry Haynes has been a great Sufferer, by the undertaking hee has born, and yet is engaged in, and that it has well nigh wrought his utter ruine, and I thinke hee is a very great Object of Compassion.'[92]

[89] S.R.O., D 603, Walter to Uxbridge, 13 July 1723.
[90] See especially, Epistle I, ll. 241–50; T.E., iii–i, pp. 45–6.
[91] *Joseph Andrews*, Bk. III, Ch. XIII; ed. cit., pp. 274–5.
[92] S.R.O., D 603, 24 June 1731. Walter's plea appears justified by Hayne's own excellent letter, which suggests this was a most conscientious and efficient man (see Hayne to Walter, 19 June 1731; also Thomas Hixon to Walter (?), 21 June 1731).

Peter Walter's attitude to money probably speaks for itself, through the evidence assembled above, and especially perhaps through the details from his account book.[93] One clinching quotation is all that is needed to confirm the picture. On 20 July 1725, Walter replied to a suggestion from Lord Uxbridge as to a loan of money to someone whom apparently they both held in esteem. Though the security offered was nominally sufficient Walter was not satisfied that the person's resources justified a further loan from Lord Uxbridge, nor that his credit was not already over-stretched 'There is noo body that cann have a greater tenderness and regard for the Gentleman you wrote about than my selfe, But our affectōns should never runn away with our money, unless in very particular Cases . . . if wee goo to the brinke, wee shall bee in danger of Drowning.'[94] 'Our affections should never runn away with our money'—this characteristic precept of Walter is a very adequate explanation of the almost complete lack of any reference to gifts or charities in the whole body of material relating to him which has come down to us.

Walter's attitude to the law is of interest because both Pope and Swift obviously suspected him of using his professional knowledge for his own ends, and because Pope asserted that Walter had been tried and barely acquitted for forgery, in 1737.[95] I have been unable to find evidence of this trial, but certain passages in the letters to Uxbridge throw light on whether Walter would have been capable of such a thing. It is probable that in most cases Walter was careful but not over-scrupulous. Pope reflected on Walter, and on lawyers in general, for making deliberate ommissions in the deeds they drew up.[96] We may recall here Robert Monckton's comment to Lord Oxford in 1711 on the way Walter drew up the Duke of Newcastle's will, which lends some support to what Pope says—Pope was of course familiar with the Earl of Oxford and his son and could have heard their opinion of that particular affair.[97] One is made more suspicious when one finds Walter casually remarking to Uxbridge, on 22 July 1729, 'The Deed by mistake is made in my name, and therefore I have by indorsement on it declared my selfe a Trustee for your Lordshipp which is the same thing . . .'[98] If so crucial a mistake could so easily be made, did Walter always take care to rectify it? Further suspicion is aroused by two later letters. In January 1733 Lord Uxbridge was once more complaining that his neighbours were poaching his fish. This time, however, the offenders claimed a 'Customary right' and litigation was in process. Once more Walter's tone is intense, and having advised an arrest, and the destruction of a poacher's net, he continues:

. . . for since wee are to enter into a Warre, wee are not to consider, right or wrong, But annoy the Enemy, in every particular wee can. The Bill

---

[93] His Account Book shows him to have been 'worth' £168,418. 12. 1 at Christmas 1730; H.R.O. (Gorhambury MSS.), IX. C. 136, p. 93.
[94] S.R.O., D 603, Walter to Uxbridge, 20 July 1725.
[95] 'Epilogue to the Satires', Dialogue II, l. 57n; T.E., iv, p. 315.
[96] 'The Second Satire of Dr. John Donne', ll. 99–100; T.E., iv, 141.
[97] See n. 45 above.
[98] S.R.O., D 603, Walter to Uxbridge, 22 July 1729.

against the rest, is before the Counsell, and shall be fyled as soon as conveniently may bee, and this being a mre. of great consequence, as well to power as property, ought to be well considered . . .[99]

Uxbridge evidently expressed surprise at Walter's advice and manner, and three days later Walter wrote again to explain his attitude, but by no means to retract his words:

I confess (My Lord) that it is not my usuall way to act in that violent and Hostile manner . . . But this is an extraordinary Case, and ought to be attended with the utmost Spirit and resolution, and therefore I repeat and say againe, That since wee are to enter into a Warr, . . . wee are not to consider right or wrong . . .[100]

We could not ask for a more clear example of Walter's moral attitude to the law, which was evidently, in cases where his feelings and opinions were deeply engaged, to use it purely as a weapon, and with a vigour and resolution calculated to daunt his opponents.

5. 'A GREAT MAN IN THE WEST'

The Walter-Uxbridge correspondence comes to an end in February 1739 with a letter on parliamentary affairs already quoted.[101] On 30 Aug. 1743 the Earl of Uxbridge died. There are few personal evidences of Walter for the last five or six years of his life, but his account book shows even more dramatic increases in his fortune than before. In 1740 his estate amounted to £245,155, having been £168,418.12.1. in 1730. It is thus reasonable to assume that Walter persisted in at least the less strenuous of his usual activities to the very end. His brief, last surviving letter, addressed to the new Lord Uxbridge and written on 11 May 1745, shows him still engaged in steward's business: he boasts he has raised 'very near' £120 'for ffines' at Drayton, 'in these difficult times for money', and left it 'attending your Lordshipps pleasure'; he also notes that at Iver the Duke of Marlborough, 'in Honor to your Ldshipp . . . payd me a short Visit'.[102] This last letter is totally characteristic; Walter's Ruling Passions were strong in death—for in less than a year's time, in January 1746, Walter himself was to die, at the age of 82. In that year *The Gentleman's Magazine*, reporting his death, stated his reputed fortune to be £300,000.[103] The account book gives the precise sum for Christmas 1745: £282,401—a huge sum indeed for those days.[104]

The story of Walter's life is not yet quite told, if that of his business career is complete. Though Walter acquired his country house and estate at Stalbridge as early as 1700, he seems to have looked on himself as a man of business (in

---

[99] Ibid., Walter to Uxbridge, 13 Jan. 1732/3.
[100] Ibid., Walter to Uxbridge, 16 Jan. 1732/3.
[101] See n. 68 above.
[102] S.R.O., D 603, Walter to the second Earl of Uxbridge, 11 May, 1745.
[103] *Gentleman's Magazine*, xvi (1746), p. 45.
[104] H.R.O. (Gorhambury MSS.), IX. C. 136, p. 123.

his own and others' behalf) for the greater part of his life. In his last ten years, however, perhaps because he had begun to consider what he should leave behind him after his death, he began to act as much in the role of a country gentleman as of a land steward. A sure sign of this may be found in his instructions as to his burial in the various drafts of his two wills. Sometime between 1737 and 1743 he added to the eight-page draft of his 1737 will a wish to be buried ('privately' as we have already seen) 'in my owne Isle belonging to the parish Church of Stalbridge . . . and that a comodious Vault or burreing place bee made there for the repose of my selfe and ffamiley.'[105] By 1743 he was able to refer to 'a Vault in Some Sort already made . . .'[106] His individualism was at last merging into a concern for the dignity and status of the family he had founded, and its posterity. Walter was possibly not, as the Carylls were not, among those who belonged to the established church, but he now joined the Carylls and countless other landed gentlemen whose sense of their local tradition and importance was expressed by the family vault in the local parish church. And Walter's expenditure on his Stalbridge estate was in other respects passing beyond the concern of an efficient land steward with the upkeep of a property. On 16 Sept. 1734 he had referred to his estate as '. . . the good Effect of my Long Labours and care, and the exalted joy of my minde.'[107] Stalbridge was beginning to have some sort of spiritual and aesthetic significance for him, and accordingly we find, in his account book, references to 'Building and repaireing ffarme Houses' giving way to details of work on the mansion itself:

. . . in this one yeare in new-fronting and reforming Stalbridge House 800 ll. att ye. Least [1736] . . . about 500 ll. in adorning the House and park [1737] . . . in building the new offices to Stalbridge House, makeing the new Church way . . . above 1000 ll. [1738] . . . in fitting upp the great room att Stalbridge and in severall other matters in and about the great House there, 200 ll. att Least [1741][108]

But the days of his parsimony were not gone, if one is to believe a recollection of him in his later years, printed in 1811:

A characteristic scene was described by a son of his bailiff, who, when a boy, attended his father in an evening on business at the manor-house [Stalbridge]. They found its possessor sitting without light in a small room communicating with the kitchen. On their approach he applied a dry raspberry stick to his fire, and lighted a small candle which stood on the table before him; but finding, on enquiry, that the present business required no light, he extinguished the candle, and continued the conversation in the dark. Notwithstanding his rigid parsimony he exacted the respect usually paid to opulence; for observing that the youth had continued with

[105] Ibid. IX. C. 4, f. 1.
[106] Ibid. IX. C. 9a, f. 1.
[107] S.R.O., D 603, Walter to Uxbridge, 16 Sept. 1734.
[108] H.R.O. (Gorhambury MSS.), IX. C. 136, pp. 105, 107, 109, 115.

his hat on, supposing no extraordinary deference due to the great man's
appearance, he rated him violently for his rusticity and inattention.

Though stated to be from an undoubted authority, this anecdote has all the
quality of folklore.[109]

It was not only from his bailiff's boy that Walter required deference, but
from all his neighbours landed and poor alike. Landed and poor alike they
resented it. Thus when, sometime before June 1739, Walter 'took upon him
to Inclose severall parts & parcells of the Waste or Commons' of Stalbridge,
'In prejudice of the Freeholders & other Tennants . . . who are Intituled to
the Herbage & Pasture', his indignant neighbours broke in and asserted
their traditional rights, damaging trees, hedges, fences and a great deal of
grass in the process, all of which Walter carefully enumerated and valued
when he filed his writ of trespass against them in the Court of Common Pleas
at Westminster.[110] One may imagine Walter's attitude from his comments
to Lord Uxbridge on similar situations; what the defendants felt about it is
well expressed in one of the statements of the case prepared for the assizes at
Dorchester:

> The Plaintiffe Mr. Walter is a great man in the west and particularly in
> and about *Stalbridge* & will do what he pleases and will not bear Contra-
> diction as he is Lord of the mannor of Stalbridge he will have the absolute
> direction of everything in the parish, tho' there are other Men in the parish
> of Moderate Fortunes and who have property's to look after within that
> parish . . . & altho' the Deft. Mr. Weston hath a good Estate in that Parish
> & in the Plts. Mannor, & hath Right of Common on the waste of the said
> Mannor, the plt. will not Consult or have any regard to his interest, but will
> inclose any part of the Common at his pleasure . . .[111]

The case was taken most seriously by both sides, the chief defendant, Thomas
Weston, joining with two tenants of the manor to bear the necessary expense.[112]
The case was tried in Dorchester in July 1743; who won we do not know,
but the enclosure of the Common went on in accordance with a complicated
system of allotments, which may have been a consequence of the trial. It is
ironical to observe that in 1751 Peter Walter the younger joined with Thomas
Weston and his mother to maintain this system against possible infringement
by the tenants of the manor and by another local landowner.[113]

What of the family to whom Walter was to leave the splendid inheritance
he had built up through (in the words of his will) 'God's Providence & my
own constant Labours'?[114] It is hard to get a detailed picture of Walter's

[109] Cobbett, ix, 482n.
[110] Somerset Record Office, Walker Heneage MSS. DD/WHh 550 (Statement witnessed by
Thomas Weston, Samuel Cave and James Banger, 29 March 1741).
[111] Ibid. 550, f. 2b.
[112] See n. 110 above.
[113] Somerset Record Office, Walker Heneage MSS. DD/WHh 550 (Agreement between Peter
Walter the younger and Betty Weston of Hargrove, July 1751).
[114] H.R.O. (Gorhambury MSS.), IX. C. 9a.

family, before the generation of his grandchildren, and his own parentage, as we have seen, is obscure. He is, however, stated to have married Diana, niece of Richard Newman, Esq., of Fifehead Magdalen in Dorset, and it is reasonable to connect this Newman with the Richard Newman who appears in the draft court book of Drayton, Harmondsworth and Iver to have been Lord Paget's steward in these manors before Walter himself.[115] From this marriage Walter seems to have had one son, Paget Walter, who died in his father's lifetime. If a reference to 'My Boy' in a letter of Nov. 1733 is to Paget Walter, then he cannot have been, as sometimes stated, an only child, but must (as the letter makes clear) have had at least two sisters.[116] The 1737 draft will makes no mention of him so he is likely to have died between 1733 and 1737. Paget Walter married Elizabeth, sister of Sheldon Mervyn, Esq., of Marston, Dorset, whose family estate was at some stage purchased by Peter Walter. Paget Walter had three sons and four daughters, one of whom, Jane Walter, was born in 1710, which suggests that Peter Walter's own marriage cannot have been much later than 1690.[117] Of Peter Walter's three grandsons, the eldest was born in 1717 and was named after his grandfather. He was Walter's principal heir in all three wills, with remainder to his sons, then to the next grandson, Edward, and his sons, then to the third grandson, Sheldon, and his, after which his estates and possessions were to 'descend & go as the Law shall direct' (in the 1737 will, however, each of his grand-daughters was mentioned in turn).[118] The family looked thriving enough when the grand-father died, yet none of the grandsons had a son. The failure of Peter Walter the younger to provide one may have convinced him that his brothers would fail likewise, though each, like him, had a daughter. In his will, which he made in 1752 the year before his death, he left the Walter estates (after the assumed death of his brother Edward without a male heir) to the heirs of the Paget family, with which the Walter fortune seems to have begun.[119]

But all this was hidden from the eyes of old Peter Walter. By 4 May 1745 his last will and codicil had been drawn up, his affairs were in order, and he could wait for death. No family could have been better established in the world, by one man's work, than his, and he looked forward to the increase of the Walter estates and wealth under his grandchildren—his will provided that they might lease any of the family properties (excepting Stalbridge itself) for 'the best & Utmost rent that can be had & obtained for the Same'.[120] The

[115] E. C. Waters, 'The Walters of Surrey, Temp. George II', *The Herald and Genealogist*, ed. G. C. Nichols (London, 1874), viii, pp. 1–3. Greater London Record Office (Middlesex Records), ACC. 446/M20 (April 1684–April 1693). Cf. Romney Sedgwick, ed. *The Commons, 1715–54*, ii, p. 517.

[116] S.R.O., D 603, Walter to Uxbridge, 22 Nov. 1733.

[117] For the Walter genealogy, see E. C. Waters, art. cit.; for the sale to Walter of the Mervyn estate, John Hutchins, *The History and Antiquities of the County of Dorset* (3rd. edn., Westminster, 1868), iv, p. 74; J. J. Howard, art. cit. (n. 25 above) for Jane Walter.

[118] H.R.O. (Gorhambury MSS.), IX. C. 9a, f. 3; IX. C. 9b, f. 2; IX. C. 4 (draft of the 1737 will), ff. 2–5.

[119] See n. 85 above.

[120] H.R.O. (Gorhambury MSS.), IX. C. 9a, ff. 2–3.

proviso was totally characteristic, and lends force to the last stroke of Pope's prose portrait of the man:

> . . . a person not only eminent in the wisdom of his profession as a dextrous attorney, but allow'd to be a good, if not a safe, conveyancer; extremely respected by the Nobility of this land, tho' free from all manner of luxury and ostentation: his Wealth was never seen, and his bounty never heard of . . . therefore the taxing of this gentleman with any Ambition, is certainly a great wrong to him.[121]

An accurate enough picture, though the three wills show a few softening touches. Those who were familiar with the contents of his final will, however, must have been edified by at least one generous sentiment, for he gave to whichever of his grandsons should first succeed him at Stalbridge £1,000 'the better to enable him to keep his house and to be indulgent to his Tenants . . .'[122] His bounty, also, was not quite unheard of in the end, for from the near £300,000 he was worth when he died, he bequeathed 'to the Poor People of Stalbridge and also to the Poor People of Hanley ffive pounds to each of those places to be distributed as my executors shall think fit . . .'[123]

The evidence here assembled affords a fuller and more balanced picture of Peter Walter than the attacks of the satirists. The chief characteristics which emerge are determination, industry and efficiency, backed by shrewd, independent and often sardonic judgement. (It is a minor but rewarding fact that this judgement often issues, in his letters, into highly effective satirical prose.) But the features which the satirists attacked are also found in the evidence, sometimes abundantly so: the relentless accumulation of wealth on a truly staggering scale; the almost equally staggering parsimony; the solemn, confident, didactic manner. Professional crookedness, by its very nature, is a quality difficult for the historian to verify; and Walter was no fool. Yet there is, from several different sources including Walter's own private letters to Lord Uxbridge, sufficient evidence to render this charge plausible, and to prove that as a general rule he pressed his financial advantage to the last possible degree with neither charity nor compassion. He was a man with a hard heart, prepared to use power ruthlessly. Yet he could show compassion, rarely; and when, at the end of his life, he called his manor 'the exalted joy of his minde' material and selfish considerations are strangely mingled with something different. Much of this picture—indeed possibly more than can be recovered today—Pope was in a position to know. As in the case of his knowledge of Kyrle, he had friends who could give him reliable information: Lord Digby, Lord Oxford, Lord Bolingbroke, above all perhaps the Earl of Burlington, who was familiar enough with Walter to get 'detestably drunke with sweet punch' in his presence 'and next day very deservedly Sicke'. Pope was well

---

[121] T.E., iii–ii, p. 102 (*To Bathurst*, l. 102n.).

[122] H.R.O. (Gorhambury MSS.), IX. C. 9a, f. 2.

[123] Ibid. f. 3. In the draft will of 1737 (IX, C. 4, f. 6) he had proposed to give £20, equally divided, to the poor of these two parishes, but only to such as were not already 'upon the common reliefe of the parishes'. Cf. *Joseph Andrews*, Bk. III, Ch. XIII; ed. cit., p. 275.

aware why Walter was 'extremely respected by the Nobility'; it was because he helped them wring the utmost from their land. He also knew, no doubt, why despite or because of this Walter had developed a reputation for sharp practice.

In his concern with Peter Walter, Pope was concerned with a man whose career was intimately involved in the characteristic economic life of eighteenth-century England: lands, labour, crops, rents, and the slowly developing industrial revolution (coal mines, the iron trade, the navigability of rivers). It seems likely that his significance in his time lies in his ability to put large estates onto an efficient and ruthless capitalistic basis. It was a career equally involved with the paperwork of landed wealth: accounts, leases, wills, deeds of all kinds, marriage treaties and lawsuits; and with the political administration of that 'great man', Walpole, whose chief aim was to allow this economic life to develop in conditions of stability. In Kyrle Pope found and praised an example of creative charity whose very peculiarity and remoteness strengthened its appeal. In Kyrle, so far as Pope was concerned, ideal and practice met—on a miniature scale but with potent suggestion. In Caryll he knew and praised a man who, for all his multifarious material preoccupations, had his sights, intermittently at least, on something beyond: 'the Gloryes of a future Day'—or the exacting will of Heaven. To Pope Caryll promised to be, and partly was, the meeting of ideal and practice on a greater scale. But Caryll's resources, his handicaps, the social and political orientation of his family, all combined to prevent his complete fulfilment of Pope's social ideal. The Carylls were swimming against the tide. Walter, on the other hand, swam tirelessly with the tide and all the strongest currents of his time. Yet against him Pope, for reasons and with results to be considered more fully in a later chapter, most implacably opposed his pen.

V. 'Christian Nobleman': William, fifth Baron Digby of Geashill (1662–1752)

1. YOUTH AND BACKGROUND

AMONG the noble clients of Peter Walter was William, Lord Digby. In Spring 1683, then twenty one and the younger son of an old Warwickshire landed family, he was on his travels in France. He had graduated from Magdalen College, Oxford, two years earlier, and it was to a Fellow of Magdalen College, Dr. Thomas Smith, that he wrote a number of letters from France which have survived.[1] These letters, often pedestrian, nevertheless give insights into the character and interests of their writer; he comments on the disappointing weather, apologises for having little to say, but is nevertheless a dutiful sight-seer.[2] Two leagues from Blois he visits the house of Beau-regard, belonging to the Queen's Chancellor, where there are pictures of 'all ye famous men of Europe that have lived these severall hundred years'; he sees two aquaducts 'still of great use to ye town' of Blois, and agrees with Smith that they must be 'Roman-work; for few such things have been made since'.[3] At Angers, in October, he notes that 'this town . . . was famous for giving rise & name to ye Hugenots' and seeks out 'with much adoe' St. Hugo's Gate, finding it at 'ye entrance into ye town, not known to ye common people by that name'.[4] He is a great collector of inscriptions, several of which he forwards to his correspondent, with comments such as: '. . . ye meaning of it I leave to you learned to find out.'[5] By the Winter he is in Paris and with other English gentlemen visits the Louvre 'to see ye K's pictures which are delicately fine . . . There are a great many of Raphiells, one of them valued at 2000,000[?] crowns . . . & a thousand others, too many to name, of all ye famous hands of the world.' He attends a ceremony in memory of the Queen-mother at Mansart's chapel of Val de Grace ('ye finest chapell I ever saw'); he describes the service in some detail and with apparent admiration ('ye Nuns sung most delicately . . .'), until a very English voice breaks in: 'I cannot describe ye foppery I saw there; insomuch yt. I fancied them rather showing tricks than

---

[1] Bodleian Library, MS. Smith. 49, ff. 17–40 (14 May 1683–22 April 1684).
[2] Ibid. ff. 27, 29.
[3] Ibid. f. 29.
[4] Ibid. f. 31.
[5] Ibid. f. 35.

WILLIAM L.D DIGBY
YOVNGEST SON TO
KILDARE L.D DIGBY.

4. Sir Godfrey Kneller, *William*, *Fifth Lord Digby*. By kind permission of the Rt. Hon. Simon Wingfield Digby, M.P.

at their prayers.'[6] The final letter, written from Paris in the Spring of the following year, describes with enthusiasm 'a mathematicall instrument . . . lately invented; it is very commode for travelling . . . it . . . serves for Demi-circle, sector, square, measuring all sorts of angles wtsoever, taking ye weight of bullets . . .' and many other uses. He proposes to take it with him to Dijon, where he will stay, before he departs for Geneva.[7] The writer of these letters was certainly a conscientious correspondent; one would say his character was not yet strongly formed, though he had it in him to be moved by works of art; clearly his strong concern was with religion.

Digby's family had, during the previous century, raised itself from gentry to nobility and wealth by serving the court and by two judicious and successful marriages. As the result of the first, the younger branch of the family had become Earls of Bristol and been granted the confiscated estates of Sir Walter Ralegh at Sherborne in Dorset. As a result of the second, the elder branch possessed large Irish estates, and its head, William's elder brother Simon, held the title of Baron Digby of Geashill in the Kingdom of Ireland.[8] Despite the pull of these Irish estates, however, the family's old bond with its manor of Coleshill in Warwickshire had been slowly re-asserting itself; both father and grandfather of William had died and been buried in Dublin, but his eldest brother had been M.P. for Warwick and had died (aged twenty three) at Coleshill, where both his mother and the present Baron Digby now lived.[9] A further marriage alliance had recently been contracted; on 27 Aug. 1683 his brother Simon had married Frances Noel, eldest daughter of the Earl of Gainsborough.

It is doubtful whether William continued his travels into Switzerland as he intended. Had he done so, further letters to Dr. Smith would probably have been found, for he had promised to write from Geneva.[10] A reason for an early return home may have been the death in childbirth, on 29 Sept. 1684 of his brother's young wife, little more than a year after her marriage. But whatever the case, he returned to face fifteen years crowded with some of the most difficult moral, political and religious decisions of seventeenth-century English history, by no means all of them happy, in which as an earnest man he could not but think his own part important and hard to play.

Public events began to move with the death, on 6 Feb. 1685, of King Charles II. The accession of the Roman Catholic James was received by the nation with a show of loyalty and obedience inconceivable five years earlier.

---

[6] Ibid. f. 37.

[7] Ibid. f. 39.

[8] John Digby (1586–1653) was created Earl of Bristol by James I in 1622, in reward for his (ultimately unsuccessful) services, as ambassador to Spain, in forwarding the proposed marriage treaty between Prince Charles and the Spanish Infanta (G.E.C., ii, p. 320). William's great-grandfather, Sir Robert Digby of Coleshill, had married Lettice, *suo jure* Baroness Offaley, heir of Gerald FitzGerald last Earl of Kildare; while his grandfather had allied the family, by his first marriage in 1626, with Richard Boyle, fifth Earl of Corke (G.E.C., iv, p. 353).

[9] G.E.C., iv, pp. 353–4.

[10] Bodleian Library, MS. Smith. 49, f. 40.

Yet naturally both 'Whigs' and 'Tories' had their misgivings. Such misgivings
are reflected in the two proposed votes of thanks with which, in May 1685,
James's parliament sought to reply to the monarch's promise to maintain the
government in church and state. The first affirmed that parliament would
stand by James 'with their lives and fortunes' in defence of the Church of
England, and requested him to put into execution the penal laws against all
recusants. Apprised that such a motion would hardly be acceptable to him,
parliament framed a second resolution wholly accepting the king's 'gracious
word, and repeated Declaration, to support and defend the Religion of the
Church of England, as it is now by law established ...'[11] At this point,
according to the testimony of Thomas Bray, a clergyman well acquainted
with the Digby family, Simon Lord Digby, one of the members for Warwick
Town, intervened and 'standing up, mov'd, That those most Remarkable
Words might be added, *which is dearer to us, than our Lives*; which coming
from so Young a Gentleman, just Return'd from his Travels, as it drew the
Eyes and Admiration of the whole House upon him, and was agreed to without Demur; So it drew the Frowns of the Court ...'[12] There is no reason to
doubt this account; certainly the motion finally adopted contains the additional
clause.[13] But one must understand the meaning of the resolution. It has in
fact no threat in it; the king's promise is accepted unequivocally ('acquiesce,
and entirely rely, and rest wholly satisfied' are the words used); absolute
loyalty to both church and throne are affirmed in a way which only the doctrine
of Passive Obedience could pretend to reconcile.

This doctrine was a vital part of the religious and intellectual background
of Simon and William Digby, both at Magdalen College where the career of
William's correspondent Dr. Thomas Smith was shortly to display the most
scrupulous observance of it, and at Coleshill where in 1682 Simon had appointed to his Rectory John Kettlewell, a Yorkshireman who was to gain
renown for the saintliness of his life and the integrity with which he adhered
to his religious and political principles.[14] Three months after Simon Digby's
intervention in the Commons, Kettlewell preached a sermon at Coleshill on
the text: '*Render unto Cæsar the Things that are Cæsar's Render unto God, the
Things which are God's.*'[15] It is probable that both William and Simon heard
this sermon; since (under the title of *The Religious Loyalist*) it was subsequently published, they certainly knew it.[16] It affords a clear statement of the
spirit which guided the attitude of so many Anglican clergymen to James II,

[11] David Ogg, *England in the Reigns of James II and William III* (Oxford, 1955), pp. 143–4;
Cobbett, iv, 1358.
[12] Thomas Bray, *A Brief Account of the Life of the Reverend Mr. John Rawlet* (London, 1728),
np. Bray regarded the clause as a warning to James, but I think it can only be understood in the
terms I here suggest.
[13] *Commons Journals*, ix, p. 721; Cobbett, loc. cit.
[14] Simon had preceded William at Magdalen College (G.E.C., iv, p. 354). For Kettlewell, see
T. T. Carter, *The Life and Times of John Kettlewell* (London, 1895); and the life included in *A
Compleat Collection of the Works of John Kettlewell* (London, 1719), i (pp. 1–88).
[15] Matthew 22:21; Kettlewell, op. cit., i, p. 806. The date of the sermon was 28 Aug. 1685.
[16] Kettlewell, op. cit., i, pp. 806–15.

and which on the accession of William lent vigour to the Non-Juror movement. Kettlewell's position is an uncompromising one; he interprets his text in the following way: 'That we pay all due Respect and Obedience to our Prince, whatever Religion he be of; so that *the Pretence of Religion must never make us ill Subjects* . . . That at the same time we reserve all due Service and Subjection to Almighty God; so that when Princes happen to err in Religion, *the Pretence of Loyalty must never draw us to embrace their Errors, and become irreligious.*'[17] If a king proves despotic (Kettlewell argues) and commands what is unlawful, his subjects 'may claim their *legal Privileges*'; if these fail they may 'have recourse to *Prayers* and *Tears*' but if force alone promises success, the redressing of the injustice must be left to God. 'Rebellion is a thing, which no Necessity can excuse . . .' and he quotes Saint Paul: '*They that resist . . . shall receive to themselves Damnation*, Rom. 13:2', where the force to be resisted was not Roman Catholic but pagan persecution. Mention is made of the Emperor Nero, and Kettlewell's congregation is implicitly reminded that James is at least a Christian prince.[18] The theme of charity to other branches of the Christian church is, in fact, a prominent one in this sermon, second in importance only to the necessity for loyalty.

> Let not your Zeal for Protestancy bereave you of your Loyalty or Christianity, and make you forget either your Duty to your Governors, or that Charity which you owe your Neighbours; even those who are most opposite in Religion to yourselves. This is to act by a Primitive Spirit like sincere servants of Christ, and true members of the *Church of England*; to whose eternal Honour it may be said, that the Clergy, and true members of it, beyond what is ordinary in other Churches, are careful to shew a just and well-govern'd Zeal for Almighty God, as dare not fly in the Face of the King, or be unchristianly violent against their Brethren for God's Sake. They are, and by their principles should be zealous against Popery. But at the same time they are zealous against Rebellion and Disloyalty, one of the most mischievous Things in Popery, and against all Unchristian Usage, and Uncharitableness towards men of different Persuasions, which the unbridled Zeal of Papists and Sectaries too commonly transports them to.[19]

Such was the attitude preached at Coleshill to the problems raised by the accession of a Roman Catholic prince to the throne of Britain. Since Kettlewell had been at Coleshill and familiar with his patron since 1682, and had no doubt often expressed his views on this subject, it is probable that the arguments of *The Religious Loyalist* were those which prompted Simon Digby's intervention in the Commons. It is certain that William Digby, who thought highly of the works of Kettlewell,[20] must have been influenced by his views as he faced the difficult political choices created by the reign of James, the Revolution, and the accession of William III.

---

[17] Ibid., p. 808.
[18] Ibid., p. 810.
[19] Kettlewell, op. cit., ii, p. 814.
[20] Birmingham Reference Library, Digby 'B' 137 (William Digby to Sir Clement Fisher, 1686), f.2.

2. THE NEW LORD DIGBY

Simon Digby and John Kettlewell are likely to have been chief among those who helped to mould the character and opinions of William during the years of his young manhood. One of his surviving prayers closely resembles *The Religious Loyalist* in sentiment, and partly for this reason may perhaps be dated within the reign of James.[21] He prays for 'ye holy Cath: Ch: yt thou wouldst give all Xtians grace to live according to yt doctrine they profess, & teach ym yt great mark of Xrists followers to be loving and Charitable one towards another. Show us all whch is ye true way . . .' He beseeches God to 'be particularly kind to ye country in whch I live and to ye Church of which I own my self a member (ye Ch: of Engl.)', to grant her peace and unity, and prevent her members from being satisfied with 'the bare profession of a pure doctrine, whilst our lives are a scandale to it . . .' Finally he prays for 'our King', asking for him to be blessed with 'wisdome, righteousness and prosperity', and so down the ranks of a hierarchically conceived society to 'the lower rank of men in these Kingdoms'.[22]

The partnership of patron and clergyman between Simon Digby and John Kettlewell had not been limited to their common approach to the political and the religious problems which were raised by there being a Roman Catholic monarch. Kettlewell had been appointed by Simon as 'the very best Pastor he could get'.[23] The subsequent amity and esteem between the two men bore fruit in two immediate ways: one symbolic, the other practical. In the belief that it was the duty of the Church of England to display 'Catholic Charity', rather than sectarian exclusiveness, to other branches of the Christian religion, they chose to make a public affirmation of the sacrament as the core of their faith. Simon made a gift to Coleshill church of a new set of communion plate, and (which shows that this was not an insignificant event at the time) Sancroft, Archbishop of Canterbury, officiated at the dedication and first use of the gift.[24] That was in 1685, the year in which Kettlewell twice preached passive obedience, once at the accession of James, once on the defeat of Monmouth.[25] More practical was Simon's determination to return to Coleshill Church the impropriated great tithes of the parish, which had since the Reformation been a part of his 'Paternal Estate', and which were worth over £100 a year.[26] In this decision Simon was obeying the injunction of Charles II, on his restoration, who had requested nobility and gentry to

---

[21] Several prayers and meditations preserved in the Digby 'B' Collection, in the B.R.L. can be ascribed to William Digby, on the grounds that: (1) they are recognizably in the same hand as that of his signed holograph letters; and (2) one of them (Digby 'B' 153/5: 'Meditations for ye Sacrament', Section 3) makes clear reference, in the first person, to his own circumstances. These items are 153/1 (which seems to link with *The Religious Loyalist*) 153/3, 153/4 and 153/5. Other items, such as the eleven 'Christian and Moral Maxims' (153/8), may be ascribed to Digby, but less surely.

[22] B.R.L., Digby 'B', 153/1.

[23] Bray, op. cit., np.

[24] Kettlewell, op. cit., i, pp. 56–8.

[25] Ibid., pp. 56, 33, 39.

[26] White Kennett, *The Case of Impropriations* . . . (London, 1704), pp. 427–8.

restore impropriated tithes to their churches, in order that the Anglican
Ministry might in this respect be truly established, and so many ill-endowed
livings be less dependent upon the conscience of patrons.[27] Between 1660
and 1685 few secular landowners had acceded to this request. Simon had,
however, made a study of the matter, and was convinced; no doubt Kettlewell
encouraged him with his usual candour and earnestness, though we are told
that he was diffident to press for a decision which would benefit himself.[28]
Simon's pious design went forward, but death prevented him seeing its fulfilment. He died, aged only twenty eight, on 19 Jan. 1686, less than two years
after his young wife, leaving £500 to the poor of the parish of Coleshill, and a
paper in which he requested his brother William, now the fifth Baron Digby,
to complete his design for the restoration of the tithes.[29] Thus, as Thomas
Bray put it, having 'laid up by these and a Multitude of other good Works,
Treasures so great in Heaven', Simon was called 'to enjoy the same', leaving
behind him the reputation of a patron who knew how 'to Protect as well as
Bestow a Church', and of a man whom Kettlewell, in his dedication to William
of the funeral sermon, could praise as 'that most dear, and exemplary Saint,
your deceased Brother'.[30]

His brother's death made a deep impression on the new Lord Digby. His
reaction was conventional, religious, and plainly deeply sincere. In the draft
of a letter he wrote to Sir Clement Fisher of Packington, 'soon after my Brothers
death', the rather dutiful tone of the tourist has changed to one of strong
evangelical earnestness. In the following words William passes on to Sir
Clement the message of his dead brother:

When he had ye vast concerns of his future state upon him, he nevertheless
thought upon you; & having then a lively idea of a peacable, and of an
accusing conscience, he Desired his old friend might know wt remorse he
felt from ye former part of his life, & wt satisfaction & comfort from ye
latter. You know very well how he spent both & therfore will easily understand this wthout a comment. Yet give me leave to put you in mind of
something whch perhaps you may not reflect upon, and I have yt confidence in yr good temper yt I dare speake freely as becomes a freind . . .
you were an intimate companion of my poor Brothers in ye former & worst
pt. of his life & you were no less so in ye latter. Consider him in both—
& see in which he is most amiable and fittest to be imitated; & you will presently blame your self for having made the worst choice . . .

He hastens to add that he does not deny Sir Clement's 'visible reformation'
and achievement of 'a sober settled way of life' but he doubts its full religious
motivation. He therefore recommends daily prayer and meditation, the
reading of 'good books such as the Wh[ole]: D[uty]. of M[an], Mr. Kettlewell's
& ye like' and keeping 'always a sense of religion in your thoughts.'

[27] Ibid., pp. 153–5.
[28] Bray, op. cit., np.; Kennett, op. cit., pp. 427–8.
[29] Kennett, op. cit., pp. 427–8.
[30] Bray, op. cit., np.; Kettlewell, op. cit., i, p. 790.

It is a great prejudice most men have against religion, that they think it a morose sort of thing, yt is not consistent wth ye pleasures & diversions of this world, I mean those we call innocent, such as bowling, hunting, shooting and ye like . . . all religion forbids is ye spending too much of our time and thoughts upon them; whch are cheifly to be employed about more useful things . . . Dear Sr C., forgive me if I have offended in wt I have said, and believe . . . that it proceeds from a more yn ordinary zeal & love I have for you . . .[31]

The interest of this letter is not chiefly in the light it throws on an unsuspected aspect of Simon's character (however it may prompt speculation on the doings of 'that most dear, and exemplary Saint' in the London of Wilmot, Earl of Rochester's last years) but rather in the way it shows the character of William, in a moment of intimacy and earnestness, to have assumed substance and form. Plainly his concern with religion is much more than a merely outward thing; he seems to have thrown his whole being into the letter, and though he is anxious not to offend he does not fear to speak out. If there is immaturity here it is perhaps in his high degree of innocent zeal.

Less than a month after the death of Simon Digby, Rachel Russell, Countess of Bedford, mentioned in her correspondence that she had

just dated my letter to my Lady Digby, of Coleshal, writ in answer to hers, by which she desires me, in pursuance of a dying brother's advice, and her son's inclination, to propose to Lord Gainsborough a marriage between the present Lord [ie. William Digby] and Lady Jane. I have done it . . . the proposition is accepted; my Lord declares himself willing to do all he can for his children; he offers 8000l. paid as with the last, and leaves out the 2000l. coming back, if Lord Campden should happen to dye . . .[32]

Thus, following his brother's advice, William sought in marriage the younger sister of that brother's deceased wife. The marriage was rapidly arranged and soon celebrated; the licence from the Vicar General is dated 22 May 1686, William being twenty four and his young wife nineteen years of age, and sixteen months later Lady Russell is able to write 'I had, as you guess, Doctor, the satisfaction of seeing Lady Digby, and her prosperous son, and hope she will maintain that house with an honourable and virtuous race.'[33] The last surviving son of a family, whose sons seemed prone to dying in their twenties or before, was now blessed with a male heir; the future of the family looked secure again. Yet the short career of this son, John Digby, was to be far from prosperous.

3. THE LOYALIST'S PREDICAMENT

While these happy domestic events were taking place in the Digby family

---

[31] B.R.L., Digby 'B' 137.

[32] *The Letters of Lady Rachel Russell*, ed. T. Sellwood (London, 1773), p. 56 (Lady Russell to Dr. Fitzwilliam, 15 Feb. 1685/6).

[33] G.E.C., iv, 354; *Letters of Lady . . . Russell*, p. 86 (22 Oct. 1687).

James II was mismanaging his kingdoms. Supported by the scrupulously loyal yet increasingly stoical Kettlewell, Digby must have watched with disquiet the steadily worsening situation of the royal government.[34] One significant episode must have engaged his particular concern, since it involved his old College, a number of personal friends, and a principle of vital importance to the maintenance of the Church of England. This was James's attempt to appoint a Roman Catholic as President of Magdalen College.[35] On 26 March 1687, William's friend Dr. Thomas Smith was visited by Dr. Younger, another Fellow of Magdalen, and also acquainted with Digby as the letters from France show.[36] Younger apprised Smith of the death of the President of the College, as yet not formally announced, declared his own decision not to stand, and advised Smith 'to look after the Presidentship, to use . . . interest in Court to procure it, and take time by the forelock.'[37] All this Dr. Smith proceeded to do, only to find that the King required a candidate 'favourable to his religion'. Smith's scrupulously correct declaration that he would advance piety and learning, keep men loyal to throne and government, and promote 'true Catholic Christianity'[38] was not sufficient for James, whose Papist advisers prompted him to recommend instead a profligate young Roman Catholic convert, Anthony Farmer, who was ineligible according to the statutes of the College. Finding the royal condition unacceptable, Smith was active in petitioning the King for a different recommendation, though when the Fellows, taking their stand upon the statutes, proposed to defy the royal *mandamus*, he advised them to defer the election.[39] Nevertheless, when they rejected this advice, he took his place and joined with them in the regular and statutable election of Dr. John Hough, chaplain to the Duke of Ormonde.[40] The rest of the story is well known: the government's support for Farmer, then Parker, Bishop of Oxford, then Bonaventura Gifford, on the one hand; on the other Dr. Hough's defiance of the Ecclesiastical Commission because 'we have a Religion to defend';[41] finally James's capitulation as his political situation deteriorated. Throughout these events Smith acted with scrupulous rectitude, deferring always a little more to the throne than the majority of his colleagues, yet never yielding a principle.[42] His conduct might have been modelled on *The Religious Loyalist*.

Two points may be made about William Digby and the Magdalen College episode. Firstly, William must have been aware of every stage of the crisis, and in particular of James's demeanour towards the College. In the late Summer of 1687 James made a tour which took him through Warwick, where

[34] Kettlewell, op. cit., i, pp. 79, 110–11.
[35] See David Ogg, op. cit., pp. 183–5; and J. R. Bloxam, *Magdalen College and James II, 1686–88* (Oxford, 1886).
[36] Bodleian Library, MS. Smith. 49, ff. 29, 37.
[37] Bloxam, op. cit., p. 3 (Dr. Smith's Narrative).
[38] Ibid., p. 4.
[39] Ibid., pp. xii–xiii.
[40] Ibid., pp. xiii–xiv.
[41] Ibid., p. xx.
[42] Ibid., pp. xiii, xxiii.

William may have seen him, and ended in Oxford where he attempted to intimidate the Fellows into admitting Parker to the Presidency.[43] His remarks on this occasion display all the mindless bullying of self-obsessed authority: '. . . you have always been a stubborn & turbulent Coll., . . . you have affronted me, know I am yr. K., & I will be obey'd . . . goe, get you gone, & elect me ye Bp of O forthwith, or else ye shall know wht it is to feel ye weight of a Ks hand . . .'[44] It was acquiescence in the face of such brainless bluster as this that the exacting doctrine of Passive Obedience required. Secondly, William was not only friendly with Dr. Smith and Dr. Younger, but probably also with Dr. Hough himself. They were certainly to become friends later.[45] The Magdalen College affair could not have been better calculated to bring out the full implications of Passive Obedience and test adherence to it. William must have been exercised whether to approve the scrupulous loyalty of his friend Smith, or that crucial extra degree of defiance in defence of the Church of England that Dr. Hough so spiritedly and successfully displayed. Precisely where William himself stood must be assessed in the light of his subsequent career, but it is of interest that Pope, as much as fifty years later, celebrated the names of Digby and Hough for their integrity, respectively for and against the Stuart cause.[46]

James's departure into exile in 1688 meant an intensification of rather than release from conflict for men of Digby's position and theological viewpoint. To the more unworldly simplicity of Kettlewell there could be no doubt; 'Better all the world be angry with me, than God and my own Conscience', and he resigned his cure, presumably soon after the passing of the Bill of Rights with its insistence on an oath of allegiance to William and Mary. With him resigned Mr. Jacomb, master of the free-school at Coleshill, and Mr. Digby Bull, rector of the nearby parish of Sheldon.[47] According to one source, Lord Digby, who had not yet legally completed the restoration of the great tithes to Coleshill Church, revoked his intention so that he might help support Kettlewell and another non-juring clergyman.[48] Kettlewell, nevertheless, ended his days in comparative poverty in London, busy with controversial writings, and with helping Robert Nelson compose his *Festivals and Fasts*.[49] He died on 12 April 1695, aged only forty two, and was buried at All Hallows Church, Barking, where the deprived Bishop Ken, a fellow Non-Juror, officiated at his funeral.[50]

[43] Ogg, op. cit., p. 184.
[44] Bloxam, op. cit., pp. 85–6.
[45] Hough, a Warwickshire man who was to marry the sister of Digby's friend Sir Clement Fisher of Packington, (Montagu Burrows, ed. *Oxford Historical Society Collectanea*, Second Series, (Oxford, 1890), pp. 402–3), composed the epitaph for Digby's mother in 1692 (John Wilmot, *The Life of . . . The Rev. John Hough* (London, 1812), p. 81); R. Smallbroke, *Some Account of . . . Dr. Hough* (London, 1743), p. 15, was later to refer to Hough's 'antient friendship' with that 'truly Honourable Lord'.
[46] T.E., iv, p. 326 (l. 240n.).
[47] Kettlewell, op. cit., i, p. 93; ii (Appendix), p. ix.
[48] Carter, op. cit., p. 153.
[49] Kettlewell, op. cit., i, pp. 170–3.
[50] Ibid., p. 187.

For Digby it was not so simple. On 22 Jan. 1689, having been elected a member for Warwick, he took his place in William's Convention, summoned to debate the constitutional situation.[51] He was thus a member of the parliament which, in offering the throne to William and Mary, imposed upon the clergy the oaths which prompted men such as Kettlewell and Thomas Smith to become Non-Jurors, and to consider themselves 'the Communion of the truly Catholick and Faithful Remnant of the *Britanick* Churches'.[52] Bearing in mind Kettlewell's influence upon him, it is not surprising to find Digby among those who at first voted that William be declared merely regent.[53] In the end he evidently acquiesced, outwardly, in William's accession, though James's defeat was by no means to be taken for granted. On 6 Feb. William dissolved his first parliament, on the 15th James left St. Germains to join his supporters in Ireland, where Digby had extensive estates. On March 20, King William's second parliament assembled, Digby being once more returned for Warwick.[54] On 7 May he was attainted, along with some 400 other nobles and gentlemen, by James's Irish Parliament in Dublin, from which he was of course absent. His inclusion in this Act of Attainder was perhaps not inevitable. If we may believe Thomas Bray, James granted Digby's Barony of Geashill to one Sir Patrick Trant, 'an obscure Fellow, but a Favourite', whereupon a noble who thought he had sufficient credit with James interposed, and asked him 'to revoke that Grant, in favour of Lord Digby, and to expunge him out of those Proscrib'd'. James refused, according to Bray, because he remembered unfavourably Simon Digby's intervention in the Commons in 1685.[55] If this story be true, it is interesting first because such an episode would be bound to dispose Digby against James to some degree, whatever his religious principles, and secondly because it shows that Digby had a friend at the court of James who thought himself powerful, and who considered Digby potentially well-disposed to the Jacobite cause.

Spring 1690 saw King William about to depart for Ireland to fight the forces of King James. The Whig interest in parliament, in order to create security for the government and put on a bold front to its enemies, proposed an Oath of Abjuration of King James, which all persons 'in employment or trust' should take, or be imprisoned without the rights of Habeas Corpus. At the second reading of the Bill, on 26 April, Lord Digby seems to have opened the debate, and spoken as follows:

It is a tender point that I am going to speak to; and, before I enter into the debate, I desire I may speak freely, without prejudice. Whatsoever concerns the constitution of the present government, I would not be thought to speak against; nor for King James, if I speak against the Bill. The foundation of

[51] Cobbett, v, 31.
[52] Kettlewell, op. cit., ii (Appendix), p. xxiv.
[53] A List of Those That Were Against Making the Prince and Princess of Orange King and Queen [5 Feb. 1689]; Sir Keith Feiling, *A History of the Tory Party, 1640–1714* (Oxford, 1924), p. 498.
[54] Cobbett, v, 546.
[55] Bray, op. cit., np.; G.E.C., iii, p. 632.

the government is the Bill of Rights; wherein the king promises his part, &c. and we swear fealty. This is our original contract; if there be any, I am of opinion that is it. This Oath I took with a good conscience, and will keep it. Till the king enlarges his part of the contract, I think we should not enlarge ours. I have heard of enemies against kingly government, and I fear this will create many more. This will not distinguish the enemies from the friends of the government, If this be, now the king is going into Ireland, it may be of dangerous consequence. These considerations weigh with me against the bill.[56]

In our attempt to penetrate Digby's attitude to King William and King James, it is useful to look ahead to 1696 when Digby, Sir Clement Fisher, and two other gentlemen, resigned their places as Deputy Lieutenants of the County of Warwick, rather than sign the Act of Voluntary Association to King William.[57] What precisely does the evidence mean? The speech against the Abjuration Bill tells us two things. It shows that Digby had taken the original Oath of Allegiance to William, and that if this had not been easy, he had found some way of settling his conscience. It also shows that, as one might expect, Digby was associating himself with the Tory interest in the House of Commons; the opposition to the Abjuration Bill was almost entirely Tory.[58] What the speech does not show, I believe, is precisely why Digby opposed the Bill. For if one considers the speech carefully one finds that the arguments are advanced, with a subtlety one might not have expected, to appeal to the Whig interest without abandoning the Tory. After carefully guarding his position against the suspicion of Jacobitism (as almost any opponent of the Bill was bound to do) he takes his stand upon the basis of a contract between King and Parliament. He is very much a Tory when he denies any contract *before* the Bill of Rights, but his appeal is to a Whig position when he argues, on the basis of *this* undeniable contract, that they should not offer more to the King than the King offers them. This speech, opening the debate as it seems to have done, was plainly a politic attempt to unite both sides of the House against the Bill. Nevertheless, one might take the speech at its face value, if all the Tory arguments for opposing were not so varied, and, more important, if Digby had not rejected the Association six years later. This last suggests that, had the Bill been passed, Digby would not have abjured King James. If this supposition be correct, then plainly the real reason why Digby opposed the Bill was that it would indeed, as the Whigs intended, distinguish the wholehearted from the dubious supporters of William, and that Digby counted himself among the latter.

[56] Cobbett, v, 595.

[57] Warwickshire Record Office, 1091 (Microfilm of letters of Henry Parker and others to the Earl of Warwick): Lord Digby, Sir Clement Fisher, Sir Charles Holt and William Bromley to the Earl of Warwick, 15 June 1696. See also here the list (*c.* 1696) of Warwickshire J.P.s 'pitched upon to take the Oathes to execute the said Office but have not taken the same' in which 'William Lord Digby' is named.

[58] Gilbert Burnet, *History of His Own Time*, ed. M. J. Routh (Oxford, 2nd. end. 1833), iv, p. 78.

A comparison of the wording of the Oath of Allegiance, the Abjuration Bill and the Voluntary Association thus helps to define Digby's real views. The first resolved that James had abdicated, that the throne was thereby vacant, and that William and Mary be declared King and Queen, the succession being settled, in the first place, on the posterity of James's two Protestant children.[59] The second implicitly denied James's *right* to the throne which the first, though it enumerated his crimes, never did. The third not only declared that William 'hath the right by law to the crown of these realms' but repudiated any right in 'the late king James', and engaged to fight him and 'all his adherents'.[60] It appears from this that Digby was not ready to deny James's right to the throne, and not prepared to take up arms against him; he was perhaps one of those, reflected on in the Abjuration Debate, who distinguished between 'a king *de facto*, and a king *de jure*' and whom the Whigs considered 'might perhaps serve faithfully as long as the government stood firm; but, as they kept still measures with the other side, to whom they knew they would always be welcome, so they would never act with that life and zeal which the present state of affairs required.'[61] One other point must be noticed: between the time of the Declaration of Rights (with its Oath of Allegiance) and the time of the Abjuration Bill, it had become clear that James was not content to have 'abdicated' his throne. If the king *de jure* claims his right by force of arms, allegiance to the king *de facto* becomes harder to defend. Hence Digby's opposition to the Abjuration Bill and Voluntary Association after taking the Oath of Allegiance to William.[62] That this was Digby's position is confirmed by a later piece of evidence still, which it is proper to mention here. In the 'Maxims & Rules for your Conduct', probably written *c.* 1708 for his son Robert, the friend of Pope, Digby was to contend:

> There is hardly any precept in ye Bible, more plainly, more frequently, more earnestly inforced than ys Obedience to Governors; & I do not see how a Man can take up Arms against his Prince wthout rebelling against God himself unless where ye Laws of ye Country do expressly allow it, whch ours do not in any Case yt I know of.[63]

This then is the nature of that firm attachment to the cause of King James which Pope speaks of; with every allowance made for the difficulty of the times, it appears less unequivocal than Pope suggests, less so, perhaps, than that of some of the unfortunate Caryll family.

4. THE COUNTRY GENTLEMAN

The directly political part of William Digby's career was now nearly over. The Abjuration Bill was dropped in the face of Tory opposition. Between 1690 and 1696 Digby acted as a Deputy Lieutenant of the County of Warwick,

[59] Cobbett, v, 108–11.

[60] Burnet, ed. cit., iv, p. 306; cf. the original wording, Cobbett, v, 991.

[61] Cobbett, v, 602 (the speech of the Master of the Rolls); Burnet, ed. cit., iv, pp. 80–1.

[62] Cobbett, v, 601 (the speech of Sir John Lowther, and his proposed emendations). The Bill was dropped.

[63] B.R.L., Digby 'B' 159, f. 5.

nd seems to have been chief of the deputies in various largely routine communications with the Lord Lieutenant. During his years as an M.P. his name
s to be found in the lists of numerous committees, recorded in the *Commons
Journals*. The plot to assassinate King William in 1696, which caused the
emporary imprisonment of John Caryll, caused him to be unusually active
s a Deputy Lieutenant in issuing warrants for Papists and persons disaffected
o the government. The resignation of his commission came on 15 June, and
vas accepted with regret by the Lord Lieutenant: 'I ... am sorry that you
till persist in the same mind, & yt you will not consider your own and Countrys
Good but leave them both exposed to the pleasure and disposal of other men;
And tho ye have now forsaken me I shall not forsake you, but will always be
eady to serve yr Lp ...'[64] On 6 Nov. 1696 he spoke in the House of Commons
gainst the attainting of Sir John Fenwick, one of the chief conspirators in the
ssassination plot, accused on the testimony of one witness alone. The debates
n this Bill of Attainder were among the longest and most difficult of the
eign, and many Tories evidently favoured it, lest in the process of ordinary
rial Fenwick should disclose details of their own equivocal relation with
King James.[65] Digby was not one of these; his speech is a plea for moderation
nd a sense of proportion in the exercise of the supreme powers of parliament.
Digby cannot but have felt sympathy for Fenwick's Jacobitism, though he is
unlikely to have approved the way Sir John went about serving his exiled king.
On 5 July 1698, Digby's last parliamentary session came to an end; his state
f mind on this occasion can be judged from a remark in a letter he wrote four
days later to his friend Edward Nicholas, the Member for Shaftesbury:
I fancy you will now be looking towards Shaftsbury: I cannot heartily wish
ou success; but rather yt. you would turn Country Gentleman, & live quietly
fter ye. example of your old friend D'[66]

It is as a country gentleman that William Digby is chiefly of interest during
he remainder of his long life, and that he was known to Pope. A series of his
etters to Edward Nicholas, written mainly during 1698 give a fairly complete
icture of this period of his life.[67] He was now thirty six, and had been married
welve years. His family now consisted of two sons, John and Robert, daughters,
is niece Frances, the daughter of his brother Simon, and another niece, the
aughter of his brother-in-law the Earl of Gainsborough.[68] Of his friends,
ohn Kettlewell, had died three years earlier, Thomas Smith, who had been
eprived of his Fellowship by Bonaventura Gifford in August 1688, and
estored later the same year, was now deprived once again through his refusal
o take the oaths to William and Mary, though Hough apparently deferred
he deprivation as long as possible.[69] Hough himself, shortly to be translated

[64] Warwickshire Record Office, 1091 (Microfilm of letters of Henry Parker and others to the
arl of Warwick): Warwick to Lord Digby and others, 16 June 1696.
[65] Ogg, op. cit., pp. 435–6.
[66] B. M. Egerton 2540, f. 100 (9 July 1698).
[67] Ibid. ff. 94–136, 142 (29 May 1698–1 Oct. 1707).
[68] G.E.C. iv, p. 354.
[69] Wilmot, op. cit., pp. 53–8.

from the see of Oxford to that of Lichfield, was to marry in 1702 the sister of another friend of Digby, Sir Clement Fisher. Another famous cleric, long to be associated with William Digby, had come under his patronage during the last decade. This was Thomas Bray whose information concerning the Digby family has already been quoted.[70] Simon Digby had heard Bray preach an Assize-Sermon at Warwick and, being impressed, had commended him to his brother William, who first appointed him to his parish of Over-Whitacre, later to that of Sheldon, on the deprivation of Mr. Digby Bull in 1690.[71] Bray's evangelical work in the early eighteenth century is well known; 1698, the year with which we are now concerned, was that in which he founded the Society for the Promotion of Christian Knowledge; Digby was closely associated with his work for the creation and preservation of parish libraries and with his work in the American colonies.[72] In 1701 Digby was to be recorded on the charter of the Society for the Propogation of the Gospel as one of its founding members.[73]

If Digby now led the life of a country gentleman, it was for the moment in Warwickshire. He considered Coleshill his seat, and had also a house in town, in Southampton Square.[74] His income must have been derived almost entirely from the rentals of his Warwickshire and Irish estates, though he may have augmented this by coal mining in Warwickshire. He seems to have spent no time in Ireland. His letters to Edward Nicholas show him concerned with a number of routine arrangements between town and country, and eager for political news. He asks, in July, that a 'Hamper of wine' be kept at the 'Castle & Falcon in Aldersgate-Street' until cooler weather, and requests that his Acts of Parliament be sent him as soon as possible.[75] Later in the month he mentions that 'Our old acquaintance Bp K[en] dined here today in his way to Ld Weym[outh] where he stays but two or three days and then into the North for exercise . . .'; in August he reports that 'We all now begin to be convinced yt. peace is coming, but long to know on what Termes . . .'; he is anxious to know of Nicholas's re-election to parliament:

> You leave me still in Suspence how you have succeded at Shaftsb: if you have gott a priviledge I shall desire some use of it; whch is yt. you will let one of your men put up a Gazette & post-Boy every post & yt. you will take ye. trouble to frank it . . . I have no Parliamentary freind at present I can be so free with.[76]

On 16 Aug. he announced his intention of 'going into Rutland on wednesday for a week wth my wife and sisters Noel. Our business is to visit my sisters

[70] See above, n. 12 and passim.

[71] *Publick Spirit, Illustrated in the Life and Designs of Thomas Bray* (London, 1746), pp. 6–7.

[72] Ibid. pp. 10–42. For the S.P.C.K. and the S.P.G. see G. N. Clark, *The Later Stuarts* (Oxford, 1934), pp. 151–2; and W. K. Lowther Clarke, *A History of the S.P.C.K.* (London, 1959).

[73] The Charter is preserved in the archive of the United Society for the Propagation of the Gospel, in London.

[74] Dorset Record Office, KG 2624,2690.

[75] B. M. Egerton 2540, f. 100.

[76] Ibid. ff. 103, 105, 109.

Estate, & see our freinds.' He asks once again for news 'this being a Criticall time' and is disturbed at the poor prospect of the peace.[77] A cryptic reference in his next letter shows he was not without an interest in joint stock companies, but the same letter hints at the possibility of gain in what was perhaps for a nobleman a more conventionally acceptable way of getting wealth. 'Hearing today that Ld. Brist: grows worse', he resolves to visit him at his seat at Sherborne; he asks Nicholas to say nothing of this journey, and mentions having had a reason for not going sooner.[78] Two further letters report the declining state of his kinsman, then on 14 Sept. came the news which Nicholas must have expected:

> My Ld Br left this world on monday last, & I cannot hide from you ye. kindness he has shewd to yr. old freind. He has left part of his Estate in ye. first place to pay his debts, as he was always ye. justest man alive: ye. rest to my Lady for her life; after that to yr. servant & his issue male . . . I am left a trustee wth others to order ye. funerall & Monuments . . .[79]

Thus the estates, though not the titles, of both branches of the Digby family were united in one man, and William Digby acquired the house and estate of Sherborne in Dorset which, some twenty six years later, was to prompt Pope to write one of his most significant surviving letters.[80]

The intention of the late Earl of Bristol's will was not unexpected; it is likely to have been in fulfilment of a family agreement, for the Dorset Record office preserves two bonds of the Earl of Bristol to William Digby, one for £1,500 in 1687, one for £3,000 in 1689.[81] Probably Digby agreed to make good his kinsman's financial needs in prospect of his succession to the Earl's estates. Doubtless because the Earl had been the last of a noble line of his family, Digby determined to give him a magnificent funeral and monument. William Russell (an eminent embalmer) was sent for from London to arrange the funeral, and his receipt, dated 20 July 1700, shows that he was paid £558.0.0. for his services, including articles that he supplied for the occasion.[82] For the monument Digby engaged Jan van Ost, or Nost, a sculptor of Flemish origin, a pupil of Grinling Gibbons and well known in his day. Nost's signed monument to the third Earl of Bristol, an outstanding work of art, can still be seen in Sherborne Abbey where Pope admired it and called it 'noble'.[83] According to Hutchin's *History of Dorset* it cost £1,500; this, however, is an exaggeration, for Nost's receipt, preserved in the Dorset Record Office, shows

---

[77] Ibid. f. 109.
[78] Ibid. f. 111.
[79] Ibid. ff. 113, 115, 117 (from which the quotation is taken).
[80] *Corr.*, ii, pp. 236–40.
[81] D.R.O., KG 2721, 2709.
[82] Ibid. KG 2728.
[83] For an account of the monument see M. D. Whinney and O. M. Millar, *A History of English Art, 1625–1714* (Oxford, 1957), pp. 249–51 and Plate 73a; and R.C.H.M. *Dorset* (London, 1952), , p. 209 and Plates 169–72.

the figure to have been £700.0.0., still a great sum for the time.[84] Once more John Hough composed an epitaph, producing a piece of balanced and measured prose which expresses an ideal of benevolent, artistocratic piety with dignity and conciseness.[85] It is fully in harmony with the spirit of Nost's sculpture, and the total work of art, form and words, must be regarded not only as a monument to the third Earl of Bristol but as an expression of William Digby's ideal of the role and destiny of his class. The Earl stands between his two wives, raised and celebrated by pedestal, corinthian column, entablature, arched cornice and achievement-of-arms, the whole effect of which is magnificent but not over-elaborate. It is expressive of the Earl's place in society: in the words of the epitaph, the 'Titles to which the merit of his Grandfather first gave lustre: And which he himself laid down unsullyd', 'the port of his Quality'. His figure stands easily yet with the feeling of pre-eminence; his features are strong and manly, well-marked and firm, yet there is in his stance, expression, the direction of his eyes, a certain quiescence. This balance is expressed also in the epitaph: '. . . Was willing to be at ease, but scorned Obscurity'. The two female figures, which are particularly well realized in space, support the central one and, with the pointing of hand, face and eye, subtly unite with it; the younger woman looks inward to the figure of the Earl, while the elder follows the direction of his eyes upwards and across to the altar of the abbey. Two putti, genuinely expressive of childlike sorrow, stand outside the columns. The sculpture and the words complement one another like the figure and legend of a medal. Some of Hough's epitaph must be quoted here:

> He was naturally enclined to avoid the Hurry of a publick Life,/Yet was careful to keep up the port of his Quality./Was willing to be at ease, but scorned Obscurity;/And therefore never made his retirement a pretence to draw/Himself within a narrower compass, or to shun such expense/as Charity, Hospitality, & his Honour call'd for./His Religion was that which by Law is Established; and the Conduct of his life shew'd the power of it in his Heart./His distinction from others never made him forget himself or them./He was kind & obliging to his Neighbours, generous & condescending/to his inferiours, and just to all Mankind./Nor had the temptations of honour and pleasure in this world/Strength enough to withdraw his Eyes from that great/Object of his hope. which we reasonably assure our selves/he now enjoy's.[86]

Important here, and characteristic of the age, is the clear sense of class-distinction between the aristocrat and the rest of society: a distinction which appears to carry with it involvement with other men as well as separation from them, and appears to confer obligations rather than release from them. In

---

[84] Dorset C.R.O., KG 2728. Grinling Gibbons was paid £100. o. o. for his monument to Archbishop Lamplugh at York, in the same year (Whinney and Millar, op. cit., p. 250).

[85] John Hutchins, *The History and Antiquities of the County of Dorset* (3rd. edn., Westminster, 1868), iv, p. 254.

[86] Taken from the monument; there is a text in Hutchings, loc. cit.

this conception, the role of an aristocrat is to benefit surrounding society, and condescension means doing this with grace. Interesting also is the presentation of religion: its outward and formal establishment is balanced by its power in the heart; this is an essential equipoise, parallel to love of retirement but scorn of obscurity. Finally, we may note how the closing words point the significance of the sculpture: the eyes of the Earl are indeed on the 'great Object of his hope' for the group is so placed, in the west wall of the south transept of the church, that it looks towards the altar. Thus the monument has a devotional significance for those who see it, while it cannot be a worldly distraction, being invisible to the great body of the congregation at worship. It is the very opposite of the kind of monumental tomb Pope was later to attack: 'Shouldering God's altar a vile image stands . . .'[87] and there can be no doubt that Nost's sculpture and Hough's epitaph together contributed to Pope's approval of Digby and his seat at Sherborne.

After the funeral of the third Earl of Bristol, the even tenor of Digby's correspondence with Nicholas resumes. There is much talk of sport: invitations to come shooting, the procuring of puppies, the killing of 'half a hundred Cocks, which is pretty well considering the weather'.[88] On 14 Jan. 1698/9 he fears 'mischeif rather than good' from a new Game-Bill, and a month later asks for more news of it.[89] He is busy planting; trees are sent from London but delay loses him a 'fine season' in which to set them. Christmas 1698 sees the family at Coleshill '. . . emprisoned in frost & snow, onely fit for feasting & dancing, whch makes it tolerable this Christm: when I have my neighbours about me every other day.'[90] Political news is a recurring topic: he doubts, on 21 Sept., that the anticipated death of the King of Spain will 'break ye peace'; he wonders, on 5 Dec., at the king's delay in returning to England to open parliament, and discusses likely candidates for being elected Speaker.[91] He rejoices 'to hear ye. Disbanding Bill goes on so merrily' and enquires as to the continuation of the Malt Tax.[92] Finally, there is a series of references which show that Digby was not content to derive his income entirely from the rents and agricultural produce of his estates. In his letter from Sherborne on 3 September he had asked Nicholas to inform him further about 'the Lead-Mine & sr. H: Mack[worth]'s proposal . . .' A few days later he agreed to see this proposal,[93] and at the end of the month he writes: 'I expected better encouragement from you about our Lead-Mine. The proposall seems rationall enough pray tell me what you hear of it; for tis hard to judg at this distance.'[94] On 8 October he declares he has 'so good an opinion of ye. project as to accept of 5 shares for the 100lb you [owe?] me, if you think fit' and in December he

[87] *To Bathurst*, l. 293; T.E., iii–ii, p. 117.
[88] B. M. Egerton, 2540, f. 132.
[89] Ibid. ff. 134–5.
[90] Ibid. f. 133.
[91] Ibid. ff. 119, 132.
[92] Ibid. f. 133.
[93] Ibid. ff. 115, 117.
[94] Ibid. f. 123.

writes: 'I find some have a mighty opinion of our Mine'.[95] It is interesting to discover Digby ready to speculate in joint-stock companies, and perhaps not surprising to find that it was to the dubious commercial activities of Sir Humphrey Mackworth, with their philanthropic, High Church Tory front, that he was attracted.[96] It is to be hoped that Digby did not sink too much of his money down Sir Humphrey's mines, for he would have had little back.

Two final letters, dated 10 Oct. 1705 and 1 Oct. 1707, remain in the correspondence with Edward Nicholas.[97] They extend the picture of Digby the country gentleman into his forty fifth year. The first is the more interesting; it discusses, first, the marriage of one of Digby's nieces to the Duke of Beaufort: an unexpectedly great match. Nicholas had been making overtures to another family on her behalf but its proposal came too late. Digby's explanation and attitude are of interest: '. . . perhaps I may be of your opinion yt. ye. Lady might be happyer wth. ye. other: & perhaps she might have chose that . . . But in ye. present Circumstances there was no refusing so great an offer, without incurring ye. censure of ye. world; & we hope to find happiness There too, as well as Grandure . . .'[98] In this affair he appears to have given way to ambition.

Digby next describes the nomination of a member for Warwick Town in the next election and then proceeds to discuss Nicholas's own political alignment with regard to the election of a new Speaker. The Member for Oxford University, William Bromley, 'a man of grave deportment and good morals, but looked upon as a violent tory, and as a great favourer of the Jacobites', had been assured of his vote, yet Digby is afraid he may have been deceived: 'Your opinion is so well known, & if your Vote should not go with it, ye world will ascribe it to something that is not very honourable. I know Temptation will be layd in your way; but give me leave to say there can be no Temptation to a man in your Circumstances; nor can there be a price for a mans Integrity in any condition.' He concludes that this is a matter of more concern 'than ye. having a sp[eake]r our friend'.[99] Bromley was in the event defeated by Smith, the Whig candidate.[100] The last letter to Nicholas declines, in terms of warm affection, an invitation to meet him and two other gentlemen at Oxford.[101]

On Thursday 7 March 1705/6 Narcissus Luttrell reported in his diary that 'Lord Scudamore is married to Mrs. Digby, daughter to the last lord Digby; her fortune 10,000l.'[102] This event, together with the alliance with the Duke

---

[95] Ibid. ff. 127, 132.

[96] See D.N.B., xii, pp. 631–3. I am indebted to Mr. R. O. Roberts, of University College, Swansea, for much helpful information concerning Mackworth's extensive mining activities in South Wales.

[97] B. M. Egerton, 2540, ff. 136, 142.

[98] Ibid. f. 136. Cf. Narcissus Luttrell, *A Brief Historical Narration of State Affairs* (Oxford, 1857), v, p. 596 (27 Sept. 1705).

[99] Burnet, ed. cit., v, p. 228; B. M. Egerton, 2540, f. 136.

[100] Burnet, ed. cit., v, p. 228.

[101] B. M. Egerton, 2540, f. 142.

[102] Luttrell, op. cit., vi, p. 23; cf. G.E.C., xi, p. 575.

of Beaufort, suggests an approximate date for one of William Digby's surviving meditations which certainly refers to one of these marriages as a near event. A passage from this MS. work, 'Meditations for the Sacrament', has a personal interest, and is in fact Digby's own review of his life so far:

Besides those great Blessings of Creation, Redemption &c. whch I enjoy in common with ye rest of Mankind, I have many particular reasons to adore ye Divine Goodness, & magnify Gods Loving kindess towards me. That I was born in so good a Country, under an excellent Govermt. in ye best part of ye Christ: Church; for an extraordinary Mother who tooke great care of my education; for giving me a contented mind & competent understanding, good Reputation, much better than I deserve, a healthfull body, a plentiful Fortune, an excellent Wife, & many hopefull Children, good success in the education & disposall of my Neice; for ye continuall preservation of me and mine, & many gracious deliverances from great dangers.

Lord how hast thou heap'd thy favours upon me! more than upon those who deserve much better: Thou hast given me all yt I can wish for in this world, & a certain prospect of Eternall happiness in ye next, if I am not strangely wanting to myself, for thou hast made my Duty easy to me.[103]

5. LAW, DOCTRINE AND PRECEPTS

To these favours the University of Oxford added, on 13 July 1708, the degree of Doctor of Civil Law.[104] Digby was not, however, to pass his fiftieth year without suffering some cruel blows from the deity who had so far heaped only blessings upon him. Once more the Digby family seemed unable to keep its sons. On 5 Aug. 1707, his eldest son John Digby wrote to him from Oxford alluding to what seems to have been a serious illness but resolving '. . . to use my utmost endeavours to raise good out of evil, in which by God's special grace I have so far succeeded . . .'[105] The nature of this illness remains obscure, but it appears that in 1710 John Digby began to suffer bouts of madness which increased in severity until even his personal servant, who had for some time been able to manage him, could no longer control his violence. On 2 Sept. 1714, a Private Act was passed in the Commons to make provision for the care of John Digby and to safeguard the estates.[106] No more is then heard of this young man, whose student notes and letters from Oxford suggest so receptive a mind; he died in 1717, aged thirty.[107] Nine years later Digby's second son, Robert, the friend of Pope, was to die at the early age of thirty four; his modest monument, bearing Pope's epitaph, was to join Nost's sculpture in the south transept of Sherborne Abbey.[108]

[103] B.R.L., Digby 'B' 153/5, ff. 5–6.
[104] G.E.C., iv, p. 354.
[105] B.R.L., Digby 'B' 78. Cf. Digby 'B' 153/30, where, amidst much other material concerning John Digby and his studies at Oxford, the dated draft of this letter occurs.
[106] *Private Acts* 1–5, George I, 1714–19, I. 4, pp. 1–4. Six letters from John Digby to Lord Digby (*c.* 1710–11?), written on tour in the Low Countries and Italy, are in the possession of Miss Fiona Digby.
[107] G.E.C., iv, p. 355.
[108] T.E. vol. vi, pp. 313–20; R.C.H.M. *Dorset*, i, p. 208.

The years 1710–13 saw Digby also troubled with legal and theological problems. The first involved him in a lawsuit with Sir Nathaniel Napier concerning debts of the late Earl of Bristol which seem to have been irregularly paid by his wife before his death, but in a way not easily proven in a court of law. On the other hand the Earl had made provision in his will for the payment of these debts, provision ignored by William Digby in the belief that they were already discharged. Napier's demand was for the sum £1,186.17.3.[109] In contesting the claim, Digby put his case in the hands of none other than Peter Walter; it is not surprising to find Digby concluding a letter to him on 22 Nov. 1712: 'I am sorry you are obliged to make ye Bill so long, which I fear will considerably encrease ye Charge. However I must leave it to you to do as you think best for Your Client & servant Digby.'[110] The Digby/Napier lawsuit was concluded on 30 April 1713 when Digby was allowed to pay £300 for his release from any obligations. He may be considered to have won his case though there is no record of what he paid Walter. Probably it was a large sum, and perhaps Digby's experience with Walter contributed to Pope's bad opinion of this interesting man: the couplet:

> 'Tis such a bounty as was never known,
> If Peter deigns to help you to your *own*:
>
> ['The Second Satire of Dr. Donne', ll. 65–6]

is applicable to this lawsuit.[111]

Digby's theological problems, if they can be called *his* problems, were prompted by his acquaintance with a very different kind of man: William Whiston, the successor of Sir Isaac Newton in the Lucasian Chair of Mathematics at Cambridge, a clergyman whose lively, unorthodox mind and determined quest for truth (however disturbing) led him to doubt the doctrine of the Trinity and hold the Athanasian Creed to be '... a gross and Antichristian Innovation and Corruption of the Primitive Purity and Simplicity of the Christian Faith among us.'[112] For these heterodox views he was in 1710 expelled from the University of Cambridge, though not before a number of eminent divines of the church had endeavoured to persuade him to abandon his views, or at any rate not to broadcast them. Prominent among these was John Hough, the 'Ever-Memorable President of Magdalen College'. Hough strongly advised him not 'to break the peace of the Church' and argued that nothing could excuse him doing so 'unless the Church holds some *damnable* Error': 'Can you think this possible? I am sure it is very unlikely. What? that any part of the Faith once deliver'd to the Saints hath been lost ever since the *Nicene* Times; and had been so still, but that my Friend Mr. *Whiston* hath found it?'[113] But Whiston could only have been deterred by convincing

[109] D.R.O., KG 2726.
[110] Ibid. KG 2752.
[111] Ibid. KG 2746A.
[112] William Whiston, *An Historical Preface to Primitive Christianity Reviv'd* ... (London, 1711), Appendix, p. 10.
[113] Whiston, op. cit., Appendix, p. 25.

scholarly argument, and this the established academics of the Church of England were reluctant to offer: 'And indeed great Care was all along taken that the Truth or Falsehood of my Doctrines should be wholly wav'd, and all set upon their contrariety to those of the Church of *England*, without so much as a pretence that any Body would answer the Arguments and Testimonies which I had to produce for them.'[114] This note sounds, increasingly obsessively, throughout Whiston's writings on this subject, and the intellectual injustice which he suffered is undeniable.[115] He ought not therefore to have been surprised when, on trying to interest Lord Digby in the founding of a Society for Promoting Primitive Christianity, in November 1712, he received a frosty reply. 'I . . . do plainly see', wrote Digby, 'ye designe of yt new Society is to make proselites to yr own Opinions. For my own part, I am so well satisfyd with ye Doctrines of ye. Ch: of E. (whch I have not taken upon trust) yt I cannot think myself obliged to hunt for others.'[116] The crux of Whiston's long and detailed reply is a basically simple one: his case was at least worthy of impartial consideration. That belief should be subject to examination in his plea;

> Nay, yt this should be done only by such motives as every honest Jew or Mahometan would equally use for his own religion, against any persuasions to Christianity; & yt. it should go so far as to cause your Lordp. to reject ye fairest proposal for Sincere men to meet in Societies on purpose to examin what is old Christianity; (which Societies & their examination must be fatal to my cause, if it be a wrong one;) is still more amazing; & shews to a demonstration yt religious Protestants, whose first principles are examination and reformation, can almost as securely sit down in ye fallible determinations of that (reformed) Church wherein they happen to be bred, as ye religious Papists do under ye (pretended) infallible determinations of their own.[117]

All this was unwelcome to Digby, who had sufficient concern for fairness and intellectual integrity to prevent him from dismissing Whiston out of hand, yet whose innate orthodoxy and conservatism could not brook the possibility that Whiston might be right. The dignified resentment of his next reply matches the unorthodox cleric in intensity; both are deeply engaged in what they write. Digby vigorously rebuts Whiston's censure, and asserts again that his beliefs are '. . . NOT taken upon trust: (I put that litle word in great letters, yt. you may not again overlook it).'

> Is there no way of examining ye truths of Christianity but by conversing with yr society? Examination, I own, is one great principle of protestants;

---

[114] Ibid., Appendix, p. 23.
[115] Ibid., Appendix, pp. 18–19, 21. Hough, to his credit, did prepare a refutation of Whiston's views (loc. cit., pp. 29–43).
[116] B.R.L., Digby 'B' 146 (29 Nov. 1712).
[117] Ibid. Digby 'B' 80 (6 Dec. 1712).

& another is yt ye Rule we are to examine by is ye Holy Scripture, not ye Apostolicall constitutions which you have too boldly put upon a levell with it. I never thought ye Authority of any Church so great as to supercede ye necessity for such examination: & I have examined ye Faith I profess according to my poor capacity, wth all ye impartiallity I cd nor shall I ever refuse to receive information. But as for your proposall, for refusing *that*, my conscience does not at all reproach me; since ye entering into a society with those we esteem Hereticks is so farr from being a Duty, yt. it seems directly contrary to ye Apostles precept.[118]

After all the professions of impartiality, there in the last sentence we have the truth. We are not concerned here with the rights and wrongs of Whiston's opinions, but the fact that, with the best will in the world, Digby could not open his mind. His convictions were as stable and established as the hierarchical conception of society expressed in his prayers. Whiston's next reply, yet fuller and more detailed and this time rather obviously patient in tone, was no doubt equally unsuccessful.[119] It is to the credit of both men that they stayed friends; on 26 May 1739, nearly thirty years later, Whiston was to write to Digby on behalf of a young curate seeking modest preferment, and was to conclude his somewhat diffident letter with the request that 'Your Lordp. will excuse the freedom of this Address in one whom you are pleased to own as an *old friend* . . .'[120]

Digby's letters to Whiston reveal a contradiction in his character that he could not resolve; they do not show that his profession of open-mindedness was insincere. That the opposite is the case may be seen from his 'Maxims & Rules', written, perhaps, some years earlier: 'Don't take yr. Religion upon trust from yr. Parents or Masters; but when yr. Understanding is ripe, examine for yr. self, & endeavour to settle in yr. Mind a Clear conviction of the Truth of Xtianity upon Rational grounds.' He is of course confident of the answer: 'Upon a Just & impartial Enquiry I dare Answer yt you will not find a better constituted Church yn. the Church of England . . .'[121] The 'Maxims & Rules' is indeed of interest, not in showing evidence of new thinking on Digby's part, but rather as a distillation of the opinions and actions of his life. This short work, which is full in the Courtesy Book tradition that culminates in Chesterfield's *Letters to his Son*, is stated to have been written 'By Lord Digby to his son Robert at Oxford about the year 1714', but may have been written in 1708.[122] It is interesting because Robert Digby was a friend of

---

[118] Ibid. Digby 'B' 147 (15 Dec. 1712).
[119] Ibid. Digby 'B' 81 (18 Dec. 1712).
[120] Ibid. Digby 'B' 82 (26 May 1739).
[121] Ibid. Digby 'B' 159, pp. 1–2.
[122] Ibid. Digby 'B' 159, p. 1 (endorsement). The full title is: *Some few Maxims & Rules for your Conduct, on 3 Heads*. Robert in fact matriculated at Magdalen College in 1708 (*Alumni Oxonienses, 1500–1714*, i, p. 403), whereas Wriothesley, Digby's fourth son, did matriculate 1713/ 14. But since the endorsement is positive about the name, while admitting doubt about the date, there is little reason to question that it was for Robert that the 'Maxims & Rules' were written. Doubtless all Digby's sons had the benefit of its contents in one form or another.

Pope, and because it was through Robert that Pope came to admire William Digby. Much that is in the 'Maxims & Rules' must, through precept, example or anecdote, have formed a part of Pope's picture of William Digby and his family. The work is arranged under three heads: 'Religion, Integrity, & Discretion', a logical progression from belief to action, from action to manners. As one might expect, the longest section is the first and contains much memorable advice directly and concisely expressed: 'Religion is an easy & pleasant thing: ye pains to be taken, no way proportionable to ye reward propos'd . . . Be strict & constant in ye observation of ye Ld's day . . . nothing contributes more to ye keeping up a sense as well as a Face of Religion . . . *Gratitude* is ye best & most generous principle of Religion . . . let yr Employments be Manly, not about Trifles, which Emasculate ye Mind . . .

> There is this wonderful difference between Vertue & Vice; In Vicious pleasures, ye more you know of ym, ye more you tast them, still ye more insipid they grow: whereas ye satisfaction a Man finds in a Virtuous Course, increases with his Knowledge & Experience. Tis ye surest character of good Wine if it bear often tasting: & of a good Author if he will bear often reading & by ye same Test we shd. be convinced of the preference of Virtue if we wd. but try ye Experiment; & tis strange we shd. not in a matter of infinitely ye greatest concern.[123]

As he concludes the first section, Digby touches appropriately on the subject of political loyalty, in a passage quoted at an earlier point in this chapter.[124]
Upon the subject of integrity Digby writes with impressive force. The maxims fall like blows:

> Take this for a first & certain principle that nothing can be a price for your Integrity.
> There is nothing so mean & contemptible in a Gentleman as to see his Opinion change with his Interests—
> Let yr. Judgement be fixt upon solid Reason & yn. immovable.
> Reflect often upon yt noble saying of a Heathen Justum & tenacem &c (Hor. Lib 3 O: 3) . . .
> An honest Porter deserves more Respect than a man of Quality who values not his Word.[125]

If there is any worldliness in the 'Maxims & Rules' it is in the third section, but it is worldliness in the sense of a sound knowledge of men. The burden of his advice is prudence: before speaking, before passing an opinion; against reflecting upon people, against satire ('it will run you into a thousand inconveniences'). He recommends civility 'to all ye World; to ye mean as well as to the Great. This is an easy way of being belov'd . . .' and advises that his son should 'Make but few intimate friends; but keep a fair corres-

---

[123] Ibid. Digby 'B' 159, pp. 1–5.
[124] See n. 63 above.
[125] B.R.L., Digby 'B' 159, p. 6.

pondence with all persons as far as possible tho' they differ from you in Opinions.'[126] Even at our present distance we can detect the character of Digby behind these precepts. His remarks on integrity recall his letter to Edward Nicholas on the same subject; his warning against taking religion on trust recall his protestations to Whiston; the remark last quoted reminds one of his continuing 'correspondence' with Whiston.[127] Digby is likely to have been a very consistent man, in precept as in practice; where there was something equivocal it is likely to have been deep down, unsuspected by himself or successfully rationalized, as in his attitude to Jacobitism and to the unorthodoxy of Whiston. His presentation of religion is interesting because he seems to have loved it, and the life which he believed it enjoined him to lead. For this reason his children probably responded to it favourably and, as Pope was to suggest to Digby himself, perpetuated it in their lives.[128]

6. POPE AND THE DIGBYS

The year 1715 saw the first Jacobite Rebellion, which Digby cannot but have regarded with alarm and misgiving, if also sympathy; the founding of Whiston's Society for Promoting Primitive Christianity, which we know he disapproved of, and the dedication at Sherborne of 'a neat Chappel for the use of the Towns-people', which, Pope goes on to tell us, Lord Digby himself had designed.[129] This modest building, rich inside with contemporary eighteenth-century fittings, still stands today.[130] 1717 is the year of Pope's first letter to Robert Digby. The letter shows the two men were already well acquainted. How they came to know one another it is hard to say, though it was possibly through the painter Charles Jervas who was friendly with John Hough, now Bishop of Worcester.[131] But Jervas may have been more directly in contact with the Digby family.[132] Pope's correspondence with Robert Digby lasted until the latter's death in 1726, and was sustained by a number of common acquaintances (notably Lord Bathurst and Lady Scudamore, the daughter of Simon Digby), by a common love of literature, classical and English, and possibly also by the fact that both men were invalids. Some remarks of Pope also suggest a degree of political sympathy: Dryden's idea of *Gorboduc* is unfavourably compared to the original, as King George to Queen Anne; Londoners '. . . stare, and roar, and clap Hands for K. *George* and the Government' but Lady Scudamore '. . . talks without any manner of shame of good Books, and has not seen *Cibber's* Play of the *Non-juror*.'[133] There can be little doubt what

---

[126] Ibid. Digby 'B' 159, pp. 7–8.

[127] See nn. 99, 118, 120 above.

[128] *Corr.*, iii, p. 52 (Pope to Digby, 8 Sept. 1729).

[129] Ibid. vol. ii, p. 239. Digby subscribed to Vols. ii and iii of Colen Campbell's *Vitruvius Britannicus*. His interest in Leoni's *Palladio* is shown by Robert Digby's letter to him, 12 March 1716/17.

[130] R.C.H.M. *Dorset*, i, pp. 209–11.

[131] *Oxford Historical Society Collectanea, Second Series*, ed. cit., pp. 403–6 (Jervas to Hough, 24 Feb. 1702/3).

[132] A section of Jervas's will is preserved in the Birmingham Reference Library, Digby 'B' 173.

[133] *Corr.*, i, 408, 472–3 (Pope to Digby, 31 March 1718).

he family of Digby the Non-Juror, the patron of Kettlewell, and friend of Bishop Ken and Thomas Smith, thought about this play, with its brash loyalty to King George and its crude hostility to those who would not take the oaths; and Pope shows his awareness of the situation. The two correspondents vie with one another in 'fine' descriptions of the countryside, and in celebrations of the virtue of country life, 'surrounded with blessings and pleasures' where we don't live unpleasantly in primitive simplicity and good humour'.[134] South Sea year enabled Robert Digby to play ironically with the concept of a new Augustan Golden Age:

> I congratulate you, dear Sir, on the return of the Golden-age, for sure this must be such, in which money is shower'd down in such abundance upon us. I hope this overflowing will produce great and good fruits, and bring back the figurative moral golden-age to us. I have some omens to induce me to believe it may; for when the Muses delight to be near a Court, when I find you frequently with a First-minister, I can't but expect from such an intimacy an encouragement and revival of the polite arts.

But with the bursting of the Bubble he fears that 'a taint of the corrupt age we live in' makes him grieve more for his friends who have suffered in the South Sea than 'for the publick, which is said to be undone by it.'[135]

The grave embarrassment of the Government at the bursting of the Bubble afforded the Jacobites a remarkable opportunity. On 28 April 1721 Pope's friend Atterbury, in fact the Pretender's chief representative in England, wrote to the *de jure* monarch that 'The time is now come when, with a very little assistance from your friends from abroad, your way to your friends at home is become easy and safe . . . The worthy Sir Henry Goring will be able to explain things more fully . . .'[136] As a papist, Pope was of course liable to penalties consequent on any further unsuccessful Jacobite attempt. Furthermore he is, somewhat enigmatically, at the centre of a pattern of indirect connections with those involved in the Plot. Sir Henry Goring was a close neighbour and friend of John Caryll.[137] Pope's friendship with Atterbury was so close that he visited him in the Tower, protested his personal loyalty in letters, including one to Secretary of State Carteret, and agreed to be a 'character-witness' at his defence in the House of Lords. Lord Digby's own name appears in the list, drawn up probably at Atterbury's direction in 1721, of 'what nobility and gentry may be inclinable to join' a new Jacobite attempt.[138] Digby may be on the list merely as a known Non-Juror; Jacobite lists of supporters do not often mean much. But this list, drawn up in England by those in a position to give a realistic assessment, may have more significance.

[134] *Corr.*, ii, pp. 44, 47; i, p. 474.
[135] *Corr.*, ii, pp. 51 (30 July 1720), 58 (12 Nov. 1720).
[136] The History of Parliament: Romney Sedgwick, ed. *The House of Commons 1715–54* (London, 970), i, p. 64.
[137] Sedgwick, op. cit., ii, pp. 72–3; B.M. Add. 28228, f. 431 (Sir Henry Goring to John Caryll, o March 1730/1).
[138] Sedgwick, op. cit., i, p. 110; see also p. 64.

The period of crisis lasted from August 1722, when Government suspicion of the Plot grew sufficient for Goring to flee to France and Atterbury be arrested and sent to the Tower; to June 1723 when Atterbury, having been found guilty of High Treason, made his farewell present of a bible to Pope, and boarded a man-of-war for France and exile. During this period Robert Digby, now M.P. for Warwick, was present at many of the crucial parliamentary transactions, describing them in a series of detailed political letters to his father, who had reason to follow them with close concern.[139] The fact that at this time Pope was in direct contact with Robert and Edward Digby[140] means that this correspondence gives us a good sense of the public news as Digby and Pope received it.

On 27 Oct. 1722 the Government asked the Commons to vote the supply for 4,000 extra troops; 'The pretence of them was ye Plot', wrote Robert Digby 'wh they say is still carrying on; but all the evidence they give us of it, is, Will you not believe ye K[ing]'s speech . . .' and went on to report a sharp exchange between Walpole and Shippen, the Jacobite leader in the Commons.[141] On 31 Oct. Walpole hinted at his scheme for a new tax of 5/- in the pound on all Roman Catholics and Non-Jurors as a reprisal for their alleged support of Jacobite plots.[142] This would affect both Lord Digby and Pope. Next Walpole moved to suspend *Habeas Corpus*, giving 'many dark hints of Plots; but Mr. Shippen observed, there was no proper evidence upon oath yet appeared, to convince . . . of the reality of the danger, and necessity of this remedy.'

> Mr. Walpole let us know in his speech yt they had Evidence enough agst ye Bp of Rochester to have taken him up long before yey did; but . . . had they done so, he wd have had an opportunity of being bayled, and being set at libery to continue and advance his schemes; this intimated enough, & so most think yt ye Evidence is not yet full agst him, enough to endanger his life.[143]

On 26 Nov. the new tax was agreed by a narrow vote in the Commons, Digby writing that 'had not many of our friends been gone into ye Country, even since ys Proposal, we had rejected it.'[144] On 6 March 1723, the Report of the Commons Committee on the Conspiracy was distributed; Digby sent his assessment of it to his father before the debate:

> . . . there has been a Plot, but that persons of great consequence have been concerned in it I cannot see . . . All ye Evidences have little weight with

[139] Letters of John, Robert and Edward Digby to Lord Digby, *c.* 1710 to 1725, in the possession of Miss Fiona Digby, Three Pines, East Road, West Mersea, Colchester. Some of these are published in Lettice Digby, *My Ancestors* (London, 1928), pp. 62–7.

[140] *Corr.* ii, pp. 161–2 (Pope to Robert Digby, Winter 1723); Edward Digby to Lord Digby 22 Nov. 1722; Robert Digby to Lord Digby, 4 and 6 April 1723.

[141] Robert Digby to Lord Digby, 27 Oct. 1722.

[142] Cobbett, viii, 47.

[143] Robert Digby to Lord Digby, 18 Nov. 1722.

[144] Robert Digby to Lord Digby, 27 Nov. 1722.

me ... but ye Committee, I believe, were better enlightened, who could
see clearly what I and many others cannot ... as to ye real danger from
this Plot I think there could be none to the Nation, but of its being made
an occasion by an Artfull Minister, of suspending its Liberties & sub-
jecting it to an increase of Forces.[145]

This fairly represents the expressed views of that loose Tory-Jacobite alliance
in the Commons to which Robert Digby seems to have belonged. But he is
less circumspect than usual; when he reports the eleven-hour debate on
Atterbury's guilt, on 11 March, he confines himself to summary of the different
speakers' arguments, with the highlight once again a clash between Walpole
and Shippen:

> W–le said it was hard if Ministers must now be censured, when Gentlemen
> had so fully seen ye horrid and desperate conspiracy yt was carrying on ...
> Shippen remarked upon W–le's manner of treating ye Bp and wished he
> had spoken with less bitterness; He said ye Whole of his Argument was,
> begging ye Question ... He told his Friend Walpole that rash conspiracies
> might greatly strengthen a Govt., if ye Persons concerned were treated with
> Mercy.[146]

Digby added the vote: 270 to 152 in favour of the Bishop's guilt. The penalty
remained to be determined: here Digby's letters show how skilfully Walpole
kept his support together by quelling suggestions of extreme punishment.[147]
On 6 April the 'moderate penalty, Deprivation and Banishment' was agreed;
when, 'Our Friends getting up in a great body and leaving ye House immediately', Robert Digby, with something like party solidarity, 'rose too and
went away with them; I thought it wd be wise in me to act in this instance
with them, tho it should be said they acted simply.'[148]

The clear evidence of the Plot we now have was not available to the Government despite their correct suspicions. If Lord Digby were indeed party to
it, he and his son may have known the truth about Atterbury. This must have
been known to many of the committed Jacobites in the Commons, and seemed
intrinsically probable to many others. At times it seems close to the surface.
What is the force of Shippen's last-quoted remark if not as a plea for mercy
for Atterbury as a 'Person concerned'? What are the implications of Atterbury's
applying to himself, in his letter to Pope of 10 April 1723, lines from the end
of *Paradise Lost*:

> Some natural Tears he dropt, but wip'd them soon:
> The World was all before him ...[149]

if not to intimate a fall as well as predict an exile? And if Pope were at all in
the confidence of Caryll, who may have accompanied him to see Atterbury in

[145] Robert Digby to Lord Digby, 7 March 1722/3.
[146] Robert Digby to Lord Digby, 9 March 1722/3.
[147] Robert Digby to Lord Digby, 30 March, 6 April 1723.
[148] Robert Digby to Lord Digby, 6 April 1723.
[149] *Corr.*, ii, pp. 165–6.

the Tower,[150] special allegation or evidence could have reached his ears, for it was public knowledge that one member of the Caryll family was entangled at the edges of the Plot. The unsavoury Philip Caryll was one of the new informers the Government managed to secure in March. Questioned on his depositions by the House of Lords Committee on the Conspiracy, the informer was 'angry, and uneasy', hoped not to be 'a Sufferer for his Candour' and said 'he would rather a Thousand Times die in Newgate than be an Evidence'. Nevertheless, he claimed knowledge of Goring's Jacobite designs, based on meetings in Goring's and Philip Caryll's own houses and elsewhere, and, most dramatically if equivocally, declared:

> It was but a Supposition of his own, that the Discourse which occasioned the Bishop of *Rochester*'s taking Sir *Harry Goring* by the Collar related to the Pretender's Affairs; but that he remembers very well Words there recited ['This is rocking the Cradle indeed!'], the Bishop did take him by the Collar; and that he, *Caryll*, did apprehend the said Discourse to have relation to the Pretender's Affairs.[151]

Thus qualified, these depositions were hardly strong new evidence against Atterbury; but they reinforce what the whole context underlines: the surprising nature of Pope's apparently total conviction that Atterbury was innocent.[152]

As Pope's correspondence with Digby continued the tone deepened; delight in the exchange of wit and fancy changes to the more frequent expression of personal regard. In a long and moving letter, on 14 Aug. 1723, Robert thanks Pope for entertaining him at Twickenham, and, with something of the wistful air of an invalid, attempts to put into words a wider gratitude:

> If I any ways deserve that friendly warmth and affection with which you write, it is, that I have a heart full of love and esteem for you. So truly, that I should lose the greatest pleasure of my life if I lost your good opinion. It rejoices me very much to be reckoned by you in the class of honest men . . . Perpetual disorder and ill health have for some years so disguised me, that I sometimes fear that I do not to my best friends enough appear what I really am. Sickness is a great oppressor . . . I have as you guess, many philosophical reveries in the shades of Sir Walter Raleigh, of which you are a great part. You generally enter there with me, and like a good Genius applaud and strengthen all my sentiments that have honour in them.[153]

Pope was soon to share 'the shades of Sir Walter Raleigh' at Sherborne in a

---

[150] Ibid., p. 173 (Pope to Caryll, *c.* 17 May 1723) and n. 1.

[151] *Lords Journals*, xxii, 1722–6, p. 155. That the informer was indeed Philip Caryll, John Caryll's cousin, is clinched by his reference to his own house, of North; see B.M. Add. 28228, f. 244 (Philip Caryll to John Caryll, 10 Sept. 1727) for the first of several letters about this house.

[152] *Corr.*, ii, pp. 168–9 (Pope to Atterbury, May 1723). Pope was perfectly familiar with the phenomenon of highly placed, often Whig, politicians corresponding with the Pretender; his allegations to Spence concerning Sunderland, which long seemed quite implausible, have recently been proved correct (see Spence, 370, and Sedgwick, op. cit., vol. i, pp. 64–5).

[153] Ibid., 191–2.

literal sense. In June 1724 this long-planned visit probably took place, and is recorded in the long letter to Martha Blount already alluded to. Pope had already expressed to Robert Digby his admiration of the father; these remarks culminate in this letter where they gain authenticity not only because Pope is now no longer speaking of Lord Digby at second-hand, but also because he is addressing a person in no way connected with the family, but with whom he was on terms of intimacy and candour. His tribute is evidently sincere, and his earnestness tells one a lot about Pope.

> The Present Master of this place (and I verily believe I can ingage the same for the next Successors) needs not to fear the Record, or shun the Remembrance of the actions of his Forefathers . . . I dare say his Goodness and Benevolence extend as far as his territories; that his Tenants live almost as happy & contented as himself; & that not one of his Children wishes to see this Seat his owne.[154]

This tribute, is not personal but social, and is much in harmony with Hough's epitaph on the monument to the late Earl of Bristol, which Pope had just seen when he wrote the present letter. It stands here for its importance in the record of Digby's life, but will be discussed in detail later.

Robert Digby died on 19 April 1726. Pope expressed his affection and admiration for him, first, two days later, to the younger brother Edward Digby, then, three years afterwards on the death of Robert's sister Mary, in an epitaph which Lord Digby must have asked him to write. This was the occasion of an exchange of letters between Pope and William Digby. Pope submitted a draft of the poem to Digby, and the sixty seven year old peer noted an ambiguity and made some small objections to which Pope deferred. The epitaph has an eloquence of both affection and dignity; Johnson's criticism of it for too great generality is too severe, partly because the general virtues cited are the measure of Pope's esteem, partly because individual touches *are* to be found: 'Compos'd in suff'rings . . .' refers to the invalid, while 'heav'ns Eternal year' connects (through the Great, or Platonic Year) with the idea of the Golden Age often mentioned in Robert Digby's letters, perhaps often discussed by the two friends.[155] The closing lines of the epitaph associate the grief of the father and the friend, and the last paragraph of Pope's letter

---

[154] Ibid., p. 239 (Pope to Martha Blount, 22 June ?1724).
[155] T.E., vi, pp. 313–14:
Go! fair Example of untainted youth,
Of modest wisdom, and pacifick truth:
Compos'd in suff'rings, and in joy sedate,
Good without noise, without pretension great.
Just of thy word, in ev'ry thought sincere,
Who knew no wish but what the world might hear:
Of softest manners, unaffected mind,
Lover of peace, and friend of human kind:
Go live! for heav'ns Eternal year is thine.
Go, and exalt thy Moral to Divine. [ll. 1–10]
Samuel Johnson, *Lives of the English Poets*, ed. G. Birkbeck Hill (Oxford, 1905), iii, pp. 263–4.

to Lord Digby formally expresses his admiration of the father in terms which, though certainly sincere, the poet must have known would be the one tribute most welcome: 'It is you My Lord, that perpetuate your Family the best way, by transmitting thro' yourself all the Virtues of it into your Posterity. Your whole family is an example of what is almost now lost in this Nation, the Integrity of ancient Nobility.'[156]

This was not Pope's last word of poetic tribute to the family. The early death of the virtuous children, the long life of the virtuous father, defeated any easy and obvious formulation concerning the disposition of providence over long and short lives, resisting the imposition upon events of an easily intelligible pattern. In a roll of virtue which moves from public and historical to contemporary and personal, Pope includes Robert and William Digby as names mediating between those of Falkland, Turenne, and Sidney (Robert, like those, one of the virtuous to meet an early death); and Belsunce, bishop of Marseilles, and Pope's own mother (William, like these, one of the virtuous to live long lives against expectation). The paragraph modulates beautifully from Providence and the public at the beginning, to Pope and the personal at the end, with the Digbys at the centre of both the passage and the paradox:

> Say, was it Virtue, more tho' Heav'n ne'r gave,
> Lamented DIGBY! sunk thee to the grave?
> Tell me, if Virtue made the Son expire,
> Why, full of days and honour, lives the Sire?
>
> [*Essay on Man*, IV, ll. 104–7]

The honour of which Pope speaks was, it is safe to say, Digby's reputation for integrity and benevolence. It is appropriate to conclude this account of his long life with his philanthropy. The fullest single account of Lord Digby's charities is by Thomas Bray, with whose activities in the S.P.C.K. and S.P.G. Digby seems to have been continuously associated. Writing in 1728, Bray tells us that 'besides the settling of the Great Tithes of Coleshil and Over-whitacre', William Digby had

> Given Ground for the Site, and been at very considerable Charge towards Erecting a very fine Parsonage-House on the former, and Rebuilt a ruin'd Chappel near his Seat in Dorsetshire, adding his own to the Royal Bounty for its Endowment (a difference of £200 a year); Founded two Libraries at Coleshil and Overwhitacre, contributed Bountifully to Two more Libraries, one at Warwick, the other at Sherborn, Built a Repository for the Parochial Library at Sheldon, another Rectory whereof he is Patron; and moreover founded Charity-Schools at Coleshil, and Sherburn: Rebuilt a Church on his Estate in Ireland, and also raised a Charity-School there.[157]

We also learn that 'William, Lord Digby, and other principal inhabitants of the town [of Sherborne], raised 1,000l. by subscription to augment the

---

[156] *Corr.*, iii, p. 52 (Pope to Digby, 8 Sept. 1729).
[157] Bray, op. cit., np.

vicarage' and that in 1743 he founded a school for the education and clothing of thirteen poor girls in the town of Sherborne, endowing it with land to the value of £27.0.0. a year.[158] Much the most imaginative of the charitable activities in which William Digby was involved, however, was James Oglethorpe's scheme for founding a colony in Georgia. This was indeed a philanthropic project, and Pope was perfectly right to speak of Oglethorpe's 'strong Benevolence of Soul'; the literature describing the founding of Georgia shows that one of the chief motives of those interested was to provide employment for poor families, including those imprisoned for debt.[159] Edward Digby, William's third and now eldest surviving son, was a trustee for the funds collected to establish the colony, and in April 1733 Lord Digby himself was appointed a member of the Common Council for Georgia.[160] He is recorded as having contributed the sum of £30.0.0. to the funds, and James Lacy, his vicar at Sherborne, £5.0.0.[161] It is interesting to notice that both Edward Digby and James Oglethorpe were associated with Bray in his concern for 'the State of the Gaols': all this was part of the same philanthropic conception, inspired, led and supported by many of the same people, among whom the Digby family played a notable part.[162]

In 1738 Pope, in the Second Dialogue of his 'Epilogue to the Satires', brought to a climax his account of a corrupted Britain by an apostrophe to the heroic muse of satire, to virtue and to light; like Milton in *Paradise Lost*, Book III, Pope turns to light after darkness:

> When black Ambition stains a Publick Cause,
> A Monarch's sword when mad Vain-glory draws,
> Not *Waller's* Wreath can hide the Nation's Scar,
> Nor *Boileau* turn the Feather to a Star.
> Not so, when diadem'd with Rays divine,
> Touch'd with the Flame that breaks from Virtue's Shrine,
> Her Priestless Muse forbids the Good to dye,
> And ope's the Temple of Eternity;
> There other *Trophies* deck the truly Brave,
> Than such as *Anstis* casts into the Grave . . .
> Such as on HOUGH'S unsully'd Mitre shine,
> Or beam, good DIGBY! from a Heart like thine.
>
> $\qquad\qquad$ [ll. 228–37, 240–1]

These examples of integrity are set in a context of great historical events, Cromwell's rise to supremacy and Louis XIV's invasion of the Netherlands; here the linking of the names of Hough and Digby denotes, not just a tribute

---

[158] Hutchins, ed. cit., iv, pp. 263, 299.

[159] See, eg., *Publick Spirit, Illustrated in the Life . . . Of Thomas Bray*, pp. 53–4; T. M. Harris, *Biographical Memorials of James Oglethorpe* (Boston, Mass. 1841), pp. 39–40.

[160] Harris, op. cit., p. 349. G.E.C., iv, p. 354.

[161] *The General Account of all Monies and Effects Received and Expended by the Trustees for . . . Georgia* (London, 1733), p. 5.

[162] *Publick Spirit, Illustrated*, [facing] p. 54.

to two men whose careers Pope respected, but their honourable record in regard to another great historical issue: the conduct and rights of James II. Pope's note confirms the point: 'The one an asserter of the Church of England in opposition to the false measures of King James II. The other as firmly attached to the cause of that King. Both acting out of principle, and equally men of honour and virtue.'[163] From what has gone before, we may see that the particular reference is to Hough's part in the Magdalen College dispute before the exile of James, and Digby's stance as a Non-Juror afterwards, each having acted against his own apparent interest. Such conduct is the mark of true nobility; not the insignia with which the Herald at Arms (Anstis) is concerned.

The lives of these two men were to touch once again. In 1743 Digby received a letter from Hough, then in his ninety second and last year, which spoke movingly of their great age and his hope for their reunion after death:

> ... I have ease (if it may not more properly be term'd indolence) to a degree beyond what I durst have thought of, when years began to multiply upon me. I wait contentedly for a deliverance out of this life into a better, in humble confidence, that, by the mercy of God thro the merits of his Son, I shall stand at the resurrection at his right hand; And when you, my Lord, shall have ended those days, that are to come (which I pray may be many and comfortable) as innocently & exemplarily, as those, that are past, I doubt not of our meeting in that state where the Joys are unspeakable & will always endure.[164]

On the 29 April 1748 Digby signed for the last time the accounts of the free-school at Coleshill, which he had done almost every year since June 1694, over half a century ago.[165] He died on 29 Nov. 1752, at Coleshill, leaving a personal estate of about £23,000.0.0. plus £14,000.0.0. to be charged on the estates of his grandson, the new Lord Digby, for the use first of paying his personal debts and legacies, and then secondly for the purchase of land for those of his grandsons not inheriting the title and entailed estates. The legacies amounted to £7,592.0.0. of which the only one of charitable interest was £100.0.0. 'for discharging poor Prisoners' in the Warwick County Gaol. However, the account of the execution of his will reveals a recent gift of £1,000 to the Almshouse of St. John the Evangelist at Sherborne. The debts came to £2,029.16.6., leaving, in the end, some £12,000 for his younger grandsons.[166] A lawsuit within the family soon ensued.[167]

But that is not our concern here. The man whom Pope singled out, in private and public, as an example of true nobility, appears from a review of his life

[163] T.E., iv, p. 326.
[164] B.R.L., Digby 'B' 79 (13 April 1743).
[165] Warwick C.R.O., H2/152a: Account Book of Coleshill Free School from 1693–1836.
[166] An Abstract of the Will and Codicils of ... William, Lord Digby ...; B.R.L., Digby 'B' 83C. An Account of the Personal Estate of ... William, Lord Digby ... administered by Wriothesley Digby, Second Schedule, c. 1753–8; Digby 'B' 161.
[167] B.R.L., Digby 'B' 83C, 162, 163; D.R.O., KG 1475, 2739, 2749.

to have been something more than the figure of stolid worth suggested by his earlier letters. He described himself as of 'competent understanding' (not better), and it is probable that he possessed his integrity of morals at the cost of inflexibility of mind. But his prayers can express strong emotion, and he could show subtlety as well as firmness in the political sphere. If his stand as a Non-Juror cost him less than Roman Catholicism cost the Carylls, he constantly devoted a great part of his wealth not merely to the clergy, but to the public, and particularly those members of it in real economic need. His conception of his role was supported by his deeds, and his character, expressive of something of the best of Augustan civilization, still communicates through the vigour of his words: 'Gratitude is ye. best & most generous principle of Religion'; 'Reflect often upon yt noble saying of a Heathen Justum & tenacem &c.'; 'An honest Porter deserves more Respect than a man of Quality who values not his Word.' But the last word must be given to his 'old friend' and theological opponent, William Whiston: '. . . the best Christian Nobleman whom I ever knew, the good Lord *Digby*.'[168]

---

[168] William Whiston, *Memoirs of his Life and Writings* (London, 1749–50), i, p. 153.

VI. 'Much injur'd Blunt'[1] : Sir John Blunt, Bt. (1667–1733)

1. A COBBLER'S SON

IN 1697 Daniel Defoe published his *Essay on Projects*. He drew, in the first section of this work, a distinction between the 'meer projector' and the 'Honest Projector', depicting the first as one who

> finds no remedy but to paint up some Bauble or other, as *Players make Puppets talk big*, to show like a strange thing, and then cry it up for a New Invention; gets a Patent for it, divides it into Shares, and *they must be Sold*; ways and means are not wanting to Swell the new Whim to a vast Magnitude. Thousands and Hundreds of thousands are the least of his discourse, and sometimes Millions; till the Ambition of some honest Coxcomb is wheedl'd to part with his Money for it, and then
>
> . . . *Nascitur ridiculus mus,*
>
> the Adventurer is left to carry on the Project, and the Projector laughs at him. The *Diver* shall walk at the bottom of the *Thames*; the Saltpetre-Maker shall Build *Tom* T--d's Pond into Houses; the Engineers Build Models and Windmills to draw Water, till Funds are rais'd to carry it on, by Men who have more Money than Brains, and then *good night Patent and Invention*; The Projector has done his business, and is gone.

The honest projector, on the other hand, is he who

> having by fair and plain principles of Sense, Honesty, and Ingenuity, brought any Contrivance to a suitable Perfection, makes out what he

[1] An earlier version of this chapter, together with a part of Chapter VIII, has been published as 'Pope and the Financial Revolution', in Peter Dixon, ed. *Writers and Their Background: Alexander Pope* (London, 1972), pp. 200–29. Though a conspicuous figure in the economic history of Britain, Blunt has never been the subject of a biography, even in D.N.B. Much light is thrown on his career, however, by two modern works: John Carswell, *The South Sea Bubble* (London, 1960), and P. G. M. Dickson, *The Financial Revolution in England* (Oxford, 1967); I am in debt to both these books, and have relied on the latter particularly for the financial detail of Blunt's activities. The present chapter adds to the account of Carswell and Dickson by adducing several further primary sources, notably Blunt's own *True State of the South Sea Scheme* (London, 1722), and his will.

5. Artist unknown, *Sir John Blunt*, Bt. By kind permission of the Trustees of the British Museum.

pretends to, picks nobody's pocket, puts his Project in Execution, and contents himself with the real Produce, as the profit of his Invention.[2]

Defoe's words show the reaction of an average, fair-minded man to that heightened sense of technical and commercial possibility which many felt in the last decade of the seventeenth century.[3] The standard of his judgement is conservative common sense (his diver and engineer are far from ridiculous in hindsight), and his false projector is a Jonsonian knave, presented with some of the pithiness of the Jonsonian grotesque. What is strange must be distrusted; what may be trusted is that which can be seen to have been devised by 'fair and plain principles of Sense'. These two sketches mark the moral extremes for any picture of that great European wave of inventiveness, enterprise and deception which broke, in Britain, with the bursting of the South Sea Bubble. In a remarkable way, they also point up the characters of the last two contemporaries of Pope who are the subjects of this study. John Blunt was by no means a simple fraud, yet he differed from his great financial contemporary John Law in raising the credit of his stock on a totally inadequate economic basis; in this sense he painted up a 'Bauble' and found indeed that ways and means were not wanting 'to Swell the new Whim to a vast Magnitude'. Ralph Allen, on the other hand, will be found a projector in a very different way, one closer to those proposals 'in general of public advantage, as they tend to the improvement of trade, and employment of the poor' which Defoe outlined in his *Essay*. Allen's scheme of postal reform was certainly based on 'fair and plain principles of Sense, Honesty, and Ingenuity'; he deprived nobody of their honest earnings in its projection, and contented himself with 'the real Produce' of its execution.

Blunt also differs from Allen, and from the other four men described in these pages, in his attitude to money. For John Kyrle and Peter Walter, money was inseparably linked with produce. The cutting of Kyrle's timber from Dymoke Wood was in effect his small income, his means of subsistence and source of charity; for him wealth in money and wealth in kind were scarcely separate. Walter, it is true, did not originally derive his enormous fortune from his own property but from the management of the property of others. But as his wealth in money increased so did his purchase of land; though he invested money, and lent it out at interest, the end of the process for Walter was the enlargement of his landed estate. An anecdote puts the point well: 'Peter Walter would not lend money or buy without seeing every acre: for, said he, "I live on bread and butter, and milk porridge; and it must be land that maintains the cows for this: whereas none of the stock companies have a single cow." '[4] Walter's characteristic irony is here directed against his own reputation for a miserly frugality, but the truth in the comment is clear: for him money derived its meaning and value from land. The Carylls and

---

[2] [Daniel Defoe,] *An Essay Upon Projects* (London, 1697), pp. 34–5.

[3] Carswell, Ch. I; David Ogg, *England in the Reigns of James II and William III* (Oxford, 1955), p. 417.

[4] John Hutchins, *The History and Antiquities of the County of Dorset* (3rd. edn., Westminster, 1868), iii, p. 671.

Digby show a slightly different attitude. The wealth of each family was founded upon land. But the Carylls, being Catholics, were in a vulnerable position. The source of their wealth was liable to be confiscated, or at least double-taxed. Thus we find this family, which in other circumstances would probably have been content to care for and live off its estates, investing in the Hotel de Ville, in Paris, as 'the best security for English Catholicks'. These investments could not, however, secure the Carylls against John Law. Digby, like the Carylls, derived his wealth primarily from landed property, but in him we have seen some concern with industrial investment for its own sake; we know that he was interested in mining, not only on his own land, but in the form of a business proposal by Sir Humphrey Mackworth inviting capital invest-ment. With the Carylls and Digby, then, the link between money and land is a little less close. With Ralph Allen, as we shall see, the link is less close still, for Allen founded his fortune on the sale and execution of an idea. But it is notable that no sooner did he find himself successful in exploiting this source of income than he established himself as a landowner and a stone-merchant; for him investment took the form of ploughing money back into his various enterprises, which, in their turn, were directed towards the greater prosperity of the local and the national community. It is perhaps true (despite some qualifications to be made) that John Blunt had a more original mind than any of these men. His attitude to money differed from theirs in that he conceived it as largely separate from such tangibles as land and trade, and he seems to have looked on the world of finance as almost autonomous. Blunt half realized what Law fully understood: that money is a human system, potentially distinct from the intrinsic value of coinage and wealth in kind, and that this knowledge may be used for the benefit of society providing that society's co-operation can in some way be secured. In such an operation public confidence is crucial, as both Law and Blunt appreciated. Unfortunately for Britain and for himself, Blunt's dawning realization of a new dimension of public finance was accompanied by an imperious ambition and a contempt, in practice, for professional and moral honesty. Thus it was that after the South Sea Bubble fiasco Blunt was treated as an overweening public criminal of a highly dangerous kind, which, though true, is certainly not the whole truth.

John Blunt was born in 1667, the son of Thomas Blunt of Rochester (formerly of Strood) in Kent, a shoemaker by profession, and Isabella Blacke, the daughter of Thomas Blacke, yeoman. The marriage of his parents took place on 27 March 1654. Little can be gathered of Thomas Blunt, except that he was the son of John Blunt of St. Sepulchre's, London, Upholder; a freeman of Rochester by purchase on 1 Sept. 1655, and a shoemaker all his life, for it is referred to in the records of his burial as well as his marriage. Another detail is significant: his religion. The register of his burial at St. Nicholas's church Rochester is specific: 'Thomas Blunt, Shewmaker, a Baptist, put into ye ground, March ye 28, 1703.'[5] That Blunt had a dissenting background is

---

[5] *The G.E.C. Complete Baronetage*, v, pp. 48–9.

interesting in view of his subsequent career, characteristic speech, and Pope's presentation of him in the Epistle *To Bathurst*. As (perhaps) in the case of Peter Walter, dissent seems to have gone hand in hand with enormous financial ambitions; certainly Walter's ironical remark to the Earl of Uxbridge: '. . . these Low puritanicall fellows are the greater picke pockitts . . .' applies well to each of them.[6] On the 5 March 1689 Blunt became free of the Merchant Taylor's Company, in the City of London, by virtue of apprenticeship to Daniel Richards, a scrivener of Holborn.[7] By profession, then, Blunt was a specialist in documents of business, and an indispensable middleman in financial transactions of all kinds. As John Carswell has put it, in his lively and detailed work, *The South Sea Bubble*, the scrivener was 'simultaneously the solicitor, the estate agent, and the business agency of that enterprising age.'[8] Four months after ending his apprenticeship, Blunt married Elizabeth Court, the daughter of a Warwickshire family.[9] By her he had seven children; we hear nothing else of her until her death on 22 March 1708.[10] On 11 March 1691 Blunt was a Liveryman of the Merchant Taylors, and a Freeman of Rochester by patrimony in June 1698.[11] The Wardmote Inquest Book for Cornhill Ward shows that he was living in this Ward—in the parish of St. Michael's—in 1699, when he is listed as one of those who '. . . being Inhabitants or Shopkeepers in the said Ward and followe Trades there haveing been duely summoned to shew to Us the Coppy of the respective ffreedomes of this Citty . . . have refused or neglected to do it.'[12] The same is recorded in 1700, but also that in this year he was on the Petty Jury of the Ward.[13] He likewise failed to show his copy in 1701, but in 1702 his compliance was for the first time recorded.[14] It may perhaps be inferred that Blunt was living under the pressure of much business.

Pressure of business did not, however, preclude him from taking an interest in the technicalities of government finance. As early as 1693 he had written to the Treasury proposing a new method of keeping accounts, and on 1 June 1702 he again wrote to convey his 'sentiments about the manner of keeping the public accounts'. His argument was that 'the majority of the first commissioners (of the Treasury) consisting of gentlemen that were bred merchants, carried the method of keeping all the accompts in the merchants way of Journal & leiger, commonly called the Italian way.' This method he considered good, and in many ways serviceable, but insufficient in some respects, and he offered instead his own new method already submitted to them nine years earlier as one which would satisfy all the ends of the Com-

[6] See Ch. IV, n. 57 above.
[7] Carswell, p. 19.
[8] Ibid., p. 19.
[9] *G.E.C. Baronetage*, v, pp. 48–9.
[10] *The Case of the South Sea Directors* (London, 1721), No. 3; *G.E.C. Baronetage*, loc. cit.
[11] *G.E.C. Baronetage*, loc. cit.
[12] City of London: Guildhall Library, Wardmote Inquest Book of Cornhill, MS. 4069/2, f. 420.
[13] Ibid. ff. 423, 425.
[14] Ibid. f. 431.

mission.[15] It is not now possible to know precisely what Blunt had proposed, but it is significant that he is rejecting the merchant's attitude to
public finance, that of the man who dealt primarily in commodities. We see
here not only the approach of a scrivener, whose job was the *paperwork* of
financial transactions, but also, and the two seem to be connected, the mind
of an economist ready to think of money, and ways of expressing financial
relationships, as matters only indirectly concerned with the substantial realm
of goods. In this letter the germ of Blunt's later public career can be seen.
Meanwhile a considerable step towards his later importance was taken,
probably in 1703, when he became secretary of the Sword Blade Bank. This
curious institution, to become so important a bulwark to the ambitious edifice
of the South Sea Company, is interestingly described by Carswell. It had
begun in 1692 as a chartered stock company for the manufacture of the
fashionable grooved sword, and was the creation of Sir Stephen Evance,
goldsmith and projector. At the end of the reign of William III, Evance failed
in business and shot himself. Through his associate, Sir Francis Child, the
company and its charter passed into the hands of Elias Turner, Jacob Sawbridge, George Caswall (whom Defoe called the 'three capital sharpers of
Britain')—and of Blunt.[16] The Sword Blade Company now ceased to concern
itself with manufacture—again a characteristic attitude is seen—and instead
employed its rights by charter to hold land and issue stock in the purchase of
forfeited Jacobite estates in Ireland. This operation, unsuccessful in the event,
showed a number of interesting features. The Company did not pay cash for
the land but instead issued stock. Neither was the stock issued for cash but
Army Debentures, vouchers for unsecured government debts for military
expenditure, which had depreciated in value.[17] The Sword Blade offered the
original nominal value for them, and the part of the Irish lands in the transaction seemed to offer convincing security. Army Debentures rapidly appreciated as a result, and the Sword Blade partners, who had previously
invested in them at the lower price, as private individuals, were able to sell
them at a handsome profit. For this operation government co-operation was
naturally needed. It was gained because the government, being paid by its
own obligations for assets (the Irish lands) which it could not profitably use,
was thus able to cancel a considerable public debt. It also extracted from the
Sword Blade partners a loan in cash, on security, which could have been the
price of its readiness to deal with the upstart company.[18] The whole transaction is remarkable in that it seems to have required no capital investment by
the Sword Blade, and while it produced the partners little cash profit, they
became at the end of it major creditors to the government, with all the business
prestige which that brought. The whole thing was an exercise in 'credit', and
for this the psychological element that makes for confidence, rational or
otherwise, was beautifully judged. The operation was based not so much on

[15] *Calendar of Treasury Papers, 1702–7*, lxxx, 4 (pp. 20–1).
[16] Carswell, pp. 30–4.
[17] Ibid., pp. 34–5.
[18] Ibid., pp. 35–6.

the lands themselves, which in practice proved hard to get possession of, but on the *idea of land*—land which as Peter Walter well knew was the most tangible and convincing of all securities.

2. THE TORY FINANCIERS

The bargain between the Sword Blade Company and the government was completed with a visit by Blunt to the Treasury on 1 June 1704.[19] It must have been observed with outrage by the Bank of England, for it was an impudent attempt to challenge the Bank at its own game. The Bank was the major landmark of the financial landscape in which Blunt worked. It provided him, in the first decade of the eighteenth century, with a challenge, a model, and above all a limitation. Blunt's career may be seen as an attempt to do in his own interest what Sir Gilbert Heathcote and the other promoters of the Bank of England had already done in theirs. It is necessary to consider briefly the nature of the Bank of England and its importance in contemporary political life. It had been founded in 1694 to meet a particular and unprecedented need. Britain was engaged, under the leadership of William III, in a continental war on a scale never previously known. None of the existing sources of revenue, and methods of collection, were adequate to supply the need for immediate funds with which to wage the war against France. New sources and new channels had to be found—and of these the Bank of England was chief. In return for a charter incorporating them as a national bank, Heathcote and his syndicate had in 1694 made a loan to the government of a million and a half pounds *in Bank of England notes*, retaining for banking the cash put up by the shareholders. Immense financial prestige, of the kind Blunt sought and partly won in his Sword Blade loan, thus accrued to the new institution. Three years later, in 1697, the Bank offered to give the government a further loan by incorporating depreciated exchequer tallies in an issue of new stock— the model for Blunt's Sword Blade loan of 1703–4. In return the Act of Parliament which provided for this operation also prolonged the Bank's charter until 1710, and entrenched its monopolistic position more securely against many rival institutions and schemes. It did not, however, secure it against the Sword Blade Company, whose charter had already been granted, though the necessary Act of Parliament had not in fact been passed.[20] The Sword Blade hardly seemed a serious rival in 1697, and the alarm with which the Bank viewed Blunt's 1704 deal must have been all the greater. A protest was now made to the government that the monopoly clause of the 1697 Act was being infringed. Nothing was done, however, until 1707 when, in return for a further loan and the extension of the charter to 1732, the government passed further legislation, designed to put an end to the Sword Blade's rivalry with the Bank of England.

Blunt and his partners in the Sword Blade were not the only ones to regard the Bank of England with a jealous eye. It was recognized as a great political

[19] Ibid., p. 36.
[20] Ibid., p. 36.

as well as financial power, and the landed gentry in particular saw in it a
threat to their parliamentary influence. Swift was to put their case forcefully
in his *History of the Four Last Years of the Queen*:

> By all I have yet read of the History of our own Country, it appears to
> me, That National Debts secured upon Parliamentary Funds of Interest,
> were things unknown in *England* before the last Revolution under the
> Prince of *Orange* . . . it was the Business of such as were then in Power
> to cultivate a money'd Interest; because the Gentry of the Kingdom did
> not very much relish those New Notions in Government, to which the
> King . . . was thought to give too much way . . .
>
> But, when this Expedient . . . was first put in practice; artful Men in
> Office and Credit began to consider what Uses it might be apply'd to; and
> soon found it was likely to prove the most fruitful Seminary, not only to
> establish a Faction . . . but likewise, to raise vast Wealth for themselves in
> particular, who were to be the Managers and Directors in it. Thus, a new
> Estate and Property sprung up in the hands of the Mortgagees, to whom
> every House and Foot of Land in *England* paid a Rent Charge free of all
> Taxes . . . So that the Gentlemen of Estates were in effect but Tenants to
> these New Landlords; many of whom were able in time to force the Election
> of Burroughs out of the Hands of those who had been the old Proprietors
> and Inhabitants . . .[21]

As early as 1695 there had been a Tory attempt to establish a rival economic
and political force to the Whig Bank of England in Robert Harley's unsuccessful scheme for a Land Bank. The idea was extremely attractive to
moderate Tories such as Harley since it seemed at once to assert the importance of land and to challenge the Bank of England at its own game. It is
interesting that the Land Bank idea played a part in Blunt's Sword Blade
operation in 1703–4.

Thus Blunt and Harley had already something in common, apart from a
very differently motivated aversion to the Bank of England, when, in August
1710, the Whig Lord High Treasurer Godolphin was dismissed, and Harley
himself assumed power. He was faced, not only with the Tory desire to find
an alternative to the Godolphin-Bank of England financial system, but also
with the fact that this system was beginning to fail under the strain of the
continuing war, and a hard winter followed by a bad harvest in 1708–9. In
addition Godolphin, to avoid new taxation, had been raising loans from
public subscription only by committing government revenue far into the
coming century, an expedient which could not be used indefinitely. There
were loans from the East India Company and the Bank of England, in 1708
and 1709; and in 1710 he resorted to a public lottery, and a further loan, from
the Swiss Canton of Berne.[22] All this Blunt followed with care, and may

---

[21] Jonathan Swift, *The History of the Four Last Years of the Queen*, ed. Herbert Davis and
Harold Williams (Oxford, 1951), pp. 68–70.
[22] Dickson, pp. 59–62.

have studied anew on the fall of Godolphin. He recounted the whole process
in minutely careful, colourless language—very different from his speech—in
a memorandum given to Swift, at the latter's request, in 1713, which concludes:

> ... so that no Money was borrowed upon the General Mortgage in 1710
> except £150000 lent by the *Swiss* Cantons: but Tallies were struck for the
> whole Summ. These all remained in the late Treasurer's hands at the time
> of his Removal, yet the Money was expended; which occasioned those
> great Demands upon the Commissioners of the Treasury who succeeded
> him . . .[23]

Blunt must have contemplated with satisfaction the failure of the system
into which he had tried to break in 1703–4. Furthermore he seems to have
been convinced that in new circumstances he himself could do better.

This possibility had probably not occurred to the Bank of England. So
highly had Godolphin been regarded by the Bank and its supporters in the
City, and so alarmed were they at the idea of his being dismissed, that Sir
Gilbert Heathcote took the unusual and ill-judged step of obtaining an interview with the Queen, and warning her of the dangerous consequences to public
credit of a change of ministers. If Godolphin were in difficulties, what was
Harley, the author of the unsuccessful Land Bank scheme, likely to make of
the situation?[24] The anxiety of the Whigs can be understood; but equally
intelligible is the Tory anger at this apparently arrogant intervention by the
moneyed interests of the City in the political affairs of the kingdom. Harley's
aim was now twofold. Firstly, he sought to bring the War of the Spanish
Succession to an end. Secondly, since the need for immediate military expenditure was as great as ever, he had to find new financial backing. Heathcote,
and the Bank of England, heavily committed to Godolphin and Whig policy,
assured themselves that Harley would never do it. They reckoned without
the sharpness of the Sword Blade. The alternatives open to Harley were few,
but the rivals of the Bank of England were naturally ready to exploit the opportunity and submit proposals. Blunt and Caswall recommended that the
creditors of the state should be incorporated, and the short-term public debt
cancelled in exchange for a commensurate issue of stock.[25] The suggestion
seems quite unoriginal; like the Sword Blade operation of 1703–4 it was an
attempt—in the circumstances most welcome to Harley—to supplant the
Bank of England in its own characteristic procedure. But there was a new
political ingredient in the otherwise old recipe: the powerful lure of the
prospect of trade with Spanish America (in slaves among other commodities),
on the successful termination of the War of the Spanish Succession. Harley
and his financial advisers together evolved a concept which could dispel the
crisis in public credit and provide the new Tory government with the necessary

---

[23] Swift, *History of the Four Last Years of the Queen*, ed. cit., pp. 71–2. Swift here refers to Blunt
as 'a Person, who is throughly instructed in these Affairs'.

[24] Dickson, pp. 62–4; Carswell, p. 40.

[25] Dickson, pp. 64–5.

financial backing. This concept was the South Sea Company. From Harley's point of view it was most adroit. The opportunity of breaking into the carefully restricted trade with the Spanish Indies was one of the chief commercial goals of the war. And as nobody, least of all the Whigs, would deny, the campaigns of Marlborough had been highly successful; it must have seemed very likely indeed that at the end of the war Britain would win the trade concessions with the Spanish Indies which she coveted. But when would the end of the war be? Here Harley's political brilliance can be seen. It was precisely the Tory desire to bring the long and expensive war to a speedy conclusion which divided them from the previous Whig administration; with great skill Harley linked the saving of public credit with the fulfilment of the Tory foreign policy. Nor was this entirely political sleight of hand. It was the war which was running the country into unprecedented public debt. No more solid solution to the country's financial problems could be devised than bringing the war to an end. From Blunt's point of view the concept of the South Sea Company was also highly satisfactory. The familiar Bank of England operation was given a completely new credibility by the prospect of the South Sea trade. This was the confidence-creating element in the new scheme, which in the Sword Blade operation of 1703–4 had been the forfeited Jacobite estates. As in 1703 Blunt had the strongest public guarantee that these tangible assets should not prove illusory—but as in 1703 they were not yet secured. Practice was teaching Blunt the dangerous lesson that a good prospect of material advantage is alone sufficient to raise public credit. Above all Blunt had helped Harley to put the Bank of England's nose out of joint. They were out and he was in. He could not have hoped for more.

The political and financial alliance between Harley the moderate Tory and Blunt the Baptist shoemaker's son, a man of the City if ever there was one, is at first sight surprising. The most compelling reason for it was expediency; each seems to have been the only one who could offer what the other needed. But the alliance was not so extraordinary as it looks. The Harleys, a Parliamentarian family in the Civil War, took care to cultivate their connections with the dissenting interest. Since 1698 Robert Harley's brother Edward had represented in parliament the prosperous Herefordshire town of Leominster, a stronghold of dissent. In the elections of 1710, following Harley's assumption of office, his family captured both the Leominster seats with the help of the family of Blunt's Sword Blade partner George Caswall, who were influential Baptists in the borough.[26]

With its own financial advisers the new government now set to work. An early but significant victory was the 1710 election of directors of the East India Company; as with the Bank of England election it was contested between Whigs and Tories, but while the Bank stayed firmly in the hands of Harley's opponents, here several of his associates, including Blunt, were successful.[27] More important was the Autumn quarterly remittance to the troops abroad,

[26] Carswell, pp. 32–3, 41; G. M. Trevelyan, *England Under Queen Anne* (London, 1930–4), iii, p. 95.
[27] Carswell, p. 41.

which Harley contrived to arrange without help from the Bank.[28] A new form of state lottery was planned, with Blunt's aid, and a pamphlet was published demonstrating the scrupulous honesty with which Blunt handled the money.[29] This skilful piece of financial window-dressing was not carried through without much opposition from Treasury officials. At first it looked as though the lottery would fail, those in the Bank of England interest being hardly eager to subscribe, but Blunt and his partners, with the Sword Blade behind them, were soon able to give a strong lead. As Swift was triumphantly to record of the parliamentary lotteries: 'The last of that kind under the former Ministry was Eleven Weeks in filling; whereas the first under the Present was filled in a very few Hours, although it cost the Government less . . .'[30] In May 1711 Harley described his proposal for the South Sea Company to the Commons; the necessary legislation was rapidly despatched, and by September the Charter had been granted. As Carswell points out, it had been personally drawn up by Blunt, and once again his reliance upon Bank of England precedent is clear. But the constitution of the Company was contrived to permit its control by a small group. The post of Governor—Harley himself was the first—was honorific, the full board, nine larger than that of the Bank, was too large for an efficient executive role; finally it was provided that a committee of directors should have full authority to act on behalf of the whole board. Five directorships went to the Sword Blade partners: John Blunt and his nephew Charles Blunt, Caswall, Jacob Sawbridge and Benjamin Tudman.[31] All were to be prominent in the notorious future of the South Sea Company, and it is an historical irony unlikely to have been lost on Pope that it was these men, above all Blunt himself, who were behind the measure so enthusiastically celebrated by Swift in his *Examiner* paper for 7 June 1711:

> The Publick Debts were so prodigiously encreased, by the Negligence and Corruption of those who had been Managers of the Revenue; that the late Ministers, like careless Men, who run out their Fortunes, were so far from any Thoughts of Payment; that they had not the Courage to state or compute them. The Parliament found that thirty Five Millions had never been accounted for; and that the Debt on the Navy, wholly unprovided for, amounted to Nine Millions. The late Chancellor of the *Exchequer* [Harley], suitable to his transcendant Genius for publick Affairs, proposed a Fund to be Security for that immense Debt, which is now confirmed by a Law; and is likely to prove the greatest Restoration and Establishment of the Kingdom's Credit.[32]

By the end of the year 1713, if not earlier, Pope was personally acquainted with Swift and with Harley himself. Pope's first letter to Swift shows by

[28] Ibid. p. 50.
[29] Ibid. p. 51. *A True Account of the Payments made by Mr. John Blunt into the Exchequer on his Receipt of the Class Lottery* (London, 1712).
[30] Swift, *History of the Four Last Years of the Queen*, ed. cit., p. 77.
[31] Cobbett, vi, 1021–3; Carswell, pp. 57–9.
[32] Swift, *The Examiner and Other Prose Pieces Written in 1710–11*, ed. Herbert Davis (Oxford, 1940), p. 170.

implication that contemporary political affairs had been the subject of discussions between them.[33] From August 1712 to May 1713 Swift was busy with his *History of the Four Last Years of the Queen*, for which he particularly sought Blunt's assistance in the discussion of financial affairs, publishing verbatim the latter's memorandum concerning the public debt in the last years of the previous administration.[34] It would be surprising if Pope did not learn from Swift how Blunt had assisted Harley to put an end to 'Negligence and Corruption' in the management of public finance, and to the over-mighty political power of the 'Money'd Men' of the Bank of England. Sometime after June 1720 Swift revised his *History*, acknowledging in a footnote his debt to 'Sir John Blunt', a Baronet since that date. Almost certainly he brought it to England with him in 1727, and Pope was reminded of its contents when, at his own house, he, Swift and Bolingbroke (one of the original directors of the Company) discussed the possibility of its publication.[35] With Blunt's part in the founding of the South Sea Company we have come to an aspect of his public career with which Pope is certain to have been familiar.

3. Appius and his Decemvirs

It is a sign of the importance of the South Sea Company, more of the need of any British government at this time for large-scale credit, that the new, Tory-created institution survived so easily the fall of Harley and St. John, and the accession of the House of Brunswick to the throne. In the 1715 Company elections the most prominent Tory politicians were removed from their directorships, and the Prince of Wales was chosen Governor. The King and the Prince both invested in Company stock, and in 1718, when the rift between father and son was public, George I himself agreed to succeed the Prince. With the change of dynasty and ministry, however, the Bank of England was back in favour, and equally with the South Sea Company a financial bulwark of the new administration.[36] The Company had nevertheless survived the political crisis. Yet behind the façade of government and royal approval all was not well. Even before the fall of Harley it had become clear that hopes for trade with the Spanish Indies were little better than a mirage. The Asiento Clause of the Treaty of Utrecht indeed conferred on Britain the contract to supply negro slaves for a period of thirty years; trading stations were established in seven South and Central American ports, and one ship a year, of not more than 500 tons, was allowed to make a trading voyage to one of these stations.[37] But against this, the King of Spain had been granted 28% of the profits of the general trade, and for a time it appeared that $22\frac{1}{2}\%$ of the overall profit would be made over to the Queen. Above all the inexperience and inefficiency of the Company in trade, the obstructive hostility of the officials in the Spanish Indies, and in 1718 the outbreak of a new war with Spain and

---

[33] *Corr.*, i, pp. 199 (Pope to Swift, 8 Dec. 1713), 207 (Pope to Caryll, 9 Jan. 1713/14).
[34] Swift, *History of the Four Last Years of the Queen*, ed. cit., pp. x–xi, 71–2.
[35] Ibid., p. xii. For Bolingbroke's directorship, see Add. MSS. 25494, f. 4.
[36] Dickson, pp. 81–2.
[37] Carswell, p. 65.

the seizure of all the Company's property on Spanish territory—spelled failure
for Blunt and his partners. History had repeated itself, only on a larger scale.
Just as the Jacobite lands in Blunt's Sword Blade operation of 1703–4 had
temporarily served to create confidence but were never gained, so now the
prospect of South Sea trade had created widespread confidence but little
profit in the end. Equally, just as the 1703–4 manoeuvre had elevated the
Sword Blade to the status of a government creditor, so now Blunt found
himself, if not a director of a successful trading company, still in an ideal
position for financial manipulation on a scale more ambitious than he had
yet attempted.

His competitive energies were not now directed against the Bank of England
alone, but also across the channel to France where, in the space of three years,
the financial genius of the age, John Law, had achieved remarkable things.
At the source of Law's policy was his conviction that contemporary monetary
practice, having evolved in piecemeal and pragmatic fashion, could be brought
under control for the greater benefit of society. Law rejected the assumption
that money should be intrinsically valuable in favour of the concept of a
truly systematic paper currency whose value should be determined by skilled
financiers, recognized throughout the land, and guaranteed by the power
of the government. Provided the value of the currency were not arbitrarily
fixed, but made to correspond to accessible wealth, such a system could be
trusted to facilitate trade, release the latent resources of an economy, and
increase general prosperity.[38] Such were the ideas which Law put to the
Regent Philippe d'Orléans, soon after the death of Louis XIV. They were
rejected; nevertheless Law had sufficient influence to advance steadily towards
control of the French economy. With his founding of the Banque Générale,
his acquiring dominant interest in the Mississippi Company, and his taking
over the French National Debt, he had gained, by August 1719, the total
control of a major national economy which he had earlier been denied.[39]

Law's steady move to a position of complete financial control in France
was viewed in Britain with apprehension and dismay. A France which had
divested itself of its National Debt, and whose economy was in the hands of
so ambitiously successful an intellect, might indeed seem to menace Britain
financially, even militarily. If Blunt shared this apprehension, for him it was
mixed with emulous excitement; he saw himself as the Law of Britain. Another
director of the South Sea Company, probably Sir Theodore Janssen, gives
us a vivid picture of Blunt at this time, under the name of Appius:

> ... the progress of the Mississippi Company about that time having in-
> toxicated, and turned the brains of most people, APPIUS's mind was
> thereby wonderfully affected, and from his natural inclination to Projects,
> so inflamed, that he could brook no longer the narrow thoughts he had
> entertained before, of engaging for one or two branches of the public Funds
> only; but carried on his views for taking in at once all the national Debts,

[38] Ibid., pp. 77–9, 81–2.
[39] For an account of Law's successive measures, see Carswell, pp. 82–94.

the Bank and East India Company included: often saying, 'That as Mr. LAW had taken his pattern from him, and improved upon what was done here the year before in relation to the Lottery of 1710, he would now improve upon what was done in France, and out-do Mr. LAW'.[40]

The allusion of this passage, and of Blunt's quoted statement, is to the relatively modest conversion into South Sea stock, in February 1719, of a particular section of the British National Debt. It had clearly been an attempt by Blunt to offset the commercial failure of the Company, and was made the more attractive to the government by a promise to lend it a sum proportionate to the value of the actual conversion. This sum the Company did not possess, and it appears to have been a calculated gamble by Blunt and his partners that South Sea stock would appreciate sufficiently to enable them to fulfil the obligation. In the event an abortive Jacobite invasion, brilliantly exploited in an unscrupulous piece of rumour-mongering, to the effect that the Pretender had actually landed and been captured, caused a happy rise in quotations for South Sea stock, with the result that the Company gained a considerable sum towards the promised government loan. By comparison with Blunt's present scheme, however, this had been trifling. Carswell doubts whether Blunt's new conception was so ambitious as to propose the taking over of the National Debt through an amalgamation of the South Sea Company, the East India Company and the Bank of England, yet all the evidence seems to point to this. It is stated by the author of *The Secret History of the South-Sea Scheme* (quoted above) and in Chancellor Aislaby's speech in his own defence before the House of Lords in 1721, where he refers to 'the funds of the Bank and the East India Company, which were proposed to be incorporated into the funds of the South Sea Company.'[41] While it is possible that Aislaby and the author of the *Secret History* were exaggerating in order to incriminate Blunt and clear themselves, the idea they attribute to him would have been characteristic both of his overbearing and ambitious style, and of the essentially imitative nature of his mind—it was after all from the Bank of England that Blunt first learnt the possibilities of converting debt into stock; now he was imitating Law also, who was apparently demonstrating to the world that such schemes could succeed.

Even so there was little chance of such a scheme being accepted without radical modification. Yet, paradoxically, it may have been a sounder scheme

[40] *The Secret History of the South-Sea Scheme*; in *A Collection of Several Pieces of Mr. John Toland* (London, 1726), i, pp. 406–7. This work, pp. 404–47 of vol. i of Toland's *Collection*, is stated to be 'enlarged and corrected' but not written by Toland (p. 404). It gives in polemical form relatively 'inside' knowledge of Blunt's activities in 1720. Hitherto no attempt has been made to establish the authorship of this important source, but a letter from Toland to the director 'Sir T[heodore] J[anssen]' (pp. 466–9; see also 469–75) stresses the same chief point as the work: the comparative innocence of the outer circle of South Sea directors. This suggests Janssen as the author of *The Secret History*. Attribution to so respected and formidable a figure would lend the work further authority, though it should be remembered that Janssen had good reason to feel resentment against Blunt.

[41] Carswell, p. 100; Cobbett, vii, 883. Dickson, pp. 94–5, accepts that this was Blunt's original proposal.

in its original form than as it emerged after negotiation with the politicians. The South Sea Company itself could hardly have been in a worse position to take over more public debt, having failed to acquire a solid basis of wealth through trade. But if the resources of all three companies had been amalgamated, the deficiencies of the South Sea might have been made good, and Blunt himself (as he doubtless intended) master-minded the operation. Blunt certainly realized the need for some confidence-creating element in his new scheme, and was perhaps still sensible enough to try for more than this. If we can trust his own retrospective account, he proposed that the Company be granted the Africa Trade, Nova Scotia, and the French part of St. Christopher's, as 'solid supports to the Stock'—a point usually forgotten in accounts of the South Sea Scheme.[42] In this instance, 'solid supports' seems to spell 'slave trade' particularly plainly.

Blunt now opened his scheme to Lord Sunderland, the head of the government so far as home affairs were concerned. He was rebuffed and referred to Chancellor Aislaby, with whom he was on bad terms.[43] Instead he approached Lord Stanhope, whom he already knew, and who was not absolutely discouraging, despite 'several objections, and a dislike of the whole in the main', for according to Aislaby he 'sent this scheme to me, and desired me to talk with Sir John Blunt about it.'[44] These talks included James Craggs the elder, one of the Postmasters General, and on the Company side Francis Hawes; the Treasurer, Knight; and Sir George Caswall, a director of the Sword Blade Bank and an old associate of Blunt. The idea of amalgamating the South Sea Company, the East India Company and the Bank of England must have been quickly rejected, as also that of the South Sea Company taking over the debts with which the other two institutions were concerned. What eventually emerged, as the result of Blunt's initiative, was that the South Sea Company would take over all the remainder of the National Debt, redeemable and irredeemable, and would convert it into stock as the government creditors came forward to make the exchange. For the privilege of becoming the government's sole creditor for this debt the Company would, in the event of a successful conversion, charge a favourable rate of interest, and also offer a very large sum as a gift to be devoted to buying off such government creditors as might be reluctant to convert their assets into South Sea stock. The value of the debt to be taken over has been calculated in round figures at £31 million; that of the reduced interest rate on the debt at £400,000 a year, and the gift was to be £3 million. This offer must have seemed a brilliant prospect to the government: a solution to the problem of the National Debt at one stroke, and one which would commend itself to the landed and trading interests of the nation, especially the country members of the House of Commons. And

[42] [Sir John Blunt,] *A True State of the South Sea Scheme* (London, 1722), pp. 18, 20. The attribution of this pamphlet to Blunt, derived from Abel Boyer, *The Political State* (London, 1713–40), xxxvi, p. 225, is accepted by L. W. Hanson, *Contemporary Printed Sources for English and Irish Economic History, 1701–50* (Cambridge, 1963), 3965 (p. 423).

[43] *Secret History*, pp. 407–8.

[44] Ibid., p. 408; Cobbett, vii, 883.

the light of Law's apparently successful activities in France all things
:emed possible—only a few cautious and penetrating minds considered the
ossible consequences of the fact that Blunt was proposing to raise credit,
ot, as Law taught, in correspondence to accessible wealth, but far beyond.
'his was especially clear when, in response to government pressure, and with
n eye on rival offers from the Bank, Blunt agreed to drop the proposal con-
:rning the Africa Trade.[45]

The secrecy and the hurry with which the promoters of the scheme urged
on seems to have precluded mature deliberation. The Court of Directors
f the Company, with no earlier warning but rumour, were now asked to
pprove Blunt's proposal to the government; on the day following, 22 Jan.
720, before they had had time to debate it, Aislaby announced the proposal
the Commons, who were immediately asked, by James Craggs the younger,
give their unanimous acceptance.[46] The reason for the secrecy and haste,
nd consequent desire to avoid proper public discussion, was of course the
ompetitive frenzy of the Company and other interested parties to steal a
narch on the Bank of England. But the Bank was not so easily excluded;
ter a long silence in the Commons, Cragg's proposal was met with the
ounter-suggestion by Thomas Broderick that the House should consider
ther tenders. This opened the way for the Bank, whose supporters now
astened to frame a proposal which would outdo that of the South Sea. They
ere half way to abandoning their own more sober judgement in favour of
ae rash boldness of Blunt and his partners. The government itself showed
ttle more moderation, Blunt himself the least of all. At this juncture, as
islaby later recounted,

we had a meeting, where the lords of the treasury, and those in the administration, were present, in order, as sir John Blunt says, to persuade
the South Sea Company to advance their proposals, and to offer four
millions certain [ie. the gift]: It was then, my lords, that I again expressed
my fears of this undertaking, and declared, that I did not see how the
South Sea Company could go through with it, if they were to give any
more money for it, without the assistance and concurrence of the Bank,
and much less, if the Bank opposed them; and upon this I proposed . . .
that the scheme should be divided between them and the Bank, which drew
from sir John Blunt this memorable saying, 'No, sir, we will never divide
the child.'[47]

Aislaby is to be trusted, the government was at this point guilty of ex-
oiting the competition between the Company and the Bank in order to
ise the already extravagant offer of the Company from three to four millions.
is quite credible that Aislaby had misgivings, and if they proceeded from
ar rather than rectitude, there was wisdom in them all the same. But Aislaby's

[45] Carswell, pp. 104–6. *A True State of the South Sea Scheme*, pp. 19–20.
[46] For the proposal in the Commons, and the moves which led up to it, see Dickson, pp. 93–8,
d Carswell, pp. 103–10.
[47] Cobbett, vii, 884.

account is most interesting for what it tells us about Blunt. His saying he
expresses his vehement sense of competition with the Bank, the lifelon
obstacle to his ambitions. It expresses his characteristic impatience and,
the words of the *Secret History*, 'high spirit' with opposition. Above all
shows the biblical bias of his thought and expression, for the allusion her
showing a certain persuasive wit on Blunt's part, is to the story of Solomon
judgement between the two harlot-mothers who claimed the same child. Th
king's command that the living child should be divided between them r
vealed the true mother who preferred to lose her child than see it hurt.
The allusion, struck off no doubt in the heat of impatience, reminded Blunt
listeners that he was the true begetter of the Scheme, and that the wisdo
of Solomon would not dispute his possession. The author of the *Secret Histo*
concisely sums up these events and their immediate outcome:

> ... and after several meetings having got over some difficulties ... th
> Scheme was entertained, and opened to the House of Commons in th
> manner every body knows: three Millions being offered without the co
> sent of the general Court, or the knowledge of the Court of Directors;
> presumption perhaps not to be parallel'd in any past transaction, b
> perfectly of a piece with APPIUS's future conduct in the manageme
> of that important affair. The Bank having thought fit to interpose, and
> bid more than the Chancellor had offered, APPIUS resolving to stick
> nothing to carry his point, got an order of Court to leave it to the S
> and Deputy Governors to offer what they should think fit; who havi
> bid seven Millions and a half, the House of Commons accepted th
> Proposal.[49]

Thus Blunt, at the cost of offering the fantastic sum of $£7\frac{1}{2}$ million, got h
way.

In consistently referring to John Blunt as Appius, the author of the *Secr
History of the South-Sea Scheme* not only avoided mentioning by name th
individual against whom the work was directed, but, more important, set h
subject in a particular moral and political light by his allusion to the even
recounted in the Third Book of Livy's History of Rome. Three hundre
years after the founding of Rome, consular government was suspended
order that a magistracy of ten, the decemvirs, might frame a new code
laws. Chief among the decemvirs was Appius Claudius; his guiding har
governed the actions of the ten; it was he who through shameless canvassir
and self-promotion got himself and the other nine a second term of offic
who then violated the constitution by attempting to retain power indefinitel
and who finally brought about the downfall of the decemvirs by a gross viol
tion of justice.[50] Like Appius Claudius, Blunt had been given special powe
for the benefit of the many. As the *Secret History* is at pains to point ou
he had successfully importuned the Company to give the Sub and Depu

[48] I Kings 3: 16–28.
[49] *Secret History*, pp. 408–9.
[50] Livy, *Ab Urbe Condita*, Bk. III, xxxiii–lviii.

overnors and (covertly) through them himself and seven other trusted
lleagues—Knight, Hawes, Houlditch, Sawbridge, Chester, Gibbon and
rigsby—powers to negotiate with the government as he thought best.
hese were the modern decemvirs. But in getting the South-Sea Scheme
cepted by Parliament Blunt, like Appius, had also been given special re-
onsibility towards the whole nation, which might be honoured or abused.
he mercurial Duke of Wharton, in the debate on the South Sea Bill in the
ords, expressed fears which the example of Appius Claudius might well
ve been cited to illustrate:

That the addition of above thirty millions new capital, would give such a
vast power to the South-sea Company, as might endanger the liberties of
the nation, and, in time, subvert our excellent constitution; since by their
extensive interest they might influence most, if not all the elections of the
members . . .[51]

bsequent events were to clarify in the minds of many the nature of the part
ayed by Blunt.

TREASURE IN THE CLOUDS

is clear that the South Sea Company could only fulfil the obligations it
d bargained so hard for if there were an enormous appreciation in the
lue of the stock. Blunt saw this, and it was 'his avow'd Maxim, a thousand
nes repeated, *That advancing by all means the price of the stock, was the only
ty to promote the good of the Company.*'[52] This cannot have been, as he
terwards claimed, a mere yielding to public demand for money-subscriptions.
e set about his task with great short-term skill. His means were money-
bscriptions and loans. Stock was offered to the public at a certain price;
ere was about the Scheme an air of excited speculation, in every sense, and
e stock was rapidly disposed of, appreciating in market value as a result.
he inflow of cash from the subscription then made possible substantial loans
om the Company to the public, which released funds for further speculation,
d drove up the price of the stock still higher. Carswell describes Blunt's
ethod concisely:

Like Law, he had constructed a financial pump, each spurt of stock being
accompanied by a draught of cash to suck it up again, leaving the level
higher than before. As fast as stock issued . . . the money received for it
was returned to the market to support the prices and take up fresh issues
at the higher price. . . . Law's pump fed an open spray, which watered, and
eventually drowned, the economy. Blunt's was meant to be a closed circuit.[53]

unt carried out this manoeuvre, with variations, four times between March
d September 1720, and on each of the first three occasions drove up the
ice of his stock higher than before.

[51] Cobbett, vii, 646–7.
[52] *Secret History*, p. 423.
[53] Carswell, pp. 135, 146.

There were several reasons for his spectacular success. The author of th
Secret History alleges that 'all ways and means, Bribery not excepted', ha
been used to get the South Sea Bill passed.[54] This 'Bribery' had consisted o
the conveying of stock to persons whom the Company wished to oblige; wher
as each party expected, the stock appreciated, it was sold back at the highe
price. The only cash to change hands was the difference between the earlie
and the later price. Among those obliged in this way were the Earl of Sunder
land, Secretary Craggs and his father Postmaster Craggs, Chancellor Aislaby
and (through Secretary Craggs) two of George I's mistresses. There is th
further *possibility* that the King and the Prince of Wales also received 'fictitious
stock.[55] In all but the last instance there was little secrecy about these trans
actions; it was in the personal interests of some of the mightiest men of th
land that the stock should appreciate, and this was known. Where the leader
of the nation had shown their interest, many were eager to follow. In additior
Blunt imitated Law in courting the interest of the polite, not merely that o
the mercantile world. In speech he went further:

> on all occasions he freely declared his opinion, without mincing the matter
> that he was not for disposing the Company's money to traders and suc
> other fair dealers; but to those who frequented the Alley [Exchange Alley]
> and to Ladies and young Gentlemen, who came from the other end of th
> town, with a spirit of gaming: for such, according to him, were the mos
> likely to advance the price of the stock.[56]

Among these polite speculators was Alexander Pope who, having remarke
to his friend Eckersall: '. . . 'tis Ignominious (in this Age of Hope and Golde
Mountains) not to Venture', had purchased £500 worth of stock, on behal
of himself and Teresa Blount, in early March of South Sea Year.[57]

Three further factors contributed to the appreciation of the stock. Th
first was the political reconciliation of the two wings of the Whigs—th
Stanhope-Sunderland group in power, and the Walpole-Townshend grou
out of power—with the forgiveness by George I of the Prince of Wales. Publi
and private reasons prompted this reconciliation. The Walpole factior
which supported the Bank of England, must have been glad of the chance t
join the administration on its high tide of South Sea success. The Stanhope
Sunderland faction must have felt a more secure political future now it wa
no longer at odds with the heir to the throne; and the well-publicised re
conciliations must have been intended to support public credit in genera
and the value of South Sea stock in particular. Among the more private motive
involved, the King's concern for his Civil List, Walpole's and the younge
Craggs's concern for certain insurance company promotions, and a *possib*
mutual interest in providing the Prince with fictitious South Sea stock, ma

[54] *Secret History*, p. 410.
[55] Carswell, p. 126. For a considered account of South Sea bribery, see Dickson, pp. 110–12.
[56] *Secret History*, p. 446.
[57] *Corr.*, ii, pp. 33–4, 38.

be mentioned.[58] In all this Craggs the younger seems to have been the chief promoter and negotiator, and Craggs was of course the one member of the administration with whom Pope was on terms of personal friendship. This reconciliation, in the glow of financial success, of the original advocates and opponents of the South Sea Scheme certainly points up the significance of the conclusion of Pope's apostrophe to Blunt in the Epistle *To Bathurst*:

> No mean Court-badge, great Scriv'ner! fir'd thy brain,
> Nor lordly Luxury, nor City Gain:
> No, 'twas thy righteous end, asham'd to see
> Senateś degen'rate, Patriots disagree,
> And nobly wishing Party-rage to cease,
> To buy both sides, and give thy Country peace.   [ll. 147–52]

The second factor was John Hungerford's parliamentary enquiry into the wave of new financial projects which was now sweeping London. The lists of these minor 'Bubbles' show very well the extraordinary mixture of genuine enterprise and Jonsonian folly in which the British financial revolution was currently expressing itself. Proposals varied from the good sense of those 'For making of iron and steel in Great-Britain', 'For paying pensions to widows, &c. at small discount', and 'For insuring from thefts and robberies', to those 'For extracting silver from lead', 'For the transmutation of quick-silver into a malleable fine metal', 'For a wheel for perpetual motion', and 'For carrying on an undertaking of great advantage, but nobody to know what it is', which sort well with the world of Jonson's *Alchemist* and the attitudes there expressed.[59] The Hungerford Committee, which reported on 27 April, revealed much that was dubious and deceptive in these projects, and proposed an act of parliament to suppress all joint stock companies not authorised by charter. It made no attempt to distinguish promising from unworthy or absurd projects. The 'Bubble Act' came into effect in June, which meant that none of the cash which Blunt now injected into the market in the form of loans would promote speculation in new forms of rival companies. The Act perfected Blunt's closed system, and cleared the way for a further rise in South Sea stock.[60]

The third factor, an ominous favour of Providence, was the news from France. Law's system, set in motion with twice the skill and intelligence of Blunt's, was getting out of control. Inflation was threatening the economy under his care, and in the middle of February he had all dealings in the stock of the Compagnie des Indes stopped. No further paper money was issued and the buying and selling of bullion was forbidden. Law was now trying to make paper currency stable and permanent in France. But the polite world which Law had succeeded in involving in his financial strategy would not be denied its stockmarket, which he was compelled to re-open. On 20 April Alexander Smith, the Caryll family's agent in Paris, who the previous August had re-

[58] Carswell, pp. 128–31, 137–40.
[59] Cobbett, vii, 657–9.
[60] Carswell, pp. 116–18, 139.

ported the 'wonderful progress' of the Mississippi and heartily wished 'the
Family had something in it at first', wrote to Lady Mary that Compagnie
shares had been falling, and had had to be fixed by the government.[61] The
Arret du 21 Mai, which sought to cut the value of paper currency and shares,
was an even more drastic and apparently arbitrary deflationary measure.
Troops were sent out into the streets of Paris, and so great was the shock and
anger the measure provoked that it had to be rescinded in a few days. Once
again the inflation resumed, and it would not be long before Lewis Innes,
writing to advise Lady Mary Caryll on the family investments in the Hotel
de Ville, urged her, after 'so many & so surprising changes in everything that
relates to public or private affaires', to invest in the Clergy of France 'becaus
it was allways thought more secure (as we now find by sad experience) to
deall with a substantiall Corporation, than with the King.'[62] The immediate
result of the great economist's failure for Blunt was that the speculators'
market shifted finally from Paris to London, driving up even further the
value of South Sea stock. Joseph Gage, the 'modest Gage' of Pope's *To
Bathurst* who had bid for the crown of Poland with his Mississippi fortune
of £13,000,000, was now in London, speculating in Exchange Alley.[63]

Those whose sturdy and unimaginative common sense still convinced them
that crown and government, nobility and gentry, were bedazzled by a mere
bubble, those who like Defoe held that stock-jobbing was no more than 'a
compleat System of Knavery',[64] expressed their view with vigour despite
everything. The Jonsonian view of Blunt's achievement is most trenchantly
and memorably put in 'A South Sea Ballad; or, Merry remarks upon Exchange
Alley Bubbles. To a new Tune, called, 'The Grand Elixir; or, the Philosopher's
Stone discovered':

I

In London stands a famous pile,
And near that pile an Alley,
Where merry crowds for riches toil,
And wisdom stoops to folly . . .

2

Here stars and garters do appear,
Amongst our lords the rabble:
To buy and sell, to see and hear
The Jews and Gentiles squabble . . .

[61] B.M. Add. 28228, ff. 19, 40.
[62] Ibid. f. 65 (17 Feb. 1720/1).
[63] *To Bathurst*, ll. 130–4 and n.; T.E., iii–ii, p. 103. Carswell, p. 143.
[64] [Daniel Defoe,] *The Anatomy of Exchange-Alley: Or, A System of Stock-Jobbing . . . By a
JOBBER* (London, 1719), p. 3.

5

'Tis said, that Alchymists of old
  Could turn a brazen kettle,
Or leaden cistern into gold,
  That noble, tempting metal:
But if it here may be allowed
  To bring in great and small things,
Our cunning South Sea, like a god,
  Turns nothing into all things.

6

What need have we of Indian wealth,
  Or commerce with our neighbours?
Our constitution is in health,
  And riches crown our labours.
Our South Sea ships have golden shrouds,
  They bring us wealth, 'tis granted;
But lodge their treasure in the clouds,
  To hide it till it's wanted.

9

. . . But should our South Sea Babel fall,
  What numbers would be frowning?
The losers then must ease their gall,
  By hanging or by drowning.

10

Five hundred millions, notes and bonds,
  Our Stocks are worth in value;
But neither lie in goods or lands,
  Or money let me tell ye.
Yet through our foreign trade is lost,
  Of mighty wealth we vapour;
When all the riches that we boast,
  Consist in scraps of Paper.[65]

It was precisely this common sense, which equated wealth directly with goods,
lands or an intrinsically valuable coinage, that Law and Blunt, with their
different degrees of skill and foresight, sought to supplant with a conception
of wealth new, dangerous, but by no means absurd.

[65] Cobbett, vii, 659–61 (c. July 1720).

Unmoved by scepticism, Blunt was now at the height of his visible success and pride. More than half the government creditors had subscribed their holdings into the Company towards the end of May, and the stock was still rising. Blunt might well have spoken of 'this Bold undertaking' which 'Providence had blessed with success, much beyond expectation'.[66] It is possible that he felt sustained by a personal and religious destiny:

He visibly affected a prophetick stile, delivering his words with an emphasis and extraordinary vehemence: and used to put himself into a commanding posture, rebuking those that durst in the least oppose any thing he said, and endeavouring to inculcate, as if what he spoke was by impulse, uttering these and such like expressions: *Gentlemen, don't be dismayed: you must act with firmness, with resolution, with courage. I tell you, 'tis not a common matter you have before you. The greatest thing in the world is referred to you. All the mony of Europe will center amongst you. All the nations of the earth will bring you tribute.*[67]

This 'prophetick stile' was clearly what Pope had in mind (knowing of him as he did from Harley, St. John, Swift and Craggs) when he wrote of his being 'a Dissenter of a most religious deportment'.[68] Blunt and the decemvirs were now popular figures. On the King's birthday, at the end of May, they were positively *fêted*, and the Duke of Marlborough actually helped the Company Accountant, Grigsby, out of his coach (though the Duchess may have instructed him to be attentive since she was just at that time selling out their enormous holdings in the South Sea to invest in the Bank). On 9 June Blunt, 'but one in thirty one' in his own falsely modest phrase, was deservedly singled out from the other thirty South Sea directors to receive the honour of a Baronetcy, 'for his extraordinary services in raising public credit to a height not known before'.[69] Thus the Baptist cobbler's son had become a Baronet of no ordinary fame.

From this point Blunt's triumph seems to have become hectic with an anxiety not at first acknowledged. It was not just that the other South Sea directors were becoming increasingly restive at his high-handedness, and increasingly hostile to his loans and money-subscriptions, apparently successful though these had been. The somewhat piqued conservatism of the more respectable directors made things more difficult for him, but must have been a minor worry compared with his inevitable fear for the future. Could the stock be maintained at its extraordinarily high level? What would happen if it started to fall? What philosophy of economics, if any, did he have to guide his policy in the coming months and years? For the moment his mind seems to have been chained to 'his avow'd Maxim', of '*advancing by all means of the price of the stock*'. He merely varied his devices so as to wring from them

[66] *Secret History*, p. 425.

[67] Ibid., p. 443.

[68] *To Bathurst*, l. 135 n.; T.E., iii–ii, p. 104.

[69] *Secret History*, p. 443; Carswell, p. 157. He was actually created a Baronet on 17 June (*G.E.C. Baronetage*, v, p. 49).

slightly greater advantage. Thus early in June he proposed yet another loan, although, as Carswell points out, it had not this time been preceded by a money-subscription.[70] He must have hoped by this to achieve an even more spectacular rise in the stocks, ready for the third and most ambitious of his Money-Subscriptions which he now bludgeoned the other directors by shock-tactics and haste to accept, and which was to be for an unlimited issue of stock at 1000, on easy terms. The books opened on 17 June, and £5,000,000 worth of stock was issued at this fantastic level.[71] The subscribers were almost all nominated—by directors of the Company, and by Sunderland, Aislaby, Charles Stanhope and Craggs. They included more than half the notables of the nation; practically nobody of influence or importance but now had some interest in the Company. Never before had the Company so thoroughly or so obviously 'bought both sides'. Blunt was now, as the *Secret History* records, in the Zenith of his Glory, by having got a Subscription at 1000: application was made to him from all quarters: young Ladies came to his *levée* to beg Subscriptions, and the pride of the Decemvirs ran so high at that time, that the best men in the land, could scarce be admitted to the speech of them.'[72] It must have been at this time that, 'one day, at the treasury . . . when a re-lation of a great man, asking sir John for a subscription, the upstart knight, with a great deal of contempt, bid him go to his cousin Walpole, and desire him to sell his stock in the Bank, and by that means he might be supplied.'[73] Blunt now lost any caution he ever had in his treatment of colleagues in the Company, and ordered a fourth loan, 'and the Cashiers lent upwards of three millions in one day, without acquainting the Committee of Treasury with it . . .' This Committee complained constantly to the Directors of the 'irregularity and confusion in the Treasury' and Blunt's answer, while it truthfully acknowledges his own method of handling people, appears to have a touch of hysteria in it:

> *The more confusion the better; People must not know what they do, which*
> *will make them the more eager to come into our measures; The execution of*
> *the Scheme is our business; The Eyes of all Europe are upon us; Both houses*
> *of Parliament expect to have it done before their next meeting: and the loss of*
> *one million or two is nothing, to the speedy execution of the Scheme.*[74]

This answer refers to the second and final stage in the conversion of the National Debt, which took place, at 800, on 14 July and 4 August, 1720.[75]

With this in train, the Scheme was at last executed, and Blunt, who thought (or seemed to think) that 'he had the world in a string', retired to Tunbridge Wells for a holiday. 'In what splendid equipage APPIUS went to the Wells,

[70] Carswell, p. 157.

[71] *Secret History*, pp. 426–7; Dickson, p. 125; Carswell, p. 159.

[72] *Secret History*, p. 427.

[73] Cobbett, vol. vii, 801.

[74] *Secret History*, pp. 429–30. Carswell (p. 170) misquotes, and probably misdates, this effusion; there seems no evidence that it occurred after Blunt's return from Tunbridge, while its place in the narrative suggests that it was before.

[75] Dickson, p. 124.

what respect was paid him there, with what haughtiness he behaved himse
in that place, and how he and his family, when they spoke of the Scheme
called it *our Scheme*, is not the subject of this discourse' writes the *Secre*
History.[76] It was perhaps now that he declared 'that in any other nation be
this, they would have given him a reward of 5000000l. for the service he ha
done to his country.'[77] But Blunt cannot have had the complete confidenc
he took care to display. On 25 June, Blunt's son Henry had joined with Turne
Caswall and Sawbridge of the Sword Blade to form a new bank into which
great sum was immediately paid, presumably to insure against disaster.[7]
From Tunbridge he wrote by every post instructing his brokers to sell part
of his South Sea stock, and we know that in June and July he began (though no
on a great scale) to buy land.[79] On 13 July he had paid £20,400 for a manor i
Essex; the next day part of the remaining debt was converted into stock a
800; four days later the price of the stock began to fall. Blunt must hav
expected it, though not a disaster of the dimensions which occurred. Fo
effectively the South Sea Bubble had now burst.

5. THE COMMITTEE OF SECRECY

The fall of the stock brought Blunt post-haste back to London from Tunbridg
Wells. He was concerned to halt the trend; he was also worried that ther
would not be enough ready money on the market to take up the stock whic
he and his partners were discreetly selling or to sustain his by now predictabl
remedy for a falling rate: yet another money-subscription. The fourth Sub
scription was a step in support of which he had already written 'very pressin
letters' from Tunbridge, but the Sub-Governor had resisted his suggestion:
In these circumstances the falling stock really alarmed him; so much so tha

> he came to town on a Sunday in great rage, and appointed a meeting fo
> the next day, where he used the Sub-Governor in a very rough manner
> saying among other things, *that he did not know but it might cost him h*
> *life, to have left off drinking the waters so abruptly; and that he had rathe*
> *given 10000l. than to have come up to town, but that there was a necessit*
> *to take another Subscription immediately*.[80]

As usual Blunt got his way, though at the cost of greater resentment, becaus
nobody else had his apparent self-confidence. On 24 August the books opened
£1,000,000 stock was offered at the previous rate of 1000, and it was this tim
aimed chiefly at the substantial moneyed interests of the City. Terms fo
payment were stiff, and it would seem that Blunt's policy was to act as thoug
prospects had never been so good. Once again the Subscription was exceeded
and some buyers were turned away; notably the list from the Court of Hanover

[76] *Secret History*, p. 431.
[77] Ibid., pp. 436–7.
[78] Carswell, p. 185.
[79] *Secret History*, pp. 431–2; *The Particular and Inventory of Sir John Blunt* (London, 1721
p. 23. See Dickson, pp. 146–7, on land purchase by Company directors.
[80] *Secret History*, pp. 432–3.

and the apparently still credulous Robert Walpole.[81] But the enthusiasm had gone out of the affair, especially on the part of Blunt himself who flouted an agreement that directors should each subscribe £3,000 by subscribing £500 only.[82] After two subscriptions at 1000 it was now unreasonable to think that speculators for capital gain could be further interested in stock at this price. Blunt had used his characteristic procedure so often that it had become self-defeating. Presumably he ought now to have tried to fix the stock at its high level, or at least to have allowed it to sink gradually with a few upward surges to discourage the idea of an irreversible fall. The only incentive with which the Company could now encourage stockholders to this end was the amount of dividend they might expect. Thus on 30 August a 30% dividend was announced for the current year, with a guaranteed 50% for the next twelve. This proposal seems out of the real world, but it was perhaps the least a government creditor who had bought stock at 1000 had a right to expect, and if credible would have prevented further falls in the stock. However, the sudden switch from a bait of capital to a bait of dividends jogged people back to their senses. The proposal was not credible, and on 2 September the stock had sunk as low as 755.[83] On 8 Sept. a General Court was held, packed with friends of the directors, and encouraging speeches were made by the Duke of Portland, the elder Craggs, and John Hungerford who exulted in 'such wonderful Things in so short a Time' and praised the Company for having reconciled 'all Parties on one common Interest, and thereby laid asleep, if not wholly extinguish'd, our Domestick Jars and Animosities', and for having enriched the nation.[84] But already the loss sustained by the courtiers, politicians, nobility, gentry, officers of the army and navy, merchants and businessmen, who had subscribed at 1000, amounted to a national disaster. Foreign money now left London for the newer Bubbles at Amsterdam and Lisbon. Worst of all, despite the Fourth Subscription, the Company had nothing like enough cash to meet its obligations, nor was there any immediate hope of profit from its almost forgotten original purpose: trade.

To such a situation, Blunt had nothing left to offer. What Carswell has called 'his one serious claim to stand beside Law as an economist', his proposal to make London a free port, was a very long-term measure, and in any case was now unlikely to be accepted, as the scheme of a discredited man.[85] For some months Blunt fades out of the picture, while Walpole adroitly comes to the fore, in his crucially balanced role as the man who had backed the Bank against the South Sea Bill, but who was now a member of the government again, and one who had himself bought South Sea stock. Walpole was well-placed to promote the one expedient which offered hope to the Company and nation: an appeal to the Bank of England. This appeal was answered in

[81] Dickson, p. 125; p. 109; Carswell, p. 177; J. H. Plumb, *Sir Robert Walpole: The Making of a Statesman* (London, 1956), pp. 315–16.

[82] *Secret History*, p. 434.

[83] Carswell, pp. 178–9.

[84] Boyer, *Political State*, xx, pp. 181–2.

[85] Carswell, pp. 172–3.

the end by two proposals, the 'Bank Contract' and the 'Engraftment Scheme', in each of which Walpole was intimately concerned, and the second of which was virtually delivered to him as a political weapon. On the 'Bank Contract', first drafted on 19 September, the Company, the King and the government now pinned their hope. But the Bank, partly because it was in difficulties and partly to exploit its advantage, held back, and on 8 Nov. finally rejected the scheme. The government was thus acutely embarrassed. Meanwhile Walpole and his banker Jacombe had evolved the second proposal (first mentioned on 11 November), perhaps more acceptable to the Bank, but with cynically shrewd timing they withheld it until 19 November. Sunderland and Stanhope, Walpole's old political rivals, now understood that their administration depended on him, and were obliged to accept the proposal. But Walpole's aim was power not revenge. It was agreed that the joint policy should now be one of reconstruction rather than recrimination, this being as personally welcome to the government, not to mention the South Sea directors, as it was likely to promote the material welfare of the nation. On this nice point turns the whole question of Walpole's subsequent role as a 'screen' for a public cheat. For it soon became clear that a powerful alliance of Jacobite, Tory and Whig back-benchers were strongly against drawing a veil over the glaring misjudgements and suspected misdemeanours of the South Sea Company and the Sunderland-Stanhope administration.

Prominent in this alliance were Shippen, the leader of the Jacobites, Sir William Wyndham, and Sir Joseph Jekyll, each of whom Pope was subsequently to praise respectively for bluntness, justice and unswerving principle.[86] In the Commons debate on the Address of Thanks for the King's speech, at the start of the new session, Shippen spoke of 'the honour of parliament, the interest of the nation, and the principles of justice'; Wyndham praised the 'firmness and resolution' with which the French parliament had dealt with the now disgraced Law; and Jekyll hoped that 'a British parliament would never want a vindictive power to punish national crimes'.[87] A clause for 'punishing the Authors of our present Misfortunes', seconded by Jekyll, was now added to the Address, and on 12 December, despite the opposition of Craggs, Horace and Robert Walpole, an immediate examination of the conduct of the South Sea Company was resolved on. On the 15th the Company was ordered to bring its documents before the House; four days later another clash between Walpole and Jekyll took place, in which the former urged that to 'unravel what had been done, they should not only ruin the South Sea Company, but instead of alleviating, aggravate the present misfortunes.' Against the morally unfastidious pragmatism of Walpole, Jekyll stood firm for an assertion of 'public faith, equity and justice, which the South Sea Managers had notoriously violated', and he implicitly denied that the 'Engraftment Scheme', hints of which Walpole kept dangling before a somewhat

---

[86] *To Fortescue*, l. 52; 'Epilogue to the Satires', Dialogue I, ll. 39–40; Dialogue II, l. 88 (T.E., iv, pp. 9, 300–1, 318).

[87] Cobbett, vii, 681–3.

indifferent Commons, could do so much to restore public credit.[88] In the end both measures went forward, but while Walpole's 'Engraftment Scheme' (though it made his political career) proved in its main point to be as much a bubble as Blunt's, the efforts of Jekyll and his supporters resulted in the setting up on 11 Jan. 1721, of a Committee of Secrecy with full powers to investigate the recent conduct of the South Sea Company.[89] Five days later the directors were restrained from leaving the country, and on 23 January Sir John Blunt was taken into the custody of the Serjeant at Arms.[90]

Blunt now came back into prominence for the last time in his life. The chief question which now arises is that of his integrity, in 1720 and before. By the standard of integrity that would have been recognized, for example, by Lord Digby, how guilty was Blunt? Was the South Sea Scheme a calculated cheat? Clearly Law's scheme was not, and Blunt's, conceived when Law's was rising to its peak of acknowledged success, was in avowed imitation of Law. If Law sought to raise credit to develop the whole economy while Blunt constructed a closed system, to benefit only the Company and the government, subscribers who bought stock at a high rate did so of their own free will. Blunt certainly misled the public, but perhaps deluded himself too; he could hardly have foreseen from the beginning the disastrous fall by which they lost their money, since such a fall would obviously be equally disastrous for himself. It is thus unlikely that Blunt, ambitious and unscrupulous though he was, framed his Scheme as a public deception. In his own words, 'there was no evil Design in the first preparing this Scheme'.[91] He must have believed that even without 'solid supports' the value of the stock could be raised and fixed high. But he seems to have been carried away, in the hectic atmosphere of mass speculation, by his own success in short-term manipulation of the market. Perhaps he hardly faced the consequences of what he was doing when he carried out the second stage of the conversion of public debt at 800. It is at this point that real duplicity appears, yet Blunt may still have half-believed that his own expertise and Providence might save the day. But after the failure of the dividend-offer, on 30 August, even half-belief was impossible. From then on he merely kept up a front. Apart from the Scheme itself, however, there were in the early months of 1721 other questions being asked, almost equally important, concerning irregularity in the conduct of the Company, the honesty with which the South Sea Bill had been procured, and the selling of 'fictitious' stock. These reflected on the integrity not only of Blunt and the directors, but also of the government, perhaps even of the court, in the most serious way.

We should know little of these matters if it were not for Blunt himself. It is the final irony of Blunt's career that he now supported Jekyll's insistence that parliament should 'discover' the 'distemper' before attempting the cure, against the screening policies of Walpole. He put himself in the power of the

[88] Ibid., pp. 684–90.
[89] *Commons Journals*, xix, p. 399.
[90] Ibid., p. 406.
[91] *A True State of the South Sea Scheme*, p. 56.

Committee of Secrecy and, unlike the Company cashier, Robert Knight, who absconded rather than reveal all he knew, agreed to tell them the truth. Blunt must have realized that he could not hope to conceal the whole truth, that he was likely to be considered chief culprit in the national disaster, but that something might be salvaged from the wreck of his fortune and career through co-operation with the Committee. It is probable too that his religion and his liking for a righteous moral stance played a part in this decision. Having confessed his own offences, he could, with some integrity, help to expose those who had not yet confessed theirs. The turning-point of his resolution is preserved in the Committee of Secrecy's First Report:

Sir John Blunt said . . . that after this examination on Friday the 27th of January last, Mr. Joye [the late Deputy-Governor of the Company] came to his lodgings, and asked him touching what had passed in his examination before your committee. That sir John Blunt told him, he had said nothing of the ministry: What! says Mr. Joye, nor of the ladies neither? To which sir John replied, that he had not.

That on Saturday the 28th. of January last, soon after sir John Blunt had been again examined by your committee at the South-Sea house, Mr. Joye came to him, and asked him what had passed; that sir John told him he was under an obligation of secrecy; that he loved him very well, and that the best way was to tell the whole truth: What, says Mr. Joye, of the ladies, and all? Yes (says sir John) the examination is very strict, and nothing but the truth will do.[92]

There is a wry irony in the spectacle of these two gravely embarrassed men holding out as long as possible before they revealed the illicit gains of the King's mistresses—'the ladies'—and in the way expediency and morality embrace in the final remark: '. . . nothing but the truth will do'. Thus it was that the politicians were arraigned. Charles Stanhope, defended by Walpole among others, was acquitted by a mere three votes, though certainly guilty. In the next trial 'Walpole's corner sat mute as fishes', and Aislaby was condemned. Sir George Caswall went the same way. The mob lit bonfires in the streets as they were taken to prison. Sunderland, the greatest of them all, was another matter. Walpole exerted all his influence to secure an acquittal. Sunderland took his stand on a flat denial of the charges, so that, as Broderick, the Chairman of the Committee, wrote afterwards: 'the question in truth, was neither more nor less than whether we should give credit to that assertion, or sir John Blunt's oath.' Attempts to falsify the oath were unconvincing, and the stronger appeal of the defence was: 'If you come into this vote against lord Sunderland, the ministry are blown up, and must . . . be succeeded by a tory one.'[93] Such was the view of the prosecution. It is hardly surprising that many, looking back on these events from the 1730s, felt them to have been crucial in the subsequent development of the political situation. Between 1713

[92] Cobbett, vii, 720.
[93] Ibid., 752, 756.

and 1732 there was no better chance of a new Tory government. Sunderland was acquitted, probably wrongly, by 233 votes to 172. The only person who could have further strengthened the evidence against Sunderland and others was the cashier Knight, then in Brabant, and it has been suggested that secret influence was brought to bear, from Britain, to prevent his extradition.[94]

There remained the punishment of the South Sea directors themselves. A South Sea Sufferers Bill permitted a levy to be made on the estates of the directors to help make good the losses of the Company. Each director was required to give a full and detailed statement of his total assets in June 1720 and March 1721. *The Inventory of Sir John Blunt* shows his estate to have amounted to £183,349.10.8¾; he was the third richest of the directors, after Janssen and Fellowes.[95] He petitioned the Commons for clemency, like the other directors, and spoke of his 'Thirty Years diligent Application to Business' by which he had acquired 'a very plentiful Estate before Christmas, 1719' and pleaded his need to provide for his seven children by his first wife and the eleven children and grandchildren of his second wife by a former husband.[96] When his case was debated on 23 May there was a clear clash between the supporters of the Committee, who wished to see him rewarded for telling them 'many secrets which otherwise they could not have known', and the supporters of Walpole who having 'screened' the Earl of Sunderland were happy to revenge themselves on 'the upstart knight'. Jekyll spoke warmly for him and moved that he be allowed to keep £10,000, but both the Walpoles went out of their way to stress his guilt as 'the chief contriver and promoter of all the mischief', his history as a fraudulent projector, and his general arrogance. In the end he was allowed £1,000, which was subsequently raised to £5,000.[97]

More resentful than ever at the avarice and ingratitude of noble persons, Blunt retired to prepare his own account of the calamity which had ruined his own career along with the fortunes of so many of his countrymen. In *A True State of the South Sea Scheme*, published in 1722, he made as restrained and plain a defence of the South Sea directors as the case would allow. This important pamphlet, ignored in books on Blunt and the Bubble, lays neither blame nor praise at the door of particular directors. Nor does it follow the course of the Committee of Secrecy in pointing to corruption in high places. It consistently blames the Bank of England for envious competition in forcing the South Sea Company to undertake the conversion of the National Debt on terms so risky that the directors had no alternative but to exploit 'the general disposition of the People' and drive up the price of the stock in response to the inordinate public demand for Money-Subscriptions.[98] 'The Spring of Money-Subscriptions', Blunt contended, 'arose from without Doors, and not from the directors themselves.'[99] Second to the Bank of England, Blunt accused

[94] Carswell, p. 243.
[95] *The Particular and Inventory of Sir John Blunt*, Abstract, p. 3.
[96] *The Case of the South Sea Directors*, No. 3.
[97] Cobbett, vii, 801-2; Carswell, p. 258.
[98] *A True State of the South Sea Scheme*, p. 20.
[99] Ibid., p. 24.

THE DISTEMPER OF THE TIMES, which captivated the Reason of Mankind in General, not only in *England*, but in all the neighbouring Countries, who leaving the usual Methods of Labour and Industry to gain Estates, were all tainted with the fond Opinion of being rich at once; which caus'd many Persons to engage much beyond their own Fortunes, not only in *South Sea* Stock, but in every *pernicious Bubble*, that could be devis'd. And here needs only an Appeal to every Man's own Conscience, and to desire him to reflect on the Operations of his own Mind at that 'Time, and what he did and saw, and knew to be done by others.

Blunt's righteous tone finally breaks through the restraint as he recalls: 'HOW did Persons of all Ranks and Stations, lay aside all manner of distance, and almost Decency, to become the humble Suitors for Subscriptions: not only to the *Directors* of the *South Sea* Company, but also to the *meanest* and *vilest* of People . . .'[100] He concluded by declaring that though the South Sea directors 'may have committed some Errors, which is common to human Frailty', 'there was no evil Design in the first preparing this Scheme', and that they were hardly 'guilty of so black Crimes, as by the popular Cry they were accus'd of.'[101] Despite its plain, factual air, Blunt's defence is evasive. No doubt the competitiveness of the Bank and the 'distemper' of the times did contribute to the disaster, but Blunt had, at the nation's peril, exceeded the one and exploited the other to have his own way.

It is possible that Blunt could not see his own irresponsibility. His will, made out in his own now shaky hand on 13 Feb. 1731/2, speaks of 'my Estate of above Two Hundred Thousand pounds which hath been most unjustly taken from me by a cruel & unjust Act of parliament' and makes provision for the eventuality of its being returned '. . . in Case it shall at any time hereafter please God to inspire ye Nation with yt due sense of Justice as to make any Restitution or satisfaction . . . in respect of all or any part of my said Estate so very unjustly taken away . . .'[102] But if the world had dealt unjustly by him, he trusted in heaven, 'thro' ye merits and Intercession of our blessed Savior & Redeemer Jesus Christ to obtain full Pardon & fforgiveness of all my sins & an Inheritance in ye Kingdome of Glory with other ye Elect Children of God . . .'[103] Strong in his faith as age came on, he lived out the remainder of his life quietly, was able to bequeath to his family £8,000 more than parliament had left him, and retired finally to Bath where since South Sea year the young Ralph Allen, the honest projector, had been struggling with his first government contracts.[104] There he died, in January 1733, shortly after having been fined by the Court of Chivalry for usurping the Arms of the family of Blount of Sodington.[105]

---

[100] Ibid., p. 41.

[101] Ibid., p. 56.

[102] Principal Probate Registry, Literary Department, Somerset House: The Will of Sir John Blunt, ff. 5–6.

[103] Ibid. f. 1.

[104] The Codicil of Blunt's will, dated 15 Jan. 1732/3, is stated to have been witnessed at Bath (f. 1).

[105] *G.E.C. Baronetage*, v, pp. 48–9.

6. BLUNT AND POPE

John Blunt was a tirelessly energetic and ambitious man, with a highly developed and hectic sense of competition, an impatient capacity to grasp at
new and startling possibilities, though not always fully to understand them.
He was a man with enormous confidence in himself and a certain contempt
for others, both in his high-handed manner, and in his readiness to mani-
pulate people usually through their own acquisitive or corrupt motives. He
was highly unscrupulous in all but the basic concepts of his two biggest enterprises: the South Sea Company and the South Sea Scheme, though the realization of each, and especially the latter, was attended by profiteering and
deception in numerous lesser instances. Finally, Blunt was, in however
ambiguous a way, a religious man. If he was hardly a good man, religion was
nevertheless an essential part of his personality, of the way he expressed
himself, and the way he seems to have thought about himself and his activities.
Indeed the 'trace of titanism' which Carswell has seen in him, and the 'neo-
Biblical oratory' which Dickson notes, together with some of the language of
his will give a very Calvinistic feel to his character, and suggest that he felt
Providence working particularly through him. It is perhaps what might be
expected if his Baptist background is considered together with the bold and
startling nature of his career. Evidence offering us a more inward picture of
Blunt has not survived. Perhaps the most intimate insight we have is that
afforded by his private conversation with Joye at the time of the Commons
investigation: '. . . the examination is very strict, and nothing but the truth
will do'. Some social details may be added from *The Particular and Inventory
of Sir John Blunt*, which lists all his effects and expenditure in 1720.

Several facts stand out, and the first concerns Blunt's second marriage.
His first wife, Elizabeth Court, had died in 1708. On 22 December 1713,
however, he married Susanna Tudman, widow of Benjamin Tudman, goldsmith, banker and South Sea director, previously widow of John Banner, a
London salter, and daughter of Richard Craddocke, a governor of Bengal in
the East India Company.[106] This was almost a dynastic marriage in the
business and commercial world of the City, and as well as useful family-and-
business connections his second wife brought him, by his own admission,
'a large Fortune' including his 'Dwelling House' at Stratford in Essex.[107]
Though Blunt had settled her own fortune on her at the time of their marriage,
it was a great point in his petition to the Commons that he should be left
enough money to keep his other 'solemn' financial promises to her.[108] Connected with Blunt's second marriage is the importance in his accounts of the
very large family of which he was head. If Pope saw Caryll in the role of a
patriarch with his family around him, Blunt and his own large business and
mercantile family could be seen in the same way. Not only did the education
and provision for his children and step-children naturally engage his concern,
but also the claims upon him of remoter and poorer relatives, as witness:

[106] *G.E.C. Baronetage*, v, pp. 48–9; Carswell, p. 63.
[107] *The Particular and Inventory of Sir John Blunt*, p. 15; Abstract, p. 1.
[108] *The Case of the South Sea Directors*, No. 3; *Particular and Inventory*, p. 15.

George Cornwall, a poor Nephew at *Buenos Ayres*, which I
intended to forgive him .... £76.16.6.
Thomas Birch, a poor Relation, lent at several times, which I
never expect again .... £152.2.4.
To Cash given Mrs. *Owen*, a poor Relation .... £100.0.0.

Once, and but once, in these accounts his charity is extended beyond the
family:

To Cash paid Mr. *Morley* for a Charity School .... £25.0.0.
[109]

These items must be set in the context of South Sea year, when Blunt must
have thought he was worth upwards of £180,000, and of his subsequent interest in minimizing his personal fortune. Nevertheless he appears a more
generous man than Peter Walter.

A third interest of *The Inventory* is the light it throws on Blunt's way of
life and social ambitions. His two houses, one in Birchin Lane near Exchange
Alley in the City, the other bought by his second wife in Stratford, seem to
have been amply and comfortably furnished (the catalogue of Birchin Lane,
incidentally, includes 37 'pictures' and 'A Book-Case . . . and some Books'),
but the one can have had no pretensions to be a fashionable town house, nor
the other a country house and estate. Yet with his 'plentiful' fortune acquired
before the end of 1719 he could surely have set himself up as a landed gentleman had he wished. Evidently he did not so wish, and even in South Sea year
the most he did to change his way of life was to have his house in Stratford
done up, and buy himself a new coach.[110] All in all Blunt was essentially a
City businessman, with little personal desire to break into the world of the
landed gentry or nobility. His land purchases in 1720 were primarily a financial
manoeuvre.[111] When he expressed his own valuation of his services to the
public, at the height of his success, he put it not in terms of lands or dignities,
but in monetary terms.[112] Naturally he accepted his baronetcy, but there is
reason to think that his usurping the arms of Blount of Sodington, at the end
of his life, was rather the result of his wife's ambition than his own![113] Such,
with these few softening touches from *The Inventory*, was the character of
Sir John Blunt, the man who more than any other individual in Britain was
responsible for the South Sea Scheme and the public calamity which followed.
While he shares many of the unlikable qualities of Peter Walter, it is fair to
say that Blunt was more ambitious, more imaginative, more rash, and perhaps
finally more human.

Public reactions to the bursting of the South Sea Bubble were firmly
based on the more conservative, sceptical and moral attitudes that had been

[109] *Particular and Inventory*, pp. 7, 21.
[110] Ibid., pp. 9–10, 21; *Secret History*, p. 431.
[111] The nature and extent of Blunt's land purchases may be seen from *The Particular and
Inventory*, Abstract, p. 1.
[112] *Secret History*, pp. 436–7.
[113] Carswell, p. 258.

expressed towards the Scheme during South Sea year, and, before that, to
stock-jobbers and projectors in general. Among these there is none more
remarkable than the view of Defoe set out in 1719 in *The Anatomy of Exchange
Alley*. Written particularly as an attack on Blunt's three partners Turner,
Sawbridge and Caswall, this work proved astonishingly prophetic of the
moral and political consequences of the ambitions of the Sword Blade partners.
The process would start, Defoe thought, with projectors (he does not mention
Blunt) 'old in the Crime (*viz.*) of *resolving to be rich at the Price of every Man
they can bubble*'; they are men who are ready when occasion offers 'to Stock-
jobb the Nation, Couzen the Parliament, ruffle the Bank, run up and down
the Stocks, and put the Dice upon the whole Town.' The occasion Defoe had
in mind was a 'degenerated Government'; it was a possibility he feared because
he had already seen instances of 'when our Statesmen come into a Confederacy
to bite the People, and when Dukes turn Stock-Jobbers'. 'What fatal things',
asks Defoe 'may these shining Planets (like the late Great Light) foretel to
the State, and to the Publick; for when Statesmen turn Jobbers the State
may be Jobb'd', and '... in time, by Strength of Money, they may *Stock-jobb*
Religion, Property, Constitution and Succession ... if the same Avarice
reigns among them that 'tis evident is their Guide now, they would ...
make a Transfer of King *George* and his Crown for a half *per Cent.*' And
while Defoe foresees that such ambitions 'will, in Time, ruin the Jobbing-
Trade', this is cold comfort, for ''twill be only like a general Visitation, where
all Distempers are swallow'd up in the Plague, like a common Calamity, that
makes Enemies turn Friends, and drowns lesser Grievances in the general
Deluge.'[114] Defoe's work is of great interest not only because of its apparent
inside knowledge of the ambitions of some of the City projectors, but also of
its shrewd reading of the possible political consequences, which in its all-
embracing pessimism resembles Tory fears of the City in 1711. Striking too
is the language and imagery—planets, plague and deluge—with which he
invests what he intends to be his prophecy. It was in fact natural to think
of South Sea year in terms of prophecy, for prediction, denunciation, an
apprehension of widespread evil and suffering, were all part of the historical
experience. Thus Pope, writing to Atterbury on 23 Sept. 1720, declared:

> I have some cause, since I last waited on you at Bromley, to look upon you
> as a Prophet in that retreat, from whom oracles are to be had, were man-
> kind wise enough to go thither to consult you: the fate of the South-sea
> Scheme has much sooner than I expected verify'd what you told me.

and went on to quote from *Job*: 'Men shall groan out of the CITY, and hiss
them out of their PLACE,' and to develop the theme of avarice and the image
of the deluge, which Defoe too had used:

> Indeed the universal poverty, which is the consequence of universal avarice,
> and which will fall hardest upon the guiltless and industrious part of man-
> kind, is truly lamentable. The universal deluge of the S. Sea, contrary to

[114] *The Anatomy of Exchange Alley*, pp. 37–8, 39–40, 62–3, '12' [in fact 20], 42, 55, 40–1.

the old deluge, has drowned all except a few *Unrighteous* men:[115]

Atterbury himself, in the debate on the state of public credit in the Lords on
9 Jan. 1721, used the other obvious image in Defoe and 'justly compared' the
ill-effects of the Scheme 'to a pestilence'.[116] It was however Pope's friend
the philosopher George Berkeley who in his important *Essay Towards Preventing the Ruin of Great Britain* (1721) was the first among the poet's circle
to connect the moral corruption of the Bubble crisis with the ideal of Augustan-
ism, and with the prospect of Britain's now declining from such civilization
as it had already achieved. He opened with the significant question: 'Whether
the prosperity that preceded, or the calamities that succeed the South Sea
project have most contributed to our undoing . . .' and went on to commend
those 'old-fashioned trite maxims concerning religion, industry, frugality,
and public spirit, which are now forgotten', and included under the fourth
head (though the 'expense suiteth ill with our present circumstances') the
erecting of 'Triumphal arches, columns, statues, inscriptions, and the like
monuments of public services . . .', the building of 'a parliament house,
courts of justice, royal palace, and other public edifices, suitable to the dignity
of the nation . . .' and the establishing of an Academy that learning also might
'inspire men with a zeal for the public . . .'[117] He launched an attack on
'bribery', and 'solemn perjury', and affirmed that the 'South-sea affair, how
sensible soever, is not the original evil, or the great source of our misfortunes;
it is but the natural effect of those principles which for many years have been
propogated with great industry.' If the calamity could now turn men's minds
from 'private aims' to 'the good of their country' then 'British worth and
honour' might revive.[118] But he assumed, in the longer perspectives of history,
a cyclical pattern of the rise and fall of civilizations and concluded with the
prospect of a degenerated Britain:

> God grant the time be not near when men shall say: 'This island was once
> inhabited by a religious, brave, sincere people, of plain uncorrupt manners,
> respecting inbred worth rather than titles and appearances, asserters of
> liberty, lovers of their country, jealous of their own rights, and unwilling
> to infringe the rights of others; improvers of learning and useful arts,
> enemies to luxury, tender of other men's lives and prodigal of their own;
> inferior in nothing to the old Greeks or Romans, and superior to each of
> those people in the perfections of the other. Such were our ancestors during
> their rise and greatness; but they degenerated, grew servile flatterers of
> men in power, adopted Epicurean notions, became venal, corrupt, in-
> jurious, which drew upon them the hatred of God and man, and occasioned
> their final ruin.'[119]

[115] *Corr.*, ii, pp. 53–4.
[116] Cobbett, vii, 697.
[117] *The Works of George Berkeley, Bishop of Cloyne*, ed. A. A. Luce and T. E. Jessop (London,
1948–57), vi, pp. 69, 80–1.
[118] Ibid., pp. 83–4.
[119] Ibid., p. 85.

Berkeley's talk of triumphal arches as a remedy for the collapse of national credit and widespread poverty may seem absurd, but public spirit is his theme; it is by public works and public symbols, as well as by 'the slow moderate gains' of an 'honest industry', that public spirit is sustained. In this insistence, and in his fear that the Bubble was 'not the original Evil' but an augury of national decline, he was expressing views which were to become Pope's own.

Pope's own image of Blunt was drawn firstly from the course of public events and secondly from those of his friends and acquaintances who had known him directly. Among these, Robert Harley, Henry St. John and Jonathan Swift, would all have been well informed about Blunt at the time of the founding of the South Sea Company. To them should be added James Craggs the younger, whom Pope had known since 1715, who had been a minister since 1717, and who was on terms of intimacy with Pope through-out South Sea year.[120] From Craggs Pope was in a position to learn much about Blunt in the last four years of the latter's public career. Thus Pope is himself a source of some authority on Blunt, and his character-sketch of him is of interest:

> Sir, JOHN BLUNT, originally a scrivener, was one of the first projectors of the South-sea Company, and afterwards one of the directors of the famous scheme in 1720. He was also one of those who suffer'd most severely by the bill of pains and penalties on the said directors. He was a Dissenter of a most religious deportment, and profess'd to be a great believer. Whether he did really credit the prophecy here mentioned [the allusion is to *To Bathurst*, l. 136 et seq.] is not certain, but it was constantly in this very style 'he declaimed against the corruption and luxury of the age, the partiality of Parliaments, and the misery of party-spirit. He was particularly eloquent against *Avarice* in great and noble persons, of which he had indeed liv'd to see many miserable examples. He died in the year 1732 [O.S.].[121]

Seen against the evidence here assembled Pope's brief summary is accurate to a degree. He is aware of the important part Blunt played in 1711 and 1720, that he was one of the most severely punished in 1721, and that he was a very vocal dissenter. By reference to *The Secret History of the South-Sea Scheme* it has been possible to demonstrate Blunt's style of declamation, and to show that Pope is not, as might have been thought, exaggerating in this respect. The *Secret History* alludes to Blunt's proneness to grumbling at ungenerous treatment, and *A True State of the South Sea Scheme* partly confirms Blunt's eloquence against corruption, luxury, party-spirit and avarice.

Let us now consider the passage to which Pope appended the above sketch, the apostrophe to Blunt in the Epistle *To Bathurst*, written shortly before the death of the 'upstart knight':

---

[120] *Corr.*, i, p. 306 (Pope to Craggs, 15 July 1715); ii, p. 51 (Robert Digby to Pope, 30 July ? 1720); pp. 53, 57 (Pope to Caryll, 19 Sept. and 28 Oct. 1720).
[121] *To Bathurst*, l. 135 n.; T.E., iii–ii, p. 104.

Much injur'd Blunt! why bears he Britain's hate?
A wizard told him in these words our fate:
"At length Corruption, like a gen'ral flood,
(So long by watchful Ministers withstood)
Shall deluge all; and Av'rice creeping on,
Spread like a low-born mist, and blot the Sun;
Statesman and Patriot ply alike the stocks,
Peeress and Butler share alike the Box,
And Judges job, and Bishops bite the town,
And mighty Dukes pack cards for half a crown.
See Britain sunk in lucre's sordid charms,
And France reveng'd of ANNE's and EDWARD's arms!"
No mean Court-badge, great Scriv'ner! fir'd thy brain,
Nor lordly Luxury, nor City Gain:
No, 'twas thy righteous end, asham'd to see
Senates degen'rate, Patriots disagree,
And nobly wishing Party-rage to cease,
To buy both sides, and give thy Country peace.   [ll. 135–52]

At its most obvious level the passage attacks Blunt through irony. Blunt is
presented as a hypocritical puritan (as in great measure he was) and Pope
deploys his irony by creating such an account of the South Sea Bubble Crisis
as Blunt the puritan moralist might have given, and in one respect *did* give.
Pope's note assures us that the wizard's prophecy is in Blunt's own vein; but
without the *Secret History* and *A True State of the South Sea Scheme* we
should not know how remarkably closely it matches the 'prophetick stile'
and apocalyptic tone of his utterances, or the self-righteous contempt with
which he told how 'Persons of all Ranks and Stations' laid aside 'all manner
of distance, and almost Decency', to get stock. But Pope also inserts into the
prophecy about Britain after the Bubble the metaphor used by Defoe, by
himself, and by many others, for the Bubble Year: that of the deluge. Again,
to those familiar with Blunt's behaviour at the height of his apparent success
(his acceptance of the baronetcy, the 'splendid equipage' in which he travelled
to Tunbridge, and the £5,000,000 from the nation which he declared to be
his just reward) the couplet beginning 'No mean Court-badge . . .' has an
especially sharp point. The phrase 'righteous end' is appropriate to the man
who claimed the special guidance of Providence. And the last couplet, while
certainly pointing to political corruption since 1721, probably also alludes
ironically to the reconciliation of the Sunderland and Walpole Whigs (pro-
ponents and opponents of the South Sea Scheme) in the Spring of 1720,
which, the following Autumn, John Hungerford had so publicly praised the
Company for bringing about. On this reading, the opening phrase: 'Much injur'd
Blunt!' ironically compliments his actual guilt and his self-righteous style.

And yet, as R. A. Brower observes, much of what Blunt 'foresees' is un-
ironically true.[122] A consideration of Blunt's career strongly reinforces the

---

[122] R. A. Brower, *Alexander Pope: The Poetry of Allusion* (Oxford, 1959), pp. 254–5.

sense that there is ambiguity somewhere in the passage. It is not just that Pope had himself speculated in the Bubble and come off with 'half of what [he] imagined [he] had',[123] but that Blunt had been in alliance with so many of his friends, and had helped further the schemes of men such as Harley, St. John and Swift, whom Pope admired. An honest satire against Blunt could hardly avoid some sense of moral involvement, or at least paradox. And indeed history provided the paradox, for had not Blunt truly revealed public corruption to the Committee of Secrecy, and had not Jekyll, the politician of principle, urged that Blunt should be less severely penalized on this account? Had not Blunt's career revealed corruption as much as caused it? Had not his accusation of avarice in great and noble persons been fully justified, as Pope's note records? From this recognition springs the less obvious significance of the passage, the double irony by which Blunt really is 'Much injur'd' since, however guilty himself, he had been treated as scapegoat for a national guilt which, in a few eminent cases, had been 'screened' and left unpunished. Indeed, as Berkeley had written, the South Sea affair was not 'the original evil' but the sign of a more ominous distemper. Pope could now see the omen confirmed, since it was out of the South Sea affair that Walpole, who screened Sunderland but showed no mercy to Blunt, had laid the foundation of his long and (in Pope's view) shamelessly corrupt ministry. Blunt's paradox is like that of a later puritan businessman, Bulstrode in Chapter 71 of George Eliot's *Middlemarch*: he is guilty, but his denunciation of others' guilt is not less true for that reason. It is with this appropriateness that Pope here puts into Blunt's mind the prophecy of what Berkeley had feared, and what St. John's *Craftsman* was now thundering against the government: the pervasive corruption of Walpole's administration and the national decline which it constituted. Thus the full force of such lines as:

> And Judges job, and Bishops bite the town,
> And mighty Dukes pack cards for half a crown.
> See Britain sunk in lucre's sordid charms,
> And France reveng'd of ANNE's and Edward's arms!

is by no means ironical in its judgement of Britain in the 1730s. Here Blunt is credited with what Pope believed to be the truth.

It is worth noting, finally, how close Pope's lines are, in their employment of the device of prophecy, in their charges against the high nobility, and in their use of the image of the deluge, to the way Defoe had written in *The Anatomy of Exchange Alley*. I do not suggest direct influence, but rather that these words and ideas arose naturally from the experience of South Sea year, and that what Defoe foresaw of the South Sea Bubble in 1719 Pope saw as characterizing the reign of Walpole in 1732. This is an instance of where history has fashioned literature in all its complexity, nor is it surprising that the Financial Revolution in Britain, the great and ominous disaster of the South Sea Scheme, and the man who was the chief projector of this scheme, should have exercised Pope's moral imagination and judgement in his darkest and most deeply probing social poem.

[123] *Corr.*, ii, p. 53 (Pope to Atterbury, 23 Sept. 1720).

VII. 'Low-Born Allen': Ralph Allen of Bath (1693–1764)

1. 'A YOUNG MAN, JUST ENTERING INTO THE WORLD'

RALPH Allen, like Peter Walter and John Blunt, came of humble and obscure birth. Like Peter Walter and John Blunt he raised himself to eminence by his native talent, but while they attained to notoriety he achieved fame. The mind of Pope was exercised by the characters of all three, but while the first two were the object of the poet's attack Allen was called by Pope both 'low-born' and 'the Most Noble Man of England'.[1] Walter attained to the situation of a landed gentleman and to a wealth well beyond this station, but concerned himself with few or none of the landed gentleman's traditional duties to the community. Blunt, unlike Walter, was not primarily concerned with landed property at all; he was a man of the City, and his speculations, inspired by a new world of high finance, soared far beyond lands, rents, and the needs of tenants and workmen. Allen resembled Blunt in being a projector; his original and main fortune was derived neither from the possession nor the management of land. Yet by his middle years he had purchased a manor and was living upon it, and in his later years he built himself a great house on his estate of Prior Park. Throughout his career he showed the strongest responsibility towards the greater community of the nation in which he lived, and the strongest concern and generosity towards the smaller community to which he had come as a young man and which was the scene of his work: Bath and the surrounding country. Here he not only cared for those who lived on his estates as well if not better than John Caryll and Lord Digby did their tenants, but he assisted in the improvement and transformation of the city into a boldly Augustan form. One reason for Pope's admiration for John Kyrle and Lord Digby was that in each case an *urban* community came within their care; but in Ralph Allen's Bath Pope saw a 'white Town' which outshone Kyrle's Ross and Lord Digby's Sherborne—both small, rustic places after all—and whose increasing public state contrasted with that greater and darker city in which John Blunt and Sir Balaam triumphed and fell.

[1] *Corr.*, iv, pp. 145 (Pope to Allen, 2 Nov. 1738) and 221–2 (Pope to Fortescue, 23 Jan. 1739/40).

6. Jan Baptiste van Diest, *Ralph Allen, c.* 1728. By kind permission of the
Victoria Art Gallery and Lord Mayor of Bath.

Allen was born in 1693, and baptized on 24 July in St. Columb in Cornwall.[2] There is no certain information about his early years, though he may have assisted Gertrude Allen (his aunt or possibly grandmother) when she was deputy postmistress of St. Columb, in 1707–8.[3] The Treasury Letter Books and General Accounts, recording salary payments to deputy-postmasters, show a payment to one Robert Allen of St. Columb in the year 1705. Robert Allen seems to have been succeeded by Reskemer Allen, and Reskemer Allen very briefly by Gertrude Allen in 1707.[4] It has been stated that the regularity and neatness with which the boy Ralph Allen helped keep the accounts at St. Columb were commended by a post office inspector, who may afterwards have helped find him a place of his own in the Postal Service. Allen may have assisted Joseph Quash, deputy postmaster of Exeter, and a postal reformer and projector, from 1708–10. In that year, according to Allen's own statement, made three years before his death, he became deputy-postmaster of Bath.[5] He was still only seventeen. His first surviving letter, a brief business note, is dated from 'Bath the 29th September 1712' and addressed to 'Mr. Thomas Bristow at/Mr. Oswald Hoskyns at, the Black/moors head In Kings Street near/the Guildhall/London.'[6] A fragment from Allen's everyday life at this time, the note hardly suggests the possibility of future friendship with the poet who in this same year was completing the earlier version of *The Rape of the Lock*. Other evidence of Allen's activities in Bath are in the Post Office records. From 1701 to 1712 Mary Collins was in receipt of salary as deputy-postmistress of Bath, but on 26 March 1712 she was succeeded by Allen himself.[7] He seems now to have been paid a salary of £170.0.0. p.a.; certainly he received this sum from 1715 to 1720.[8] In 1719 Allen made the proposal to the government which was to be the foundation of his fortune, and from 1720 onwards

[2] Benjamin Boyce, *The Benevolent Man: A Life of Ralph Allen of Bath* (Cambridge, Mass., 1967), p. 1. Boyce's study surpasses the previous biography, R. E. M. Peach, *The Life and Times of Ralph Allen* (London, 1895), in amplitude and accuracy of fact, as well as in breadth of interest. The present chapter, drafted before Boyce's book appeared, draws on the major primary sources he has used, but, following the themes of my own study, differs from his in several points of focus and interpretation.

[3] Herbert Joyce, *The History of the Post Office . . .* (London, 1893), p. 146; Boyce, op. cit., pp. 2–3.

[4] General Accounts in G.P.O., i (1701–10); 1705, p. 14; 1706, p. 18; 1707, p. 17; 1708, p. 16. Boyce, p. 2.

[5] A. M. Ogilvie, ed. *Ralph Allen's Posts* (London, 1897), p. 8. This is an edition of the Narrative prepared by Allen to explain his Bye and Cross Posts System to the Postmasters General, three years before his death in 1764. Several MSS. of the Narrative exist, for Allen sent copies to the Postmasters General in 1761, Lord Bessborough and Mr. Hampden; to Henry Potts, the Secretary to the Post Office; to the Duke of Newcastle and to the Solicitor General. Newcastle's copy is now in the British Museum; another is in the Bath Reference Library; another, in the Public Record Office, is that edited by Ogilvie. A. E. Hopkins, in his edition, *Ralph Allen's Own Narrative* (London, 1961), for the Postal History Society, does not state which MS. he has used. I have therefore preferred to quote from Ogilvie. An interesting brief account of the postal projects of Joseph Quash is to be found in Boyce, op. cit., pp. 14–17.

[6] Bath Reference Library, BB (B 827.55): A. M. Broadley, *The Friendship of Pope the Poet and Allen the Postmaster . . .* (compilation of documents made in 1910), p. vii.

[7] General Accounts, G.P.O., i (1701–10), ii (1711–20); Boyce, op. cit., p. 5.

[8] General Accounts, G.P.O., ii.

his relation to the Postmasters General was to be put on a completely different footing.

To appreciate the significance of Allen's proposal it is first necessary to consider the nature of the Postal Service in England at the time when Allen first came to Bath. This may be done in the words of Allen's own 'plain narrative'; Pope himself may have heard something of the story in similar words when, some sixteen years after Allen's proposal was accepted, the friendship between the two men began.

In the Year 1710, and in the ninth Year of her late Majesty Queen Anne, an Act passed for the Establishment of a General Post Office thro' out all Her Majesty's Dominions: in which act it is expressly declared, 'that divers Deputy (or Country) Postmasters did then collect great quantity's of Post Letters, called *Bye or Way Letters*, and, by clandestine and private agreements amongst themselves, did convey the same, in their respective Mails or Bye Bags, according to their several directions without accounting for the same, or endorsing the same on their Bills, to the great detriment of her Majesty's Revenue.

In order to suppress this scandalous abuse the said Law enacts, 'that whoever, after passing thereof, should be found guilty of embezling the Postage of any *Bye or Way Letters*, to the Prejudice of the Revenue, should forfeit and pay five pounds for the Postage of every Letter so embezled; and one hundred pounds for every week for which he or she continued in such inequitous practice.'

But this was the least part of the evil, which the Legislature had in their view to redress by this penal clause. The unsafe, the uncertain, and precarious conveyance of these Letters was, by the perpetual interruption of Correspondence, of infinite hurt and detriment to Trade and Commerce. And as the negligent and absurd manner of conveyance served to cover the embezlements, so the Embezlers took care that, that negligence and absurdity should go on and increase, in proportion to the amount of their unjust gains.

Allen now gives a rather graphic account of what was actually done with the letters:

The Bye and Way Letters were thrown promiscuously together into one large Bag, which was to be opened at every Stage by the Deputy . . . to pick out of the whole heap, what might belong to his own delivery, and the rest put back again into this large Bag, with such Bye letters as he should have to send to distant places . . . But what was still worse . . . it was then the constant practice to demand and receive the postage of all such Letters before they were put into any of the Country Post Offices. Hence (from the general temptation of destroying these Letters for the sake of the Postage) the joynt mischief of embezling the Revenue and interrupting and obstructing the commerce, fell naturally in, to support and inflame one another. Indeed they were then risen to such a height, and consequently the discredit and disrepute of this conveyance grown so notorious, that many Traders and others in divers parts of the Kingdom, had recourse to various contrivances of private and clandestine conveyance for their speedier and safer Correspondence; whereby it became unavoidable but that other branches of the Post Office revenue should be greatly impair'd, as well as this.

Allen describes the failure of government measures to put matters right, ending in the survey undertaken early in the reign of George I:

> On the accession of King George the first to the Crown, Lord Cornwallis and Mr. Craggs were made Postmasters General: who . . . appointed six Surveyors, and sent them into the several and different parts of the Kingdom and especially into the great Manufacturing and distant parts of it . . . to examine minutely into the true state of the Post Office concerns, in all its Branches; but to have a more particular attention to the proper conveyance, and faithful accounting for the *Bye and Way Letters*.
>
> These Officers, after they had spent a considerable time . . . returned to the Postmasters General their various reports; some of them very Voluminous; but none of them pointed out the least shadow of a reform for the safer conveyance of the *Bye and Way Letters*; or for the suppression of the frauds committed in accounting for the produce of them . . .[9]

Bye and Way Letters were letters sent from one point to another along a postal route to or from London, but which did not pass through the capital itself. *Cross Road Letters* were letters sent cross-country from one main route to or from London to another. Letters sent to or from London itself were termed *London Letters*; letters sent through London from one provincial town to another were called *Country Letters*.[10] The problem which the young Allen had found out by personal experience was that corruption could only be prevented in respect of mail which went through London. The Postmasters General had found no way of controlling the other postal routes. Something of Allen's character may be inferred from these paragraphs of his *Narrative*. He does not write well, and gives the impression of trying to add sophistication and dignity to his practical subject by rather abstract diction ('. . . various contrivances of private and clandestine conveyance . . .') But his basic attitude, if not his language, is essentially practical; a particular picture emerges in spite of himself when he describes the letters 'thrown promiscuously together into one large Bag' and his contempt for the six surveyors and their voluminous reports is clear. Again, though his subject *is* a serious one both from the public viewpoint and his own, his tone is uniformly solemn and moral.

The situation of the Postal Service described in the quoted paragraphs gave Allen the opportunity to make his fortune. Experience had, he believed, taught him how to introduce effective reforms, and he hoped there were particular reasons why the government would be disposed to listen to so

[9] Ogilvie, ed. cit., pp. 5–7.
[10] Peach, op. cit., pp. 58–9.

humble a person as himself. The first of these reasons was his own good record in the Postal Service. When on the accession of George II the new Postmasters General had sent out Surveyors to examine the conduct of the country postmasters, the surveyor 'in whose department it fell to visit the Post Office at Bath, had, on the strictest examination and by the clearest accounts, found that Mr. Allen, from entering on his employment to that time, had faithfully accounted to the Government for the postage of all the *Bye and Way Letters* which had been committed to his care: And this truth that Surveyor was even forced to report to the Board.'[11] Allen was, in other words, an efficient and strictly honest manager, and made sure that other people knew it. The second reason was a political one. Bath was suspected of Jacobite sympathies in the early eighteenth century, and on the outbreak of the Jacobite Rebellion in 1715 Colonel George Wade was despatched to the city with two regiments of dragoons. It was Richard Jones, Allen's clerk of works in his building projects, who seems first to have stated that Allen helped Wade uncover a Jacobite conspiracy in 1715. The story was set down some considerable time after Allen's death, and was repeated later still (1806) by the novelist Richard Graves, who declared that Allen got news of a wagon-load of arms coming up from the West for Jacobite use, and reported it to Wade. Allen's early biographer R. E. M. Peach dismissed the story on unconvincing grounds; Wade is known to have discovered a deposit of Jacobite arms at Bath at 1715; and in 1752, in a letter to the Duke of Newcastle in which Allen recites his services to the House of Hanover, he alludes to the opportunity he had of showing his attachment: 'Marshal Wade was a witness to it in the Rebellion of 1715.'[12] Allen had thus some claims on the government's favour, though his strongest point was that his proposal would be as much in the interest of the king's revenue and the public as of himself.

In 1719, therefore, Allen waited on Lord Cornwallis and Mr. Craggs, the same Postmasters General who five years earlier had attempted to reform the Postal Service. They heard him, according to Allen, with great 'candour and attention' and asked him to explain to them his scheme of reform. This Allen, displaying a remarkable sharpness, refused to do. He obviously feared he would gain no advantage by disclosing his ideas so easily. Instead he offered to take over the running of the *Bye Way* and *Cross Road Letters* himself, for a period of seven years, and at his own cost raise its present annual revenue of £4000 to £6000. A contract to this effect was signed, and in 1720, at the age of twenty seven, Allen found himself free to tackle that task which would either make him or break him. If he succeeded in raising the revenue of the *Bye Way* and *Cross Road Letters* above £6000 a year, all in excess of this sum

---

[11] Ogilvie, ed. cit., p. 9.

[12] Bath Reference Library, B 926: *The Life of Richard Jones* (c. ?1776), an autobiographical MS. probably made from Jones's dictation, transcribed 'Jan 26. 1858 by C.G.', p. 12; Richard Graves, *The Triflers* (London, 1806), pp. 62–3; Peach, op. cit., pp. 54–6. See D.N.B. lviii, pp. 414–15 on Wade. B.M. Add. 32729, f. 291 (Allen to Newcastle, 16 Sept. 1752). It should be noted that Wade was acquainted with James Craggs the younger, son of one of the Postmasters General in 1719 (B.M. Add. 15936, f. 258 (Wade to Henry Worsley, 26 Sept. 1719)).

would be his own; if he did not then his promises to the government would be exposed as merely a young man's boasts, those who stood surety for him would have to pay his debts to the Post Office, and he would probably have to look elsewhere for his living.[13] The risk must have been frightening; and Allen was to encounter unforeseen difficulties enough to daunt (in his own phrase) any 'Young Man, just entering into the world'.[14]

2. A FIGHT AGAINST CORRUPTION

Allen's first problem must have been to find friends who would stand surety against his possible failure. These he refers to in his *Narrative* but does not name.[15] His own salary from 1715 to 1720 can have allowed him to save little compared with the annual sum he was now bound to pay the Postmasters General. It has been suggested, and it is possible, that Marshal Wade was among those who had sufficient confidence in 'his personal character' and 'singular abilities' to guarantee 'a full and undoubted security of £6000, for the true performance of his Contract' but there is also another probable source.[16] Miss E. A. Russ has established, against inaccurate accounts, that Allen was first married on 26 Aug. 1721, and to Elizabeth Buckeridge, daughter of the late Seaborne Buckeridge, a London merchant, and sister of Anthony Buckeridge, Esq. of Ware.[17] Allen may have received promises of assistance, as well as of a substantial dowry, from his brother-in-law to be. The next problem which arose was the discovery that the revenue of the *Bye Way* and *Cross Road Letters* was actually £300 a year less than Allen had been mistakenly informed when his contract was executed; yet he was still bound to pay the full £6000 each year.[18] More disturbing still, many of the country postmasters were unalterably hostile to Allen's design. They represented to the Postmasters General that the projected changes in the *Bye Way* and *Cross Road Posts* might indeed benefit through surer communications the commerce of the kingdom (which Allen claimed as his ultimate purpose) but would only diminish the postal revenue by drawing mail from the *Country Letter* branch (the improvement of which was no profit to Allen, being outside his contract) to the *Bye Way* and *Cross Road* branch (every improvement of which would now add to Allen's personal wealth). Many of the more corrupt or inefficient postmasters must have rationalized their fear of Allen's scheme by means of this argument. Efforts were now made to establish a practical, working distinction between all *Country Letters* and all *Bye Way* and *Cross Road Letters*, but without success. It was discovered that the revenue from

[13] Ogilvie, ed. cit., pp. 8–9.
[14] Ibid., p. 14.
[15] Ibid., pp. 14–15.
[16] Ibid., p. 14; Jones, op. cit., pp. 11–12; Peach, op. cit., p. 60. It is not true that Allen married Wade's natural daughter; see E. A. Russ, 'Ralph Allen of Bath', *Notes and Queries*, cxci, pp. 127–9 (21 Sept. 1946). This error has recently been perpetuated in Romney Sedgwick, ed. *The Commons, 1715–54*, ii, pp. 501–2, in its account of Wade.
[17] Russ, art. cit.
[18] Ogilvie, ed. cit., pp. 9–10.

the *Country Letters* had recently declined, and Allen now offered, in addition to his contract, to support this further revenue at its existing level, once again taking all in excess of the agreed level for his own expenses and remuneration. By this means the Postal revenue could be guaranteed, while Allen's enemies among the postmasters would be unable to sabotage his plan by covertly diverting *Bye Way* and *Cross Road Letters* into the *Country Letter* branch. An explanatory contract to this effect was now drawn up, but owing to a demand by the Postmasters for further security from Allen, which he could not meet, it was never executed. Allen had nevertheless to make sure that no decline in the *Country Letter* branch took place, and whether through the efforts of his enemies or his own care it was found at the end of his first period of contract that this branch of the revenue had actually increased. Though at more cost to himself than he originally anticipated, Allen had won through.[19]

Allen's success did not spring from the easy application of a brilliant idea, whatever his original reticence to the Postmasters General may suggest. It was a good practical idea, based on common-sense, and the conviction that men cannot be relied on to be honest; their honesty must be organized. In his own words, 'the consciences of the fraudulent go on pretty much at the same rate (only with more or less caution), whether under penaltys, or under none.'[20] Furthermore his idea could not be applied easily; it required, especially at first, the most elaborate and efficient nation-wide organization, with constant vigilance and constant travelling on his own part. In essence his scheme was to oblige each postmaster to check the performance of the other. In the words of his *Narrative*:

He so contrived, that every Postmaster on the same Road, and in all the Branches in the same Road, should check and be checked, by, every other: nay further, this security against fraud was extended even to operate reciprocally between the Postmasters on different Roads and on different Branches of different Roads, by means of certain Regulations which he kept in places where these different Roads are intersected by Cross-road Branches; and which for this reason, he chose to call *Key Towns*. These are all supported . . . by the constant . . . inspection of Surveyors sent as Mr. Allen discovers or apprehends a cause, with Instructions to transmit to him an exact state of the Case in question . . . by which he may be enabled to suppress the very first attempts towards fraudulent practices. And what full employment he finds in first discovering and then Speedily, as well as effectually supressing every rising abuse, in so extensive and intricate concerns, is much easier conceived than explained . . .[21]

Allen's headquarters were in Bath, but in the early days of his contracts he himself travelled throughout England that he might trace, 'fully and minutely, thro' all their wendings', the irregularities and frauds which were depriving

---

[19] Ibid., pp. 10–16.
[20] Ibid., pp. 7–8.
[21] Ibid., p. 8.

the government of its revenue, and which would deprive him, as the chief contractor from the government, of his profit. Few men in the eighteenth century can have travelled England and Wales so widely as Allen. Once he had established the system he desired, however, and the machinery was working, it became possible for him to check irregularities from his head-quarters in Bath. The following letter is typical of the vigilance which had constantly to be maintained; Allen is writing to one of his itinerant surveyors, and we may see a part of his system in action:

> Upon Your Arrival at Monmouth You will find that the Ballance due from the Postm̄ at that place at Xmas last was £36:12:1 & instead of Discharging his Debt Quarterly as formerly, He for some time past Alledges that the under Deputy at Abergaveny, who Depends on this stage keeps back his Money. While you are at Monmouth, I must desire You will fully Enquire into this particular, and not only Collect what is now due but like-wise to use Your best Endeavours to prevent any future Arrears from this Stage. Another particular which gives me some pain & must be Effectually removed before you quitt that Country, is the great Arrears which the New Deputy at Hereford have already Contracted, for this Officer's Debt at Xmas last is increased to £97:10:8 tho' by several Letters, I have in the Strongest Manner pressed for his Payment. Therefore I must desire that During your Survey at Monmouth you will . . . ride over to Hereford and Cause the Immediate payment of the Arrear . . . and Acquaint that officer with the necessity of making his payments with Exactness for the future.[22]

As the end of the period of his first contract drew near, Allen was disappointed. In a petition to the Lords Commissioners of the Treasury, on 28 Jan. 1726, he was obliged to point out that some of the chief postal routes had still not been brought under his regulations, and that he had been 'under so great an expence by the opposition & perverseness of the officers who formerly sunk & embezzell'd this part of the Revenue' that in the first three years, far from making a profit for himself from his labours, he had actually lost 'above £270.0.0.' Since 'most of these people still wait with earnest expectation for an end of the present Lease that they may again throw this business into its former disorder and confusion', Allen pressed with equal earnestness that his contract might be renewed.[23] The two Postmasters General were now Mr. Carteret and Mr. Harrison. On looking into the matter they can hardly have found it difficult to recommend a renewal of Allen's contract for another seven years. The state had already benefited greatly from Allen's work, having received £300.0.0. more from the *Bye Way* and *Cross Road Letters* than the increase of £2,000.0.0. guaranteed by him, together with an improved revenue from the *Country Letters* from which he himself derived no profit at all. The

[22] Bath Reference Library, A.L. 1502: photocopy of Allen's Book of Instructions to Surveyors, 1729–40, belonging to the G.P.O. (Allen to John Carter, 13 Jan. 1738/9).

[23] Bath Reference Library: photocopies of G.P.O. Records of Contracts and Reports [concerning Allen], pp. 275–6 (Allen's petition to the Lords Commissioners, 28 Jan. 1725/6).

contract was thus renewed on exactly the same terms as before. No attempt was made to reimburse Allen his lost £300, nor to reach an understanding on the subject of the *Country Letters*—for in this way the government gained a valuable unpaid service. And equally, no notice was taken of the hint Allen had thrown out at the end of his petition that he might be allowed to pay a little less for his contract than before, as relief from the hardships he had undergone. At the same time it is quite clear that Allen had begun to make a profit after his first three years, for had the contrary been the case he would certainly have said so in his petition.[24] His *average* profit per annum over the period of the first five years of his contract was in fact computed by the Treasury, on his own returns, to amount to £556.9.2.[25]

Further evidence that Allen now felt the way clear ahead of him is that in 1727 he had the headquarters of his postal system moved to his house in Lilliput Alley, which was now considerably enlarged and dignified.[26] Part of this building still stands, showing not only Allen's conception of the importance of his work and the stateliness appropriate to the place from which his system was conducted, but also that he possessed good taste in architecture of an ambitious kind. Allen did indeed develop wider interests from now on, but they were to be financially sustained by the increasing success of his system of postal reform. Though his energies were soon to be shared by other and newer projects, they were never withdrawn from the field in which he had made his first successful venture, for the reason that he wished to grow rich, and to grow rich if possible by a means which would benefit the communications and prosperity of his country. When the period of his second contract came to an end, in 1734, it appeared that the annual produce of the *Country Letters* had actually increased by nearly £10,000. This was the result of Allen's care in keeping the *Bye Way* and *Cross Road Letters* separate from the *Country Letters*, and of the much greater reliability of the posts under his management.[27] So impressed were the Postmasters General at this time by Allen's achievement in securing and improving the revenue from these two branches of the posts, and by his 'signal service to the trade and commerce of the Kingdom', that they declared 'it was but justice to him, that he should have their best support and encouragement for the management of this Branch for the remainder of his Life; in order, that a plan so well formed and so honestly executed, might receive all such further extension and improvement as only he appeared capable of giving it.'[28] The new contract obliged Allen to maintain the annual produce from the *Country Letters* at its improved level and to make over to the government any further increases; on the other hand it allowed him 'full

[24] Jones (op. cit., p. 10) states that Allen paid £4,000 a year for his second contract, £6,000 for his third, and £8,000 for his fourth. But Allen's own Narrative states to the contrary, and no G.P.O. papers appear to contradict him.

[25] Bath Reference Library: photocopies of G.P.O. Records, pp. 277–9 (Carteret and Harrison's Report, 27 March 1727, on Allen's Petition, 28 Jan. 1725–6).

[26] Peach, op. cit., pp. 68–70; John Wood, *An Essay towards A Description of Bath*, 2nd. edn. (London, 1749), ii, p. 245.

[27] Ogilvie, ed. cit., pp. 15–18.

[28] Ibid., pp. 18–19.

liberty' to manage the *Bye Way* and *Cross Road Letters* in whatever way he thought best in the interest of 'the extension of commerce', 'the improvement of His Majesty's Revenue', and 'his own private advantage'. In addition, Allen was for the future absolved from the duty to render accounts to the government of his annual private profits from the *Cross Posts*.[29] These profits must have been thought considerably increased by the time for the next renewal of Allen's contract, for the Postmasters General now 'judged it but reasonable to expect some addition to his rent of £6,000.0.0. a year for the *Cross Posts*', and he did not deny it. He made instead a very characteristic proposal: either he would pay a simple increase in this rent to the government, as suggested, or he would bring about a more considerable improvement to the revenue, 'by means of extending and quickening the correspondence of London and several of the most considerable of the Trading Towns and Cities ... a project which would be of infinite advantage to commerce.' The Postmasters General wisely chose the second alternative, which, it should be noticed, gave Allen control of *London Letters* for the first time—though without any private increase of profit therefrom.[30] The two subsequent renewals of Allen's contract were arranged in the same spirit: increased revenue for the Crown was brought in by further and more ambitious extensions of the *every day post* between London and other parts of the country, quickened communication gradually spreading to the South-West, the North-West and the North-East. In the year 1760, when the death of George II terminated a contract otherwise due to expire two years later, an extended system of *Cross Posts* was also agreed on, which must have greatly augmented Allen's income in the last years of his life.

These last improvements were 'the completion of an enlarged Plan, very early formed, long meditated upon, and by degrees, from time to time, carried into execution', a design for extending and accelerating commercial correspondence, to a degree unknown to other Countries—as Allen explained in his own *Narrative*.[31] According to his own calculations, made at the end of his life, his reformation of the postal system had benefited His Majesty's revenue some £1,500,000 during the forty-odd years of his contracts—besides the incalculable advantage to commerce which Allen was never tired of pointing out. Throughout the negotiations for his contracts, Allen appears to have acted with moderation. A greater reward for the benefits he conferred on the nation might perhaps have been his due, but moderation was in his interest if he wished to keep his contract, and, after his first seven years, his profits seem to have been great enough for him to afford to be moderate. The precise extent of these profits is hard to assess, but it is of some importance for an appreciation of the man to try to do so. His annual income must have ranged from some £550, during the difficult years of his first contract when he scarcely knew whether he would succeed or fail, to some £12,000 in the year ending Midsummer 1761, which Allen was careful to point out to the Postmasters

29 Ibid., pp. 19–21.
30 Ibid., pp. 21–2.
31 Ibid., pp. 22–4.

General had been an untypically good year.[32] Bearing in mind the extremely ambitious and generous projects which Allen entered into after 1730, together with the fact that only after the first seven-year contract did he complain of any hardship, we shall be wise to assume that his average annual profits from the *Bye Way* and *Cross Road Letters* were very much nearer the higher than the lower figure. The general improvement in the postal system must have benefited him all the time, and it is important to notice that all his extensions to the *London Letters* must indirectly have produced a greatly increased *Bye Way* correspondence. By means of his schemes for postal reform, and the favour of successive Postmasters General, Allen created for himself a fortune far in excess of that five to six hundred pounds a year with which John Kyrle aroused the admiration of Pope. His annual income was in excess, even, of the three thousand five hundred a year which Lord Caryll, at the end of the seventeenth century, considered necessary to sustain a Barony with honour; and considerably more, in all probability, than that from which 'the good Lord Digby' supported so many pious projects. Endowed with as strong a 'benevolence of soul' as these, if not a stronger, Allen is the only one of the representative good men described in this book whose wealth approached that of John Blunt at the precarious pitch of his speculations, or of Peter Walter at the impregnably wealthy end of his long and miserly life. To see how Allen acquitted himself of the responsibility given him by his wealth and his principles, we must now return to the first year or so of his second contract, when, still in his early thirties, he was at last able to feel power and influence growing under his hands.

3. GREAT WORKS IN BATH AND LONDON

'After he had worked some time in Bath', wrote Richard Jones, Allen's clerk of works, in his own *Life*, 'Mr. Allen bought all the quarries on Coombe Down, and the estate thereunto belonging. About the year 1727 the said Mr. Allen carried on great works, and in the year 1731, I was clerk to carry on all stone work and buildings and learned myself to draw, which I did to my master's satisfaction . . .'[33] From this testimony it may be seen that while Allen had been labouring at his postal reforms he had also looked at the city of Bath with the eye of a businessman. But he was a businessman of a special kind. As in his postal work Allen was looking for an opportunity to exercise his gift for projection and organization, and for a project in which his personal profit would coincide with an important public interest; as in his postal work Allen wished to create something, or to help create. To a man with imagination, but an imagination which could issue in practical proposals, Bath was a challenging city. Compared with London, Bath was a small provincial town ruled by a group of townsmen, its Corporation. In such a situation it was possible for an individual with vision and the respect of his fellow-townsmen

---

[32] For the first figure see n. 25 above; for the second, Ogilvie, ed. cit., pp. 1–2. Jones's statement (op. cit., p. 11) that Allen got £16,000 per annum clear profit from the contract can hardly be true unless he lied to the Postmasters General.

[33] Jones, op. cit., p. 2.

to wield considerable influence; Allen had, as it happened, been elected onto the Bath Corporation on 4 July 1725—just at the time when his postal scheme was beginning to pay.[34] At the same time Bath was not an ordinary provincial town; in the late seventeenth century and the early eighteenth the fame of its hot springs was already attracting visitors of a more illustrious kind than other country towns of a similar size could hope to see. Queen Anne herself, early in her reign, had twice visited Bath, and it was clear to all that a prospect of great affluence lay in the succession of noble, wealthy or distinguished people who were increasingly prepared to make Bath their regular resort.[35] An inseparable historical association with the hot springs of Bath also distinguished it from other provincial towns; more obviously and memorably even than London, Bath had been a famous Roman town. This may not at first have been of much significance to a man such as Allen, but to any with education in the classics the prospect of rebuilding in Bath, in the English Augustan period, must have seemed a peculiar inspiration and challenge. It was certainly felt by the two great Bath architects, the elder and the younger Wood, whose conceptions of the Circus and the Crescent are so grandly Roman.[36] Wood the elder, who became a resident of Bath in 1727, found in the city the opportunity not only to design particular buildings but to conceive of and in part execute bold schemes of town-planning, such as would have been impractical in London. Allen was clearly alert to these possibilities; they were, as he saw, part of what Bath had to offer him.

For Bath was also well endowed by nature for building projects. Not only did it have its own quarries, from which a soft but serviceable stone for building had for many years been produced, but the river Avon, once made navigable, was a practical means of conveying the stone to building-sites in the city, and indeed of sending it down to the port of Bristol, if buyers from farther afield could be found. The great period of building in Bath in fact began when in 1724 a subscription was opened by John Hobbs, a Bristol merchant, for making the Avon navigable. Without doubt Allen had his eyes upon this interesting development, and according to Richard Jones he purchased shares in the Navigation.[37] Perhaps the news of the project meant most of all to the young man who was to become the first great architect of Bath: the twenty year old John Wood, the son of George Wood, a local builder of the town.[38] Working in Yorkshire on the estate of Lord Bingley at Bramham Park, he at once had a plan of Bath sent to him, and formed two designs, one for the north west corner of the city, the other for the north east. They were of the most ambitious public nature.

> . . . in each Design, I proposed to make a grand Place of Assembly, to be called the *Royal Forum* of *Bath*; another Place, no less magnificent, for

[34] E. A. Russ, art. cit., p. 128.
[35] A. Barbeau, *Life and Letters at Bath in the Eighteenth Century* (London, 1904), pp. 18, 21–2.
[36] Wood, op. cit., i, p. 232.
[37] Ibid., p. 232; Jones, op. cit., p. 9; Boyce, op. cit., p. 25.
[38] H. M. Colvin, *A Biographical Dictionary of English Architects, 1660–1840* (London, 1954), pp. 688–91.

the Exhibition of Sports, to be called the *Grand Circus*; and a third Place, of equal State with either of the former, for the Practice of medicinal Exercises, to be called the *Imperial Gymnasium* of the City, from a Work of that Kind, taking its Rise at first in *Bath*, during the time of the *Roman* Emperors.[39]

With these grandly Roman concepts inspiring him, Wood now attempted to negotiate with the two owners of the land he was interested in: the Earl of Essex, and Mr. Robert Gay, 'an eminent Surgeon, in *Hatton Garden*'.[40] The Earl must have rejected his proposals, but the surgeon only discouraged him by causing him to shorten one of his proposed streets.[41] Wood settled in Bath in May 1727, undertook the execution of the Avon navigation scheme, and put before the Bath Corporation 'a Plan for rebuilding the Town before it should be extended'. The Corporation, however, 'thought proper to treat all my Schemes as Chimerical; tho' there were some of the Members of that Body of Citizens that acted otherwise, and as Men capable of being guided by self-evident Principles.'[42] Subsequent events strongly suggest that Allen was among these latter. It was at any rate Wood whom in this year Allen employed to design the additions and alterations to his house in Lilliput Alley, now the headquarters of his postal system.[43] This was perhaps the first house which Wood designed in Bath; he describes it with considerable satisfaction: '. . . he [Allen] now fronted and raised the old Building a full Story higher; it consists of a Basement Story sustaining a double Story under the Crowning; and this is surmounted by an Attick; which created a sixth Rate House, and a Sample for the greatest Magnificence that was ever proposed by me for our City Houses.'[44] It is interesting to consider how a man of Allen's background and occupation had acquired a concern with architecture. There can be no doubt that he was aware of the commercial possibilities of rebuilding ín Bath for anyone who could gain an interest in the nearby quarries. There is no doubt that the restyling of the house in Lilliput Alley was in part a prestige operation, and Allen certainly chose the right architect for 'Magnificence'. But in his approval of the young and as yet largely untried architect's design for his house Allen also showed appreciation and good taste. Once again it is General Wade who is likely to have advised Allen, for *c.* 1720 Wade had had a house built for himself in the Abbey Church Yard at Bath closely

---

[39] Wood, op. cit., i, p. 232.

[40] Ibid., p. 232.

[41] Wood, op. cit., ii, p. 242.

[42] Ibid., pp. 242–3.

[43] Ibid., pp. 244–5. Walter Ison, *The Georgian Buildings of Bath from 1700–1830* (London, 1948), assumes that Wood was not the designer of this addition, but Wood's own statements appear to be perfectly clear on the point. M. A. Green, *The Eighteenth-Century Architecture of Bath* (Bath, 1904), p. 45 and Plate xxxi, considered Wood to have been the architect, on this evidence. So far as Allen's support for Wood is concerned, it is interesting that Allen seems to have negotiated a loan of £1,500 for Wood from Mrs. Buckeridge, his brother-in-law's widow, in 1735 (MSS. displayed in the Bicentenary Exhibition, *Ralph Allen and His Circle*, Bath Art Gallery, 27 June to 18 July 1964, and in the possession of Mr. Michael Allen; Allen to Mrs. Buckeridge, 29 Nov. 1735).

[44] Wood, op. cit., vol. ii, p. 245.

modelled on the house by Inigo Jones in Lincoln's Inn Fields. The architect is unknown, but Colen Campbell's *Vitruvius Britannicus* (which illustrates the Jones house) had come out in 1715. In 1723 Lord Burlington himself designed a London house for Wade, which shows that the latter was no casual follower of architectural fashion but a man with the keenest interest in it, as perhaps one would expect of a friend of Richard Temple, Viscount Cobham.[45] Wade is by far the most likely to have opened up this largely aristocratic or professional interest to Allen.

Palladianism, with its prospect of a new era of building, came to Bath at a time when the Avon Navigation opened opportunities for the sale of Bath stone beyond Bath—in cities such as Bristol and London. Allen was alert to the possibilities of the situation, for at the earliest possible moment, as soon as he was satisfied of the success of his postal system, he used what must have been nearly all his newly won capital to buy some of the local quarries. The precise dates of these transactions are uncertain (the first purchase was in 1726), but as early as December 1729, little more than two years after the termination of his first postal contract, he felt sufficient confidence in his resources as a stone merchant to put out a successful tender to supply stone for the rebuilding of St. Bartholomew's Hospital in London.[46] A document of 1731 refers to his earlier purchase of the Priory Estate with its quarries on Combe Down, and to his construction of a wagonway on this land.[47] It is striking, even bewildering, to find Allen, who must have hoped for a long and profitable period of extending his postal reforms, launching so soon into an entirely different, and extremely ambitious and hazardous enterprise. Even if we grant that Allen was ambitious, it has never been adequately explained why he felt it necessary to engage at once in two full-time enterprises, at their most early and chancy stage. The answer most probably lies in the insecurity Allen felt in the tenure of his government contract. We have seen that he had enemies in the postal service who hoped to see his scheme abandoned after the first seven years. Again, if he were successful, might not one or other administration attempt to operate his system themselves? Allen must have thought it wise to diversify his source of wealth at the earliest possible opportunity, and to buttress the income he derived from his career as a successful projector with the 'solid supports' (to use John Blunt's phrase) of wealth in kind: in stone. It was also true that if Allen were to make a fortune by the sale of Bath stone, he would have to get in quickly.

At the same time, Allen's quarrying business has all the marks of a carefully worked-out scheme. It must have been planned at the very time he was struggling to succeed with his government contract, if not earlier still. His aim was that of a clear-sighted and imaginative business entrepreneur. He

---

[45] John Summerson, *Architecture in Britain, 1530–1830* (Harmondsworth, 1953 (4th. revised and enlarged edn. 1963)), pp. 226, 231. For Wade's friendship with Cobham, see B.M. Add. 15936, f. 258.

[46] St. Bartholomew's Hospital, Ha 19/7/29: Allen's agreement, 4 Dec. 1729, to supply the stone for and build the first part of James Gibbs's design.

[47] Quoted in R. E. M. Peach, op. cit., pp. 78–81.

sought to promote the sale of Bath stone by a drastic reduction in its price.[48]
This he achieved in two ways. First he reduced the wage-rate of masons,
but was able to guarantee them more work and therefore finally more money.
He built cottages for them near their place of work at the quarries, or at his
stone works by the river.[49] Secondly he availed himself of the latest technology to handle and transport the stone. John Padmore of Bristol was commissioned to design special cranes for the work: four horse cranes for drawing
the stone from the quarries, another 'to lay the stone down to square it' and
another by the river-side to load block stone onto barges. According to Richard
Jones these cranes cost £240.[50] Of greater importance was the wagonway,
or primitive railway, which Allen constructed to transport his stone from the
quarries to the riverside. According to Defoe's *Tour* (the Bath section being
written perhaps by Samuel Richardson), this too was the work of Padmore,
but the idea was taken from the early railways used in the collieries at Newcastle-
on-Tyne. Wood himself tells us that 'the late Mr. *Hedworth* sent proper
models to *Bath*' of the carriage roads which 'Gentlemen in the North of
England had made between their Collieries and the River *Tyne*, that heavy
Carriages might be drawn along it with such little Strength, as would reduce
the Transportation of the Stone to the Water Side, to half the Price of carrying
it down in common Wagons.' Allen's railway was apparently an improved
version of those at Newcastle.[51] A further refinement was a double-track
railway between quarries and the riverside, by which the loaded down-going
wagons drew the empty ones to the top for their next load—'an exceedingly
good contrivance' as Richard Jones called it when he laid claim to the idea,
in his *Life*.[52] When Pope praised Allen's manner of life, in the later 1730s,
he was praising a use of wealth which had been won, at least in part, through
some of the characteristic technology of the slowly oncoming Industrial
Revolution.

Allen now began to supply stone for building in Bath, making it available
with a good deal more efficiency and despatch than had been possible before.
Meanwhile John Wood, undaunted by discouragement from the Bath Corporation, had become absolute contractor with Gay for the land required for
the most immediately practical of his projects: Queen Square.[53] Not one of
the grand designs originally put to Gay and the Earl of Essex, Queen Square
(1729–36) was nevertheless a piece of unified town-planning of a kind which
London had still seen little of, since Inigo Jones built the Covent Garden
piazzas, and which Bath had never seen before. In conceiving the design
Wood drew on his experience as a younger man working for Edward Shepherd

[48] Wood, op. cit., ii, p. 425; and see Boyce's discussion, op. cit., pp. 31–2.
[49] R. E. M. Peach, op. cit., p. 100.
[50] Jones, op. cit., pp. 2–4; J. T. Desaguliers, *A Course of Experimental Philosophy* (London,
1763), i, p. 187; ii, pp. 283–5.
[51] Daniel Defoe, *A Tour Thro' the Whole Island of Great Britain*, 4th. edn. (London, 1748), ii,
p. 300; Wood, op. cit., ii, p. 425; Desaguliers, op. cit., ii, p. 283.
[52] Jones, op. cit., p. 15. I am indebted to Dr. Arnold Pacey for helpful advice on Allen's
technology.
[53] Wood, op. cit., ii, p. 243.

in the latter's unsuccessful bid to create a Palladian unity of the new Grosvenor Square in London. Where Shepherd failed, Wood succeeded, and behind this success was the new industry of Ralph Allen which quarried and delivered the stone. According to Richard Jones, Allen also donated £50 to the erection of Wood's massively Jonesian design for St. Mary's chapel (1732–4), Queen Square. This strong reminiscence of St. Paul's, Covent Garden is a clear indication of the source of Wood's inspiration for this part of the new city.[54]

Wood's next major work was the General Hospital, originally proposed as early as 1716, two years after the expiry of the law which allowed diseased, handicapped and poor people free use of the mineral baths of the city. As more and more of the fashionable and wealthy visited Bath to take the waters, the poor were not forgotten, and the ideal of free access to the healing springs, despite much tighter regulation, was not abandoned. Wood himself expressed this concern in the following way:

> There being many poor Objects in the several Parts of this Kingdom, who tho' they may be provided elsewhere with Physick and the Advice of Physicians, yet for want of the Assistance which only the Waters of the *Bath* can give, continue in a languishing and helpless Condition; in Compassion to the deplorable Case of such Persons, and in a View of the Improvements which under the present Design may be made in the Knowledge of the Nature and Virtue of these Medicinal Waters, some well disposed Persons have set on Foot, and hope to establish an Hospital at *Bath*, for the Reception of sixty poor diseased Persons, who are to be provided with Lodging and Diet; together with a Physician, Surgeon, Apothecary, and Medicines.[55]

A subscription was opened in 1723, and it is worth noting that though Allen would undoubtedly have been interested in the project his name is not in the lists of contributors for that year. At that critical time in his postal enterprise Allen had no money to spare. In 1728, however, he was added to the committee sponsoring the project, and in 1731 Gay gave the land needed, and Wood published the designs. On 6 July 1738 Sir William Pulteney laid the foundation stone.[56] For the building, according to Richard Jones, Allen now gave stone, lime and paving stone to the value of 'upwards of £960'.[57] On Tuesday 18 May 1742 the Hospital was opened, a building, in Wood's words, 'erected as much for Futurity as any Structure of its Kind can be'.[58] Allen gave still further aid to the Hospital; and in the October of the same year William Warburton, introduced to Allen by Alexander Pope, lent to

[54] Summerson, op. cit., p. 231; Jones, op. cit., p. 5. It is clear from Jones's description that 'the building in the square called Wood Street' is in fact Queen Square. For Allen's donation, see Jones, p. 36.

[55] Wood, op. cit., ii, pp. 286–7. Measures were taken, however, to prevent poor people flocking to Bath in enormous numbers.

[56] Ibid., ii, pp. 275–99.

[57] Jones, op. cit., p. 5; see also p. 36 where the estimate of cost is £60 less.

[58] Wood, op. cit., ii, p. 293.

the institution the support of a timely sermon in the Abbey Church.[59] By 1739, when Queen Square had been complete for over two years, and work on the Hospital had gone on for one, experience had convinced the Corporation of Bath that Wood's schemes were not wholly chimerical.

The time was now ripe for Wood to begin work on that 'grand place of Assembly, to be called the *Royal Forum* of *Bath*' which had been one of his most ambitious original conceptions. In July he became absolute contractor for the land, in the Bath Garden, and preparations began for the work which, not fulfilling his intentions adequately, was to become the Parades.[60] Richard Jones makes clear the nature of Allen's backing for the project:

> In the year 1739 began the great work in Bath Garden for the Parades, the north side begun first, and the common sewer, under the directions of Mr. Wood, architect. The stone for these four piles of buildings was all brought up by water with carriage roads in two barges, and came with two carriages in each barge four times a day, and hauled up by a capstan . . . He [Allen] caused to be built in Bath Garden for his use, five long houses which cost £10,000 at least. All the time Bath Garden work was going on (which was the Parades) four carriages were going [to] the hill constant, and over the water;—four ditto loading on the hill;—two ditto loading block to each to Dolemead;—four ditto spuare, if any misfortune should happen: each carriage cost £40.[61]

We do not always get consistency of detail from Jones, and he is untrustworthy on figures, but his general picture is plausible and illuminating. It is clear that the highest degree of organization went into the supplying of stone for the Parades; the detail of the four spare carriages show how important it must have been to prevent increases of time and cost by a rapid and punctual supply from the quarries. It is also interesting to note that Allen's support for Wood was, at this stage, not merely commercial. Whatever the actual cost of the 'five long houses' for his own use (since we never hear again of his owning them he probably sold them on the completion of the Parades), it is clear that Allen must have given Wood both financial and moral backing at a crucial stage of his project. In these ways Allen, Wood, and Richard Jones the mason and clerk of works, co-operated to transform Bath. As they did so, it must have become evident to all that the charitable projects and Roman forms were but parts of a commercial enterprise of enormous scale, complexity and promise, in which the whole city could take part.

While Allen was supplying Wood with stone in Bath he was also supplying stone to realise a different project by a different architect in London: the designs for rebuilding St. Bartholomew's Hospital by James Gibbs. Allen

[59] See Jones, op. cit., p. 36, who says Allen gave £11 a year until his death, and Peach, op. cit., p. 119, who says Allen gave £500 in 1741, and £21 a year until his death. For Warburton's sermon, see Peach, op. cit., pp. 118–19.

[60] Wood, op. cit., ii, p. 248; Summerson, op. cit., p. 232.

[61] Jones, op. cit., pp. 16, 13–14. The date is probably correct since Wood states (op. cit., ii, p. 248) that he became contractor for the land in 1739.

must have sought an opportunity of a sufficiently public kind to make the Bath quarries rapidly well known in the capital. The Governors of St. Bartholomew's Hospital gave him this opportunity. There was clearly much hostility among London architects to the idea of using Bath stone, which, it is stated, they insultingly compared to Cheshire cheese. Wood states that when, in 1728, Allen submitted a tender to supply Bath stone to the Governors of Greenwich Hospital, specimens of Bath and other stone were laid before a meeting of the governors, and of Campbell, Hawksmoor, Gibbs and Wood. Campbell by mistake took up the wrong sample, and drew attention to defects which he alleged were peculiar to Bath stone. This seemed to expose an unreasonable prejudice in the London architects, but had the immediate effect only of enabling Greenwich Hospital to obtain Portland stone more cheaply, which 'entirely defeated Mr. Allen's proposals'.[62] That there is some truth in this anecdote is suggested by Allen's later reference to the 'different sorts of oppositions which was, then made to all kinds of Tryal of my Stone', and by his letter to William Tims, of Bartholomew Hospital, on 18 July 1730, in which he states that £1700 is the lowest sum he can undertake to erect their first building for 'without a certain Loss'.

> However since the Govern[ors] have acted in so obliging a manner by me as to shew so strong an inclination to cause a Publique introduction of my Stone into London, I wil out of the seventeen hundred pounds make a Compliment of one hundred to the Hospital If the Governo: instead of a parapet wal do chuse Rail & Banisters on the top of the building that alteration shall be made without any new charge.[63]

Allen was at first desperately keen that his stone should be used, and the governors were, through the thirty four years in which the whole re-building dragged on, determined to use it despite all obstacles, since it was the cheapest they could get. That they were well aware of the bad reputation of Bath stone is made clear by the precautions they took against the possibility of its deterioration. In the indenture between Allen and the governors dated 14 Aug. 1730 it was provided that if any of the stone-work should decay within the space of thirty years after completion he should make good the defect at his own charge. At the same time he transferred to them his shares in the Sun Fire Office (to the value of £1600) as security for the full performance of his covenant.[64] For their part, the governors asked whether Allen would not agree to supply stone for the remaining three piles of the Hospital on the same terms, and Allen's answer 'was that I choose a Charitable Work to Introduce my Stone that from the beginning I might be a Contributor to so Laudable a Work, and therefore if they design'd to carry on their other

      [62] Wood, op. cit., ii, pp. 426–7.

      [63] Bartholomew's Hospital Archives, Ha 19/30/7 (Allen to William Tims, 7 Feb. 1746/7, Ha 19/29/6 (Allen to Tims, 18 July 1730). Another customer for Allen's stone was John Sydney, Earl of Leicester, with whom he corresponded on the subject on 19 May ?1734 (Bath Reference Library, MS. A.L. 385).

      [64] Bartholomew's Hospital, Ha 19/10.

Buildings without any Considerable interuption, I was willing to agree to it . . .'[65]

Difficulty upon difficulty now followed. Allen was obliged to buy the freedom of the City of London for his Bath workmen, various disputes caused delay, but the first really painful disappointment came when, the first pile having been completed, the Hospital would not sell its stocks to pay him 'because there had been a fall of Late'. After his generous treatment of the Hospital, Allen might well complain that: 'Few things cou'd be more surprising or indeed painful then this piece of News . . .'[66] However matters were compounded, and after a five year delay such as the governors had promised to try to avoid work began on the second pile, which was completed in 1738.[67] Now Allen was nominated a governor of the Hospital, and his shares in the Sun Fire Office were returned to him in exchange for his bond.[68] Allen received no further instructions from the other governors until 1743 'when the Spanish War was begun and the French War apprehended'. This raised almost insuperable difficulties in transporting the stone by sea from Bristol to London; his ships had to await convoy, and the crews were vulnerable to the press-gang despite the Hospital's claim to protect them. Allen was now only too anxious to get free of what was turning into an impracticable obligation. He offered to give the Hospital £500 to finish the building with another stone, but the careful governors instead agreed to postpone further building for a year. Next a ship of which Allen had bought the fourth part to carry stone to London was wrecked, costing him £200, and in 1746, with the war still on, the governors peremptorily requested him to deliver the stone for the third pile. They were strictly within their rights, but their request was impossible. Allen offered them £550 worth of free Bath stone if they would undertake transportation; they had no alternative but to wait for the peace, when the third pile was built and completed in 1749.[69] Instead of proceeding at once to build the fourth pile, the Hospital again delayed, only requesting Allen to send further supplies of stone when the Seven Years War was fairly begun.[70] The fourth pile was eventually started in 1763, with the Hospital paying for at least part of the freight. It was completed in the year of Allen's death.

The rebuilding of St. Bartholomew's Hospital took thirty four years, the greater part of Allen's adult life. He is unlikely to have made money from it. He offered generous terms at first to get his stone introduced into London, even more generous terms later to get free of his obligation. He had not bargained for the Hospital's shortage of funds which caused both delays in the building and the governors' tenacious determination to use none but Bath stone. Neither Allen nor the Hospital had bargained for Britain's involvement

[65] B.H. Ha 19/30/7 (Allen to Tims, 7 Feb. 1746/7).
[66] B.H. Ha 19/29/9; Ha 19/29/12; Ha 19/29/14; Ha 19/29/19 (Allen to Tims, 8 July 1732).
[67] B.H. Ha 19/30/7 (Allen to Tims, 7 Feb. 1746/7).
[68] B.H. Ha 1/11 (St. Bartholomew's Hospital Journal, 1734–8).
[69] B.H. Ha 19/30/7 (Allen to Tims, 7 Feb. 1746/7, also Ha 19/31/19 and Ha 19/31/21).
[70] B.H. Ha 19/31/21 (Allen to Tims, 30 March 1758).

in two European wars, with the consequent difficulties in shipping stone from
Bristol to London. This must have put an end to Allen's hopes for a big London
market for his stone; as he said in February 1746/7. 'I have not Sold so much
as one Tun of Stone in London since ye. Commencement of the War . . .'[71]
But Allen was not wholly in the business for money. The interest of this
protracted episode lies in the way it displays his attitudes as stone merchant
and a supporter of building enterprises; he had no need to write many letters
to do business in Bath, thus there are few personal records of his support for
Bath enterprises. The correspondence with Bartholomew's Hospital reveals
a man in whom commercial and philanthropic concern were very evenly
blended, a man who sought constantly the coincidence of private with public
interest. It shows a man of imagination and enterprise, though not so far-
seeing or cautious as to anticipate some of the difficulties he encountered; a
man with a practical knowledge of building and the costing of architectural
designs, whose strong sense of practicality adjudicated between the commercial and philanthropic sides of his nature. What his imagination and sense
of practicality unfortunately did not reveal to him was that, in the atmosphere
of London, Bath stone was indeed little better than Cheshire cheese. In 1763,
a defect was observed in the stone, just one year after the expiry of the period
in which Allen was obliged to make it good. In 1845 a report was prepared
on the state of the stonework, in which it was stated that 'Bath stone is a
very inferior building stone—it is oolite and calcareous, easily decomposed
by the action of the weather and particularly by the atmosphere of London.'
It recommended that all the facing of Bath stone be removed and replaced
by the Portland stone which, it noted, had been employed in every other
building by James Gibbs.

4. 'THE MOST NOBLE MAN OF ENGLAND'

Pope first visited Bath in the Autumn of 1714 in company with Parnell.
Allen had been in the city four years, working in the Post Office; another
seven were to pass before his first contract for the *Cross-Posts*. The two men
are unlikely to have met at this time; the scene of Allen's painstaking labours
was very different from that in which Pope wrote to his friend Martha Blount:

> If Variety of Diversions & new Objects be capable of driving our Friends
> out of our minds, I have the best excuse imaginable for forgetting you.
> For I have Slid, I cant tell how, into all the Amusements of this Place:
> My whole Day is shar'd by the Pump-Assemblies, the Walkes, the Chocolate
> houses, Raffling Shops, Plays, Medleys, &c.[72]

Bath was certainly a gay place at this time, but it did not yet possess the public
dignity to be given it by the majestic schemes of John Wood and of his son.
Pope was in Bath again the next year, again the year after, and again for a long
visit twelve years later in 1728.[73] The next time was in September 1734. On

[71] B.H. Ha 19/30/7 (Allen to Tims, 7 Feb. 1746/7).
[72] *Corr.*, i, p. 260 (6 Oct. 1714).
[73] *Corr.*, v, p. 56.

this occasion Pope, now the author of the Epistle *To Burlington*, probably noticed certain changes in the city. Wade's house in the Abbey Church Yard, modest, economic and elegant, and Allen's in Lilliput Alley, ornate yet grandly dignified, had been there in 1728 and may have caught his eye before. What had not been there before was Wood's first great architectural achievement of Queen Square, now only two years from completion, and in particular the Chapel of St. Mary, to be officially opened three months later.[74] There could be no more explicit tribute to Inigo Jones's achievement in St. Paul's Covent Garden than Wood's Chapel of St. Mary. It had not quite the monumental simplicity of Jones's 'handsomest barn in England' whose massive portico does not echo, as in Wood, but is itself the end of the building, and Wood allowed himself just a little decoration. But both chapels, in their dramatic use of the column in deeply moulded porticos—Wood's 'west' end in fact faced south thus gaining full advantage of the light—and in their whole cultivation of plainness and strength, a massively fundamental architecture, are products of masters of a like mind.[75] There can be no doubt that Wood's building would make a deep impression on the poet who had so recently recommended that Burlington should

> Jones and Palladio to themselves restore
> [*To Burlington*, l. 193]

and with ambitious schemes by the same architect nearing completion in Queen Square and beginning in the Parades, Pope must have realized that a considerable Palladian rebuilding was in progress in Bath—a transformation that was to continue long after his death. On the same visit, as Benjamin Boyce has shown, Pope is likely to have read Mary Chandler's poem, *A Description of Bath*, which the poetess revised to include welcoming words for the Princess Amelia, also in the city at this time. The poem contains a glowing tribute to Ralph Allen, praising all aspects of his activities in Bath, and hailing him as grand patron of the city and an example to the age. Miss Chandler had read Pope, and much of what she had to say about Allen was couched in terms recognizably Pope's own.[76] Her poem would impress upon Pope that Allen was a powerful supporter of all that he saw developing in Bath, that he was indeed a man of 'Great Designs', whether commercial, architectural or philanthropic. It was with the last two types of activity that Pope was to be most concerned.

Henry Fielding said of his Allworthy, thought on good grounds to have been modelled on Allen, that 'though he had missed the advantage of a learned education, yet, being blessed with vast natural abilities, he had so well profited

---

[74] Ison, op. cit., p. 72; the first stone of the chapel was laid on 25 March 1732, and it was opened on Christmas Day 1734 (Green, op. cit., p. 61).

[75] Ison illustrates Wood's 'west' end, op. cit., p. 71. For a not very revealing photograph of the since demolished chapel, see Green, op. cit., p. 61 and Plate xli.

[76] For this point I am in debt to Benjamin Boyce's very interesting essay, 'The Poet and the Postmaster: The Friendship of Alexander Pope and Ralph Allen', in Paul Baender and C. A. Zimansky, eds. *Essays in English Neoclassicism* (Iowa City, 1966), pp. 115–16.

by a vigorous, though late application to letters, and by much conversation with men of eminence in this way, that he was himself a very competent judge in most kinds of literature.'[77] This detail is unusual in a portrait of an eighteenth-century gentleman who had *inherited* a large fortune and estate, and we may take it as one of the points where Fielding revealed rather than disguised his model. Allen evidently possessed a lively and eager understanding, which turned almost as readily to matters literary and artistic, as to postal communications and the support of architectural projects. Undoubtedly he must have read Mary Chandler's poem; quite possibly he appreciated its debt to Pope, and realized that an acquaintance with that 'Mr. Pope, the Famous Poet' who on 28 Sept. 1734 the London newspapers declared to be 'dangerously ill' at Bath might assist him in his latest 'Great Design': to break into the realm of aristocratic creation by erecting a Palladian mansion on his Priory Estate overlooking the city.[78] For this he had already commissioned John Wood, which at a stage, when he could easily have procured a London architect, shows his continuing approval of Wood's work. Nor did he blindly accept Wood's conceptions; according to the architect himself an original scheme of great magnificence, 'wherein the Orders of Architecture were to shine forth in all their Glory', was eventually rejected in favour of a less ambitious scheme.[79] If the grounds on which Allen rejected the utmost magnificence John Wood was capable of conceiving are likely to have been primarily financial they were not therefore unconnected with taste. As Pope had observed:

> 'Tis Use alone that sanctifies Expence,
> And Splendor borrows all her rays from Sense.
> [*To Burlington*, ll. 179–80]

The building of Prior Park began in 1735, and Wood's designs are likely to have been complete the year before. If Pope met Allen during his 1734 visit, as the fact that Allen called on him at Twickenham eighteen months later perhaps suggests, he is likely to have heard of, perhaps seen, these splendid designs. As John Summerson has shown, Wood's conception is one of several deriving from the seminal designs of Colen Campbell for Wanstead House in Essex.[80] It is impeccably in the English Palladian tradition, and yet too it is the work of John Wood. In each building the elevation showing the giant hexastyle portico displays an analytic purity of relationship and proportion, but with Wood there is a greater sense of weight, perhaps owing to the hipped roof rising above the parapet and pediment, and a more massive dignity and plainness. Wood's evolution of a simple and strong architecture in Prior Park is even more clear in the south front of the mansion, and most of all in his

[77] *Tom Jones*, Bk. I, Ch. X. Arthur Murphy, in the Life of Fielding written for his edition of *The Works of Henry Fielding, Esq.* (London, 1762), speaks of Allworthy as having, in the general opinion, been modelled on 'the features of a worthy character yet in being'; elsewhere in the Life he warmly praises Allen by name (i, pp. 40, 46). Richard Graves, op. cit., p. 75, declares Allen had 'only a writing-school education'.

[78] *Corr.*, iii, p. 346.

[79] Wood, op. cit., ii, p. 427.

[80] Summerson, op. cit., pp. 192–4.

designs for the two office wings where the inspiration of the Jones of St. Paul's Covent Garden is again strongly evident, without the least limitation on the creative originality of the later architect.[81] In asking the advice of Pope on some details of this mansion, Allen had no reason to be ashamed of what he was doing; and Pope had every reason to admire it.

It may have been against the background of some exchange in Bath about Prior Park that he ventured, eighteen months later, to call on Pope at Twickenham. There was now another topic for discussion; in 1735 one of the unauthorized editions of Pope's correspondence had appeared, and Allen perhaps curious to deepen a slight acquaintance with this distinguished visitor to Bath, read the volume, forming the 'highest opinion of the other's general benevolence and goodness of heart'.[82] On this visit to Twickenham, in what Boyce has well described as 'one of his characteristic bold plunges', Allen proposed that Pope allow him to publish an authorized edition of the correspondence at Allen's own expense.[83] With an elaborate display of self-deprecation, and of anxiety lest Allen be too generous, Pope, in effect, accepted. Allen's offer was essentially that of the patron, respectfully couched though it clearly was in terms referring to the public good.[84] With due modesty and complete tact Allen was assuming towards Pope the attitude of the generous and enlightened aristocrat. This explains the great show Pope made in drumming up further subscriptions for the volume; to be independent of patrons had been a constant care of Pope's life and perhaps the chief personal aim of his enterprise in the Homer translations. Allen's moral support for the volume was accepted more frankly, but it was with open confidence and eager expectation that Pope accepted all Allen's numerous gifts to him in *kind*—'. . . daily fresh proofs of your kind remembrance of me, the Bristol waters, the Guinea Hens, the Oyl & wine (two Scripture Benedictions) . . .', curious stones for his Grotto.[85] In return, Pope gave Allen 'a young Bounce', a puppy that 'can but just lap milk', recommended Allen's stone to Lord Peterborough, and was ready to advise Allen about the decorations for his hall at Prior Park:

I saw Mr. Morice yesterday who has readily allowed Mr. Vandiest to copy the Picture. I have enquired for the best Originals of those two Subjects which I found were Favorite ones with you, & well deserve to be so, the Discovery of Joseph to his Bretheren, and the Resignation of the Captive by Scipio. Of the latter my lord Burlington has a fine one done by Ricci . . .

A Man not only shews his Taste but his Virtue, in the Choice of such Ornaments: And whatever Example most strikes us, we may reasonably imagine may have an influence upon others, so that the History itself (if wellchosen) upon a Rich-man's Walls, is very often a better lesson than

[81] See Ison, op. cit., pp. 135–44 (144 for the elevation of the west wing of Prior Park as originally designed). See also Plates 57–61. Green, op. cit., pp. 82–100, gives the most lavishly illustrated and comprehensive account of Prior Park. The mansion may still be seen.

[82] William Warburton, ed. *The Works of Alexander Pope* (London, 1751), ix, p. 312.

[83] Boyce, art. cit., p. 116. His whole discussion of this episode is interesting.

[84] *Corr.*, iv, p. 19 (Pope to Allen, 5 June 1736).

[85] Ibid., p. 145 (Pope to Allen, 2 Nov. 1738).

any he could teach by his Conversation. In this sense, the Stones may be said to speak . . .[86]

It is of great interest that Pope accepts Allen's aristocratic role (though he knows he is also 'low-born Allen') but constantly stresses what he takes to be the moral foundation of the aristocratic ideal: to do good to his fellow-men in ways beyond the means of most men of goodwill. Thus the human subjects, sacred and profane, which mean most to Allen personally, and which he can as it were project on the walls of that almost public place, the hall of his great house, are mind-full and can enlighten others. Pope's whole point is made beautifully particular and relevant to Allen at the end of the passage: '. . . the *Stones* [my Italics] may be said to speak . . .'

So far as others were concerned, Pope was happy to encourage Allen's efforts as a patron. In the case of the historian Nathaniel Hooke, then working on the first volume of his *Roman History*, Pope passed on to him a gift from Allen to aid his subscription, concealing the source not apparently because Allen had asked him to, but because he had not 'Explicitely' asked him not to.[87] Pope was probably taking seriously Mary Chandler's couplet on Allen:

> You chide the Muse that dares your Virtues own,
> And, veil'd with *Modesty*, wou'd live unknown[88]

and, because he much approved such unostentatious generosity, made sure that Allen was exactly true to the ideal. It is probably this incident, together with Mary Chandler's lines on Allen, which prompted Pope to write his own well-known lines:

> Let low-born ALLEN, with an aukward Shame,
> Do good by stealth, and blush to find it Fame.
> ['Epilogue to the Satires', Dialogue I (original version), ll. 135–6]

On another occasion Pope vied with Allen in generosity to a 'poor Woman' who had evidently come to the end of Pope's garden to beg:

> I can't help telling you the Rapture you accidentally gave the poor Woman (for whom you left a Guinea on what I told you of my finding her at the End of my Garden.) I had no Notion of her Want being so great, as I then told you, when I gave her half an one; But I find I have a Pleasure to come, for I will allow her Something yearly . . . I am determined to take this Charity out of your hands . . .[89]

Pope's somewhat competitive attitude is partly real generosity, but partly also an anxiety that, despite Allen's incomparably greater wealth, he should not have a monopoly on gentlemanly patronage when Pope was at hand, and in his own home.

[86] Ibid., pp. 175 (Pope to Allen, 5 May 1739), 41 (Pope to Allen, 6 Nov. 1736), 13 (Pope to Allen, 30 April 1736).

[87] Ibid., p. 36 (Pope to Allen, 7 Oct. 1736).

[88] Mary Chandler, *Poems on Several Occasions* (London, 1734), p. 17; Boyce, art. cit., p. 115.

[89] *Corr.*, iv, p. 92 (Pope to Allen, 28 April 1738).

It would seem that in the first years of their acquaintance Pope and Allen enjoyed a good deal of intellectual conversation together. Allen had a lively intelligence and if the possession in his library (now preserved at Hartlebury Castle) of works such as Norris of Bemerton's *Ideal World* tells us anything, it is probable that he had an interest in religious speculation. One of their common acquaintances may possibly have been James Craggs the younger (see n. 12 above), whom Pope often recalled with affection after his sudden death in 1721, and whose father was Postmaster General when Allen's proposal for the *Cross-Posts* was first accepted. Perhaps Pope spoke of Craggs in the religious way in which he had once written of him to Swift: '. . . Yet am I of the Religion of Erasmus, a Catholick; so I live; so I shall die; and hope one day to meet you, Bishop Atterbury, poor Craggs, Dr. Garth, Dean Berkley, and Mr. Hutchenson, in that place, To which God of his infinite mercy brings us, and every body!'[90] If at the same time Pope mentioned Atterbury, as another dead friend he had loved and admired, Allen would have been keenly interested; some of the unauthorized editions of Pope's letters included correspondence with Atterbury, and as one who had helped Wade strike a blow against the Jacobites in 1715, Allen is likely to have been curious about the famous bishop, exiled in 1723 for plotting to restore the House of Stuart. It is curious in this connection that Allen's painter Van Diest should soon be copying for him a painting in the possession of Atterbury's son-in-law William Morice—a painting which does not appear to be a model for one of Allen's favourite biblical or classical subjects.[91] The point of interest was possibly that the painting had been Atterbury's. A similar motive must account for what would otherwise be a very surprising gesture by Pope: his gift to Allen in 1739 of the bible which Atterbury had presented to him on his departure into exile.[92] This gift may imply that Allen came to share something of Pope's esteem for Atterbury—with perhaps a consequent broadening of his political and religious views. Again Pope may have recalled to Allen what he had written to Atterbury in defence of his remaining a Roman Catholic: '. . . after all, I verily believe your Lordship and I are both of the same religion, if we were thoroughly understood by one another; and that all honest and reasonable christians would be so, if they did but talk enough together every day . . .'[93] This was perhaps the background of discussion to Pope's remembering and mentioning a hymn he had written, some twenty years earlier, with the idea of linking up into one picture different approaches to the deity. Allen expressed definite interest, and Pope asked their mutual

---

[90] *Corr.*, iii, p. 81 (Pope to Swift, 28 Nov. 1729).

[91] See n. 86 above. For Pope-Atterbury correspondence which might have attracted Allen's interest, see *Letters of Mr. Pope, and Several Eminent Persons. From the Year 1705 to 1735. N.B. This Edition contains more Letters, and more correctly Printed, than any other extant* (London, 1735), pp. [261]–3. C. W. Dilke, in his MS. notes to the British Museum copy (Pressmark 12274.e.14) thought that Pope connived at this volume to gain advantage of Curll, and that the Atterbury and following letter were added to bear out the title. R. H. Griffith, *Alexander Pope: A Bibliography* (1922; new edn. London, 1962), ii, pp. 316–17, 308–9.

[92] *Corr.*, ii, p. 169, n. 1.

[93] *Corr.*, i, p. 454 (Pope to Atterbury, 20 Nov. 1717).

friend Nathaniel Hooke to transcribe a revised version of the poem, and so sent it to his friend: 'I've sent you the Hymn, a little alterd, & enlargd in one necessary point of doctrine, viz: the third Stanza, which I think reconciles Freedom & Necessity; & is at least a Comment on some Verses in my Essay on Man . . .'[94]

Architecture, painting, philanthropy, politics, and religion—almost the whole spectrum of human activity seems to have been the subject of their conversation and correspondence, as the surviving letters casually record. Pope found Allen 'low' in nothing but his birth, for he was responsive to almost all which for the poet meant civilization, and he was vigorously and variously active in pursuit of the human and artistic ideals most dear to Pope's heart. Despite what has sometimes been said of Pope's calling Allen 'low-born' (later 'humble') in his 'Epilogue to the Satires', there is more praise than condescension in his words, precisely because Allen's low birth made his voluntary assumption of the interests and responsibilities of the idealized landed aristocrat the more remarkable. Pope's attitude is similar to what he had recently written of John Kyrle: 'My motive for singling out this man, was twofold: first to distinguish real and solid worth from showish or plausible expence, and virtue fro' vanity: and secondly, to humble the pride of greater men . . .'[95] Allen did far more than Kyrle, was far more prominent than Kyrle, but he was not, as Kyrle had been, of gentle birth. Pope's point is really the same in each case: to distinguish real worth from what might conventionally be expected to accompany it, as he says in the lines of his poem following his mention of Allen:

> *Virtue* may chuse the high or low Degree . . .
> ['Epilogue to the Satires', Dialogue I, l. 137]

There is no evidence that Allen was offended at the phrase 'low-born'—indeed he gave Pope permission to state that he was 'no Man of high birth or quality'—nor that he requested the substitution of the word 'humble', a more comprehensive term, which yet somewhat blurs the point Pope makes in the poem.[96] Pope had already made it clear to Allen: 'If the Memory I every day have of your Friendship were to be told you, it would be a more constant Address than most people offer to their Best Benefactor, and a thousand Times more Sincere than Any ever offerd to an Earthly Prince on the Throne. So much higher is my Respect for Virtue than for Title . . .'[97]

But of all Allen's claims to Pope's high opinion, it was significantly his philanthropy which won from him the highest praise—praise the sincerity of which we can be doubly sure of because it was not addressed to Allen himself, in the way by which Pope loved to give pleasure to his friends, but to a mutual acquaintance, William Fortescue. Pope was right in thinking Allen unusually generous and public-spirited with his wealth, though it is

---

[94] *Corr.*, iv, p. 31 (Pope to Allen, 8 Sept. 1736).
[95] *Corr.*, iii, p. 290 (Pope to Tonson, 7 June 1732).
[96] *Corr.*, iv, p. 93 (Pope to Allen, 28 April 1738), 144–5 (Pope to Allen, 2 Nov. 1738).
[97] Ibid., p. 108 (Pope to Allen, 6 July 1738).

hard to get a precise and comprehensive picture of Allen's benefactions up till the time Pope knew him. Particular public donations can sometimes be established, but Richard Jones, who attempted in his *Life* of himself to give a more general account, must be guilty of wild exaggeration. Nevertheless, even if his figures are treated with scepticism, what he says is still evidence of a remarkable generosity on Allen's part:

> His private charities, I believe, exceeded his public ones. He caused to be paid by his clerk not less than £100 per week for a considerable time, and little less till towards his latter end: he did not employ less than 100 men of all kinds, so that his death was a great loss to this part of the country . . . The poor of the parish, and of the neighbouring parish had a great loss in him. He gave to the poor of Weymouth yearly money, and did many good deeds there: he kept a poor man that came out of his country to ask for work and charity, and kept him as long as he lived, which was about 5 years, giving him six shillings a week besides lodging and eating . . .
>
> Gave, towards building Queen's Square Chapel . . . . [£] 50
> Ditto, towards St Michael's Church . . . . [£] 50
> To the General Hospital, all the stone, lime, and paving,
> value . . . . [£] 900
> To Hampton Church, all the stone, lead and timber
> which cost . . . . [£] 400
> To the Bath Hospital yearly till his death . . . . [£] 11
> To Exeter Hospital, annual . . . . [£] 10..10..0
> To Charity School, Bath: annual . . . . [£] 10..10..0
>
> . . . Mr. Allen lived in a good hospitable manner, and kept a good house; plenty was given to all comers and goers . . . He gave towards building a new Church at Portland £50 . . . He gave to one Samuel Perry, of Monkton Combe, towards rebuilding his house after it had been burnt down, £36. He gave money to any countryman of his that came to ask for charity . . . [98]

Some features of this information are worth pointing out. The ambiguity of the second sentence (does it refer to outright charity or to the payroll?) is difficult to resolve, but it is interesting that Jones mentions employment in the same breath as charities; it suggests that, as one of Allen's workpeople, he was aware of his master's benevolence expressing itself through his provision of employment. Again, it is interesting to note that Allen was ready to *maintain* someone old and poor for the remainder of his life, which suggests he thought anyone in that position had a good claim to support from those fortunate enough to supply his need. Finally we must consider Jones's emphasis on Allen's hospitality. Clearly it is not just hospitality to noble and famous men that we have here, or to impecunious men of genius such as Henry

[98] Jones, op. cit., pp. 21, 31–2, 36, 37–8. For Allen's hospitality, see also Graves, op. cit., pp. 66–7.

Fielding. Richard Jones was one of Allen's workmen, albeit in a responsible and skilful job; furthermore his reference to 'all comers and goers' makes it plain that something very like that old-fashioned housekeeping, for which Pope had praised John Caryll at Christmas 1717, was being practised by Allen. The qualities and deeds of Ralph Allen recorded by Richard Jones are at once recognizable in the letter of Pope to Fortescue, written from Bath on 23 Jan. 1739/40:

> I should be sorry to be detain longer here, as if it should thaw, tis to be feard I must, and yet I would almost rather suffer any Confinement than *hear* of the Poor perishing round me by Want & Cold. I say *hear* of it, for I *See* nothing of it in this Place; the Good Man of it suffers no misery near him; He actually employs on this occasion some hundreds, (all the neighbouring Parishes can send him) of labouring Men, & has opend a new Quarry on purpose which he has yet no sort of occasion for. Whoever is lame, or any way disabled, he gives weekly allowances to the wife or children: Besides large supplies of other kinds to other Poor. God made this Man rich, to shame the Great; and wise, to humble the learned. I envy none of you in Town the Honours you may have received at Court, or from the Higher Powers: I have past this Christmas with the Most Noble Man of England.[99]

This is a crucial passage for an understanding of Pope's social poetry. Like his letter to Martha Blount about Sherborne, sixteen years earlier, it expresses in terms unraised and unintensified by poetic expression what moved him most deeply, what he most admired, in the society in which he lived. It shows the positive values of his social poetry. It is revealing how close the plain English of this letter takes us to the 'Honest Muse' which, in his epistle *To Bathurst*, had recounted the life and deeds of John Kyrle, the Man of Ross. Pope praises both men for their goodness in thinking of human *need* rather than *desert*. What moves Pope is that Allen provides employment for its own sake—because men have need of it—and that for the same reason he gives allowances to those depending on the sick; it is in fact a very modern ideal. While, as we have seen, Pope had many other grounds for calling Allen noble—not the least of which were his support for literature and architecture—it was his social conscience which in the end caused the poet to rank him morally a nobleman.

5. THE PATRIOT HOPE FULFILLED

Allen was forty seven in the year when Pope praised him so highly to Fortescue. His life must have seemed successful in almost every way. His postal organization was well-established and, with the help of his brother Philip Allen, steadily expanding, much to his own and the nation's profit. His quarries were highly organized and expanding; though the coming wars were to spoil

[99] *Corr.*, iv, pp. 221–2 (Pope to Fortescue, 29 Jan. 1739/40). This letter is quoted from, but not commented on, in Boyce, *The Benevolent Man*, pp. 89–90.

his chances of selling Bath stone in London, Bath itself, already transforming itself into a stately Palladian city, was a market of enormous promise and one which could be supplied with economy. His estates were already extensive, and, overlooking the city and scene of his various labours, the central building of his new mansion was almost complete.[100] In his family too he was happy, though not quite with the good fortune which favoured his public activities. His infant son George had died, just above two months old, in Dec. 1725, and there is no record of his having other children.[101] His first wife, Elizabeth, *née* Buckeridge, died sometime after 1725, but in March 1737 Allen married again, not this time to the daughter of a London merchant, but of a local landed gentleman, Richard Holder, whose family may have been in financial difficulties at the time.[102] The surviving correspondence of Allen shows the solicitude with which he guarded the interests of his family and relations, whether it was his sister who wrote for his help in 'a trubelsum and chargeabel dispute', or William Warburton, the proud and ambitious husband of his favourite niece, for whose ecclesiastical preferment he successfully petitioned the Duke of Newcastle.[103] It is not my purpose, however, to attempt a full and balanced account of Allen's life (of which a highly detailed picture has been provided by Boyce) but to trace through some of the salient features of his career those concerns which are relevant to a study of Pope's social values.

For this reason I shall dwell only briefly on the personal relations between Pope and Allen during the last four years of the poet's life. They are certainly of interest, but from a chiefly personal point of view. Throughout 1740 the flow of presents from Allen and of thanks and compliment from Pope continued; they knew one another well enough now for Pope to allow his tone to modulate into genial comedy—'Just now I hear of another Cargo of your Stone for my Grotto. I may properly be said to be *loaded* with your favours; but that they may not be *heap'd upon my head*, I have taken care to support them by many Cramps . . .'—or, on the subject of his letters to Swift, into unconcealed anxiety.[104] The winter of 1740–1 Pope spent with Allen at Bath, returning to Twickenham in February. Allen's chief service to him this year was to help him to invest £1000 in the Sun Fire Office, whose shares were much in demand.[105] In November Pope was once more staying with Allen, this time in the new mansion; it was on this occasion that Warburton was introduced at Prior Park, and also that much of *The New Dunciad* was written.[106] Warburton now dedicated to Allen the new edition of his *Critical*

---

[100] On 14 May 1741, Pope was to ask him: 'Are You got into your New House?' (*Corr.*, iv, p. 344).

[101] E. A. Russ, art. cit., p. 128.

[102] Boyce, op. cit., pp. 71–2; Peach, op. cit., pp. 71–2.

[103] Bath Reference Library: A. M. Broadley, op. cit., ii, p. vii (19 July 1743); she may have been Mrs. Buckeridge. For letters concerning Warburton's preferment, see B.M. Add. 32729, f. 291 (16 Sept. 1752); 32875, f. 163 (17 Oct. 1757); 32732, f. 141 (30 June 1759); 32900, f. 218 (20 Dec. 1759).

[104] *Corr.*, iv, 253 (Pope to Allen, 17 July 1740), 273–4 (Pope to Allen, 3 Oct. 1740).

[105] Ibid., p. 340 (Pope to Allen, 17 April 1741).

[106] Ibid., pp. 373 (Pope to Allen, 22 Nov. 1741), 387 (Pope to Allen, 8 Feb. 1741/2).

and Philosophical Commentary on Mr. Pope's Essay on Man, which commemorates the association of the three men.

Pope's friendship with Allen continued strong until Summer 1743 when,
during a stay at Prior Park, there occurred a mysterious quarrel involving
the Allens, Pope and Martha Blount. It is hard to reconstruct what happened,
though it is plain beyond dispute that Pope and Martha Blount were mortally
offended with the Allen family, and that the incident caused an utterly frank
exchange of letters between these two old friends, the absolute sincerity of
which it is impossible to doubt. Pope confessed to Martha Blount 'the bitter
Reflection that I was wholly the unhappy cause of it', and one at first thinks
of the poet's unsuccessful attempt to persuade Allen to make over one of his
smaller country houses for a temporary period to the use of Pope and George
Arbuthnot. This Allen declined to do, 'he making it a kind of Villa, to change
to, & pass now & then a Day at it in private' as Pope recognized; furthermore
Allen seems to have been proudly anxious to have Pope and his distinguished
friends about him at Prior Park. It is quite possible that Pope took Allen's
generosity too much for granted in his request, accustomed as he was to
unusual attention and allowance from his friends, and that an atmosphere of
some strain was thus created.[107] But it is impossible this should have caused
the Allens to treat Martha Blount, in her words to Pope, with 'much greater
inhumanity than I could conceive any body could shew'; something involving
both Pope and Martha Blount is required, and it is probable that Boyce has
the answer: '. . . Allen's favorite niece, sixteen-year-old Gertrude Tucker . . .
occupied the chamber next to Pope's and observed the odd fact that Miss
Blount early every morning made a surreptitious visit to Pope's room.'[108]
Pope was an old and ailing man; Martha Blount was his oldest and most
intimate female friend; they had known one another since childhood and
gone through many of the vicissitudes of their lives together. It does not take
much imagination to see that there must have been nursing services which the
invalid Pope might prefer done by Martha Blount than by Allen's servants.
But from this a stupid and narrow-minded scandal arose, originating with
Allen's niece, and encouraged by Mrs. Allen. This same niece figures vividly
in Richard Jones's *Life*, as one who got Allen's chaplain unjustly dismissed
for being 'a little free' with her, when in Jones's opinion, he could not help
being 'great' with her, 'for she would play with him in an indecent manner'.
She it was, who as wife of the Bishop of Gloucester, on Allen's death, 'put off
all the old servants', and would hardly speak to Jones himself, though 'her
poor Uncle never brought her up to be so arbitrary'.[109] She sounds like a
maker of trouble. But Allen, the model for Fielding's Allworthy, was, despite
the best of intentions, capable of being deceived, and of unjust dismissal. He
was no doubt deceived on this occasion. Pope himself, in the midst of his
letter of angry and mortified consolation to Martha Blount, seemed to recognize

---

[107] Ibid., pp. 461–3 (Pope to George Arbuthnot, Martha Blount to Pope, Pope to Martha Blount,
23 July–Aug. 1743).

[108] Boyce, art. cit., pp. 120–1; op. cit., pp. 148–9.

[109] Jones, op. cit., pp. 33–5.

this: 'however well I might wish the Man, the Woman [ie. Mrs. Allen] is a Minx, & an impertinent one, & he will do what She would have him—' and he adds of Warburton, who in the charged atmosphere of Prior Park after Pope's departure had ignored poor Martha Blount, 'W. is a sneaking Parson, & I told him he flatterd.'[110] A month later, after Allen had had a serious illness, Pope was large-minded enough to write letters of reconciliation to Allen and Warburton;[111] the following March Allen visited Pope at Twickenham and they had the matter out, Pope loyally defending his old friend and criticizing Mrs. Allen's conduct. Allen 'utterly denied any Unkindness or Coolness'—no doubt it was all he could do—and Pope at length let things rest.[112] Pope's last surviving letter is to Allen; just over two months later the eight years' friendship ended with the poet's death.[113] In his will, made after his letters of reconciliation but before Allen's visit, Pope left his friend £150, 'being, to the best of my calculation, the account of what I have received from him; partly for my own, and partly for charitable uses.'[114] It is absurd to suppose that Pope is here referring to the hospitality, services and gifts in kind he had had from Allen. It must rather allude to some financial payment. It is quite possible that Pope much under-estimated his debt, as Allen himself implied when informed of the bequest, but that it was intended as a slight is inconsistent with the fact that Pope also bequeathed to Allen and Warburton his library. Rather Pope, by this bequest, was emphasizing the nature of their relationship; Allen had been a most generous friend, but he had not been Pope's patron.

This is not quite the end of the story of Pope and Allen. To complete the picture it is necessary to introduce one final theme, not commercial, architectural or philanthropic, but political. Pope's praise of Allen in the winter of 1740 was in the first place purely social, yet in Pope's mind at least it also came to have political implications. In a poem which clearly refers, amongst other charity, to Pope's recent experience of Allen, 'On the Benefactions in the late Frost, 1740', we recognize in the first four lines the poetic language of the Patriot opposition to Walpole, from the two dialogues of his 'Epilogue to the Satires':

> Yes, 'tis the time! I cry'd, impose the chain!
>   Destin'd and due to wretches self-enslav'd!
> But when I saw such Charity remain,
>   I half could wish this people might be sav'd.
> Faith lost, and Hope, their Charity begins;
>   And 'tis a wise design on pitying heav'n,
> If this can cover multitudes of sins,
>   To take the only way to be forgiven.[115]

---

[110] *Corr.*, iv, p. 464 (Aug. 1743).
[111] Ibid., pp. 471 (Pope to Warburton, 4 Sept. 1743), 471–2 (Pope to Allen, 13 Sept. 1743).
[112] Ibid., pp. 510–11 (Pope to Martha Blount, 25 March 1744).
[113] Ibid., p. 522 (7 May 1744).
[114] Joseph Warton, ed. *The Works of Alexander Pope* (London, 1797), ix, p. 461.
[115] T.E., vi, p. 389.

At the time when Pope had arrested his readers with his vision of a degraded
Britain:

> ˙ Hear her black Trumpet thro' the Land proclaim,
> That 'Not to be corrupted is the Shame.'
> ['Epilogue to the Satires', Dialogue I, ll. 159–60]

Allen's charity made Pope hope that, if not in the words of his poem 'One
Thousand Seven Hundred and Forty', '. . . one man's honesty redeem the
land', at least the corrupted scene might display redeeming features.[116] In
this poem Allen is included in the people which had lost both faith and hope;
the reference is general, but it is interesting to note that in the earlier part of
his career Allen was probably not dissatisfied with the government of Sir
Robert Walpole. Until the last years of his life the evidence of his political
views is sparse. Clearly he was a more than vigorous opponent of Jacobitism,
as his assistance to Wade in the 1715 Rebellion shows, and this continued, for
in 1745 when Marshal Wade was again in the field against the House of
Stuart, Allen raised a company of men clothed in blue and red, with guns,
drums, halberds, pikes, belts and swords, at his own expense, against the
unnatural rebellion. They exercised in the Market Place of Bath before some
thousands of spectators, 'and gave great satisfaction'.[117] It is Wade who is
the key to Allen's politics in his earlier career. Wade had probably encouraged
him to put his postal proposals to the government in 1720 and had probably
stood surety for their success. After the Marshal's death in 1748 Allen had
erected in the grounds of his mansion a statue of him in Roman garb, which
depicted round the pedestal his road-building achievements in Scotland after
the 1715 Rebellion. It is clear that Wade was at first Allen's patron and thereafter his advisor and friend. Now Wade was an M.P. as well as a soldier; in
1715 he was the member for Hindon in Wiltshire, and from 1722 to his death
in 1748 he was one of the two M.P.s chosen by the Corporation of Bath to
represent it at Westminster. 'The corporation consisted for the most part of
country gentlemen and substantial tradesmen, proud of their independence
and integrity; and the Members had either strong local connections or were
national figures. There was no Patron; Government had little influence; and
bribery was unknown. It was a unique and, in many ways, a model borough.'[118]
Over this Corporation, however, Allen came to have something like complete power. At least at first Allen probably accepted Wade's political views,
and if later he ever doubted them, it is most improbable that he would have
interfered with what his old friend and patron chose to do or say. Wade was
on the whole a government man, and more so after the accession of Walpole
than before. In 1716 he voted with the government for the Septennial Bill,
in 1719 for the Bill for strengthening the Protestant Interest, and for the

---

[116] 'One Thousand Seven Hundred and Forty. A Poem', l. 98; T.E., iv, p. 337.

[117] According to Richard Jones all this cost Allen £2,000 (op. cit., pp. 25–6, 30. On p. 30 '1715'
is clearly a slip for '1745').

[118] Cobbett, vii, 36; viii, 11; xiv, 77. Sir Lewis Namier and John Brooke, ed. *The Commons,
1754–90* (London, 1964), i, p. 366.

Peerage Bill.[119] He proudly recalled in 1734 how he had voted against the govenment's disastrous decision to allow the South Sea Company to take over the National Debt, observing that '... though I have generally joined in opinion with those who were in the administration, yet I have likewise upon many occasions differed from them.'[120] Despite this statement, Wade voted with Walpole on every crucial issue in the latter's administration for which lists are recorded, even the widely unpopular and ill-fated Excise Bill.[121] He was not, however, closely associated with Walpole, and spoke in the Commons chiefly on military matters.

Likewise Allen himself is not to be thought a placeman of Walpole because he held an important government contract throughout the latter's administration, and it is going too far to speak of Walpole as Allen's patron.[122] It was not the Postmasters General of any Walpole administration who originally accepted Allen's proposals. On the first renewal of his contract in 1727, Walpole might indeed have intervened, as Allen perhaps expected, but there would have been little point in his doing so. Allen had solved a problem which several previous governments had failed to solve, and his continuing success was in a very obvious way in the interests of future administrations, whatever their political inclination. It was not obvious that anyone else but Allen could serve them better. This was still the conclusion after 1742. On the fall of Walpole John Barbutt, secretary to the Postmaster General, was removed from office and went bankrupt, but as Pope then wrote to Allen: '... you were secured a better way than by him'.[123] In short Allen, by this time, might feel himself able to judge independently in politics, however he might still defer to Wade. It is clear that friendship with Pope and acquaintance with some of Pope's friends must have put before him the alternative view to that of the supporters of Walpole. The passage of Pope's Dialogue I of the 'Epilogue to the Satires' in which Allen was praised culminated in the most glowing and intense denunciation of Walpole's England that Pope ever wrote, or that ever issued from the pens of the Patriot Opposition. In the great 'Epilogue' Pope took the cry of 'Corruption' from the pages of *The Craftsman* and Bolingbroke's *Patriot King*, and orchestrated it into an unforgettable poetic expression of anger, shame and pride. There are particular reasons why what Pope said might be expected to strike home to Allen. Corruption for him was not just an abstract term, nor was it, as Pope and Bolingbroke felt, the ominous mark of a civilization declining from its Augustan zenith. It was rather that recalcitrant, narrow-minded dishonesty with which for years he had had to struggle in seeking to establish an efficient and publicly responsible system of communications independent of London. Pope himself must have heard about this struggle and may have made the

[119] Cobbett, vii, 372, 587, 625.
[120] Cobbett, ix, 305–6.
[121] Cobbett, viii, 705, 917, 1311; ix, 305–6, 482; x, 290, 316; xi, 947, 975, 989; xii, 37, 1033, 1055. See also Romney Sedgwick, ed. *The Commons, 1715–54*, ii, pp. 501–2.
[122] Boyce, art. cit., p. 118.
[123] *Corr.*, iv, p. 405 (Pope to Allen, 19 July 1742).

connection between this corruption and corruption on a greater scale.

Pope also introduced Allen to certain key-personalities in the contemporary Patriot Opposition. Of these Lyttleton was perhaps the most significant.[124] Lyttleton was mentor and secretary to the Prince of Wales, whom at this time the Patriots hoped would bring better days to Britain when he came to the throne. It had been to Lyttleton that Bolingbroke had originally addressed his, as yet unpublished treatise, *The Idea of a Patriot King*, and it was he who now, in the very thoughts and words of this work, besought Pope to exert his ennobling influence upon the heir to the throne:

> Be therefore as much with him as you can, Animate him to Virtue, to the Virtue least known to Princes, though most necessary for them, Love of the Publick; and think that the Morals, the Liberty, the whole Happiness of this Country depends on your Success. If that Sacred Fire, which by You and other Honest Men has been kindled in his Mind, can be pre-serv'd, we may yet be safe; But if it go out, it is a Presage of Ruin, and we must be Lost. For the Age is too far corrupted to Reform itself; it must be done by Those upon, or near the Throne . . .[125]

Within the next ten days Pope tried to effect an alliance between Sir William Wyndham, leader of the more resolute section of the opposition in the Commons, and Lyttleton and the Prince of Wales.[126] It is interesting to speculate what effects upon Allen his acquaintance with Lyttleton had. It is even more interesting to note that Pope and Lyttleton were also acquainted with another politician who frequented Bath: one of the most fiery and promising of the 'Boy Patriots', William Pitt; Lyttleton conveyed Pitt's regards to Pope at the end of the letter quoted above.[127]

Pitt had entered parliament in 1735, and at once joined the opposition to Walpole. With his friend Lyttleton he tried to come to terms with Walpole on the latter's fall, but without success. He was not included in the new ministry. However he backed the administration in the year of Pope's death, and supported it for the next ten years. Out of office in 1754, he became premier for the first time in 1756, only to be dismissed the following April. In the same month Thomas Potter wrote to Allen alluding to 'The Part you have taken in the Honours lately done to Mr. Pitt by the Corporation of Bath' and it is clear that advances had been made to Pitt to change his con-stituency to Bath at the coming election. On Pitt's dismissal some members of the Corporation had misgivings, but Allen does not seem to have been among them. By June Pitt was premier once more, and had accepted Bath's invitation, having, in his own words, 'long ambition'd the honour of a Seat there'.[128] He wrote two letters, one to the Mayor of Bath, another more intimate to Allen, to whom he attributed the invitation:

124 Ibid., p. 144 (Pope to Allen, 2 Nov. 1738).
125 Ibid., pp. 138–9 (25 Oct. 1738).
126 Ibid., pp. 142–4 (Pope to Lyttleton, c. 1 Nov. 1738).
127 Ibid., p. 139 (Lyttleton to Pope, 25 Oct. 1738).
128 Peach, op. cit., pp. 159–63.

Dear Sir,—The repeated Instances of your kind friendship, and too favour-
ible opinion of your faithfull Servant, are such and so many, that Thanks
and acknowledgements are quite inadequate. give me leave to present them
to you, with a heart so truely yours as, on that account, makes me hope
your goodness will accept them for something.[129]

Pitt relied on Allen to arrange for his adoption as candidate for Bath in his
enforced absence, which was duly managed. On the event Allen wrote briefly
to Pitt, '. . . just to say that it is Impossible for you to be more satisfied with
the pleaseing Event . . . than I am with the honest and faithfull discharge of
my Duty to my Country . . .'[130] It was as the member for Bath that Pitt now
led Britain in the conduct of one of its most successful wars of the century;
his brief but glorious administration fulfilled a number of the Patriot hopes
cherished in the last years of Pope's life. The humiliatingly pacific policy
towards France and Spain, associated with Walpole, was now triumphantly
abandoned; Pitt had already brought a new probity to the holding of political
office, and he had eventually come to power in spite of the wishes of the court.
The connection between Allen and one of Britain's most brilliant prime
ministers takes its origin almost certainly in the eight years' friendship of the
postmaster and the poet. In 1760, a century after John Kyrle had witnessed
the celebrations of the restoration of Charles II, the relationship between
Pitt and Allen was at its height of warmth and mutual admiration. Consenting,
in December, to renew his connection with Bath at the next election, Pitt
wrote to Allen:

Dear Sir,—The very affecting token of esteem and affection which you
put into my hands last night at parting, has left impressions on my heart
which I can neither express nor conceal. If the approbation of the good
and wise be our wish, how must I feel the sanction of applause and friendship accompany'd with such an endearing act of Kindness from the best
of men? True Gratitude is ever the justest of Sentiments, and Pride too,
which I indulge on this occasion, may, I trust, not be disclaim'd by Virtue.
May the gracious Heaven long continue to lend you to mankind and particularly to the happiness of him who is unceasingly, with the warmest gratitude, respect, and affection,

My dear Sir,
Your most faithfull Friend and
most obliged humble Servant,
W. Pitt.[131]

Allen died on 29 June 1764. It is not possible to compute the extent of his
wealth, at his death, since so much of it was in the form of land and equip-
ment which were not then valued or immediately sold. His legacies in cash,

[129] Ibid., pp. 163–4; I have corrected the text by the MS. original displayed in the Bicentenary
Exhibition (see n. 43 above).
[130] Ibid., p. 167.
[131] Ibid., p. 171.

which amounted to some £63,000, were to his family, his friends and his servants, in descending order of value. No specific sum was left to charity, but £1,000 was bequeathed to his wife 'for such charities as she shall see proper'.[132] Numerous annuities were also left to various members of his family. That Allen died very wealthy indeed there can be no doubt. But in his lifetime he had put his wealth to great uses. Of the four 'good men' described in this book, Allen was certainly the most rich at his death. But of the six men considered he was not the most wealthy. Peter Walter's £282,401.0.0., the result of years of abstinence from expenditure, stands unrivalled.[133]

Pitt, it is said, wrote to Mrs. Allen on the death of her husband: 'I fear not all the example of his virtues will have power to raise up to the world his like again.'[134] But perhaps the last, and less rhetorical, word may be given to the 'sneaking Parson' whom Pope accused of flattery:

> I have studied his character even maliciously, to find where the weakness lies, but have studied in vain ... And of all friendly men, I never knew one so easily paid. He has no idea, in his commerce with those he loves, that there can be anything disguised or feigned: and so reasonable with all men, that he wishes the reason of the thing may prevail, whether, for or against himselfe ... It is true he has raised a Fortune by the Public, but not out of it. He has this in Common with many others, that he has got considerably by being concerned for the Public; but he is one of those few by whom the public has largely got, in their concerns with him ... But what perhaps more particularly distinguishes him is, his having preferred ... the public benefit to his own; and what is more, the giving much of his own to advance that service.[135]

---

[132] Ibid., p. 235. Allen's will is printed here, pp. 226–41, minus the codicils dated 28 June 1763. It may be compared with Bath Reference Library, MS. 1103, Class No. 929. 36, a copy of the same will, with the five codicils, and some additional matter concerning their proof.

[133] Richard Graves thought he recalled (op. cit., p. 79) that Allen left debts and legacies amounting to £70,000, which his executors had no more than £30,000 to discharge without selling freehold property, which the will empowered them to do.

[134] Peach, op. cit., p. 188.

[135] Ibid., p. 140 for the first sentence of the quotation; for the rest B. M. Egerton MSS. 1952, f. 48 (Warburton to Charles Yorke, 22 Sept. ?1755).

Part Three: The Poetry

VIII. The Betrayal of Society

1. THE THEME OF FALSE STEWARDSHIP

IN the preceding seven chapters, predominantly biographical, literature has been adduced either as biographical evidence (as the poems in the Caryll papers), or as yielding accounts or impressions which could be compared with a pattern of facts independently established (as Pope's account of John Kyrle in *To Bathurst*). It appears that Pope was for the most part well-informed and accurate in his statements about these six characters; and it has, further, been possible to present fuller and more detailed pictures of them than is given by what the author has said. There is much in these pictures with which it is entirely reasonable to presume Pope was familiar, though this must remain probable only, not proven. There have, finally, been details in Pope's statements (for example his remark on Peter Walter's being tried for forgery in 1737) for which I have failed to discover evidence. The purpose of the three following and final chapters is different. An independent basis of knowledge having been established, these chapters seek, first, to examine more fully the images of the six characters as they manifest themselves in the poems of Pope and certain of his contemporaries, secondly, to abstract from such passages the values which Pope attacks or affirms therein, and to trace these into the wider poetic expression of his social standards and views. In the present chapter I shall use the lives of Peter Walter and Sir John Blunt as the starting-point for an exploration of what Pope felt to be most deplorable and menacing in the English society of his time.

Peter Walter first made his way in the world as a steward. It was a form of work he expanded enormously throughout his career. As land-steward to the Duke of Newcastle, and other powerful members of the nobility, he stretched his stewardship to almost national proportions. As a Westminster attorney he extended his work into legal fields, and by 1712, if not before, was being applied to by members of the nobility to handle their legal disputes. His stewardship consisted in his being a man of law as well as a man of business. And like the 'faithful and wise steward' of Christ's parable, 'whom his lord shall make ruler over his household, to give them their portion of meat in due season', Walter as an eighteenth-century steward had a twofold obligation: to his lord, the landowner or noble, and to the dependants, tenants, labourers

and poor who fell under his practical care.[1] It was in respect of this double
obligation, and the way in which they thought Walter betrayed it, that writers
such as Swift and Pope launched their attack. Swift, in his *Answer of ...
William Pulteney to ... Sir ROBERT WALPOLE* (1730), is explicit and
trenchant:

> How many great families do we all know, whose masters have passed for
> persons of good abilities, during the whole course of their lives, and yet
> the greatest part of whose estates have sunk in the hands of their stewards
> and receivers; their revenues paid them in scanty portions, at large dis-
> count, and treble interest, though they did not know it; while the tenants
> were daily racked, and at the same time accused to their landlords of in-
> solvency. Of this species are such managers, who, like honest *Peter Waters*,
> pretend to clear an estate, keep the owner pennyless, and after seven years,
> leave him five times more in debt, while they sink half a plum into their own
> pockets.[2]

Walter frequently 'accused' tenants of insolvency to their landlord, and could
be suspected of incompetence or double-dealing by as old an acquaintance
and employer as Lord Uxbridge, on at least one occasion.[3] Swift knew what
he was talking about, and further information, imagination, or both, filled
out for him the character of the false steward. In a poem begun in the same
year but not published until 1735, 'To Mr. Gay on his being Steward to the
Duke of Queensberry', Swift enlarged on the theme of true and false stewardship with much asperity and some humour:

> Next, hearken GAY, to what thy Charge requires,
> With *Servants*, *Tenants*, and the neighb'ring *Squires*.
> Let all Domesticks feel your gentle Sway;
> Nor bribe, insult, nor flatter, nor betray.
> Let due Reward to Merit be allow'd ...
> Each Farmer in the Neighbourhood can count
> To what your lawful Perquisites amount.
> The Tenants poor, the Hardness of the Times,
> Are ill excuses for a Servant's Crimes:
> With Int'rest, and a *Præmium* paid beside,
> The Master's pressing Wants must be supply'd;
> With hasty Zeal, behold, the Steward come,
> By his own Credit to advance the Sum;
> Who, while *th'unrighteous Mammon* is his Friend,
> May well conclude his Pow'r will never end.
> A faithful Treas'rer! What could he do more?
> *He lends my Lord, what was my Lord's before* ...

---

[1] Luke 12:42.

[2] Jonathan Swift, *Miscellaneous and Autobiographical Pieces* ..., ed. Herbert Davis (Oxford,
1962), p. 117.

[3] See Ch. IV, n. 84 above.

> Should some *imperious Neighbour* sink the Boats,
> And drain the *Fish-ponds*; while your *Master* doats;
> Shall he upon the *Ducal* Rights intrench,
> Because he brib'd you with a Brace of Tench?
>
> [ll. 53–7, 65–76, 89–92]

The accusation of tenants' poverty reappears in this passage; and the picture of the steward lending to his master, which few can have been in a position to do but which we know Walter did, points forward to the identification which is to come: 'Have *Peter Walters* always in your Mind . . .' (l. 101).[4]

The connection between the false steward and 'the mammon of unrighteousness', which alludes to another New Testament parable of stewardship, brings us close to Pope's earliest reference to Walter.[5] In the Epistle *To Bathurst* (1733) we find Pope

> . . . fairly owning, Riches in effect
> No grace of Heav'n or token of th' Elect;
> Giv'n to the Fool, the Mad, the Vain, the Evil,
> To Ward, to Waters, Chartres, and the Devil.   [ll. 17–20]

These lines put Walter in bad company. Ward was a convicted forger, and one thought to have been involved in an attempted fraudulent conveyance of a part of Sir John Blunt's estate, when due for confiscation in 1721. Charteris was a notorious cheat, usurer and debauchee, also a strong supporter of Walpole.[6] However the artistry of the last couplet must not be interpreted minutely; there was no appropriateness in implying that Ward was foolish, Walter mad, Charteris vain. All the men named are plainly seen to be vicious, and the list leads down by a natural gravitation to 'the Devil' their master. Pope returns to the attack later in the poem:

> Wise Peter sees the World's respect for Gold,
> And therefore hopes this Nation may be sold:
> Glorious Ambition! Peter, swell thy store,
> And be what Rome's great Didius was before.   [ll. 125–8]

Like the biblical steward, Walter is presented here as one who puts his trust in '*th' unrighteous Mammon*' and like the false steward of Swift's poem concludes that by so doing 'his Pow'r will never end'. There are political implications here, as in Swift's poem, which will shortly be discussed. Meanwhile we may see Pope's following references to Walter take up Swift's point about his untrustworthiness with property. In the satire *To Fortescue*, after glancing lightly back at *To Bathurst* ('Scarce to wise *Peter* complaisant enough'), he has his friend warn him not to 'laugh at Peers that put their trust in *Peter*', and in the satire *To Bethel*, more philosophically, Pope asks:

---

[4] See Ch. IV, n. 13 above.
[5] Luke 16:9.
[6] T.E., iii–ii, pp. 85–6.

> What's *Property*? dear Swift! you see it alter
> From you to me, from me to Peter Walter,
> Or, in a mortgage, prove a Lawyer's share . . .[7]

Four years later, in his Epistle *To Augustus*, Pope with mock-modesty praises the role of the poet in the state:

> To cheat a Friend, or Ward, he leaves to Peter;
> The good man heaps up nothing but mere metre,
> Enjoys his Garden and his Book in quiet . . .   [ll. 197–9]

However, Pope's fullest attack on Walter as a false steward and treacherous lawyer was made in his imitation of 'The Second Satire of Dr. John Donne' (1735). Pope had already written a modern version of Donne's second *Satyr* in 1713 when he had retained Donne's name, Coscus, for the grasping and dishonest lawyer whose portrait forms the central part of the poem. Always alert for contemporary point in his imitations, Pope probably realized that he had a good modern Coscus in Walter, and that it would be worth revising his early version of Donne's 'Satyr II' to make a pair with the imitation of 'Satyr IV' which he had composed two years before. Much of what Donne had written was given point when applied to Walter, and Pope filled out the portrait with certain authentic details from his own knowledge:

> One, one man only breeds my just offence;
> Whom Crimes gave wealth, and wealth gave impudence . . .
>   Curs'd be the Wretch! so venal and so vain;
> Paltry and proud, as drabs in Drury-lane.
> 'Tis such a bounty as was never known,
> If Peter deigns to help you to your *own*:
> What thanks, what praise, if Peter but supplies!
> And what a solemn face if he denies! . . .
> His *Office* keeps your Parchment-Fates entire,
> He starves with cold to save them from the Fire;
> For you, he walks the streets thro' rain or dust,
> For not in Chariots Peter puts his trust;
> For you he sweats and labours at the Laws,
> Takes God to witness he affects your Cause,
> And lyes to every Lord in every thing,
> Like a King's Favourite—or like a King.
>   These are the talents that adorn them all,
> From wicked Waters ev'n to godly [Paul] . . .
> In shillings and in pence at first they deal,
> And steal so little, few perceive they steal;
> Till like the Sea, they compass all the land,
> From Scots to Wight, from Mount to Dover strand . . .
> Piecemeal they win this Acre first, then that,

---

[7] *To Fortescue*, ll. 3, 40; *To Bethel*, ll. 167–9; T.E., iv, pp. 5, 9; 69.

> Glean on, and gather up the whole Estate:
> Then strongly fencing ill-got wealth by law,
> Indentures, Cov'nants, Articles they draw;
> Large as the Fields themselves . . .
>
> [ll. 45–6, 63–8, 71–80, 83–6, 91–5]

This is not one of those portraits in which Pope transforms his subject into a creature of poetic imagery, as he does Lord Hervey in *To Arbuthnot*. To read this passage after Walter's correspondence is to recognize real qualities of the man that Pope has conveyed. These points of truth or probability are weakened, however, by the pervasive attitude, in the portrait, of aristocratic contempt for a *parvenu* and self-made man. 'Paltry and proud . . .', 'In shillings and in pence at first they deal . . .', '. . . If Peter deigns to help you to your *own*:' these are the phrases which give away that Pope's attitude is here somewhat less than fully moral, and that his identification with the tone of an exasperated and superior landowner is complete—and limiting. Limited also is the quality of the poetry; Pope's lines are pointed, have some expressive variation of tone, and certainly build up well to that very Popian line of Donne: 'Like a King's Favorite—or like a King' with its suggestive political implications. But the passage lacks vividness. Pope's attitude to Walter as a false steward, thus far, has led to the expression of a fairly direct and well-supported moral viewpoint, enlivened by sarcasm, and limited by its association with a somewhat routine class outlook, born of Pope's long association with landowning gentry and aristocrats. Socially representative, but not humanly and poetically impressive, it is closer to what readers often expect of Pope's social poetry than his more frequent best.

There was, however, another reason why Pope was moved to re-write Donne's *Satyr II* as a poem about Walter. Walter had, as we have seen, become a landowning gentleman, with a country seat and estate at Stalbridge, near Lord Digby's great house at Sherborne in Dorset. And Donne's poem not only recognized the remorseless accumulation of land by men like Coscus, but added lines on the hospitable ideal of 'housekeeping', an ideal quite neglected by such new landlords. We have seen, in considering the lives of John Kyrle, John Caryll, William Digby and Ralph Allen, something of how this ideal was alive and centrally important to Pope. Thus when Pope, immediately following his portrait of Walter, proceeds to render Donne's lines on neglected 'housekeeping', a wider social perspective opens up, one in which it is less relevant to see Walter the land-steward, than Walter the wealthy country gentleman and lord of his own manor:

> The Lands are bought; but where are to be found
> Those ancient Woods, that shaded all the ground?
> We see no new-built Palaces aspire,
> No Kitchens emulate the Vestal Fire.
> Where are those Troops of poor, that throng'd of yore
> The good old Landlord's hospitable door?

> Well, I could wish, that still in lordly domes
> Some beasts were kill'd, tho' not whole hecatombs,
> That both Extremes were banish'd from their walls,
> Carthusian Fasts, and fulsome Bacchanals;
> And all mankind might that just mean observe,
> In which none e'er could surfeit, none could starve.
> These, as good works 'tis true we all allow;
> But oh! these works are not in fashion now:
> Like rich old Wardrobes, things extremely rare,
> Extremely fine, but what no man will wear.   [ll. 109–24]

In a sense the country gentleman is a steward still, entrusted by God with wealth and land for the good of the immediate neighbourhood, but now the stress is on an obligation to the poor rather than to a human master. By this wider communal standard also Pope judges Walter; it was a standard by which Caryll had not been found wanting: 'good works', like 'old wardrobes', Pope had told Caryll in 1717, using the simile from Donne's *Satyr II*, should not be entirely forgotten lest they should come into use again some day. We have seen enough of the Carylls to know that Pope's praise was in some measure justified. We have seen enough of Walter to know that he felt little interest in such traditional ideals with their wider sense of communal obligation; '. . . our affections should never runn away with our money', he wrote to Lord Uxbridge, 'if we goo to the brinke, wee shall bee in danger of Drowning'.[8] If affection could not make him generous, social duty was not likely to, and in fact did not, as the almost total absence of references to charity or alms in his letters and accounts makes clear. Walter, as we have seen, was ready enough to see society in the traditional hierarchical pattern ('All government from a King to the Masr. of a family depends upon Subordination . . . If inferiour men should bee permitted to trample upon Superiour ones, wee should soon fall into Confusion') but was not ready to acknowledge that those who were born or had struggled to 'Superiour' positions had human obligations to neighbours, tenants and poor.[9] The one-sided nature of Walter's social attitude is perfectly brought out by the anecdote in which he was visited by his bailiff and the bailiff's boy: sitting in darkness, he lit a candle on their approach, but put it out when he found it was not needed. 'Notwithstanding his rigid parsimony he exacted the respect usually paid to opulence.'[10] Walter did indeed leave £1000 to his heir, the better 'to keep his house and to be indulgent to his Tenants'. This may be taken at its face value, but the light in which it should probably be regarded is that of his actual bequests to the poor in his will. The 1737 draft left £20 to the poor of Stalbridge and Hanley, with the proviso that they should not already be getting relief from the parish. The actual will, however, cut the proviso—and the sum, leaving out of a total

---

[8] See Ch. IV, n. 94 above.
[9] See Ch. IV, n. 89 above.
[10] See Ch. IV, n. 109 above.

wealth of £282,401.0.0., £5.0.0. to the poor of each parish.[11] Pope might well write of Walter, and others like him,

> Where are those Troops of poor, that throng'd of yore
> The good old Landlord's hospitable door?

Turning again to the Epistle *To Bathurst*, we find Pope giving us a similar picture to that at the end of 'The Second Satire to Dr. John Donne', expressing the same concern, and the same values, but without reference to Walter:

> Old Cotta sham'd his fortune and his birth,
> Yet was not Cotta void of wit or worth:
> What tho' (the use of barb'rous spits forgot)
> His kitchen vy'd in coolness with his grot?
> His court with nettles, moats with cresses stor'd,
> With soups unbought and sallads blest his board.
> If Cotta liv'd on pulse, it was no more
> Than Bramins, Saints, and Sages did before;
> To cram the Rich was prodigal expence,
> And who would take the Poor from Providence?
> Like some lone Chartreux stands the good old Hall,
> Silence without, and Fasts within the wall;
> No rafter'd roofs with dance and tabor sound,
> No noontide-bell invites the country round;
> Tenants with sighs the smoakless tow'rs survey,
> And turn th' unwilling steeds another way:
> Benighted wanderers, the forest o'er,
> Curse the sav'd candle, and unop'ning door;
> While the gaunt mastiff growling at the gate,
> Affrights the beggar whom he longs to eat.   [ll. 179–98]

The success of this passage lies in the way Pope has embodied his moral, social and human point in a *scene*. Or rather two related scenes, for just as Pope's description of the Man of Ross showed first a distant prospect of his works, and then entered the market-place to see the more immediate and practical working of his charity, so here a similar tactic is adopted, but in reverse. Here we are first in the cold unused kitchen and overgrown court, and thereafter afforded a more distant prospect of the hall, in relation to 'the country round' and the unsatisfied expectations of the neighbourhood. In almost every line our attention is drawn to some human detail which, while it contributes to the scene, attests also to a tradition, a hope and a need which is unfulfilled, so that the passage displays a humanly negative prospect in a poetically positive way. The sense of coldness where there had once been warmth, silence where there had once been revelry, the unopening door where there had once been welcome—emptiness where there was once community—

---

[11] See Ch. IV, nn. 122, 123 above.

is made vivid indeed, and culminates in the final, cruel image of the savageness of one deprived creature to another. In a small way, Cotta's hall shows a failure in civilization, and the detail of the nettle-infested courtyard earlier in the passage subtly anticipates the suggestiveness of the last image. The passage expresses Pope's specific and genuine concern with 'housekeeping' and its attendant associations, but it has through this a more general meaning, and is in itself an image of communal disintegration. It contrasts markedly in this respect with Pope's account of the Man of Ross in the same poem, this contrast being a major feature of the structure of this epistle.

Literary and biographical background tell us something more about the passage and the values expressed in it. In Pope's canon the ancestor of 'The Second Satire of Dr. John Donne' and of this passage is his 1713 version of Donne's *Satyr II*. A small but telling detail in all three is the mention of the kitchen, and the opposed extremes of old and young Cotta are anticipated by Pope's wish, in the 1713 version,

> That both Extreams were banisht from their Halls,
> *Carthusian* Fasts, and fulsom *Bacchanalls*:
> And all mankind wou'd that blest Mean observe . . .

—the blessed Mean which in *To Bathurst* becomes the Man of Ross.[12] This shows that Donne himself is Pope's real ancestor here, and that his attitude to neglected 'housekeeping' is close to the Elizabethan one. And indeed a comparison of Pope's lines on old Cotta with the description of neglected 'housekeeping' by that other Elizabethan satirist Pope so admired, Joseph Hall, in the Second Satire of his Fifth Book, shows a sufficient similarity of attitude and visual detail to suggest that Pope might have drawn something from the older satirist.[13] It may be seen that the whole subject was a traditional one—traditional in society as in literature—and that it would therefore be wrong to consider the portrait of Old Cotta as having been prompted by the life of one man only: Sir John Cutler (1608?–93), the London merchant, the closest scholarship has come to finding an historical 'original'. Pope's technique of leading his audience into self-identification by hinting at a number of possible originals, and by basing his portraits on the firm substratum of some general moral type, such as the miser or the spendthrift, is now well understood.[14] For Pope's contemporary reader, no doubt, the portrait of Old Cotta glanced at many people of his own and the previous age. Peter Walter is simply one caught up in this web of social allusion, by virtue of Pope's later making him the modern subject of his 'Second Satire of Dr. John Donne'. But Walter's 'sav'd candle' agreed well enough with old Cotta's—indeed this is almost a folklore detail in the eighteenth-century presentation of the miser— and if asked what was the contemporary relevance of Old Cotta Pope would

[12] Ll. 122–5; T.E., iv, p. 142.

[13] Arnold Davenport, ed. *The Poems of Joseph Hall* (Liverpool, 1949; 2nd. edn. 1969), pp. xxvii–viii, n. 5.

[14] T.E., iii–ii, pp. 108–9 (l. 179 n.); E. R. Wasserman, ed. *Pope's Epistle to Bathurst* (Baltimore, 1960), pp. 56–7.

probably have referred to Peter Walter among others.[15] Walter's rigidly one-sided attitude to society certainly led to that irresponsibility to human claims, that communal disintegration, which it was essentially Pope's purpose to express in this portrait.

It is for this reason that the moral and social touchstone running all through the epistles *To Bathurst* and *To Burlington* is the attitude to the poor. We are relentlessly reminded of it. ''Tis thus we riot, while who sow it, starve . . . Perhaps you think the Poor might have their part?/Bond damns the Poor, and hates them from his heart . . . "God cannot love (says Blunt, with tear-less eyes)/The wretch he starves"—and piously denies . . . And who would take the Poor from Providence . . . Behold the Market-place with poor o'er-spread . . . Cutler saw tenants break, and houses fall . . . His givings rare, save farthings to the poor'; 'Yet hence the Poor are cloath'd, the Hungry fed . . . Whose chearful Tenants bless their yearly toil'—these and many more less explicit lines stress that irresponsibility to the poor is a prime mark of the abuse of wealth and of the neglect of a properly inclusive conception of society.[16] This is because the poor, in Pope's view, are least in a position to help themselves, more dependent than any other part of society on the morality of others. Yet wealth is finally for the benefit—though not (by Pope's book) the equal benefit—of the whole of society, the 'common weal' as Pope calls it, and those who come to be ruled by 'th' unrighteous Mammon', letting wealth rule them rather than they ruling wealth, are a block to this benefit. The responsibility is theirs, whether they neglect it or not, and when Pope turns from the individual life to look for some kind of justice in the longer patterns of providence—a providence to which he is clearly unwilling to resign the poor—he entertains the view that

> Who sees pale Mammon pine amidst his store,
> Sees but a backward steward for the Poor.
>
> [*To Bathurst*, ll. 173–4]

The qualified optimism conveyed by the word 'backward' is not endorsed by the Epistle *To Bathurst* as a whole, but otherwise it is thus Pope thought of the false stewardship of Peter Walter the country gentleman.

A consideration of what the writings of Pope and Swift, associated as they are with aristocratic and gentry attitudes, make of the career of Walter as land-steward and landed gentleman prompts speculation of a partly social and partly psychological kind. 'Housekeeping' in the traditional sense was not dead by the earlier eighteenth century, though it was on the wane. It seems probable that a major factor in its decline was the possibility of that highly efficient business management of the estate economy, of which Walter was perhaps the chief early eighteenth-century exponent. No doubt for this very reason he was in demand by so many members of the aristocracy. But the kind of pure cost-accountancy which Walter and others repeatedly carried

---

[15] Note the similarity to an anecdote about 'Vulture' Hopkins and Thomas Guy, *Notes and Queries*, 2nd. Series, viii, No. 193 (10 Sept. 1859) p. 208.

[16] *To Bathurst*, ll. 24, 101–2, 105–6, 188, 263, 323, 348; *To Burlington*, ll. 169, 183.

out for the Duke of Newcastle highlighted the traditional hospitalities in kind, the financial implications of which it had previously been easier to ignore. On the other hand, many landowners valued these often generous practices for their own sake, as well as for the popularity and electoral influence they helped preserve. Newcastle is a clear case of a landowner in this conflict; he certainly practised traditional housekeeping on his Sussex estates until told to stop by his economic advisers.[17] Walter, himself a substantial and parsimonious landowner, and ruthless money-lender to landowners in distress, confronted aristocrats and gentry with an unwelcome choice of roles: greater wealth and efficiency, or the keeping up of various customary paternalist forms. Most must have chosen the former, and proportionately detested the indispensable Walter and those like him as its extreme embodiments. Writers such as Pope and Swift shared this dilemma at one remove, for to praise certain kinds of artistocratic expenditure might be to condone wealth conserved or increased by the methods of a Walter; here the satirists are perilously close to the tragic contradiction at the heart of the economic process. But their case against Walter has not yet been fully exposed.

The third and final sense in which Pope and Swift regarded Walter as an instance of false stewardship is political, and takes us back to those political connotations noted but not explored in quotations made earlier in this chapter. Walter, it will be remembered, was a member of parliament from 1715 to 1735, and his political record was strongly Whig. In the 1722 election, after the first year of Robert Walpole's twenty one year period in power, Walter was referred to as the government candidate elected for Bridport, and in all the subsequent important divisions in the Commons, of which lists have been preserved, he voted with the government.[18] The only occasion on which Walter and Walpole were on opposite sides of the House was the passing of the bill to modify the Occasional Conformity and Schism Acts in 1719. But at this time Walpole was in opposition, and Walter was voting with the government of the day. Walter was kept firm to the government of Walpole, no doubt, through the influence of the Duke of Newcastle, who in 1724 made him Clerk of the Peace for Middlesex, in effect a political place.[19] He was acquainted personally with Walpole, who on 13 April 1734 used him as a go-between to make the proposal to Lord Uxbridge which the latter appears to have rejected with indignation. It was almost certainly a political proposal, and presumably offered Lord Uxbridge some form of incentive which he did not accept. Walter conducted himself with subtlety. Though (as he claims in his next letter) he disapproved of the proposal, and expected Lord Uxbridge to disapprove, he evidently said nothing of this in the original letter. He thus fully satisfied 'the great man' who 'compelled me to it', while in no way at first committing himself lest, by any chance, Lord Uxbridge should have responded favourably to the proposal. When he responded unfavourably,

[17] Ray A. Kelch, *Newcastle, A Duke Without Money* . . ., p. 82.
[18] See Ch. IV above; for Walter as government candidate for Bridport, see n. 53.
[19] See Ch. IV, n. 47 above.

Walter had no difficulty in agreeing with him.[20] Though he was a government man he was probably not entirely in Walpole's pocket. For Pope and Swift, on the other hand, he was a creature of the regime which they believed was systematically corrupting Britain.

This plainly appears in Swift's *Answer of William Pulteney*. The attack on Walter which it contains is not merely a sideshot at an unpopular figure. Knowledge of Walter's political career shows that he has a more integral place in this broadside against Walpole. Swift is working out an analogy between Walter and Walpole. 'A freeborn *Englishman*', he urges, '. . . can find little satisfaction at a minister overgrown in wealth and power from the lowest degree of want and contempt; when that power or wealth are drawn from the bowels and blood of the nation, for which every fellow subject is a sufferer, except the great man himself, his family, and his pensioners.'[21] He proceeds to stress the danger involved in a master making a wrong choice of servant and the prince making the wrong choice of courtier or minister. It is in this connection that the paragraph on Walter is introduced, and it becomes clear that, as he is seen as a dishonest steward to landowners and nobles, so Walpole is seen as a dishonest steward to the king. In both cases the people are oppressed. In both cases the master is deceived. However, the parallel is more fully developed in Swift's epistle 'To Mr. Gay'. The occasion of this poem has in itself political significance. It commemorates Gay's refusal of the offer of a very minor place at court (Gentleman Usher to the Princess Louisa) and acceptance instead (as Swift believed) of the post of steward to the Duke of Queensberry, a prominent opposition nobleman. The court and government, Swift implies, have shown their false values by offering so celebrated a man so humiliatingly minor a post, but Gay has found a patron with true values among the opposition. Swift begins by praising Gay for his decision, and showing in fanciful vein how a poet will never break trust. The tone then changes to violent invective as Swift conjures up a picture of the political arch-enemy:

> A bloated *M[iniste]r* in all his Geer,
> With shameless Visage, and perfidious Leer . . .   [ll. 33–4]

The parallel between Gay as a good steward and Walpole as a bad one is next explicitly developed:

> Now, let me show how *B[ob]* and you agree.
> You serve a *potent Prince*, as well as He.
> The *Ducal* Coffers, trusted to your Charge,
> Your honest Care may fill; perhaps enlarge.
> His Vassals easy, and the Owner blest;
> They pay a Trifle, and enjoy the rest.
> Not so a Nation's Revenues are paid:
> The Servants Faults are on the Master laid.

[20] See Ch. IV, n. 67 above.
[21] Swift, *Miscellaneous and Autobiographical Pieces* . . ., ed. cit., p. 112.

> The People with a Sigh their Taxes bring;
> And cursing B[ob], forget to bless [the King].   [ll. 43–52]

When Swift wrote of the steward who 'while *th' unrighteous Mammon* is his
Friend,/May well conclude his Pow'r will never end', he was thinking of
Bolingbroke's somewhat optimistic attack upon Walpole in his *First Vision
of Camilick* (1726), which set the pattern for much of *The Craftsman's* polemic
against the government. The *Vision* tells how a man 'with a purse of gold',
'a bluff, ruffianly manner', and 'a smile, or rather a sneer' on a face 'bronzed
over with a glare of confidence' marched to the throne, spurned the constitution,
enslaved the senators, and pacified all criticism by showers of money. 'This
he did till his purse became empty. Then he dropt it; but then too, in the
very same moment, he himself dropt with it to the ground. That, and the
date of his power, at once expired ... Heaven and earth resounded with
liberty! liberty! and the HEART OF THE KING WAS GLAD WITHIN
HIM.'[22] Thus false stewards, on both the local and the great level, may
maintain themselves by money—as long as it lasts. And thus the line of
advice to Gay already quoted: 'Have *Peter Waters* always in your mind'
is coupled with a line which clinches the parallel we have been tracing: 'That
Rogue of *genuine ministerial* Kind' [ll. 101–2]. Swift's poem does not, however,
share the optimism of *The First Vision of Camilick*. The situation with which
he was concerned was not one simply in which when the rogue runs out of
money he runs out of power. A rogue in power will *not* run out of money
unless his master dismisses him, or the old master is succeeded by a new.
The First Vision was written with high hope in 1726 and published in one
of the opening numbers of *The Craftsman*.[23] When Swift came to write,
nearly five years later, Walpole was still in power and had actually survived
a change of monarch, as the poem bitterly recognizes. This fact, for men
like Pope and Swift, opened up some longer and more gloomy perspectives.
If a minister maintains himself by corruption for some years, will not the
nation itself become corrupt? A monarch may be deceived; may he also be
bought? It is with these fears in mind that Swift, at the end of 'To Mr. Gay',
can conclude:

> Thus Families, like R[eal]ms, with equal Fate,
> May sink by *premier Ministers of State* ...
>   In ev'ry Court the Parallel will hold;
> And Kings, like private Folks, are bought and sold:
>   [ll. 115–16, 135–6]

It may be seen that these two works of Swift do not merely recognize a connection between Walpole and Walter—and historically there was such a

---

[22] Henry St. John, Viscount Bolingbroke, *Works* (London, 1754), i, pp. 187–8.

[23] *The Craftsman*, i, No. 16 (27 Jan. 1727), pp. 91–6. The importance of *The Craftsman* for an
understanding of Pope's later poems has long been apparent. Our knowledge of the relationship
has recently been extended by two excellent studies: Isaac Kramnick, *Bolingbroke and His Circle*
(Cambridge, Mass., 1968) and Maynard Mack, *The Garden and the City: Retirement and Politics
in the later Poetry of Pope* (London, 1969).

connection—but propose an analogical relationship between them; just as a manor might be seen as '*a Kingdom in Miniature*' and its lord the king of a small local domain, so the parts played by these two men in society were intrinsically similar, differing only in scale and prominence.

More significance may now be seen in Pope's second reference to Walter in *To Bathurst*. Walter sees 'the World's respect for Gold' and therefore 'hopes this Nation may be sold'. What seems a rather inflated attack on the steward and country gentleman becomes explicable when the Swiftian analogy between Walter and Walpole is remembered. This is truer still of the following couplet.

> Glorious Ambition! Peter, swell thy store,
> And be what Rome's great Didius was before.   [ll. 125–8]

The Roman lawyer Didius Salvius Julianus actually bought himself the place of Emperor, when it was put up for the highest bidder by the Praetorians on the death of the Emperor Pertinax in A.D. 193. Swift talked of the sinking of a realm through false stewardship, and the shameful episode from the decline of the Roman Empire is intended to bring home to the reader what kind of man hastens a similar decline in Britain. Walter too was an unscrupulous and enormously rich lawyer. The whole allusion is couched in a tone of ironic exaggeration, without which Pope would be guilty of losing his sense of proportion, but at the heart of the exaggeration there is an intelligent point. Pope's readiness to see Walter as a symptom of a malaise which involves the highest in the kingdom is also seen in Dialogue I of his 'Epilogue to the Satires':

> Is it for *Bond* or *Peter* (paltry Things!)
> To pay their Debts or keep their Faith like Kings?   [ll. 121–2]

This, coming in the passage in which Pope asks: '. . . shall the Dignity of *Vice* be lost?', is an extremely oblique couplet. Bond (a fraudulent director of the mismanaged Charitable Corporation for the relief of the poor) and Peter Walter are getting above themselves. Social distinction and order are being lost. But they are being lost because what now characterizes the great is vice, and in this it is only too easy for others to emulate them. It was with a similar oblique irony that Peachum sang, at the opening of *The Beggar's Opera*,

> And the statesman, because he's so great,
> Thinks his trade as honest as mine.[24]

Greatness, Peachum argues, hardly gives the right to claim the virtues of the humble. The inoffensive surface morality of the lines, however, contrasting lowly virtue with eminent vice in pastoral fashion, becomes suddenly searing when we realise the nature of Peachum's 'Trade', and that to 'think' your own trade as honest as Peachum's is to acknowledge that it is as bad as

---

[24] Gay, *The Beggar's Opera*, I, i, ll. 7–8; ed. E. V. Roberts (London, 1969), p. 6.

Peachum's. Thus the meaning is rather: that the great recognize their trade is villainous and yet persist in it. This conforms with the charge of brazen confidence which the Tory opposition made so often against 'the great man' that both these passages have in mind: Walpole. It is interesting that Pope was probably responsible for the pointed yet involute significance of the lines from *The Beggar's Opera*.[25] Both instances prompt the reader to see society as involved in a spreading web of broken faith and deception, which will ultimately destroy distinction both social and moral.

Pope's final reference to Walter, in Dialogue II of the 'Epilogue to the Satires', implicitly recognizes the connection with Walpole, but its main function is to show the poet's own slightly self-mocking awareness of his repeated attacks (this is his tenth separate allusion) on the industrious lawyer, landowner and politician. Taken to task by the *adversarius* for the bold, far-reaching yet particular nature of his satiric attacks, which hurt high and low alike, Pope leans towards attacking the great:

> Then better sure it Charity becomes
> To tax Directors, who (thank God) have Plums;
> Still better, Ministers; or if the thing
> May pinch ev'n there—why lay it on a King.
> > *Fr.* Stop! stop!
> > *P.* Must Satire, then, nor *rise*, nor *fall*?
> Speak out, and bid me blame no Rogues at all.
> > *Fr.* Yes, strike that *Wild*, I'll justify the blow.
> > *P.* Strike? why the man was hang'd ten years ago:
> Who now that obsolete Example fears?
> Ev'n *Peter* trembles only for his Ears.
> > *Fr.* What always *Peter*? *Peter* thinks you mad,
> You make men desp'rate if they once are bad:
> Else might he take to Virtue some years hence—   [ll. 48–60][26]

The mention of 'Ministers' and Wild indicate that once again Walpole is at the centre of the passage. The notorious receiver, informer and businessman in theft, Wild, had of course been the model of Gay's Peachum, whom (among others) *The Beggar's Opera* invited its audience to parallel with Walpole. Wild, being dead, can hardly be reformed by attack, while the *example* of his life would be of relevance chiefly to Walpole and those like him. But the example is obsolete, no longer feared; Walpole and the state of the nation are worse than ever. Even Walter, related to Walpole and Wild as an instance of unscrupulous doubledealing, is in danger of punishment *only* for forgery—by implication he is worthy of punishment for crimes far graver than this. The tone is now lightened by Pope's acknowledgement, through the *adversarius*, that he has indeed 'gone on and on' about Walter (though his reason was implicit in the foregoing lines) and he then turns the point by making his

[25] Gay, *The Beggar's Opera*, ed. F. W. Bateson (London, 1934), p. 111.
[26] A further, brief and problematical, reference to Walter occurs in the fragment '1740', l. 26; T.E., iv, p. 333.

critic inadvertently admit Walter's 'bad' nature—'Else might he take to Virtue some years hence . . .' Walter was already in his seventies when this poem was written; such a turning to virtue would only mean he was beyond making profit.

The theme of false stewardship has taken us from the reputedly and probably dishonest character of Walter's professional life, to a consideration of Pope's attitude to the structure of society, and from this to the betrayal of vital trust at the most important point of all: the office of first minister, steward over the nation to the king. At each of the three levels there has been a breaking of the bonds of responsibility, a betrayal. On the first level the result has been the mismanagement of estates and the decline of rents. On the second level the disintegration of a traditional and morally sanctioned social structure binding the wealthy to the poor has been the consequence. On the third level nothing less than the moral and civil decline of a nation has been seen to to ensue. Throughout it has been clear, from an investigation of the biographical background and the poetry, that Pope's repeated sniping at Walter is more than a series of isolated attacks upon a rather unattractive and notorious public figure. It has been impossible to keep Walter separate from Pope's broad social and political preoccupations—much to the credit of his satire—indeed the probing of Pope's hostility to Walter has served to demonstrate the connectedness of the poet's personal, social and political standards. The next natural stage of this exploration would be to consider the theme of financial corruption in Pope's social poetry at large, and particularly in the Epistle *To Bathurst*. But this would be to anticipate what is more properly the subject of the second half of this chapter, taking its rise from Pope's response to the career of Sir John Blunt. Here I want to extend the originally biblical theme of false stewardship further still to a theological and mythical level, and to suggest that this extension of meaning through a sense of hierarchical connection and gradation (shown in another form in *An Essay on Man*) was not alien to Pope's mind. It is once again Swift who gives us our lead. In *The Answer of William Pulteney* he adds to his discussion of ministerial false stewardship the declaration that: 'Wisdom, attended by virtue and a generous nature, is not unapt to be imposed on. Thus *Milton* describes *Uriel, the sharpest-sighted spirit in heaven*, and *regent of the sun*, deceived by the dissimulation and flattery of the devil . . .'[27] This prompts us to introduce into the contemporary political context the image of what for the Christian is the original and greatest of all betrayals of trust, and the most ruinous in its consequence: Lucifer's rebellion against God and successful temptation of man. Swift sees Walpole as abusing the trust and close confidence of his master. It is well known that the very firm relationship between the chief minister and the court, in the reign of George II, was based partly on an understanding with Queen Caroline, and that understanding maintained through the confidential agency of the Vice-Chamberlain, John, Baron Hervey of Ickworth. Pope's great attack on Lord Hervey in the Epistle *To*

---

[27] Swift, *Miscellaneous and Autobiographical Pieces . .* , ed. cit., p. 116.

Arbuthnot, approached from this angle, is seen to have a political dimension often neglected in criticism of the poem—neglected for the good reason perhaps of the extraordinary richness of connotation in that splendidly controlled exorcism of evil. Yet this part of Pope's meaning has importance.

> Whether in florid Impotence he speaks,
> And, as the Prompter breathes, the Puppet squeaks;
> Or at the Ear of *Eve*, familiar Toad,
> Half Froth, half Venom, spits himself abroad,
> In Puns, or Politicks, or Tales, or Lyes,
> Or Spite, or Smut, or Rymes, or Blasphemies . . .
> Amphibious Thing! that acting either Part,
> The trifling Head, or the corrupted Heart!
> Fop at the Toilet, Flatt'rer at the Board,
> Now trips a Lady, and now struts a Lord.
> *Eve*'s Tempter thus the Rabbins have exprest,
> A Cherub's face, a Reptile all the rest;
> Beauty that shocks you, Parts that none will trust,
> Wit that can creep, and Pride that licks the dust.

[ll. 317–22, 326–33]

The political strand, one among others, is first attested to by the image of Hervey as the puppet-actor; who was the 'Prompter' but Walpole? Though he was much more also, Hervey was after all Walpole's spokesman at court.[28] The word 'Impotence', in the first line quoted, is sexually suggestive indeed, but also points at the political impotence of the go-between. 'In Puns, or Politicks, or Tales, or Lyes' (Pope's new, grim version of 'Puffs, Powders, Patches, Bibles, Billet-doux') the one solid word, equivalent to 'Bibles' in the earlier line, is 'Politicks'—but whereas there 'Bibles' were found in a confusion of trivial things, here 'Politicks' is fatally involved in a tangled net of corruption. This is precisely the charge of Bolingbroke and the Tory opposition to Walpole. The word 'corruption' had become a political rallying-cry, and in a *Craftsman* paper in 1732 the writer described a vision of 'the TREE OF CORRUPTION, which bears a very near Resemblance to the Tree of Knowledge, in the Garden of *Eden* . . .'[29] Thus Pope's phrase 'the corrupted Heart', in the next line, like the earlier 'Impotence', has also a political connotation. Sporus is assisting in the political corruption of the realm. Finally, one need not labour the point that flattery in a courtier has always had politically negative associations. Swift had likened his false steward to the devil on account of 'dissimulation and flattery'. All this, along with the sexual, personal, literary, and social connotations of the passage, are taken up into its mythical pattern, which likens Sporus to Milton's Lucifer: the satanic serpent to Queen Caroline's Eve. Hervey, by virtue of his confidential role at court, is 'at the Ear of *Eve*, familiar Toad . . .' His cosmetic beauty

[28] As John Butt recognizes in his edition of *To Arbuthnot* for Methuen's English Texts (London, 1954), p. 37.
[29] *The Craftsman*, ix. No. 297 (25 March, 1732), p. 52.

is an appalling, fallen replica of the cherubic, and his pride, like that of Milton's Satan, becomes a serpent and licks the dust in the end. Satan's pride was brought to nothing, but he accomplished the fall of man. Pope saw the archetypal situation being echoed again; by helping to perpetuate the administration of Walpole the false steward, Hervey abused his intimacy with the court, and seemed to be forwarding the fall of the nation.

2. THE THEME OF CORRUPTION

Despite his legal and parliamentary activities, Peter Walter was a man of the country. Land was what he understood, and land was the form of wealth he sought. It makes good sense that his name should occur in Pope's poetry in connection with the ideal of the country house society, and with the neglect of that ideal. Sir John Blunt, by comparison, we have found above all a man of the City. It makes equally good sense that Pope, in writing his Epistle *To Bathurst*, Of the Use of Riches, should devote a great part of this work to a consideration and poetic presentation of City and Financial Revolution, which equally with the Revolution Settlement of 1688 was a new and vitally important factor in the fortunes of the nation. For Pope to have ignored the City in such a work would have meant that his social attitudes and values were not traditional but moribund: that he was neither capable of recognizing a fundamentally new situation, nor of bringing his traditional social values into confrontation with it. In fact it is this confrontation between City and country ways, City and country interests and values, as a way of thinking about national corruption, which is the grand subject of the Epistle *To Bathurst*, and which forms the strongest feature of its design as a work of art. Pope achieves in the poem a traditionalism of an alert and alive kind which does not evade the challenges and menaces of his time.

It is interesting to trace Pope's recognition of the financial world of the city as the poem proceeds. It begins with the slightest of allusions and builds up into a formidable prospect. Read with hindsight, Pope's assertion, early in the epistle, that riches are no 'token of th' Elect' [l. 18] hints at the quasi-Calvinistic feel of many city businessmen's attitude to their wealth—Blunt as we have seen was an example of this. The allusion to Ward, in the next line but one, reminds us of this member of parliament's suspected involvement in a scheme for the fraudulent conveyance of part of Blunt's estate in 1721. Religious claims and a corrupt actuality are already being implicitly linked. 'Trade it may help', Pope soon after says of money, 'Society extend';

> But lures the Pyrate, and corrupts the Friend:
> It raises Armies in a Nation's aid,
> But bribes a Senate, and the Land's betray'd.   [ll. 31–4]

The most prominent recent instance in Britain when money had raised 'Armies in a Nation's aid' was of course the founding of the Bank of England in 1694 to help finance William III's wars against France—wars which were, as part of the Protestant cause in Europe, to help secure the nation of Holland.

The most prominent recent instance of money bribing a senate and betraying
a land was undoubtedly Blunt's promotion of the South Sea Scheme. Both
these positive and negative instances of the use of money were City operations;
no other financial interest in the land could have mounted them, and their
scale, even in the 1730s, must have seemed unprecedented and ominous.
There now follows the mordantly comic fantasy which restores to contemporary
political corruption the 'bulky Bribes' of old—in the tilting at Walpole's
pacific policy towards Spain critical satire is modulated into the fullness of
laughter:

> A Statesman's slumbers how this speech would spoil!
> 'Sir, Spain has sent a thousand jars of oil . . .'   [ll. 43–4]

—and concludes with reference to 'the nation's last great trade, Quadrille!'
This seems at once rather an exaggerated and random stroke until one detects,
as I believe one should, the allusion to the Bubble, when the nation ruined
itself, as was repeatedly pointed out, by attending not to trade or industry
but to gambling. Wealth in kind, Pope observes, would make corruption
comically difficult; even gold, which makes it easier, sometimes betrays double-
dealing (as in the case of 'Old Cato', Sir Christopher Musgrave, a Tory patriot
in the pay of William III); but the new invention of paper credit makes
corruption easiest of all. And with the apostrophe to 'Blest paper-credit!'
we are unambiguously back in the world of City finance. Here the sense of
how much the 'money'd Interest' was capable of achieving is powerfully
heightened:

> Blest paper-credit! last and best supply!
> That lends Corruption lighter wings to fly!
> Gold imp'd by thee, can compass hardest things,
> Can pocket States, can fetch or carry Kings;
> A single leaf shall waft an Army o'er,
> Or ship off Senates to a distant Shore;
> A leaf, like Sibyl's, scatter to and fro
> Our fates and fortunes, as the winds shall blow:
> Pregnant with thousands flits the Scrap unseen,
> And silent sells a King or buys a Queen.   [ll. 69–78]

In his note to these lines Pope draws attention to 'many Princes . . . sent
about the world, and great changes of Kings projected in Europe' in his
time; he gives several instances of which the case of King Stanislaus and
'The Crown of Poland, venal twice an age' is the most apposite for his argument.[30] A further note interestingly glosses the line about banished senates
by a reference to the Regent of France banishing the parliament of Paris to
Pontoise in 1720, for opposing the financial schemes of John Law. From John
Law it is a short step back to the South Sea Bubble; the allusion in the final
line is to a rumour that Robert Knight, the notorious absconded cashier of

---

[30] T.E., iii–ii, p. 93 and *To Bathurst*, l. 129.

the Company, had succeeded in persuading Queen Caroline to accept a large 'present' from him.[31] These sinister suggestions are most effectively conveyed by the appropriately light tone—'A single leaf shall waft an Army o'er', so light and easy is corruption by paper-credit—and easy familiar diction—'pocket', 'fetch or carry', 'ship off', 'scatter'—which ironically counterpoints the weightiness of senates and armies, and the gravity of the affairs of which Pope speaks.

Pope next considers what money can and cannot reasonably provide, the minimum standard which man can legitimately expect from it ('Meat, Fire, and Cloaths'—l. 82). This leads on naturally to the theme of the poor, and with the naming of Dennis Bond and allusion to the Charitable Corporation scandal ('Bond damns the Poor . . .'—l. 102), it is brought directly into relation with the City, for Bond had opposed the Corporation lending small sums to the poor, as its charter prescribed, in favour of lending large sums at higher interest to the rich: '"Damn the Poor, let us go into the City, where we may get Money."'[32] The Charitable Corporation was significant to Pope, it is fair to assume, because it attempted to extend to urban labour the country house ideal of care of the poor. Blunt's remark about the poor now follows, and shows that (in Pope's view) he was among those who regarded riches as a token of the elect; it is to be inferred from these instances that the City had little interest in the good of society as a whole, for the touchstone, concern for the poor, has been applied and has shown it to be wanting. A few lines later, the first direct reference to the South Sea Bubble ('What made Directors cheat in South-sea year?'—l. 119) serves to maintain a focus of attention already created in more allusive ways. The comparison of Peter Walter with the lawyer Didius, now following, gains credibility from the preceding passage on the power of paper credit (backed by contemporary instances) and leads up to the presentation of a third wave of financial ambition which assumes the mad proportions and mythical force of a Jonsonian comic vision: Volpone or Epicure Mammon. Yet it is the truth, not just Pope's treatment, that has this character:

> The Crown of Poland, venal twice an age,
> To just three millions stinted modest Gage.
> But nobler scenes Maria's dreams unfold,
> Hereditary Realms, and worlds of Gold.
> Congenial souls! whose life one Av'rice joins,
> And one fate buries in th' Asturian Mines.   [ll. 129–34]

Joseph Gage, one of the most notoriously successful speculators in the Mississippi and South Sea Schemes, had made financial offers for both the crown of Poland and the crown of Sardinia. Lady Mary Herbert, another enormously successful speculator in Mississippi stock, was said once to have refused the hand of the Duke of Bouillon, seeking to marry nobody lower than a sovereign

[31] Ibid., p. 93.
[32] Ibid., p. 99.

prince. The two did indeed marry, and Gage did indeed mine for gold in the Asturias.[33]

The accumulating references to City finance, the Mississippi and the South Sea now culminate in the apostrophe to Sir John Blunt, which considers the South Sea Bubble explicitly and at length for the first time in the poem. The allusions noted have been pointing more and more clearly to the Bubble, its nature, causes and consequences, so this is a logical and human development in the epistle. The passage has been examined in detail in Chapter VI; it is sufficient here to observe how its grand theme, corruption, has been repeatedly anticipated by more glancing references to corruption in the preceding lines.[34] Like Kyrle, Blunt is just behind the scenes in the poem, when he is not actually on stage. There follows the intervention of the 'sober sage' with his attempt to rationalize 'Extremes in Nature' and 'Extremes in Man' into a benevolently providential pattern, as if in answer to the career of Blunt. The discursive conversational procedure of the poem now begins to take on a more schematic structure. The central portrait of the Man of Ross—the moral and spiritual centre of the epistle—is flanked by two pairs of contrasting portraits each illustrating avarice as against profusion: Old Cotta against Young Cotta, Cutler against Buckingham. The tale of Sir Balaam then concludes the poem. Still tracing Pope's concern with the City and City figures, we must note that if indeed, as is probable, Old Cotta was originally modelled on Sir John Cutler, Pope has given us a City man, whose wealth was drawn originally from trade not land, in the situation of a landed country gentleman. He has thus brought country and City together, and shown how the second will fail to understand and fulfill the human obligations of the first. One recalls Swift's hostility to 'setting up a mony'd Interest in opposition to the landed . . .' for 'the possessors of the soil are the best judges of what is for the advantage of the kingdom: If others had thought the same way, Funds of Credit and South-sea Projects would neither have been felt nor heard of.'[35] Though Cutler was actually a landowner, Swift's conservative point would still hold: the 'miserly seclusion' in which Cutler had lived, when in possession of an estate, was because it was to him a mere mercantile acquisition; he was unfamiliar and unconcerned (it is implied) with the tradition of housekeeping, and its attendant obligations to the community. This theme is touched on again when Cutler appears unambiguously and by name, in the second pair of portraits:

> Cutler saw tenants break, and houses fall,
> For very want; he could not build a wall.   [ll. 323–4]

If the financial world of the City, Swift's 'mony'd Interest', has been in Pope's sights for much of this epistle, it is never so unmistakably focused

---

[33] Ibid., p. 103–4; the line beginning 'Hereditary Realms' need not, as Bateson speculates, refer to her alleged descent from a mistress of James II. The contrast is simply between her seeking the hand of an hereditary prince, while Gage had sought only an elective throne.

[34] For a discussion of Pope's apostrophe to Blunt, see Ch. VI, Section 6, above.

[35] *Corr.*, ii, p. 70 (Swift to Pope, 10 Jan. 1720/1).

upon as at the end, in the tale of Sir Balaam. The setting and the character-type identify themselves at once:

> Where London's column, pointing at the skies
> Like a tall bully, lifts the head, and lyes;
> There dwelt a Citizen of sober fame,
> A plain good man, and Balaam was his name;
> Religious, punctual, frugal, and so forth;
> His word would pass for more than he was worth.   [ll. 339–44]

We are again confronted, in this tale, with Pope's artfully ambiguous portraiture. We have seen how the same figure—Sir John Cutler—can be used as the original model in one portrait, and be presented explicitly by name in another, in the same poem. We have also seen how the first portrait, that of Old Cotta, nevertheless carried a contemporary relevance which would have been reduced considerably had Cutler been connected with the portrait by name. Pope wished to keep the alternatives open because in the end they were not really *alternatives* at all but parts of the same truth; he wished his reader to *think* of 'Cutler' for 'Cotta', but be sufficiently uncertain to entertain more contemporary identifications also.[36] So it is with the portrait of Sir Balaam. Clearly the portrait can stand on its own feet as a piece of literature with general human significance. It does not largely depend on historical reality as does the apostrophe to Blunt. Nevertheless Pope could not afford to let his readers forget that he was dealing with their own society, possibly with individuals they knew themselves. Thus certain specific pointers are given, and one of these is to Thomas Pitt, sometime Governor of Fort St. George, Madras. Pitt, it has been pointed out, 'made a great deal of money in underhand ways, was remarkably pious, owned an estate in Cornwall, and bought and represented the rotten borough of Old Sarum.'[37] Furthermore Pitt bought 'a Gem', the famous Pitt diamond, when he was in India, and made an astronomical profit by selling it, through the agency of John Law, to the Duke of Orleans. Plainly Pope wanted his readers to think of Thomas Pitt—but then to think again of others. For Pope is satirizing a London citizen, not an Indian *nabob*, and thus in the poem the 'Gem' is 'pledged' to Balaam in England, not bought in a far country. Other details point not at Pitt but at someone like Blunt. Blunt like Balaam was a confirmed city dweller; his house in Birchin Lane was hard by Exchange Alley, where he was indeed 'Constant at . . . Change' [l. 347]. The line 'His word would pass for more than he was worth' [l. 344] has a sharp relevance if one thinks of Blunt; his whole career was based on the manipulation of credit rather than on the solid basis of industry or genuine trade. Balaam having made a fortune from the 'Gem',

> The Tempter saw his time; the work he ply'd;
> Stocks and Subscriptions pour on ev'ry side,

---

[36] T.E., iii–ii, p. 108 (l. 179 n. (iv)); *Pope's Epistle to Bathurst*, ed. cit., pp. 56–7.
[37] Ibid., p. 121 (l. 342 n.).

> 'Till all the Dæmon makes his full descent,
> In one abundant show'r of Cent. per Cent.,
> Sinks deep within him, and possesses whole,
> Then dubs Director, and secures his soul.　　　　[ll. 369–74]

Thomas Pitt had little concern with stock companies; trade (especially diamonds) and land were the forms of wealth he sought. On the other hand 'Stocks and Subscriptions', stock companies and lotteries, were the very stuff of Blunt's life. And the profusion with which they shower down (a new, sinister Jove in a shower of—paper credit) suggests really spectacular successes such as the South Sea Company and the South Sea Scheme when each was first launched. Pitt was never a 'Director', while Blunt was the chief director of the Company which drew from the public the biggest shower of stocks and subscriptions England had seen. Balaam seems to be knighted a second time when the devil 'dubs' him director.[38] Pitt was never knighted or ennobled, but Blunt was created a baronet at that point when the shower of stocks and subscriptions, which he had contrived, seemed to have raised public credit 'to a height not known before'. Blunt had then bowed at court and grown polite. He too had married a second time—though the parallel does not hold as to the nature of the marriage, except in so far as Blunt's second wife had cravings to be armigerous.[39] Balaam's fall conforms to the lives neither of Pitt nor Blunt, but is much closer to Blunt's, for both Balaam and Blunt are unmasked as having betrayed the nation, are arraigned by parliament, and forsaken by the court. Many members of parliament certainly felt that Blunt should forfeit his life, and Pope at one point appears to have expected this.[40] But if his life was not forfeit, his wealth was, and Pope must certainly have felt that the king, who had been deeply involved in South Sea speculation, and who had since 1721 been closely tied to Walpole and his 'screening' policies, was an indirect beneficiary of Blunt's downfall. These facts, I suggest, lie behind the conclusion of the tale:

> Wife, son, and daughter, Satan, are thy own,
> His wealth, yet dearer, forfeit to the Crown:
> The Devil and the King divide the prize,
> And sad Sir Balaam curses God and dies.　　　　[ll. 399–402]

Taken as a whole, the life of Sir Balaam is the tale of a man who abandons faith in divine providence in favour of chance and the world; what he *had* thought 'God's good Providence' he later regards as 'a lucky Hit', with all the associations of an atheistic, Epicurean theory of creation, which this last phrase carried.[41] It was chance and the lust for worldly gain which ruled the South Sea affair; the whole Bubble was really the most fantastic gamble on

---

[38] *Pope's Epistle to Bathurst*, ed. cit., p. 53.
[39] See Ch. VI, nn. 105, 113.
[40] *To Bathurst*, l. 135 n.; T.E., iii–ii, p. 104.
[41] See Howard Erskine-Hill, 'The Lucky Hit in Commerce and Creation', *Notes and Queries*, N.S., xiv, No. 11 (Nov. 1967), pp. 407–8.

everybody's part; as Defoe had foretold, Blunt and his colleagues had 'run up and down the Stocks, and put the Dice upon the whole Town'.[42] Here too, the portrait of Sir Balaam seems to grow out of the life of Blunt. Finally, it has been observed that the tale of Sir Balaam unites in one man both the avarice and the profusion which have been dominant themes in the contrasting portraits of the central part of the epistle.[43] In a curious way the life of Blunt also shows these extremes, not only in that he was abandoning his earlier, simple way of life when, at the height of his apparent success, he travelled to Tunbridge in his new chariot, but also because in the South Sea affair he recklessly staked his own and the nation's fortunes on his success—and lost. He caused such profusion in others that they ruined themselves buying what they could neither afford nor pay for.

The portrait of Sir Balaam, it may be seen, is based as much on Blunt as it is on Pitt. It comprehends much of the lives of both men, but is not confined to them in its meaning. Its implications are at their widest in its religious content: in the way it shows a narrow, mechanical piety ('Religious, punctual, frugal, and so forth . . . Constant at Church, and Change') easily overthrown by the precarious bonuses of chance, which a broader and more ardent apprehension of divine providence and human need might have resisted. Once his 'blessings' are no more than results of luck or his own wit, he has, unlike Job, no faith, no larger comprehension, to save him when things go ill and end in disaster. Hence the savagely near-negative conclusion: 'sad Sir Balaam curses God and dies'—just perceptibly modified by the laconic understatement of the word 'sad', one sense of which suggests, what indeed the whole portrait intimates, that Balaam is unfortunate; his frugal, regular, materialistic world of the City, dominated by its hypocritically lying monument, could not provide him with the spiritual and human breadth to help him resist evil. For what *appeared* chance to the City knight, was from Pope's Christian view which dramatizes the tale, the work of Satan himself.[44] It is this narrowness in Balaam which serves Pope's wider purpose so well, for he is seen to pursue wealth for its own sake and follow where it leads—in the same way as Blunt became obsessed with driving up the price of his stocks and could not extricate himself from the fatal course. But the life of these remarkable lines is perhaps not finally to be found in these considerations, greatly though they contribute, but in Pope's familiar handling of the ways of life he describes: 'He takes his chirping pint, and cracks his jokes . . . two puddings smoak'd upon the board . . . His Compting-house employ'd the Sunday-morn . . . My Lady falls to play . . .' with the appropriate, vivid stress upon the homely

---

[42] See Ch. VI, n. 114.

[43] *Pope's Epistle to Bathurst*, ed. cit., p. 53.

[44] The religious meaning of the passage has been investigated with great penetration, though perhaps an overplus of learning, by E. R. Wasserman in the important introduction to his edition of *Pope's Epistle to Bathurst*, pp. 44–55. Another, more human, dimension of the portrait has been expressed, and perhaps slightly exaggerated, by T. R. Edwards, Jr. in his book *This Dark Estate: A Reading of Pope* (Berkeley and Los Angeles, 1963), pp. 60–3. My own discussion is indebted to both these works; also to R. A. Brower, *Alexander Pope: The Poetry of Allusion* (Oxford, 1959), p. 257.

and material.[45] It lies in Pope's handling of diction to modulate tone: the familiarly low: '... he lives like other folks'; the ironic heightening and distancing: not just 'two puddings' but 'And lo! two puddings ...'; the homely and emphatic: '... one Christmas-tide/My good old Lady catch'd a cold, and dy'd' [ll. 383–4] this last line being in itself a miracle of tonal poise, with the blend of patronage and affection in the first phrase making her super-fluousness clear and a little pathetic, the vividly, authentically mundane: 'catch'd a cold', and the laconic, callous, common-sense of the additional 'and dy'd'. Never did Pope weigh ordinary words to better effect. By moving close in to, and then out from, the subject, the tone itself takes the measure of Sir Balaam. The life of the passage lies, finally, in the handling of the story-line: the economy and speed with which it establishes setting and type, the accession of new interest as at each stage we find a new viewpoint or a new chance ('The Dev'l was piqu'd ...', 'Asleep and naked ...', 'A Nymph of Quality ...') yet all relevant; and the final shape: the rounded rise and fall of Balaam's life.

The subject of the Epistle *To Bathurst* demanded an exploration of the new financial world of the City of London. Of all the city figures to whom Pope refers, the most historically important, the most apposite for his conservative argument, and the man whom he was in a position to know most about, was Sir John Blunt. That Blunt should play an important role in the epistle is thus not surprising. His life, and those of others such as Bond and (somewhat distorted by history) Cutler, did emphasize that inability to conceive, or unwillingness to regard, the good of the whole community, which Swift, Bolingbroke and the Tories felt to have been the peculiar evil in the notion of creating a new, a moneyed interest, in opposition to the landed interest, and of acquiring influence, in London at least, by the establishment of great corporations.[46] To think in terms of the good of the nation required a com-prehensive view of society; the ownership of land, the Tory argument con-tended, obliged even the most miserly to face the needs of others; the lives of Blunt and Balaam, on the other hand, showed an increasingly narrow obsession with money for its own sake, irrespective of communal obligation. Pope's poem concurs in this view, though it also recognizes that a great landowner such as Peter Walter could be as miserly on his estates as a great merchant like Cutler. To be a nation of landowners and tenants might be in the common good, but it was far from being the prevention of all social ill. Only Christian living could achieve that. But the epistle is not limited to a merely political viewpoint in its exploration of the City. The presentation of Blunt (in the apostrophe) and Balaam (in the tale) is in fact less narrowly hostile and more human than the presentation of Walter. We have seen, in the apostrophe,

---

[45] *To Bathurst*, ll. 358, 360, 380 (note also 381–2), 395; T.E., iii–ii, pp. 119–21.

[46] This view perhaps originated with Harley and St. John early in the eighteenth century. An early statement of it is the passage from Swift's *History of the Four Last years of the Queen*, quoted in Ch. VI, Section 2 (n. 21) above. Swift's letter to Pope, 10 Jan. 1721 (quoted above, n. 35) follows his earlier statement.

the ambiguity in accordance with which Blunt is attacked and yet credited
with a true prophecy couched in the actual style of his declamations; and in
accordance with which his guilt is recognized but his role as scapegoat for
the guilt of the more eminent implicitly recognized too. We have seen how
Sir Balaam's world seemed to give him no weapon against the devil. Pope
has rounded out his political viewpoint with a fullness of human response to
the historical and social facts. A consideration of Blunt's life in relation to
the Epistle *To Bathurst* does, I think, call in question the dismissive view of
the Twickenham editor: 'Pope's indignation with the wicked capitalists of
the City of London is obviously second-hand and worked up . . . for the
occasion . . . he is here simply Bolingbroke's mouthpiece . . . in this poem
Pope too often gives the impression that he doesn't know what he is talking
about.'[47]

Inextricably involved in Pope's concern with the 'mony'd Interest' of the
City is the theme of corruption. Indeed a broad definition of what Pope
meant by corruption might be the preference of narrow personal or sectional
interests before the good of the nation as a whole. But a definition cannot
really hope to encompass the range of connected meanings, the moral depth,
and the historical forebodings which, in *The Craftsman*, the writings of Bolingbroke, and the poetry of Pope, this word comes to assume. In such a case it is
perhaps better to survey than define. As early as 1711 Swift was already
accusing the politico-financial system of Godolphin and the Bank of England
of being corrupt.[48] By this he seems to have meant that the nation was being
improvidently run into debt, that there was inefficiency, and that the system
was beginning to break down. It was, as we have seen, George Berkeley in
his *Essay Towards Preventing the Ruin of Great Britain* (1721) who was the
first of Pope's friends to connect the concept of corruption (of pressing
relevance at the time) with the notion of Britain declining from civilization
into slavery and ruin. He foresaw men of the future looking back on his own
time to say: '"This island was once inhabited by a religious, brave, sincere
people, of plain uncorrupt manners, respecting inbred worth rather than
titles and appearances, asserters of their liberty, lovers of their country . . .
Such were our ancestors during their rise and greatness; but they degenerated,
grew servile flatterers of men in power, adopted Epicurean notions, became
venal, corrupt, injurious, which . . . occasioned their final ruin."' The word
corruption here has an altogether more evil meaning; Berkeley specifies
'Bribery' and 'solemn Perjury' and it is now associated with servility, flattery,

---

[47] F. W. Bateson, T.E., iii–ii, p. xxxiv. Bateson's last judgement is actually a comparative one:
Pope does not know what he is talking about compared with the Fielding of *Pasquin* and *The
Historical Register*. As evidence Bateson advances the fact that Pope often relied on newspapers
for his information. How does this prove his ignorance? Perhaps the most important thing to
remember is that neither Bolingbroke nor Swift ever produced so extended and detailed an exploration of the business interests of the City as Pope does in *To Bathurst*. Can it be second-hand
in any damaging sense?
[48] See Ch. VI, n. 32 above.

atheism and injury.[49] The association with Epicureanism is interesting in view of Pope's later touching on this theme in the portrait of Sir Balaam. Bolingbroke was next to use the idea of corruption in *The First Vision of Camilick*. Here a vision of Britain is displayed in which the fields (scenes of war and desolation before) '... were now covered with golden harvests. The hills were cloathed with sheep. The woods sung with gladness. Plenty laughed in the valleys. Industry, commerce, and liberty danced hand in hand through the cities.' This scene of happiness and freedom is then corrupted by the sneering and malign confidence of the man with the purse of gold, before whom all prostrate themselves or are chained in slavery.[50] Berkeley's fears have now been given a more specific form. The rule of Walpole, the man with the purse of gold, dated for purposes of Bolingbroke's attack from 1721; and the degeneration which, writing in that year, Berkeley had dreaded is seen by Bolingbroke, writing in 1726, to be coming about through Walpole. However the connection between South Sea year and the rise of national corruption is asserted more explicitly in another, less known, *Craftsman* paper, which appeared at the end of March 1732, some nine months before the publication of the Epistle *To Bathurst*. Its writer had evidently learned much from *The First Vision of Camilick* but he did not employ its orotund biblical style; he allowed himself more detail, and he was less hopeful. Using the convention of the dream, he first follows Bolingbroke by painting a picture of an island fertile, well-peopled, happy and free:

> But as I was pleasing myself with some Reflections on the Felicity of such a Nation, I happen'd to cast my Eyes towards the *North-East Part of it*, and took Notice of a *Tree*, which appear'd to be of so extraordinary a Nature, that I had the Curiosity to examine it very narrowly. At first, it seem'd to be only about the size of a common *Yew-Tree*, in a Country Churchyard; but it shot up with such amazing Velocity ... that it soon lost its Head in the Clouds and darken'd the whole Land with the Extension of its Branches. At the same Time, I saw it put forth a vast Quantity of beautiful Fruit, which glitter'd like burnish'd Gold, and hung in large Clusters on every Bough. I now perceived it to be the TREE OF CORRUPTION, which bears a very near Resemblance to the *Tree of Knowledge*, in the Garden of *Eden*; for whoever tasted the Fruit of it, lost his Integrity and fell, like *Adam*, from the *State of Innocence*.
>
> Perched in the Middle of the *Tree*, like K. *Charles* in the Oak, I spy'd *a round portly Man*, of a swarthy Complexion ... He sate enthron'd ... and, plucking the *golden Apples* on every Side, toss'd them down amongst the Croud beneath Him ...
>
> By this Time, methought, the Ground was cover'd with an infinite

---

[49] A. A. Luce and J. E. Jessop, ed. *The Works of George Berkeley* (London, 1948–57), vi, pp, 83, 85. The *Essay* is quoted by Isaac Kramnick in his valuable discussion of the South Sea crisis and corruption (op. cit., pp. 63–70), but he does not appear to recognize its authorship. The significance of the *Essay* having been written by one of Pope's close friends and advisers is considerable.

[50] Bolingbroke, *Works*, ed. cit., i, pp. 186–8.

Variety of little Plants, or Suckers, which sprung from the *grand Root*, and pullulated one from another in a regular Subordination. Some of them shot up to a great Height . . . and bore a plentiful Crop of Apples . . . As I had a nearer View of *these Apples*, I thought I saw some Words in-scrib'd round the Superficies of them . . . and plainly discover'd the Words *charitable Corporation* indented in natural Characters upon one of them; on another I read, *forfeited Estates*; on a third, *Army Debentures*; and on a fourth, *Bank Contract*. But there were two Inscriptions, which I could not thoroughly understand. The first was *East India*, . . . The second was *South-Sea*, . . .[51]

This passage, which I quote at length because *The Craftsman* is still so little known, yet so important in moulding opinion during Walpole's regime, establishes a connection in the eyes of its author between the South Sea episode and the subsequent menace of political corruption from the govern-ment itself. Of particular interest is the inscription '*Bank Contract*' since this shows that the way in which Walpole exploited the crisis to come to power in 1720/1 was regarded by the Tory opposition as his first corrupt step. More interesting, however, is the way in which the emblem of the tree of corruption expresses the nature of the concept: corruption is at once attractive and oppressive; it is now not haphazard but systematic, the corrupt society being represented here as 'in a regular Subordination': the negative mirror-image of the traditional hierarchical pattern. Finally, the image is ominous because the tree of corruption is also like a genealogical tree extending itself and ramifying from generation to generation, and because the fall, so many having partaken of the fruit of corruption, could only be national and historic.

These passages help to explain why Pope fashioned his apostrophe to Blunt, in the Epistle *To Bathurst*, around the idea of a prophecy of future corruption. Blunt had himself been corrupt, and corruption, on a great scale, had taken its origin in Britain from the episode for which Blunt had been responsible. It had occurred before, but had then been stemmed by leading politicians:

> 'At length Corruption, like a gen'ral flood,
> '(So long by watchful Ministers withstood)
> 'Shall deluge all; and Av'rice creeping on,
> 'Spread like a low-born mist, and blot the Sun . . .
>
> [ll. 137–40]

Now, by implication, there is a Minister who does not withstand corruption. The Miltonic overtones to these lines are worth noting. The image of the 'low-born mist' at first suggests that avarice is a consequence of low birth, and this on the whole may apply to Pope's misers, though 'low-born' Allen

---

[51] *The Craftsman*, ix, No. 297 (25 March 1732), pp. 51–5. The article is signed 'D' which may here indicate the authorship of 'Caleb D'Anvers', i.e. Nicholas Amhurst, the editor. I am indebted to Mr. J. S. Bull for drawing my attention to this number of *The Craftsman*.

was the reverse of miserly. But it also seems to recall Satan entering Eden 'as a mist by night'—'like a black mist low creeping'—and thus evading Uriel and the cherubim, the watchful ministers of heaven. This was a stage towards the temptation and the fall: the utmost Satan could do to make man blind to God, to 'blot the Sun'.[52] Satan, these lines just suggest, is working through corruption to encompass the fall of Britain. If these delicate implications are admitted, the lines may be seen to point on to the Sporus portrait in *To Arbuthnot*, where three of the chief figures responsible for Britain's political situation, Hervey, Queen Caroline and Walpole, are more explicitly involved by the poet in the myth of temptation and fall. We have already discussed the Sporus portrait in connection with the theme of false stewardship, but it is important to see it here as perhaps Pope's most vivid expression, not of the effects of corruption, but of *the quality itself*, personal, literary, social, political and theological, as embodied in one figure. At this point we may see how Pope's negative values begin to draw together into concepts and images which are ultimately religious. As Bolingbroke wrote in his *Dissertation on Parties* (Letter XVIII, first published in *The Craftsman* on 21 Dec. 1734, twelve days before the publication of *To Arbuthnot*), 'He who undertakes to govern a free people by corruption, and to lead them by a false interest, against their true interest, cannot boast the honor of the invention. The expedient is as old as the world, and he can pretend no other honor than that of being an humble imitator of the devil'; and as he was to write in *The Idea of a Patriot King* (completed three years after *To Arbuthnot*): 'Depravation of manners exposed the constitution to ruin ... Men decline easily from virtue; for there is a devil too in the political system, a constant tempter at hand ...'[53]

Bolingbroke now took up the concept of corruption again, and in the last letter of his *Dissertation on Paries* (published in *The Craftsman* during 1735) proposed two 'means of corruption' as having arisen since 1688: 'the establishment of the civil-list' and the creation of 'public funds'.[54] In his comments on the latter, we are back in the world of Sir John Blunt: '... the whole mystery of iniquity [corruption] ... arises from this establishment [of public funds] ... and ... the main springs that turn, or may turn, the artificial wheel of credit, and make the paper estates, that are fasten'd to it, rise or fall, lurk behind the veil of the treasury.' He dreads the effects on the public if some 'veteran sharper' or 'ministerial jobber' should administer the treasury. At this point, Bolingbroke's pretence to be speaking hypothetically is thin.[55] However, the tone of the *Dissertation on Parties* is sober compared

---

[52] Milton, *Paradise Lost*, Argument to Bk. IX.

[53] *The Dissertation on Parties*, Letter XVIII, published in *The Craftsman*, No. 442 (21 Dec. 1734), xii, p. 133; *Works*, ed. cit., ii, p. 230. (The Letters were first published together in 1735.) For the second passage, see Bolingbroke, *Works*, ed. cit., iii, p. 75. *The Idea of a Patriot King* was not published until 1749, though it was in Pope's possession long before, and privately printed by him before his death (see H. T. Dickinson, *Bolingbroke* (London, 1970), pp. 278–82, 290–2).

[54] Bolingbroke, *Works*, ed. cit., ii, pp. 243–5.

[55] Ibid., pp. 343–5.

with the clarion call against national corruption which Bolingbroke issued
in his Letter to Lord Cornbury *On the Spirit of Patriotism* (1736). Here
the earlier forebodings of a national decline become almost an announcement
of it.

> We will suppose a man imprudent, rash, presumptuous, ungracious,
> insolent, and profligate in speculation as well as practice. He can bribe,
> but he cannot seduce: he can buy, but he cannot gain: he can lye, but
> he cannot deceive. From whence then has such a man his strength? from
> the general corruption of the people, nursed up to a full maturity under
> his administration . . . This would be an answer, and it would be a true
> one as far as it goes; but it does not account for the whole.

> We must want spirit, as well as virtue, to perish. Even able knaves would
> preserve liberty in such circumstances as ours, and highwaymen would
> scorn to receive the wages, and do the drudgery of pick-pockets. But all is
> little, and low, and mean among us! . . . This could not happen, if there
> was the least spirit among us. But there is none. What passes among us
> for ambition, is an odd mixture of avarice and vanity: the moderation we
> have seen practised is pusillanimity, and the philosophy that some men
> affect, is sloth. Hence it comes that corruption has spred, and prevails.[56]

At such a juncture, those duly ashamed of the moral degeneration of their
society might well be caught up in a kind of historical fatalism arising from
that most common way of thinking about the long perspectives of history:
the concept of the rise, maturing and decay of civilizations.

> It may be said, that governments have their periods, like all things human;
> that they may be brought back to their primitive principles during a certain
> time, but when these principles are worn out in the minds of men, it is a
> vain enterprise to endeavour to renew them; that this is the case of all
> governments when the corruption of the people comes to a great pitch,
> and is grown universal; that when a house is old and quite decayed . . .
> every man in his senses runs out of it, and takes shelter where he can . . .
> But, my Lord, if CATO could not save, he prolonged the life of liberty
> . . .[57]

It is in the context of this kind of thinking about the state of the nation
that much of Pope's later poetry must be seen. The ironic praise of the king
in the Epistle *To Augustus* (1737), the vivid sketch of the politician intent
on 'Pow'r and Place' in *To Murray* (1738), the very full political and social
reflections of the Epistle *To Lord Bolingbroke* in the same year—

> There, London's voice: 'Get Mony, Mony still!
> And then let Virtue follow, if she will.'   [ll. 79–80]

—all this takes on deeper implications when we remember Pope's constant

---

[56] Bolingbroke, *Works*, ed. cit., iii, pp. 9, 19.
[57] Ibid., p. 16.

admiration of Bolingbroke, and his obvious recognition, seen for example in the couplet quoted above, of Bolingbroke's current anxieties and prescriptions. But it is in the two Dialogues of the 'Epilogue to the Satires' that Pope's poetic preoccupation with the theme of corruption, as Bolingbroke conceived its contemporary relevance, is to be found at its most intense. I shall quote first from the opening discussion of Dialogue I, to show that the personalities with whom this chapter has originally been concerned are still present in Pope's mind, as details in the darkening scene against which he now stands protagonist. ''Tis all from *Horace*:' says his carping and pusillanimous '*Friend*' in the dialogue:

> > *Horace* long before ye
> Said, 'Tories call'd him Whig, and Whigs a Tory;'
> And taught his Romans, in much better metre,
> 'To laugh at Fools who put their trust in *Peter.*'
> > But *Horace*, Sir, was delicate, was nice;
> *Bubo* observes, he lash'd no sort of *Vice*:
> *Horace* would say, *Sir* Billy *serv'd the Crown*,
> Blunt *could do Bus'ness*, H-ggins *knew the Town*,
> In *Sappho* touch the *Failing of the Sex*,
> In rev'rend Bishops note some *small Neglects*,
> And own, the *Spaniard* did a *waggish thing*,
> Who cropt our Ears, and sent them to the King.
> His sly, polite, insinuating stile
> Could please at Court, and make AUGUSTUS smile:
> An artful Manager, that crept between
> His Friend and Shame, and was a kind of *Screen.*   [ll. 7–22]

The thought of this passage is complex. It presents us, first of all, with a series of symptoms of widespread national corruption, of which the dishonesty of Peter Walter is the first and much the least serious; in this case laughter is still appropriate. The other instances include John Huggins, the corrupt warden of the Fleet prison. He was thought guilty of breaches of trust, extortion and cruelty, but acquitted of the charge of murder of a prisoner, in 1729, after having called great numbers of 'gentlemen of the first quality' to testify to his good character, thus showing that he '*knew the Town*'.[58] They include Lady Mary Wortley Montagu ('*Sappho*') now a symbol to Pope of gross sexual promiscuity. But most of the other instances concern Walpole, the references to Blunt and to the '*Screen*' taking us back yet again to the South Sea Bubble. Yet this is far from being just a catalogue of the old opposition slogans and accusations, because attention is focused not on the panorama of actual corruptions, which is taken for granted here, but on *how* the social poet should speak about them. The 'Friend's' presentation of Horace is at once a perversion of the Roman poet (he ends up his 'praise' of Horace by allying him with the two-faced manoeuvrings of Walpole in 1721)

---

[58] T.E., iv, p. 367.

but in another sense what he says of Horace is true and can be supported from the poet's own precepts.[59] Horace was not a fraudulent '*Screen*' for vice, and yet he was a master of a characteristically delicate and tactful manner. The point Pope is making is that the times are different. 'Augustan' Britain and Augustan Rome, whatever might earlier have been felt, have now nothing in common. Tact now *would* be to screen vice; then it was not. The final brilliance of the passage, however, lies in the paradox that though Pope is renouncing the polite Horatian manner as no longer appropriate to his corrupt country and time, his actual instances of Horatian tact are (in the context of what we know of the subjects) mordant in the extreme. 'Blunt *could do bus'ness*' —how pregnant with sinister meaning those harmless words really are, in the light of what we know of Blunt, and of the significance attached by Pope and Bolingbroke to the South Sea Bubble episode. In short the general significance of the opening of Dialogue I is that it shows us Pope bringing his awareness of a corrupt Britain into relation with his Augustan idealism, and as a consequence re-thinking his own role as a satirist. As he faces the darkening scene, he prepares to don the mantle of Juvenal, the satirist of Rome's decline.

The poetic consequence of this decision—a decision which Pope does not inform the reader of merely but dramatizes through the central part of the dialogue—is the vision both appalling and splendid of a completely corrupted Britain with which the poem ends:

> *Vice* is undone, if she forgets her Birth,
> And stoops from Angels to the Dregs of Earth:
> But 'tis the *Fall* degrades her to a Whore;
> Let *Greatness* own her, and she's mean no more:
> Her Birth, her Beauty, Crowds and Courts confess,
> Chaste Matrons praise her, and grave Bishops bless:
> In golden Chains the willing World she draws,
> And hers the Gospel is, and hers the Laws:
> Mounts the Tribunal, lifts her scarlet head,
> And sees pale Virtue carted in her stead!
> Lo! at the Wheels of her Triumphal Car,
> Old *England*'s Genius, rough with many a Scar,
> Dragg'd in the Dust! his Arms hang idly round,
> His Flag inverted trails along the ground!
> Our Youth, all liv'ry'd o'er with foreign Gold,
> Before her dance; behind her crawl the Old!
> See thronging Millions to the Pagod run,
> And offer Country, Parent, Wife, or Son!
> Hear her black Trumpet thro' the Land proclaim,
> That 'Not to be corrupted is the Shame.'
> In Soldier, Churchman, Patriot, Man in Pow'r,

[59] Cf. Horace, *Sat.* I, iii, ll. 49–54; see Pope, *Horatian Satires and Epistles*, ed. H. H. Erskine-Hill (Oxford, 1964), p. 172.

'Tis Av'rice all, Ambition is no more!
See, all our Nobles begging to be Slaves!
See, all our Fools aspiring to be Knaves!
The Wit of Cheats, the Courage of a Whore,
Are what ten thousand envy and adore.
All, all look up, with reverential Awe,
On Crimes that scape, or triumph o'er the Law:
While Truth, Worth, Wisdom daily they decry—
'Nothing is Sacred now but Villany.'

Yet may this Verse (if such a Verse remain)
Show there was one who held it in disdain.   [ll. 141–72]

Pope's attack upon national corruption culminates in this passage. This is
owing not only to the comprehensive meaning of its personifications ('. . .
Parent, Wife, or Son . . .', '. . . Soldier, Churchman, Patriot . . .', 'Old
England's Genius . . .', Vice and Villany) which draw into one vision the
many particular references which have gone before, but also to the fact that
Pope's pessimism has been pushed a stage further. This is the triumph of
Vice; the '*Fall*' foretold earlier by Pope, Bolingbroke and *The Craftsman*
has taken place—it is, as we see, moral, national and religious—but Britain
has degenerated even from the Biblical pattern; the fallen are here not exiled
from bliss but exalted. Hence the hyperbole which refashions the oft-repeated
cry of *The Craftsman*: now 'Not to be corrupted is the Shame'. And hence,
as Warburton was at pains to point out, the 'aukward Shame' with which low-
born and humble Allen, mention of whom in the poem precipitates this
whole spendid passage, performs good deeds in a degenerate age.[60] Allen's
was, as we have seen, true worth; though 'low-born' his intrinsic qualities
made him 'the Most Noble Man of England'. Because his values were firm
he could in some measure withstand the age. But in the following vision of
the triumph of Vice there is no corruption which worldly success will not
excuse and exalt. And here Pope's passage may make general allusion to
Juvenal's Tenth Satire and its account of the fall of Sejanus. Juvenal's stress
is on the unprincipled fickleness of the people who now revile the man they
were ready to worship as long as he maintained himself in power. Dryden's
version is couched in suggestive language:

Sejanus with a Rope, is drag'd along;
The Sport and Laughter of the giddy Throng . . .
     But the same very Mob; that Rascal crowd,
Had cry'd *Sejanus*, with a Shout as loud;
Had his Designs, (by Fortune's favour Blest)
Succeeded, and the Prince's Age opprest.
But long, long since, the Times have chang'd their Face,

[60] *The Works of Alexander Pope*, ed. William Warburton (London, 1751), iv, pp. 312–13.

> The People grown Degenerate and base:
> Not suffer'd now the Freedom of their choice . . .[61]

The thronging procession of a degenerate Rome in Juvenal is matched by the 'thronging Millions' of the procession in Pope, but Pope, if he indeed recalled the Juvenal satire, significantly reversed the position. What he displays here is what Juvenal knows would have happened if Sejanus had triumphed; what in Juvenal was hypothetical in Pope has become actual. It was of course the case that the name Sejanus, the type of a wicked minister, had often been levelled accusingly at Walpole by *The Craftsman*, as an earlier couplet in Dialogue I acknowledges:

> *Sejanus, Wolsey*, hurt not honest FLEURY,
> But well may put some Statesmen in a fury.   [ll. 51–2]

Pope's Sejanus, unlike Juvenal's in the Tenth Satire, was riding high. Systematic corruption at home, and a humiliatingly subservient foreign policy, reveal 'Old *England*'s Genius, rough with many a Scar' not rebellious but 'Dragg'd in the Dust', with 'Flag inverted' trailing on the ground. And to emphasize Walpole's supremacy Pope makes his whole passage allude to a very recent event. As J. M. Osborn has shown, in a convincing and suggestive article, the vision of vice triumphant alludes on one level to Walpole's recent marriage to his mistress Molly Skerrett, whom, once owned by greatness ('the great man'), the highest nobility in the kingdom competed for the honour of presenting at court.[62] Ll. 143–6 describe the effect of this marriage with particular precision. But the companion of this allusion is another, not contemporary but historical, to the Byzantine Empress Theodora, 'a Whore' until her amazing marriage to the Emperor Justinian I, which it was necessary to repeal a special law to permit. This sensational episode from the history of the eastern empire, like that of the lawyer Didius in the western empire, Pope, basing his view on that of the probably biased historian Procopius, regarded as a shameful instance of corruption in the highest place and a mark of imperial decline.[63] Of these two allusions, the first must have been recognizable and pointed at the time of publication, though not afterwards insisted on owing to the early death of the new Lady Walpole. The second, though demonstrable on contextual evidence, is barely discernible in the text itself, and Warburton felt compelled to secure it by a footnote in 1751. Like the more noticeable allusion to Juvenal, it is interesting in showing that the connection between eighteenth-century Britain and the decline of empire was

---

[61] The Tenth Satire of Juvenal, ll. 100–1, 116–22; *The Poems of John Dryden*, ed. James Kinsley (Oxford, 1957), ii, p. 723.

[62] J. M. Osborn, 'Pope, the Byzantine Empress and Walpole's Whore', *Review of English Studies*, N.S., vi (1955), pp. 372–82.

[63] The analogy cannot, however, be pressed far; Justinian was one of the most spectacularly successful of the Eastern Emperors in theological, legal and military fields. I think the allusion is made too indirectly to suggest a kind of grudging compliment to Walpole. For the reader of this passage, as opposed to the informed scholar, the parallel with the Empress Theodora is in itself faint enough.

in Pope's mind when he wrote the poem. But the 'Byzantine Empress and Walpole's Whore' were very properly subordinated by Pope to the combined visual effect and more comprehensive meaning of the total vision. Similarly Walpole as Palinurus, nodding at the helm in the finally yawning darkness of the end of *Dunciad* IV, is a significant part, but only a part, of the total effect. Here, as Warton put it so well, it is the 'groupe of allegorical persons worthy of the pencil of Rubens' that captures out attention.[64] The copiousness of the crowded line: 'Her Birth, her Beauty, Crowds and Courts confess', together with the 'Chaste Matrons' and 'grave Bishops' of the next, suggests the plentiful variety of those who now proffer their unanimous homage; the opulent flow of the line which balances the two harmonious, not opposite, terms 'golden Chains' and 'willing World' expresses the ease and outward splendour of Vice's service. The easy, lofty magnificence of the next line: 'And hers the Gospel is, and hers the Laws:' by the very conjunction of movement and meaning implies protest: how can so much so easily become the creature of Vice? But now Vice, as the woman of the Apocalypse, 'arrayed in purple and scarlet colour, and decked with gold ... drunken with the blood of the saints', lifts her head in the judgement-seat, and—in a line which brings the vision down to the streets of eighteenth-century London— 'sees pale Virtue carted in her stead!'[65] Now as in a Roman triumphal procession the vanquished is exhibited in the train of the conqueror, the spirit of a defiant and independent England, 'rough with many a Scar', is led captive by Corruption, and Pope's oratorical style—'Lo! at the Wheels ...'— temporarily hardens in sympathy with what it describes, as the strong down-to-earth diction and enactive *enjambement*—'... Dragg'd in the Dust!'— shows. 'Old *England*'s Genius' is now incapable of activity, Hector dragged at Achilles' chariot wheels, but degraded England is active enough, with youth dancing before and age crawling behind; they pay frenzied homage to no Christian shrine but one of an outlandish and pagan kind, as the word 'Pagod'—last used by Pope in association with 'The mosque of Mahound' for describing the King's 'Presence' at court—conveys to us.[66] The picture now broadens; Pope has given us the foreground in vivid colour and vigorous strokes, but the middle distance is crowded with representative supporting figures: nobles, churchmen, soldiers and patriots. Finally, the throng becomes almost totality: 'All, all look up with reverential Awe ...' All are slaves of the 'black Trumpet' which enforces corruption throughout the land, and this epithet, strangely arresting in its blend of visual and aural, dominates the remainder of the passage. Yet not quite completely. Corruption has not claimed quite all. Just as in Nicholas Poussin's *Adoration of the Golden Calf* the orgiastic worship of the image forms the brightly coloured foreground and middle distance, with the false prophet Aaron very prominent, while in dim light on the left the distant figure of Moses dashes the sacred tablets to the

[64] Pope, *Horatian Satires and Epistles*, ed. cit., p. 178.
[65] Revelation 17:4-6.
[66] 'The Fourth Satire of Dr. Donne ... Versified', ll. 238-9; T.E., iv, p. 45.

ground, so Pope allows the orgy of corruption to dominate the picture he paints, while giving himself a diminished yet defiant place in it:

> Yet may this Verse (if such a Verse remain)
> Show there was one who held it in disdain.

Throughout the poem Pope has been dramatizing the poet's choice of a role when faced with national corruption. The defiant final couplet stresses the heroic nature of his chosen stance, and keeps the poem dramatic to the end.

The treatment of corruption in the second dialogue of the 'Epilogue to the Satires' is not greatly different from the first, but the mood and the picture has changed when we come to Pope's final word on the theme of corruption, in Book IV of *The Dunciad*. 'We must want spirit, as well as virtue, to perish', Bolingbroke had written in his Letter *On the Spirit of Patriotism*; vice may itself have a kind of vigour, but systematic corruption at length must reduce a people to degeneracy. In his account of the travels of the noble young Aeneas *de ses jours*, Pope depicts a Europe in which the battle has been finally lost:

> . . . where the Seine, obsequious as she runs,
> Pours at great Bourbon's feet her silken sons;
> Or Tyber, now no longer Roman, rolls,
> Vain of Italian Arts, Italian Souls:
> To happy Convents, bosom'd deep in vines,
> Where slumber Abbots, purple as their wines:
> To Isles of fragrance, lilly-silver'd vales,
> Diffusing languor in the panting gales:
> To lands of singing, or of dancing slaves,
> Love-whisp'ring woods, and lute-resounding waves.
> But chief her shrine where naked Venus keeps,
> And Cupids ride the Lyon of the Deeps;
> Where, eas'd of Fleets, the Adriatic main
> Wafts the smooth Eunuch and enamour'd swain.
>
> [ll. 279–310][67]

How different from the Roman spirit of the original Aeneas, forebear of the Augustan empire! And how different is Venus; the guardian goddess of Virgil's poem is here transformed into the siren-temptress of an all-too yielding hero. The Virgilian Venus has become a Spenserian Acrasia. And the amazing sensuous beauty of the passage makes the ironical point that this is the happiness of slavery; there is nothing here which is sturdy or independent, nothing like 'Old *England*'s Genius, rough with many a Scar'. The Seine is subservient and yields silken courtiers to absolute monarchy (which in the person of Louis XV of France is itself hardly inspiring or manly) while the Tiber yields

---

[67] *The Dunciad*, Bk. IV, ll. 297–310; T.E., v, pp. 373–4. For a discussion of this passage in *The Dunciad*'s pattern of allusion to the *Aeneid*, see Howard Erskine-Hill, *Pope: The Dunciad* (London, 1972), pp. 22–4.

itself to the now decadent values of Italy. The Italian abbots have yielded up their true calling to wine and sleep and have become merged with the object of their pleasure. It is in this sense that they are happy, just as the singing and dancing which follows is the singing and dancing not of a free people but of slaves. The political undertones, and the idea of national decline, become clear again in the last three lines with their allusion to the lapsed naval power of the Republic of Venice, and the Pope-Warburton note brings out the warning for Britain: 'The winged Lyon, the Arms of Venice. This Republic heretofore the most considerable in Europe, for her Naval Force and the extent of her Commerce; now illustrious for her *Carnivals*.' This Europe has lost its liberty and independence; the moral landscape is so beautiful because its inhabitants no longer realize what they have lost, and are happy. It is sensuously beautiful because they have yielded themselves up to the gratification of the senses, yet the result is 'the smooth Eunuch and enamour'd swain' rather than the vitality of a true love. In its final stages Corruption merges into Dullness, in Pope's widest sense; mankind is thoroughly reduced in stature, and the end of the process is the final plunge back into Nothingness which comes at the end of this poem. Blunt, Walter, Walpole, and the many others who are bringers of darkness in Pope's eyes, are gathered up into the 'Great Negative' at the conclusion of *Dunciad* IV.

Pope's poetic dealing with the moneyed interest of the city, and with the concept of corruption itself, demonstrates what the different levels of false stewardship also showed: the final connectedness of his thinking about man, society and God. His handling of Walter and Blunt, seen in the light of an examination of their lives, suggests that Pope's smallest attacking references can rarely have been wanton or mechanical. I am far from suggesting that there is anything as intellectual as a system or philosophy behind it all: rather that a hostile impulse in Pope's mind nearly always involved in some measure the deeper loyalties and antipathies of his life. If we begin by probing comparatively local and particular references in his social poetry we shall find ourselves being led steadily outward to the full compass of his mental world. And we shall, as I have tried to show in some small degree, understand this world better in the process.

IX. The Country House Ideal

1. THE TRADITIONAL IDEAL

IF we consider the moral opposite of Old Cotta's inhospitable hall, in *To Bathurst*, we have the country house ideal. Pope's lines

> Benighted wanderers, the forest o'er,
> Curse the sav'd candle, and unop'ning door [ll. 195-6]

imply the moral and social standard expressed positively by the seventeenth-century poet Thomas Carew, in his praise of a country house which fulfilled the need that Old Cotta denied:

> Those chearfull beames send forth their light,
> To all that wander in the night,
> And seeme to becken from aloofe,
> The weary Pilgrim to thy roofe ... [*To Saxham*, ll. 35-8][1]

It is to G. R. Hibbard, in his essay 'The Country House Poem of the Seventeenth Century', that we owe our realization of the considerable continuity of attitude, concerning social values and practice, between the Elizabethan, Jacobean and Caroline ideal of housekeeping and Pope's Epistle *To Burlington*.[2] Since, however, the continuity is not complete, the seventeenth-century poems which express this ideal afford a useful perspective upon Pope's judgement of his own society.

The 'thin but clearly defined tradition', as Hibbard discerns it, consists of Jonson's 'To Penshvrst' and 'To Sir Robert Wroth'; Carew's 'To Saxham' and 'To my friend G.N. from Wrest'; Herrick's 'A Country life: To his Brother, M. Tho: Herrick' and 'A Panegerick to Sir Lewis Pemberton';

---

[1] Quotations from the Country House poems are taken from the following editions: *Ben Jonson*, ed. C. H. Herford and Percy and Evelyn Simpson (Oxford, 1925-52), vol. iv; *The Poems of Thomas Carew*, ed. Rhodes Dunlap (Oxford, 1949); *Herrick's Poetical Works*, ed. L. C. Martin (Oxford, 1956); *The Poems and Letters of Andrew Marvell*, ed. H. M. Margoliouth (Oxford, 1927; 2nd. edn., 1952).
[2] G. R. Hibbard, 'The Country House Poem of the Seventeenth Century', *Journal of the Warburg and Courtauld Institutes*, xix, Nos. 1-2 (1956), pp. 159-74. L. C. Knights, *Drama and Society in the Age of Jonson* (London, 1937) contributes importantly to this recognition.

and Marvell's 'Upon Appleton House, to my Lord Fairfax'. The opening
lines of 'To Penshvrst' introduce the moral and aesthetic contract between
prodigal ostentation on the one hand, and plainness and naturalness on the
other:

> Thou art not, PENSHVRST, built to enuious show,
>   Of touch, or marble; nor canst boast a row
> Of polish'd pillars, or a roofe of gold:
>   Thou hast no lantherne, whereof tales are told;
> Or stayre, or courts; but stand'st an ancient pile,
>   And these grudg'd at, art reuerenced the while.
> Thou ioy'st in better markes, of soyle, of ayre,
>   Of Wood, of water: therein thou art faire.   [ll. 1–8]

The measured and slow utterance, laying a thoughtful and feeling weight
upon certain words ('reuerenc'd . . . of soyle, of ayre,/Of wood . . .'), seem
fully appropriate to Jonson's subject and attitude. The same concern is
prominent in 'To Sir Robert Wroth' (to some degree an imitation of Horace's
Epode 2: *Beatus ille*); Wroth is praised for shunning the ostentatious show of
court and city, and for living at home 'Free from proud porches, or their
guilded roofes' [l. 15]. Carew, in 'To my friend G.N. from Wrest', writes:·

> Such pure and uncompounded beauties, blesse
> This Mansion with an usefull comelinesse,
> Devoide of Art, for here the Architect
> Did not with curious skill a Pile erect
> Of carved Marble, Touch or Porpherie,
> But built a house for hospitalitie . . .
> No Dorique, nor Corinthian Pillars grace
> With Imagery this structures naked face . . .   [ll. 19–24, 29–30]

Likewise Marvell commends Nunappleton House, after glancing at those
who erect superfluously huge buildings through pride, since

> · . . . all things are composed here
> Like Nature, orderly and near: . . .
>
> *Humility* alone designs
> These short but admirable Lines,
> By which, ungirt and unconstrain'd,
> Things greater are in less contain'd.
>   ['Upon Appleton House', ll. 25–6, 41–4]

In these poems ostentation is seen to satisfy only vanity and pride, while an
unpretentious plainness is ultimately connected with the concept of 'Nature'
as exemplified in a rural life. Not that ostentatious show-places could not be
erected in the country as well as the town. It is rather that the writers of these
poems saw that such houses neglected, in Pope's term, the 'genius' of the
countryside, where nothing seemed uselessly artificial and every thing served

a fundamental need. Houses such as Penshurst and Wrest are shown to have
an intimate connection with the country.

The criterion of plainness and naturalness here is that of use. 'The vse of
things is all, and not the *Store*', Jonson was to write in *The Staple of Newes*
(I.vi.26), and in 'Penshvrst' it is clear that everything in and around the house
exists to serve human need, particularly human consumption:

> Thou hast thy walkes for health, as well as sport . . .
> Thy copp's, too, nam'd of GAMAGE, thou hast there,
>   That neuer failes to serue thee season'd deere,
> When thou would'st feast, or exercise thy friends
>   The lower land, that to the riuer bends,
> Thy sheepe, thy bullocks, kine, and calues doe feed:
>   The middle grounds thy mares, and horses breed . . .
> The blushing apricot, and wooly peach
>   Hang on thy walls, that euery child may reach.
>   [ll. 9, 19–24, 43–4]

Above all the use of the house for generous and friendly hospitality is stressed.
In 'Penshvrst' hospitality to the poet himself, then to King JAMES, 'With
his braue sonne, the Prince', is described; in 'To Sir Robert Wroth' it is the
tenantry and rural neighbours we see made welcome:

> The rout of rurall folke come thronging in,
>   (Their rudenesse then is thought no sinne)
> Thy noblest spouse affords them welcome grace;
>   And the great *Heroes*, of her race,
> Sit mixt with losse of state, or reuerence.
>   Freedome doth with degree dispense.
> The iolly wassall walkes the often round . . .   [ll. 53–9]

Hibbard is perhaps right when he says that it is precisely because there is
general acceptance of the idea of degree, that degree can here be dispensed
with;[3] Carew, in 'To my friend G.N. from Wrest', puts even greater stress
than Jonson on the public hospitality of housekeeping, but here degree is
observed in the seating of the guests:

> The Lord and Lady of this place delight
> Rather to be in act, then seeme in sight.
> Instead of Statues to adorne their wall,
> They throng with living men their merry Hall,
> Where at large Tables fill'd with wholesome meates,
> The servant, Tennant, and kind neighbour eates.
> Some of that ranke, spun of a finer thred,
> Are with the Women, Steward and Chaplaine fed
> With daintier cates; Others of better note
> Whom wealth, parts, office or the Heralds coate

---

[3] Hibbard, art. cit., p. 166.

> Have sever'd from the common, freely sit
> At the Lord's Table, whose spread sides admit
> A large accesse of friends to fill those seates
> Of his capacious circle . . .   [ll. 31–44]

Herrick, in the 'Panegerick to Sir Lewis Pemberton', and Marvell, in 'Upon Appleton House', make a similar emphasis, though not so full a picture. It may be seen from this passage of Carew that the largely ornamental manner of 'To Saxham' has now been left behind; the clear undecorative description of a society in its different degrees eating together in one hall, accords with his affirmation of the principle of 'reall use' and what is 'fit for service' [ll. 55–7]. The epistolary middle style in which the poem is couched enables Carew to use well what he has learned from Jonson: the force which poetry of plain statement may possess: '. . . But built a house for hospitalitie . . . Rather to be in act . . . They throng with living men their merry Hall . . .' Our sense of the civilization of the country house community—a society which is made to appear both comprehensive and harmoniously ordered—is heightened in this poem, not by references to London or the court, but to the rigours of warfare and (as Hibbard says) the unhumanized landscape of the Border, where 'the wilde North/Brings sterill Fearne, Thistles, and Brambles forth' [ll. 7–8]. The picture of Wrest is framed by references to this outer, harsher reality, and is perhaps implicitly the human heart of what Carew and others were in arms to protect.[4]

From 'Penshvrst' and 'Wrest' particularly it is clear that these poets see the country house as accommodating a cross-section of the whole community. The king, 'With his braue sonne, the Prince', those 'of better note', neighbour, tenant, servant, poor, the chance stranger, are all involved in the country house hospitality. Society is hierarchically conceived, but in the country house this stratification seems to mean not segregation, but familiar contact between different levels of an ostensibly integrated community. The prime-mover of these harmonies between man and nature and between man and man is the lord of the manor. It is his decision whether to exercise a valuable function of his house in society, or rather to make the prime sphere of his activity the court or the city, as Jonson, in 'To Sir Robert Wroth', implies many did. One might speak of him as a patron, but to realize how these poets would interpret the term one must see, with Herrick, the lord of the manor as leader of a dance:

> No, thou know'st order, Ethicks, and ha's read
>   All Oeconomicks, know'st to lead
> A House-dance neatly, and can'st truly show,
>   How farre a Figure ought to go,
> Forward, or backward, side-ward, and what pace
>   Can give, and what retract a grace;
> What Gesture, Courtship; Comeliness agrees

---

4 Ibid., pp. 166–7.

> With those thy primitive decrees,
> To give subsistance to thy house, and proofe,
> What *Genii* support they roofe,
> *Goodnes* and *Greatnes*;   [*A Panegerick* . . ., ll. 89–99][5]

The lord leads the dance of community, bringing into contact the highest and lowest levels of society, conferring benefits at each level as monarch and tenant alike have conferred benefits upon him, and, as Jonson and Herrick insist, basing his conduct, and that of his family and house, on virtue.

How far great houses as depicted by Jonson, Carew and Herrick represented earlier seventeenth-century English society, apart from court and city, is a question only a social historian of the period can hope to answer with conviction. Hibbard argues that to Jonson Penshurst was 'the norm, slightly idealized' citing some evidence for his view; Raymond Williams, noting the degree to which the good way of life at Penshurst and Saxham is defined by negatives (and this is true too of Wrest), suggests that such houses were 'islands of charity': 'the gentle exercise of a power that was elsewhere . . . mean and brutal.'[6] The dispute is subtler than it appears. Perhaps both critics underestimate the degree to which these poems are panegyrical— rich and successful exercises in the art of praise—and are not therefore direct social evidence, either of an exception or a norm. Their art of praise certainly asserts an ideal; the extent to which it also describes a practice must remain in doubt until more historical evidence is brought forward. The definition by negatives may be read in different ways; it is surely a panegyrical device, designed to dramatize opposing moral qualities, but whether beyond this it suggests that Penshurst and Wrest were striking exceptions to the rule, or that a normative Country House practice was being increasingly violated, remains an open question. What does seem clear historically is the dominance of the noble household over the greater part of provincial England; the poems do thus, in a broad sense, describe a real social structure, while (to a greater or lesser extent) idealizing its operation. All but the largest provincial cities were under the wing of the lord of the manor. The network of such families and houses, spread over the face of England, might well be thought to represent the greater part of English society, and each could potentially, if it did not actually, approximate to the role panegyrically expressed by Jonson and Carew. To this extent the ideal advanced by these poets is neither narrowly individualistic nor wildly utopian; it has the force of a comprehensive and coherent conception, the possible fulfilment of which is demonstrated, at the very least, by an act of creative imagination synthesizing the ideal with a sense of everyday experience calmly and firmly conveyed. Especially in 'To my friend G.N. from Wrest', so strikingly circumstantial, it is hard to

[5] Cf. Sir Thomas Elyot, *The Boke Named the Gouernour*, ed. H. S. S. Croft (London, 1880), i, pp. 235–45.

[6] Raymond Williams, 'Pastoral and Counter-Pastoral', *Critical Quarterly*, x, No. 3 (Autumn 1968), pp. 277–95. Hibbard's discussion of these poems has the wider range of social-historical reference, while Raymond Williams has recently extended his general thesis about the Country House into a consideration of later literature (see *The Country and the City* (London, 1973)).

believe some country house living was not like this.

A different but related question is raised by Raymond Williams's suggestion that these poems gloss over the hard realities of labour, through their stress upon the fruitfulness of the land, and the communal manner in which all conditions of men enjoy these fruits. Is the ideal of the country house, even in the poems themselves, entirely convincing? In support of his view that it is not, William refers to Herrick's vigorous and vivid poem 'The Hock-cart, or Harvest home', where the fact of labour is fully acknowledged:

> Come Sons of Summer, by whose toile,
> We are the Lords of Wine and Oile:
> By whose tough labours, and rough hands,
> We rip up first, then reap our lands.   [ll. 1–4]

The centre of the poem is taken up with a description of the rich hospitality of the 'Lords Hearth', much in the manner of the country house poems, but at the end Herrick returns to the reality of the labouring year in its seasonal cycle:

> Feed, and grow fat; and as ye eat,
> Be mindfull, that the lab'ring Neat
> (As you) may have their fill of meat.
> And know, besides, ye must revoke
> The patient Oxe unto the Yoke,
> And all goe back unto the Plough
> And Harrow, (though they'r hang'd up now.)
> And, you must know, your Lords word's true,
> Feed him ye must, whose food fils you.
> And that this pleasure is like raine,
> Not sent ye for to drowne your paine,
> But for to make it spring againe.   [ll. 44–55]

Having drunk their lord's health, the men must, like the animals, go back to their work; and (Williams argues):

> It is crude in feeling, this early and jollying kind of man-management, which uses the metaphors of rain and spring to ratify the drink as a way of getting more labour (and more pain). But what is there on the surface—
>
> Feed him ye must, whose food fills you
>
> —is the aching paradox which is subsumed in the earlier images of natural bounty.[7]

This is a timely warning against uncritical historical readings; but something may be said in defence of Herrick and the country house poets. The 'aching paradox' has a moral for landowners in that it affirms an interdependence of lord and labourer. The absentee landlord could forget this

---

[7] Williams, art. cit., p. 290.

reciprocal relationship; to the landlord in residence his human obligations were more obvious. This is not to say this is an interdependence of equals. The force of Herrick's 'must' is partly that of a command, partly, indeed, the statement of something presumed almost as inevitable as a natural law. The word unmistakably implies the principle of subordination in society, but I think nothing in the country house poems—not even Jonson's 'Freedome doth with degree dispense' in 'To Sir Robert Wroth'—calls in doubt their writers' fundamental adherence to this principle. When not absolutely explicit, as in 'To my friend G.N. from Wrest' it was surely taken for granted. So too, I suggest, were the facts of labour. The sheep, bullocks, kine and calves of Penshurst imply a farm in which work is done, Carew speaks of grinding the yellow goddess into food, Marvell bases a sequence of reflective conceit upon the 'tawny Mowers' of the meadows.[8] Labour is not a major theme of the country house poems, as it is of 'The Hock-cart', but it is repeatedly implied, and was, I suggest, too obvious a fact of life in the minds of the country house poets and their readers to be 'extracted' or 'mystified' by the poems themselves.[9] These poems are simply panegyrical in mode, recognizable to their readers as such, and lay their chief stress on bounty and kindness: a communal sharing of the fruits of the earth.

At the same time 'The Hock-cart', germane to the preoccupations of the country house poem, should disturb anyone prepared to think the ideal fully satisfying and humane. I do not think Herrick equates man with animals when he says that the labourers must lead back the oxen to the yoke, and all return unto the plough, but he comes perilously near when he reminds them that the 'lab'ring Neat/(As you)' must have their fill. He does not say that the harvest feast is to procure more labour and more pain, but rather that it is part of a natural process of renewal of new life and labour. The labourers would have had to return to work with or without their harvest feast. Simply *because* of the hard facts of life, the merry-making is more than an employers' confidence trick. But this brings us up against that final compulsion (so easily taken for granted by men of one degree when applied to another) which marks the limits of the country house ideal. It is at such a point that one realizes the social tensions behind Christian's dialogue with Apollyon in *Pilgrim's Progress*:

> *Apol.* . . . I perceive thou art one of my Subjects; for all that Countrey is mine, and I am the Prince and God of it. How is it then that thou hast run away from thy King? Were it not that I hope thou maiest do me more service, I would strike thee now at one blow to the ground.
> *Chr.* I was born indeed in your dominions, but your service was hard, and your wages such as a man could not live on; 'for the wages of Sin is death:' therefore when I was come to years I did, as other considerate

---

[8] 'To Penshvrst', l. 23; 'To my friend G.N. from Wrest', l. 68; 'Upon Appleton House', ll. 388–456. Marvell's lines include an allusion to the Levellers, the one point in the Country House poems where an alternative to hierarchy appears.

[9] Williams, art. cit., p. 288.

persons do, look out if perhaps I might mend myself.
Apol. There is no Prince that will thus lightly lose his Subjects, neither will
I as yet lose thee: but, since thou complainest of thy service and thy wages,
be content to go back; what our Countrey will afford, I do here promise
to give thee.[10]

It is not the final religious import of the exchange, but the metaphor conveying it, which is remarkable here. Bunyan's viewpoint is totally different
from that of the country house poets, chiefly because he came of the 'rout of
rurall folke' generalized in the country house poems, and was writing for a
public which included people like him; partly too, perhaps, because the
political upheaval of the Civil War, and the driving forces of religious non-
conformity, had now made the traditional pattern of society seem a less un-
alterable thing. This helps us place the country house ideal socially. It is one
springing from an outlook intimately associated with the gentry and aristocracy.
It accepts subordination and hierarchy without question. Its view of the poor
is an external one.

Yet the ideal had value. To think of the poor entirely externally was bad,
but to neglect them altogether was worse. To accept strict social subordination
was (from our modern view) bad, but a subordination in which the poor
worked for the rich and the rich owned no obligation to the poor was worse.
This is one of the moral contrasts with which the drama and poetry of Jonson
were concerned; as Hibbard has observed, the following passage from 'To
Sir Robert Wroth' brings us close to the worlds of *Volpone* and *The Alchymist*:

> Let this man sweat, and wrangle at the barre,
>> For euery price, in euery iarre,
> And change possessions, oftner with his breath,
>> Then either money, warre, or death:
> Let him, then hardest sires, more disinherit,
>> And each where boast it as his merit,
> To blow vp orphanes, widdowes, and their states;
>> And thinke his power doth equall *Fates*.
> Let that goe heape a masse of wretched wealth,
>> Purchas'd by rapine, worse then stealth,
> And brooding o'er it, sit with broadest eyes,
>> Not doing good, scarce when he dyes.   [ll. 73–84]

It is in contrast with this that the landowner who lives on his estates, cares
for his tenantry, helps the poor and needy, and has all his human obligations
before his eyes, embodies a positive social standard. In contrast with this the
country house hospitality is a positive social value because it brings different
orders of men together, and affirms the existence of something like a total
community. Hibbard's view that it is the country house ideal which forms
the implicit moral basis of Jonson's comedy is a compelling one, and is of

---

[10] John Bunyan, *The Pilgrim's Progress*, ed. J. B. Wharey; second edition revised by Roger
Sharrock (Oxford, 1960), pp. 56–7.

special relevance here in that our concern is now with the social values of Pope, the next great *social* satirist of our literature.[11]

2. CONTINUITY OF PRACTICE

Two letters of Pope help place him in relation to the traditional country house ideal. The first is to Lady Mary Wortly Montagu, written in September 1718, and describes the decaying country mansion of Stanton Harcourt, to which Pope had retired to work undisturbed on his Homer translation. It is apparent from Pope's account that Lord Harcourt and his family no longer lived in the house. The letter is long and determined to amuse. The most relevant and least insistently amusing paragraph concerns the great hall:

> The great Hall is high & spatious, flankd with long tables (images of ancient hospitality) ornamented with monstrous horns, about 20 broken Pikes, & a match-lock Musquet or two, which they say were used in the Civil Wars. Here is one vast archd Window, beautifully darken'd with divers Skutcheons of painted Glass . . . One shining Pane bears date 1286 . . . In this Hall, in former days have dined Garterd Knights & Courtly Dames, with Ushers, Sewers, and Seneshalls; And yet it was but tother night that an Owl flew in hither, and mistook it for a Barn.[12]

This passage gives a full sense of the lapse of time between Pope and the age of the country house poems—with the reference to muskets 'which they say were used in the Civil Wars'. It gives a good sense, too, of the balance in Pope's attitude to earlier times: detached amusement is in equipoise here with a sympathetic fascination which almost anticipates the poems of Scott. Most important is his association of 'ancient hospitality' with the traditional great house. We must be careful, however, not to treat this letter as evidence that in the early eighteenth century country house practices were utterly dead. Pope is describing a decrepit and virtually abandoned mansion; by no means all the old country houses were in this situation.

The second letter describes another country house, this time one lived in by its owner for a substantial part of every year. It is the letter to Martha Blount about Sherborne, probably written on 22 June 1724, and already quoted from briefly in my account of the life of William Digby. The letter is long, and in procedure follows that of a country house poem such as 'To Penshvrst' in that it attends first to the house, then to the gardens and grounds, and finally to the character of the owner.

> The House is in the form of an H. The body of it, which was built by Sir Walter Rawleigh, consists of four Stories, with four six-angled Towers at the ends. These have since been joind to four Wings, with a regular Stone Balustrade at the top & four towers more that finish the building. The Windows & Gates are of a yellow Stone throughout, and one of the flatt Sides towards the Garden has the wings of a newer Architecture with beautiful

[11] Hibbard, art. cit., p. 163.
[12] *Corr.*, i, pp. 505–6.

Italian Window-frames done by the first Earl of Bristol, which, if they were joind in the middle by a Portico covering the Old Building, would be a noble Front. The design of such an one I have been amusing myself with drawing, but tis a question whether my Lord Digby will not be better amus'd than to execute it.[13]

Sherborne, like Penshurst, is no modern showpiece but stands 'an ancient pile'. Indeed, while Pope desires to initiate a piece of architectural improvement, he implicitly admires Lord Digby for being 'better amus'd' than to execute it. Pope is attentive, too, to the historical associations of the house; as emerges more clearly later, they are all part of the human significance of the scene. Pope now turns to the grounds:

This stands in a Park, finely crownd with very high Woods, on all the tops of the Hills, which form a great amfitheatre sloping down to the house. On the Garden Sides the Woods approach close, so that it appears there with a thick Line and Depth of Groves on each hand, & so it shows from most parts of the Park. The Gardens are so Irregular, that 'tis very hard to give an exact idea of 'em but by a Plan. Their beauty rises from this Irregularity, for not only the Several parts of the Garden itself make the better Contraste by these sudden Rises, Falls, and Turns of ground; but the Views about it are lett in, & hang over the Walls, in very different figures and aspects ... you see the town of Sherborne in a valley, interspersed with trees ... The Honisuckles hereabouts are the largest and finest I ever saw. You'l be pleasd when I tell you the Quarters of the above mentiond little Wilderness are filld with these & with Cherry trees of the best kinds all within reach of the hand ...[14]

What pleases Pope about the gardens at Sherborne is their naturalness—their beauty rises from their 'Irregularity'. The grounds are rich in surprising beauties, also in honeysuckle and cherry trees, which like the 'blushing apricot, and wooly peach' in 'To Penshvrst', grow within reach of the hand. Among the prospects which open from the gardens is the town of Sherborne: visually, as morally, within the range of the great house. Pope next turns to the ruins of the old castle:

On the left, full behind these old Trees, which make this whole Part inexpressibly awful & solemn, runs a little, old, low wall, ... which ... brings you to the Ruins, to compleat the Solemnity of the Scene. You first see an old Tower penetrated by a large Arch, and others above it through which the whole Country appears in prospect ... views, which are more romantick than Imagination can form them ...

What should induce my Lord D. the rather to cultivate these ruins and do honour to them, is that they do no small honour to his Family; that Castle, which was very ancient, being demolishd in the Civil wars after

[13] *Corr.*, ii, pp. 236–7.
[14] Ibid., p. 237.

it was nobly defended by one of his Ancestors in the cause of the King.[15]

Even at this early date we have a garden which is not innocent of a deliberate ruin and a 'Hermits Seat (as they call it)', which Pope briefly noted at an earlier point of this letter.[16] But he is more interested in the genuine ruins and in their human significance: the loyalty of the Digby family to Charles I. This sense of an heroic background expressed in the dramatic views of and through the ruins seems to lie behind Pope's admiring use of the word 'romantick'. Reflections on the history of the family lead directly to the tribute to Lord Digby himself:

> The Present Master of this place (and I verily believe I can ingage the same for the next Successors) needs not to fear the Record, or shun the remembrance of the actions of his Forefathers. He will not disgrace them, as most Modern Progeny do, by an unworthy Degeneracy, of principle, or of Practise. When I have been describing this agreable Seat, I cannot make the reflection I've often done upon contemplating the beautiful Villa's of Other Noblemen, raisd upon the Spoils of plunderd nations, or aggrandiz'd by the wealth of the Publick. I cannot ask myself the question, 'What Else has this man to be lik'd? what else has he cultivated or improv'd? What good, or what desireable thing appears of him, without these walls? I dare say his Goodness and Benevolence extend as far as his territories; that his Tenants live almost as happy & contented as himself; & that not one of his Children wishes to see this Seat his owne. I have not lookd much about, since I was here: All I can tell you of my own knowledge is, that going to see the Cathedral in the town hard by, I took notice as the finest things, of a noble Monument and a beautiful Altar-piece of Architecture; but if I had not inquird in particular, he nor his, had ever told me that both the one & the other was erected by Himself: The next pretty thing that catchd my eye was a neat Chappel for the use of the Towns-people, (who are too numerous for the Cathedral) My Lord modestly told me, he was glad I lik'd it, because it was of his own architecture. . . . Believe me ever yours, with a sincerity as old-fashiond, and as different from Modern Sincerity, as This house, this family, & these ruins, are from the Court, & all its Neighbourhood.[17]

This tribute is expressed with unusual fervour, and is the more obviously sincere because there can be no question here of that complimentary style with which Pope loved to please his friends. His letters to Martha Blount are among the most frank in their judgement of others that Pope wrote. His admiration for Sherborne is excited by a number of things: It is no modern showpiece, and, as Jonson said of Penshurst and Herrick of Sir Lewis Pemberton's house, it is in Pope's judgement 'rear'd with no man's ruine,

[15] Ibid., pp. 238–9.
[16] Ibid., p. 238.
[17] Ibid., pp. 239–40.

no man's grone'.[18] The gardens are pleasing for their irregular beauty and naturalness. The ruins are taken as an emblem of past bravery and integrity of the family, and are a standard by which 'The Present Master of this place' and his heirs are tried and not found wanting. The letter culminates in the social praise of Lord Digby; his character and works extend throughout the whole community, his family, the tenantry, and 'the town hard by'. The great house is seen as the fount of benefits for the whole neighbourhood; all appears to rest on a moral basis. And as Lord Digby is at the centre of the moral scene of Sherborne—as Sir Lewis Pemberton was leader of the dance of community in Herrick's poem—so at the centre of all his activities is religion: the chapel, the monument, the altar-piece. The conclusion of the letter, with its contrast between the old-fashioned sincerity of the country house and the modern sincerity of the court adds the final similarity between this letter of Pope and the country house poem.

The letter has in fact nearly all the important ingredients of the traditional country house poem in a similar order to that of 'To Penshvrst'. What we miss is any mention of housekeeping in the old sense. Even in 'To Penshvrst', which does not specifically mention hospitality to the tenantry and poor, the country people are made humanly real. The tenants whom Pope dares say live 'almost' as happy and content as Lord Digby himself seem more remote. And while one doesn't want to generalize on the strength of a letter based on a short visit (Pope has not 'lookd much about' before writing), it is probably true that large landowners and their friends were more remote from their tenantry in the eighteenth than in the seventeenth century. Yet it is still clear that in Pope's view the great house and its lands and influence could comprise a naturally, morally and artistically satisfying community— could still stand for much that was best in English society, and that was opposed to the values of the court and city. In Pope's mind, it seems, something very like the country house ideal of the earlier seventeenth century was still a relevant way of thinking about his own society. This is to say that it enshrined values which were meaningful and important to him personally, and that the economic and social structure through which they could be, and to some extent were, embodied was still in existence. This structure was the dominance of the great house over its immediate neighbourhood in provincial England. It is this which chiefly accounts for the similarity between Pope's letter about Sherborne and the country house poem, though Pope's knowledge of 'To Penshvrst', 'To Sir Robert Wroth', and 'To my friend G.N. from Wrest' is a probability, and may have unconsciously shaped his reactions.[19] We must also remember that when Pope wrote this letter he had just seen, in Sherborne abbey, Nost's 'noble Monument' and probably read John Hough's eloquent epitaph to the third Earl of Bristol inscribed on it. This epitaph celebrates the role of the aristocrat in society and expresses

---

[18] Cf. 'To Penshvrst', ll. 45–7; 'A Panegerick to Sir Lewis Pemberton', ll. 115–30.

[19] For Pope's knowledge of some of Jonson's poetry, see Spence, 267; Joseph Warton, *An Essay on the Genius and Writings of Pope*, i (London, 1756; 3rd edn. 1772), pp. 95–6. For his knowledge of Carew, see Spence, 455 and 408 (headnote).

values which are germane to the country house ideal. It is especially relevant that it should have stressed that retirement from 'the Hurry of a publick Life' is not necessarily retirement from human responsibility. In many respects the epitaph applied equally well to William Digby, since the time when he had left 'the Hurry of a publick Life' and, in his own words, 'turned Country Gentleman'.

Pope's letter about Sherborne shows that there was certainly continuity of thought and probably of practice between the earlier seventeenth and eighteenth centuries in respect of the country house ideal.[20] In different ways and to different degrees the lives of John Kyrle, John Caryll, William Digby and Ralph Allen have provided further evidence of continuity of practice. If full evidence has not survived, 'It is', as an economic historian has recently written, 'prudent always to bear in mind that detailed bits of evidence constitute the sole genuine records of high or even moderate re-liability that the past bequeaths to us.'[21] Of the two men born into the position of landed country gentlemen, Caryll and Digby, there are, as we have seen, several forms of evidence to suggest something like traditional housekeeping at the Caryll houses. The case of Lord Digby is slightly different. Pope's Sherborne letter is of course evidence in itself, and we must remember that Pope was at least very familiar with Robert Digby before his visit there. At the same time Digby's charity seems different and might best be des-cribed as Anglican philanthropy. He was concerned with settling the tithes back upon the clergy, with building and rebuilding parsonages, churches and chapels, founding libraries and charity schools. All these charitable acts were indeed on his own estates, in Warwickshire, Dorset and Ireland. But he was concerned with wider projects, also; through his association with Thomas Bray, with the S.P.C.K. and the S.P.G.; and through his son Edward and James Oglethorpe with the plight of those imprisoned for debt, and the efforts to establish the new colony of Georgia. In all this we are aware of Digby the fervent churchman, whose outlook and deeds were moulded in that remarkably earnest and evangelical phase of Anglicanism, at the end of the seventeenth century and beginning of the eighteenth, which fostered the rise of the charity schools, and in which so many of the Non-Jurors were involved. In this sense his charity was of a more modern, and of a more specifically religious, kind than that of the papist Carylls. Heavily taxed as they were, the Carylls were perhaps not wealthy enough to undertake philan-thropy on this scale, and it is perhaps also true that the Catholic gentry and nobility, where still able to live on their estates, were likely to be at once more old-fashioned and less enterprising in the ways in which they devoted money to the benefit of others.

The other two good men we have considered came from lower levels of

---

[20] The letter is not cited by Hibbard in his article. It supports his contention about Pope, while at the same time suggesting the survival of some aspects of country house practice later than Hibbard seems ready to allow.

[21] Jacob Viner, 'Man's Economic Status', in J. L. Clifford, ed. *Man Versus Society in Eighteenth-Century Britain* (Cambridge, 1968), p. 22.

society. John Kyrle, born indeed into the gentry, was the son of a lawyer and M.P. possessed of very little land or wealth. Allen's birth was humble and obscure. Yet once his fortune was secure, and he began to live as a landed gentleman, he showed a generosity towards dependants and those in need which falls into the pattern of the country house ideal. Indeed Lord Caryll's line in *Naboth's Vineyard*: 'The Poor, if strong, imploy'd; if weak, maintain'd' applies with precision to Allen's practice. Richard Jones, Allen's clerk of the works, and Pope, his distinguished literary visitor, stressed the same things:

> His private charities ... exceeded his public ones. He caused to be paid by his clerk not less than £100 per week for a considerable time ... he did not employ less than 100 men of all kinds, so that his death was a great loss to this part of the country ... The poor ... had a great loss in him. ... he kept a poor man that came out of his country to ask for work and charity, and kept him as long as he lived ... He gave money to any countryman of his that came to ask for charity ...' (Jones)[22]
>
> The Good Man ... suffers no misery near him; He actually employs on this occasion some hundreds, (all the neighbouring parishes can send him) of labouring Men, & has opened a new Quarry on purpose ... Whoever is lame, or any way disabled, he gives weekly allowances to the wife or children: Besides large supplies of other kinds to other Poor ... (Pope)[23]

Furthermore Allen conformed to the country house ideal in his hospitality: 'Mr. Allen lived in a good hospitable manner, and kept a good house; plenty was given to all comers and goers ...'[24] Allen's unusual wealth made possible, but did not account for, the extent of his 'benefactions'—Peter Walter was also unusually wealthy but certainly not unusually generous. If Allen's generosity is partly explained by the survival of the country house ideal and practice, it may also owe something to first-hand experience of comparative poverty. His special charity to 'any countryman of his' suggests that his very early experience formed a motive for his readiness to help those in need.

John Kyrle, with his five hundred pounds a year, was much less well off than Caryll, Digby and Allen. His small house in a street of the country town of Ross had not the remotest resemblance to the great houses of the other three: Ladyholt, West Grinstead, Coleshill, Sherborne and Prior Park. In some ways he lived the life rather of a prosperous yeoman than a gentleman, '... and went so very plain in his Dress, that when he work'd in the fields with his own Labourers, (which he frequently did) he was not distinguished from them by anything more than a certain Dignity ...'[25] He was not lord of any manor. He inherited no special moral responsibilities to

[22] See Ch. VII, n. 98 above.
[23] See Ch. VII, n. 99 above.
[24] See Ch. VII, n. 98 above.
[25] See Ch. I, n. 18 above.

the local community with his small and scattered pieces of land. This is probably what Pope meant when he described Kyrle as 'a private country gentleman'. Yet Kyrle's life, as we have seen, was directed more towards the public good than that of many a richer man. With very modest resources he fulfilled the values of the country house ideal. His hospitality was of a public kind: 'He kept two public Days in a Week; the Market Day, and Sunday. On the former, the Neighbouring Gentlemen and Farmers dined with him . . . On Sunday he feasted the poor people of the Parish at his House; and not only so, but would often send them home loaded with broken meat and jugs of beer.'[26] He was a friend to old, poor and infirm labourers. His legal knowledge was put at the service of the community.[27] He believed in 'good husbandry'—the making 'use' of an estate rather than striving to grow 'richer and richer' and all his planting and building activities were dedicated to use and enjoyment by the public.[28] Like many an aristocratic and wealthy landowner, he transformed a landscape by these activities. Behind everything, finally, one senses the importance of Kyrle's religion.

The life of John Kyrle does not add to the evidence for a continuity of country house practice in the early eighteenth century. Kyrle's case seems too unusual to have any representative value, but its very unusualness was partly what attracted the attention of Pope. In Kyrle Pope found a private individual, with limited resources, fulfilling the traditional obligations of those born to a more affluent and public role in life. He saw the country house ideal fulfilled—without the country house. Moreover Kyrle, of his own perhaps surprising choice, had decided to live as a kind of gentleman-yeoman in a remote country town, rather than pursue the more obvious alternative for a poor gentleman with university and legal training: a professional career. This meant that he had led a life, in Pope's words, 'obscure and . . . distant from the sphere of publick glory, this proud town'.[29] During sixty years of public crisis in London, the years which saw the Exclusion Crisis and Popish Plot, the downfall of the Catholic James II, Britain's entry into the wars with France, and the Financial Revolution, the coming of the Hanoverians, the South Sea Bubble and the rise of Walpole, all which developments Pope looked on with differing degrees of disfavour and anxiety, Kyrle was living humbly in Ross, working in his fields, feeding the poor, settling legal differences and planning his projects for the local good. Clearly Kyrle's life had a pastoral meaning for Pope, and one which involved no evasion of rural hardship. This point leads on to a final and more speculative reason why the life of Kyrle was moving and important to Pope. We have already noted the seeming remoteness of the tenantry in Pope's letter about Sherborne. Yet in the Epistle *To Bathurst*, as we have also seen, the claims of the poor are insistently stressed, and the attitude adopted to these claims is used by Pope as a moral touchstone—

[26] See Ch. I, n. 29 above.
[27] See Ch. I, n. 24 above.
[28] See Ch. I, n. 35 above.
[29] See Ch. I, n. 98 above.

> Perhaps you think the Poor might have their part?
> Bond damns the Poor, and hates them from his heart. [ll. 101–2]

If the life of the poor was humanly remote from Pope and from the aristocrats and gentry with whom he chiefly associated—and by 'humanly remote' I mean that there was no shared experience or intimate knowledge—something in him nevertheless made it impossible for him to forget or dismiss it. And here the closeness of Kyrle's life to that of the country poor ('. . . he worked in the fields with his own labourers . . .') may have struck Pope as a positive value, as a genuine human bond between classes, going beyond that which the communal hospitality of the seventeenth-century house had once sustained.

3. THE POETIC EXPRESSION

If we exclude the 1713 version of Donne's 'Satyr II', Pope's poetic pre-occupation with the country house ideal begins with his notes about Kyrle (recorded by Spence in May 1730): '. . . (public buildings, alms houses, walks, road; The Man of Ross divides the weekly bread; public table twice a week for strangers, etc.) . . .', continues with the composition and publication of the Epistle *To Burlington* (1730–1) and the Epistle *To Bathurst* (1730–3) for which the note on Kyrle was a brief draft, and concludes with the imitation of Horace *Sat.* II. ii, *To Bethel* and the later version of Donne's *Satyre II*, published in 1734 and 1735 respectively. After the notes Pope leapt at once to a major poetic expression of the ideal, unanticipated by any of his previous poems, but a clear development from the values and attitudes of the Sherborne letter. Each of the relevant passages of *To Bathurst* and *To Bethel* then gives a markedly different emphasis to the ideal, while in 'The Second Satire of Dr. John Donne' Pope returns, as we have seen, to the negative aspect.

Though the Epistle *To Burlington* was completed and published before the Epistle *To Bathurst*, its opening lines, perhaps by design, seem to assume preceding discussion of a miserly abuse of wealth such as *To Bathurst* was to provide. Coming to the poem from *To Bathurst*, as in Pope's final ordering of the Epistles, we seem at first to be confronted with a lighter, more risible and more superficial aspect of human behaviour. The dark world and desperate ironies of much of *To Bathurst* are behind us, and in an ambience of easy intimacy and leisurely superiority Pope converses with the Earl of Burlington on the absurdities of false taste. No pressing human drive or need is apparent, the subject is little more than that of aristocratic and gentlemanly pastimes, and with Burlington and the reader Pope plays the game of knowing everyone and knowing better than everyone so beautifully that it almost suggests the parade has a special purpose. The poor are nowhere to be seen.

> 'Tis strange, the Miser should his Cares employ,
> To gain those Riches he can ne'er enjoy:
> Is it less strange, the Prodigal should waste
> His wealth, to purchase what he ne'er can taste?
> Not for himself he sees, or hears, or eats;

> Artists must chuse his Pictures, Music, Meats:
> He buys for Topham, Drawings and Designs,
> For Pembroke Statues, dirty Gods, and Coins;
> Rare monkish Manuscripts for Hearne alone,
> And Books for Mead, and Butterflies for Sloane.   [ll. 1–10]

This is the dominant tone. Implicitly the voice of common sense is quietly protesting—at, for example, the collocation of 'Music' and 'Meats' and at the artistic direction of the latter as well as the former—while from time to time a sharper and more plainly moral note is heard. 'Dirty Gods' carries more than its literal meaning and, just beyond the passage quoted, 'fine Wife, alas! or finer Whore' pushes the gentlemanly exchange in the direction of moral challenge. Pope soon makes the first of a series of shifts from the negative to the positive example, as he addresses Burlington:

> You show us, Rome was glorious, not profuse,
> And pompous buildings once were things of Use.   [ll. 23–4]

The introduction of Rome appears abrupt until one remembers the occasion of the poem (Burlington's publication of 'the Antiquities of Rome by Palladio') and recalls how a concern through antiquities with the past, and a concern through building with the future, were in Pope's day equally dominated by Roman achievement. This poem, no less than Pope's earlier Epistle *To Mr. Addison*, mediates between a recognition of the glory of ancient Rome and the emulation of that glory in the present and future. But here there is to be a new and important ingredient; it is hinted at in the announcement of the principle which lay behind the country house poems of Jonson, Carew, Herrick and Marvell: the principle of use.

Other examples of false taste are now laid aside as Pope concentrates upon building and, presently, landscape gardening. If the precepts and examples which Burlington has published will all too probably 'Fill half the land with Imitating Fools' [l. 26], it will be through neglect of the particular decorum, purpose and use of different kinds of building. There is a nice complexity in the word 'vain', used to describe a church loaded with 'old Theatric state', and the implications about the builder who makes his garden gate into a triumphal arch are delightful. To build Rome anew it is not necessary to feel like a conqueror every time you enter your garden—and the line looks ahead to the first appearance of Timon:

> My Lord advances with majestic mien,
> Smit with the mighty pleasure, to be seen.   [ll. 127–8]

The implied comedy now breaks into the open with 'Proud to catch cold at a Venetian door,' [l. 36] and another movement of the poem has been completed. Pope again switches the focus of attention onto the positive example:

> Something there is more needful than Expence,
> And something previous ev'n to Taste—'tis Sense: [ll. 41–2]

This time Pope does not turn back immediately to consider the abuse of a positive principle, but dwells on the positive side of the question. The 'Sense' referred to is amplified in a discussion of how creation must be in harmony with nature not in opposition to it. There is humility in the advice 'Consult the Genius of the Place in all', and 'In all, let Nature never be forgot' [ll. 57, 50], which is entirely in keeping with Jonson's praise of Penshurst for rejecting 'enuious show' but joying in 'better markes, of soyle, of ayre,/Of wood, of water . . .' It is a kind of pride to impose a rigid or alien form upon nature; rather one should appreciate its spontaneous and irregular beauties, as Pope did in the gardens of Sherborne. At Sherborne also Pope had admired 'the tops of the Hills, which form a great Amfitheatre sloping down to the house', and here it is 'the Genius of the Place' which

> helps th' ambitious Hill the heav'n to scale,
> Or scoops in circling theatres the Vale.   [ll. 59–60]

The metaphor may come from Palladio himself, who remarked of the site of his famous Villa Rotonda that the house was 'surrounded by other charming hills—that give the effect of a huge theatre . . .'; and because this villa enjoyed 'the most lovely views on all sides' Palladio designed it in harmony with its surroundings, making loggias on each face of the building.[30] Nature is not a static situation in which to build or plant, but a living and co-operating force for those with the sense and taste to see it:

> Still follow Sense, of ev'ry Art the Soul,
> Parts answ'ring parts shall slide into a whole,
> Spontaneous beauties all around advance,
> Start ev'n from Difficulty, strike from Chance;
> Nature shall join you, Time shall make it grow
> A Work to wonder at—perhaps a STOW.   [ll. 65–70]

A transitional passage now leads Pope subtly back to the negative example. As T. R. Edwards well says, time is on the side of the man who builds and plans in harmony with nature ('Time shall make it grow'), but against those who go to great lengths to impose too grand or too limited an effect.[31] The 'Imperial Works' of Louis XIV and Nero pass from fashion and finally crumble; Villario contrives too long and exquisitely, only to prefer a field in the end; Sabinus loves trees so much that his son, mistaking reverse of wrong for right, creates the flat and depressing prospect of 'One boundless Green'. Then we are back to the themes of pride, extravagance and 'enuious show' with the opening of the celebrated narrative of the visit to Timon's Villa.

The structure and procedure of the epistle is now becoming more clear. It is an alternating procedure, by which Pope turns from the negative to the positive example and back, but amplifying more on each side as the poem

---

[30] J. S. Ackerman, *Palladio* (Harmondsworth, 1966), p. 70.

[31] T. R. Edwards Jr., *This Dark Estate: A Reading of Pope* (Berkeley and Los Angeles, 1963), p. 69.

goes on. The visit to Timon's Villa is the furthest swing of the pendulum to the negative side, just as the statement of the Augustan ideal with which the epistle is to conclude is the longest swing in the positive direction; the two present the final comprehensive statement and counter-statement of the poem. Growing more plain also, at this stage of the poem, is the heart of Pope's human subject: the country house. Almost imperceptibly his discussion of antiquarian hobbies, of Ancient and Renaissance inspiration, of building and landscape gardening, has placed the country house at the centre of his focus. The words 'At Timon's Villa' bring us face to face with what the 'Garden-gate', the 'circling theatres', Stowe, Villario and Sabinus have been moving us towards, and we realize that if, like *To Addison*, this poem treats of Roman glory and those emulous to recreate it in the present, Pope is here anxious to relate each to a full picture of the human community as it is and as it might be. This is the new ingredient which the Epistle *To Addison* lacked.

Having started in easy, conversational fashion, the poem now gathers momentum. The apparently casual associations and transitions are gone and in their place we have a relentless and systematic demonstration of the abuse of taste, wealth and sense. The earlier tone of aristocratic intimacy has been imperceptibly modified and deepened, growing in open seriousness and power, growing in mordant satirical humour. There is an added energy in the utterance:

> Greatness, with Timon, swells in such a draught
> As brings all Brobdignag before your thought.
> To compass this, his building is a Town,
> His pond an Ocean, his parterre a Down:
> Who but must laugh, the Master when he sees,
> A puny insect, shiv'ring at a breeze!
> Lo, what huge heaps of littleness around!
> The whole, a labour'd Quarry above ground. [ll. 103-10]

Greatness here is not one of the twin *Genii*, '*Goodnes* and *Greatnes*', celebrated by Herrick, but a greatness crudely equated with sheer size. The word 'draught', with its separate but allied meanings of 'a quantity drawn' and an architect's or planner's 'draft', effectively conveys this point, which is then forcefully stressed by the giant dominance and extravagance of 'Brobdignag' at the centre of the next line. Images of vast and pointless size follow on, and then, by contrast, Pope turns to something of minute dimensions: the master of all this greatness, who cannot but seem physically insignificant by comparison. And not only physically small—he is spiritually small who must perpetrate such vastness in celebration of himself. It is thus that the buildings and landscape which express Timon are 'huge heaps of littleness'. The passage concludes with a conceit which carried both contemporary and traditional associations. Pope had written of Blenheim Palace, in September 1717, 'I never saw so great a thing with so much littleness in it ... it is the most inhospitable thing imaginable ... In a word, the whole is a most expensive

absurdity; and the Duke of *Shrewsbury* gave a true character of it, when he
said, it was a great *Quarry of Stones above ground.*[32] Timon's Villa is not
particularly Blenheim, any more than it is (as used to be thought) Cannons.[33]
The significance of the conceit is rather to associate Vanbrugh's high baroque
with Pope's picture of a heavily majestic and over-elaborate building, and
to remind us that such pomp might, as Pope said in his Sherborne letter, be
'rais'd upon the Spoils of plunderd nations, or aggrandiz'd by the wealth of
the Publick.' Jonson, on the other hand, had praised Penshurst for being
'rear'd with no man's ruine, no mans grone.' Shrewsbury's remark about
Blenheim is also, as Hibbard points out, reminiscent of Marvell's lines on
Appleton House:

> Within this sober Frame expect
> Work of no Forrein *Architect*;
> That unto Caves the Quarries drew . . .

and Pope, turning from the great buildings to their owner, in the image of
the 'puny insect', was, as Maynard Mack has pertinently observed,[34] close
to the thought of Marvell when *he* asked:

> What need of all this Marble Crust
> T'impark the wanton Mote of Dust . . .
>   [*On Appleton House*, ll. 1–3, 21–2]

If Timon's Villa is crude in its sheer size, his garden is crude too in its
imposition of a rigid symmetry upon nature, whose beauty rises from irregularity, and in its absurd violation of the principles of use and fitness.
The summer-house offers no shade, and the ornamental urn of Nile is dry.
With the appearance of Timon himself, the poem rises from the descriptive
to the fully dramatic. After the triumphal advance of the dwarfed master—
Brobdingrag and Lilliput still linger in our mind—the sudden caution is
brilliant:

> But soft—by regular approach—not yet—   [l. 129]

and the theme of hospitality sacrificed to self-importance is introduced. The
principle of use is next violated in the study, and here too the dramatic manner
brings the scene before our eyes, with the lordly showman and the suffering
guest whom he has turned into a sightseer:

> To all their dated Backs he turns you round . . .   [l. 135]

'Turns you round' is wonderfully expressive of the arrogance of the man

---

[32] *Corr.*, i, p. 432 (Pope to Mrs. ——, Sept. 1717). Shrewsbury's remark seems to have been
well known (see T.E., iii–ii, Appendix C, p. 187).

[33] T.E., iii–ii, Appendix B, pp. 164–8. It has recently been suggested that it partly alludes to
Walpole's Houghton (see Maynard Mack, *The Garden and the City: Retirement and Politics in the
Later Poetry of Pope* (London, 1969), pp. 122–3).

[34] Maynard Mack, op. cit., p. 93. His whole discussion of Pope and the Country House tradition
is of great interest.

who has no concern with the response or independent volitions of his guest, and the emphatic 'dated backs' stresses the external nature of Timon's concern with books. In 'Lo some are Vellom . . .' we detect the voice of the poet in ironic commentary, and in the next line it emerges into a plain style of attack:

> For all his Lordship knows, but they are Wood.   [l. 138]

This plain speech modulates into satirical ambiguity in the ensuing account of Timon's chapel; it is perhaps the most poetically rich satire in the poem. Even 'the Chapel's silver bell', whose sound summons the reader with Timon's guests to holy matters, cannot after what follows escape the charge of wealthy ostentation. The sharpened, alliterative paradox 'Pride of Pray'r' (to which the bell in fact summons the household) achieves superb concentration, and seems to alert to their utmost the poet's and our critical faculties. Thereafter, to stare 'devoutly' at the saints of Verrio or Laguerre which 'sprawl' on the ceiling is ambiguous; it may be the devotion of religious worship, or worship of the painting, or of the fleshly delights which 'in fair expansion' the painting displayed. It is in more than one sense that these paintings 'bring all Paradise before your eye' [l. 148]. But if the paintings offend religion by their indecorum, the 'Cushion and soft Dean', one little more or less than the other, offend by over-decorum, and the plain word 'Hell' is taboo.

A more truly solemn ceremony now follows: dinner. Here the expressively vulgar word 'sprawl' in the account of the chapel is matched by the equally expressive and satirically appropriate 'spew', and the pleasures of eating are to begin. The theme of false hospitality is once again to the fore; the seventeenth-century country house poems laid stress on the importance of hospitality in the great house, and Jonson and Herrick devoted lines to the exposure of false hospitality, drawing partly on the Fifth Satire of Juvenal, which Hall had imitated in his satire against bad housekeeping.[35] All this tradition lies behind Pope's account of his dinner with Timon. No inferior food is offered him, nor does a servant stand behind to stop him eating too much; here it is the swiftness of the succession of courses which leads to starving in plenty. But the essential effect is the same. The comfort and entertainment of the guest is sacrificed to an ostentatious show. This kind of perversion pervades everything at Timon's Villa, the treatment of nature, the 'use' of library and chapel, the entertainment of guests. The feeling of satisfaction and harmony in the country house poems arises from the way in which, in the life they describe, human needs are generously fulfilled. Here the reverse is true:

> In plenty starving, tantaliz'd in state,
> And complaisantly help'd to all I hate,
> Treated, caress'd and tir'd, I take my leave,
> Sick of his civil Pride from Morn to Eve;

[35] 'To Penshvrst', ll. 61–75; 'A Panegerick to Sir Lewis Pemberton', ll. 5–36; Joseph Hall, *Virgidemiarum*, V, ii, ll. 112–50 in *The Poems of Joseph Hall*, ed. Arnold Davenport (Liverpool, 1949; reprinted 1969), pp. 82–3.

> I curse such lavish cost, and little skill,
> And swear no Day was ever past so ill.   [ll. 163–8]

The feeling of frustration and anger behind the satire, in *To Burlington*,
arises from Timon's complete indifference to these needs. The poet's rejection
of all that Timon tries to accomplish is the more forcibly expressed by the
sudden access of freedom with which the mask of the subtly ironic satirist—
'On painted Cielings you devoutly stare'—is dropped, to reveal that capacity
for plain speech which has been more briefly shown at several earlier points
in the epistle. Here it builds up through 'all I hate', 'Sick of his civil Pride',
to the body-blow of the last line, where even the pointed antithesis of the
line before is laid aside for a simpler strength. It is notable that in these lines
for the first and only time in the poem Pope exchanges the normal 'you'
(and 'us') for the first person singular: 'all *I* hate', '*I* take my leave . . .', '*I*
curse such lavish cost . . .' The moment is admirably chosen. The sense of
personal anger thus conveyed makes us feel the false hospitality the more
vividly, and adds a further dimension to the poem. We have come a long
way from the easily superior tone of the opening, and it seems probable that
Pope deliberately accentuated that tone for the sake of the contrast that was
to follow.

The true climax of the epistle, and its most humanly impressive moment,
is however still to come. After the round condemnation with which the
Timon passage ends, and the personal anger with which it has been informed,
the most easy and obvious sequence would have been an immediate swinging
back of the poem to a splendid and uncompromising idealism, in which
anger and the highest moral values could have been most satisfyingly—too
satisfyingly—joined. Instead, with a striking change of moral viewpoint,
Pope starts to make points in favour of Timon:

> Yet hence the Poor are cloath'd, the Hungry fed;
> Health to himself, and to his Infants bread
> The Lab'rer bears: What his hard Heart denies,
> His charitable Vanity supplies.   [ll. 169–72]

If the focus of attention widened between the opening lines of the epistle
and the end of the account of Timon's Villa, it has widened still further
here. For the first time we become aware of people who can neither offer
nor suffer hospitality of Timon's kind. In consideration of the poor and
hungry, of the labourer and his family, what looked as if it would be an easy,
final, and sweeping condemnation of Timon and all his works suddenly
becomes difficult. Of course it is better that wealth should support need
directly through kindness rather than indirectly through vanity, as Pope will
soon argue, but, the world being what it is, can society do without its Timons?
This is the train of thought which halts the confident momentum of the
preceding passage, which emerges in the uneasily stopped and pausing movement of the four lines following, and which causes the poet to put aside,
though not repudiate, his earlier contempt and anger. These lines have been

the target of severe criticism. F. W. Bateson likens their thought to the 'Private Vices, Public Benefits' paradox of Mandeville, which is 'much more cogently argued', and Hibbard finds them facile, arguing that 'There is something lacking in the moralist who assumes that the very vice he is attacking has its place in the proper working of things.'[36] Each assumes that cogent argument and a simple and consistent morality would have made the poem more admirable at this point, and indeed it may be thought that a good satirist should appear supremely confident throughout. Yet for Pope to have fulfilled these demands would have been in fact the easier alternative, and would have ignored his human problem. As it is, either Pope is here directly expressing something of his own conflict, or the subtly changing *persona* which is the 'poet' of the epistle is so dramatized by Pope that a mood of conflict and hesitation succeeds a mood of anger, as *that* has succeeded the initial mood of easy confidence. Pope gains maximum dramatic effect for this hesitancy by allowing it to follow, not one of his balanced and judicious passages, but a passage of anger and forcible repudiation. In a footnote Pope invokes 'Providence' to reconcile his dual attitude to Timon, but it is clear that through these troubled lines (the 'cogent' arguments of Mandeville would have been quite inappropriate) Pope is recognizing the claims of a wider community than could have joined him and Burlington in their justifiable condemnation of Timon's garden, house and hospitality. He is not content to be enclosed within a *milieu* in which bad taste and bad manners (however clearly traced to arrogance and pride) can be proposed as the absolute evil. He must break out into a wider view, however external his conception of 'the Poor' and 'the Hungry' may be, and however much this may arrest the momentum of his anger, and postpone the final statement of his positive ideal. In the end these lines add to the dramatic variety and the human complexity of the epistle, not impairing it but enriching it artistically.

However it is equally plain from what follows that Pope will not allow his humane recognition of the two sides of Timon's vanity to compromise his own ultimate ideal. If, in the present, one hesitates to recommend the sweeping away of an unsatisfactory compromise lest it may be replaced by a worse, one may still in consistency conceive and work for a better future. Vanity and extravagance are not the only or the most obvious way of having wealth serve the wider community. Pope's sense of a happier and more natural future is poetically·given in the next paragraph:

> Another age shall see the golden Ear
> Imbrown the Slope, and nod on the Parterre,
> Deep Harvests bury all his pride has plann'd,
> And laughing Ceres re-assume the land. [ll. 173–6]

The difference in movement between these four lines and the four preceding is remarkable. With the phrase 'Another age' the doubts and qualifications clear away, and a buoyant, connected, forward-moving rhythm takes over

---

[36] T.E., iii–ii, p. 153; G. R. Hibbard, art. cit., p. 174.

the poem. This rhythm becomes one with the visual richness of the first two lines, whose 'golden' and 'brown' make almost simultaneous our sense that this is a vision of a both useful and beautiful future; the corn is grown for food (thus, more directly, are the hungry fed) but the vision of golden harvests clothing the landscape is, like the 'chest-nut tree, great-rooted blossomer' in Yeats's 'Among Schoolchildren', an image of something at once natural and perfect. The phrase 'Deep Harvests' gathers up what has gone before into a developed image of richness and strength, against which the word 'plan' seems particularly pale and feeble, while 'laughing Ceres' brings that sense of quick life, spontaneity and joy which contrasts so completely with the heavy house and inert symmetries through which Timon sought to express his own importance. And as R. A. Brower well observes, 'in using a phrase that echoes the *laeta seges* of the *Georgics*, Pope reminds us that his vision of nature and art and society has a great historical model.'[37]

With the words 'Another age' the expected swing back of the focus of attention to the positive example has begun. The visionary glow of this passage is succeeded by lines of sententious compliment to Burlington and Bathurst (''Tis Use alone that sanctifies Expence . . .' [l. 179]) and the epistle settles down, in more tranquil and practical manner, to saluting what in Pope's society comes closest to the positive values he has expressed: the use of wealth to work in harmony with nature for the good of man. This is the country house, not as a showpiece, but as the centre of a community as Jonson, Carew, Marvell and Herrick saw it:

> His Father's Acres who enjoys in peace,
> Or makes his Neighbours glad, if he encrease;
> Whose chearful Tenants bless their yearly toil,
> Yet to their Lord owe more than to the soil;
> Whose ample Lawns are not asham'd to feed
> The milky heifer and deserving steed;
> Whose rising Forests, not for pride or show,
> But future Buildings, future Navies grow:
> Let his plantations stretch from down to down,
> First shade a Country, and then raise a Town.   [ll. 181–90]

These lines arise from Pope's awareness of a continuous tradition. They are backward-looking, and would have expressed to his satisfaction the fundamental social values of Jonson, early in the seventeenth century. They are very close to the country house ideal of Lord Caryll in his Character of Naboth, late in the seventeenth century. They look also to Pope's own lifetime. They arise from Pope's conviction of the economic, moral and social importance of 'those fine old Seats of which there are Numbers scatterd over England' (the Sherborne letter) and the way in which particular good men of his acquaintance seemed to use their country houses to lead an altruistic life. His praise of the Carylls' housekeeping at Ladyholt and West Grinstead, his

[37] R. A. Brower, *Alexander Pope: The Poetry of Allusion* (Oxford, 1959), pp. 250–1.

praise of Lord Digby's life on his estate at Sherborne, later his praise of Allen's wise and open-hearted way of life at Prior Park, all help to form the significant background to this part of *To Burlington*. Here the poetry arises from contemporary social practice and experience. Finally, the passage looks to the future. There is nothing nostalgic or sentimental about the writing, no tender attempt to protect something which has passed or is passing away. The mood is forward-looking and confident, with the emphasis on 'rising Forests', 'future Buildings', 'future Navies'. In addition the country house ideal as expressed here seems to offer something more than, for example, the relationship described by Herrick in 'The Hock-cart'. For Lord Caryll to write: 'The Poor, if strong, imploy'd; if weak, maintain'd', for Pope to write: 'Yet to their Lord owe more than to the soil' and for him to praise Allen for employing more labourers than he had need of, is to pay tribute to somewhat higher practice than that of:

Feed him ye must, whose food fills you.

It is notable, finally, how this passage of Pope's poem conveys a sense of life and growth. The creativeness which it describes works through time rather than against it. In this respect it is interesting to compare the letter which Lord Caryll wrote from exile to his brother Richard, in 1694. I do not want to suggest causal connections: but rather to illustrate the general correspondence which is to be found between the expression of an ideal in Pope's social poetry and a practical letter concerning country house affairs:

As for my self, considering my age ... I can intertain no reasonable hopes ... of seeing my friends again at home ... All our ioy and confort heer is in our Nursery, which is as thriving and promising as can be wisht; & the pleasure of it is to me like that which you take in the young trees planted at Ladyholt, which probably your sone & g. children may see come to perfection ... I am extremely glad that my sister is throughly reconciled to Ladyholt upon so good a motive, as her inioying better health then formerly; since Hartg. is like to be the Mansion of the family heerafter, I would not have it want any thing for health and convenience, that so the owners of it may love home, wherby Estates & familys are best preservd. I can not think the old house will be much lived in, but yet I would not have it drop down in my time for old acquaintance sake ...[38]

Caryll's plans are not the plans of pride. They take into account decay, death and disappointment, but see beyond to rebirth and new growth: young trees, young children, and the continuance of a family, its house, and its estate. Caryll's attitude to the country house he knows he will never see again is also unpretentious and practical. It is worth the money to make sure that Ladyholt wants nothing—not 'for pride or show', but 'for health and convenience'. Caryll's attitude to Ladyholt, and Pope's to the country house in *To Burlington*, appear to rise from identical values. A suggestive relationship between poetry and social history is here plainly established.

[38] See Ch. II, n. 45 above.

We have been tracing the development of the two major themes in the Epistle *To Burlington*: what may be called the Roman theme, and the country house theme. They express two separable but not necessarily conflicting ideals. After the climax of: 'Yet hence the Poor are cloath'd . . .,' the latter theme has received its fullest positive expression in the poem, as the first part of that final swing away to the positive example with which Pope will conclude. The Roman theme, which has been kept in suspense for some time though we sense it behind the vision of the golden harvests which will re-assume the land in the future, is now brought to its own full and final development. With the paragraph beginning

> You too proceed! make falling Arts your care,   [l. 191]

the country house ideal merges into the Roman ideal, as a smaller river flows into a greater, and Pope's concern with houses and estates expands into a concern with the country, indeed with civilization, as a whole. This passage will be more fully examined in the final chapter; here it is sufficient to note how it completes that alternating swing of the attention from the negative to the positive example and back, which is the characteristic procedure and form of the epistle, and completes also that steady expansion of view through the poem, which pinpoints, for example, 'Books for Mead, and Butterflies for Sloane' at the beginning, and yet encompasses 'Imperial Works' and obedient rivers rolling through the land at the end.

The Epistle *To Bathurst*, as we have seen, is a poem predominantly con-cerned with the abuse of wealth, and the corrupting effect of this abuse on man and society. Unlike *To Burlington*, *To Bathurst* deals with both City and country. Corruption is by no means confined to the City, and in the des-cription of Old Cotta's inhospitable hall we are given the negative aspect of the country house ideal. Nowhere in *To Bathurst* is there an example of City probity or benevolence. Instead there are brief tributes to the 'better part' of the Earls of Bathurst and Oxford, who are in the social and economic position of Timon in *To Burlington*, while possessing the sense, taste and charity which he lacked—*and* there is the portrait of the Man of Ross. The account of John Kyrle and his life is thus the only extended positive example of the right use of wealth in this very long epistle. This very disproportion, an important aspect of the structure of the work, is a statement about the world. A great moral and artistic weight may be seen to rest upon the portrait. Much significance for an understanding of Pope's pattern of values as a whole is to be attributed to the kind of ideal that he here advances, and, in addition, it is particularly vital for Pope that the passage should be a convincing artistic success. In Chapter I this passage was examined in relation to that body of information about Kyrle which is likely to have been available to Pope; it was found to be factually true to a high degree. In this sense Pope's is indeed an 'honest Muse'[39] and the air of regaling his reader with some plain in-

---

[39] See Rachel's Trickett's judicious study, *The Honest Muse* (Oxford, 1967), pp. 201–2.

formation, part of the artistic approach of the passage, is perfectly justified on non-artistic grounds.

> But all our praises why should Lords engross?
> Rise, honest Muse! and sing the MAN of ROSS:
> Pleas'd Vaga echoes thro' her winding bounds,
> And rapid Severn hoarse applause resounds.
> Who hung with woods yon mountain's sultry brow?
> From the dry rock who bade the waters flow?
> Not to the skies in useless columns tost,
> Or in proud falls magnificently lost,
> But clear and artless, pouring thro' the plain
> Health to the sick, and solace to the swain.
> Whose Cause-way parts the vale with shady rows?
> Whose Seats the weary Traveller repose?
> Who taught that heav'n-directed spire to rise?
> The MAN of ROSS, each lisping babe replies.
> Behold the Market-place with poor o'erspread!
> The MAN of ROSS divides the weekly bread:
> Behold yon Alms-house, neat, but void of state,
> Where Age and Want sit smiling at the gate:
> Him portion'd maids, apprentic'd orphans blest,
> The young who labour, and the old who rest.
> Is any sick? the MAN of ROSS relieves,
> Prescribes, attends, the med'cine makes, and gives.
> Is there a variance? enter but his door,
> Balk'd are the Courts, and contest is no more.
> Despairing Quacks with curses fled the place,
> And vile Attornies, now an useless race.
> 'Thrice happy man! enabled to pursue
> 'What all so wish, but want the pow'r to do!
> 'Oh say, what sums that gen'rous hand supply?
> 'What mines, to swell that boundless charity?'
> Of Debts, and Taxes, Wife and Children clear,
> This man possest—five hundred pounds a year.
> Blush, Grandeur, blush! proud Courts, withdraw your blaze!
> Ye little Stars! hide your diminish'd rays.   [ll. 249–82]

Kyrle and the scene of his works fulfill the country house ideal as it is expressed in *To Burlington*. His works change the terrain without denying nature; they draw out the resources of nature for the benefit of man. His trees offer both beauty and shade, and his fountain is no mere showpiece but a thing of use. He is a constant helper of the labouring poor, and of all needy, whether young or old. Like Lord Caryll's Naboth he is a peacemaker. He is at the centre of the community that he serves. As Brower says, 'he plays the familiar role in Pope of the idealized country gentleman who is a landscape improver and a patron of the poor.'[40] It is a measure of the central importance Pope found in the country house ideal that he should have given it this lonely prominence in the poem. But equally clearly, this is the country-house ideal with a difference. In the first place there is the ostentatiously announced fact of Kyrle's modest wealth. Even without this there are less conspicuous features of the passage which would qualify any conventional notion of a seventeenth or eighteenth-century country gentleman. 'Enter but his door' suggests a very easy access; 'divides the weekly bread' seems to indicate a regular personal participation in feeding the poor; and with the line: 'Prescribes, attends, the med'cine makes, and gives' we see that Kyrle is being praised for actively ministering to the needy in a way which was nowhere specified in *To Burlington*. Kyrle does play the role of the idealized country gentleman, but in a special way. He seems more humble, more directly active, in much closer touch with those he helps. Pope may see the market-place with poor o'erspread, but Kryle, we infer, sees it full of the people he knows. Perhaps this is why Brower's phrase 'patron of the poor' is not quite sensitive to the picture Pope is offering us. We are shown the country house ideal, not only without the country house, but without some of those less tangible distinctions which separated the gentry from the poor. *To Bathurst* is a poem of extremes; if it explores the depths of corruption the positive example it displays must be of a contrastingly high kind. With fewer resources than a Bathurst, Burlington or Oxford, Kyrle's altruism transcends theirs in single-minded personal activity and direct knowledge.

Nevertheless it would be wrong to argue that the surmounting of a class barrier is a major feature of Kyrle's life as Pope depicts it. The few details we have noted in Pope's lines suggest that he was aware of this aspect of Kyrle's life, but for the poet they are details in an essentially religious picture, whose familiar outlines effectively prevent us from thinking long about John Kyrle in terms of the structure of society. It is E. R. Wasserman who has pointed out the biblical and Christian overtones of the portrait: 'Who hung with woods . . .' with its very lofty language suggests the remote analogue of divine creation; 'From the dry rock who bad the waters flow?' recalls more distinctly Moses striking water out of the rock. The two extremes which Kyrle's fountain in the Prospect avoided, ostentatious waste by being thrown up or cast down, are religiously evocative: 'proud falls' of the fall of Lucifer, 'useless columns' of a temple unworthy of the God. Being, instead, 'clear and artless, pouring thro' the plain' is in fact the golden mean, the end of which is the benefit of man: 'Health to the sick, and solace to the swain.' Attention is focused upon the church spire whose rise is not useless since it is 'Heav'n-directed' and summons man to thoughts of God. Kyrle feeds the hungry, helps the poor, heals the sick, and banishes 'vile Attornies' (such as Peter Walter) by being a peacemaker. Kyrle's life is thus made to seem markedly Christlike, and it is through the mouths of children that his good works are recognized. Here Wasserman has compared the effect of Kyrle's life to Christ's

---

[40] Brower, op. cit., p. 258.

casting the money-changers and merchants out of the temple and being acclaimed as 'son of David' by the children: 'Out of the mouth of babes and sucklings thou hast perfected praise.'[41] Kyrle's love of his fellow men has been so presented that his surmounting of class division is subsumed in the presentation of something like Christian perfection.

In his portrait of the Man of Ross, therefore, Pope gives us the country house ideal, accommodated to a lower station in society and more limited means than have usually been associated with it, modified so as to suggest some genuine contact once again between gentleman and poor, and suffused with a more explicitly Christian spirit than was to be found in *To Burlington*.

The chief artistic challenge for Pope, in the shaping of his information about Kyrle, was perhaps the problem of how to blend religious suggestiveness with an account which retained its air of the convincingly factual. This was largely solved by the basic decision to portray Kyrle through the scene of his works. As noted earlier, the passage is really divided between a distant prospect of Ross—the town in a wider landscape—and a closer view of Kyrle's charity, in the market-place itself. It is this which gives the passage much of its development and unity. But, through the landscape, and the diction, Pope is able delicately to echo, for example, God's creation of nature, and Moses (often glossed as an antetype of Christ) striking water from the rock. To have stated that this 'Private Country Gentleman' was godlike would have been incongruous and crude. Instead Pope unostentatiously intimates that there is a certain harmony between Kyrle's life and the great doctrines of the Christian religion. The same is true of the more faintly heard resonances in the description of the fountain—'proud falls' and 'useless columns'—which quietly place Kyrle between the extremes of satanic rebellion and false worship. Equally delicate are the implications of the children acknowledging Kyrle's goodness, and the spire which seems to sum up the nature of his life as it serenely dominates the scene. It is thus in a subtle fashion that Pope at first permeates the portrait with a religious and Christian spirit. When, however, we are taken closer in to the scene of Kyrle's charitable activities, the Christian parallels become firmer and more factual: Kyrle's feeding the hungry, healing the sick, and reconciling of disputes are not delicate intimations in the background but bold strokes in the foreground. And here we must recognize the sureness of Pope's instinct in keeping the portrait so firmly particular, and fixing our attention again and again on practical problems and practical actions:

> Him portion'd maids, apprentic'd orphans blest . . .

Brower has spoken of 'the Goldsmithian tenderness' and 'too idyllic quality of the scene' but it must be said that Pope evades much of the danger in describing an entirely good man, a scene filled with human kindness, by his practical and factual emphasis.[42] The 'honest Muse', concerned with the

---

[41] E. R. Wasserman, ed. *Pope's Epistle to Bathurst* (Baltimore, 1960), pp. 41–2; Matthew 21: 12–16.

[42] Brower, op. cit., p. 258.

business of living in this world, is in obvious control in every part; the poetry does not evaporate into vague praise or pale abstraction.[43] And if indeed we feel 'the precariousness of the [Kyrle's] achievement in the actual England Pope knew',[44] this is exactly what the design of the whole epistle, with its enormous imbalance between the broad domain of corruption and the narrow domain of love, is designed to convey. 'Precarious, but not impractical,' Pope seems to be saying, 'goodness in harmony with heaven, but issuing in acts which are effective in the everyday world.' And yet for all this Pope does not entirely escape the common fault; his poetic conveying of complete goodness does not hold the interest throughout as it should. It is not perhaps that Kyrle is too good, but that the list of his acts of charity, varied though it is in tone and level, still becomes predictable before it concludes. The limitation of portraying a man entirely through his works also makes itself felt here; some sense of Kyrle as a person in the quick of life—

> To all their dated Backs he turns you round—
> [*To Burlington*, l. 135]

might perhaps have given the portrait that final degree of human and verbal life which it lacks. Certain other failings also make themselves felt. Pope surely builds up too ostentatiously to his final revelation of the relative modesty of Kyrle's fortune ('Oh say, what sums that gen'rous hand supply?/What mines . . .?'). The 'honest Muse' producing five hundred pounds a year from her conjuror's hat is perhaps slightly tedious and absurd. The other, more serious fault, is literary and human, and very much part of the conventional assumptions of Pope's age. Gallant though Pope is in his persistent stress on the importance of the claims of the poor—plainly and rightly he can't forget them—still his treatment of them will not do. The ineptness of the phrase 'with poor o'erspread' has been noted; it is almost as though the collective poor were an object, a special drape for the market-place on busy days.[45] It is a sad slip, resulting all too obviously from the mental and verbal habit of thinking all the time of 'the poor' instead, as Swift might have said, of 'John, Peter, Thomas and so forth'.[46] At another point Pope's handling of personification is unhappy in an even more revealing way. 'Where Age and Want sit smiling at the gate' seems odd because the kind of satisfaction must be different in each case. For Age to smile if it has been made happy is natural enough, but what can it mean to say that *Want* does the same? This is not a mere surface-illogicality; surely it unintentionally betrays the fact that (for Pope) Want remains Want for all Kyrle's kindness. Individual acts of charity may indeed mitigate hardship but will never, in Pope's view, make the poor anything other than the poor. Society can never change. And of course it is not at all surprising to find Pope making this assumption; the

[43] Trickett, op. cit., pp. 1–2.
[44] Brower, op. cit., p. 258.
[45] Ibid., p. 258.
[46] *The Correspondence of Jonathan Swift*, ed. Harold Williams (Oxford, 1963–5), iii, p. 103 (Swift to Pope, 29 Sept. 1725).

criticism here is that, momentarily, the language claims more than it or the Man of Ross can perform.

But this is almost to accuse the epistle of not having been written a hundred years later. Our experience of *To Bathurst*, underlined by reading the whole poem in its social and economic context, arises from the sense it yields of a rare encounter with this serenely creative practical life: rare, yet central, both in Pope's creed and the structure of the poem. Pope was himself quite deliberate about the expressive balances and imbalances which compose this structure and consequent reading-experience. 'To send you any of the particular verses', he wrote to Tonson, in thanking him for information about Kyrle, 'will be much to the prejudice of the whole; which if it has any beauty, derives it from the manner in which it is *placed*, and the *contrast* (as the painters call it) in which it stands, with the pompous figures of famous, or rich, or high-born men.'[47] To read the poem in context is to recognize the pervasiveness of its concern with the new City capitalism, and the connections of this (through the South Sea and Mississippi experiences) with individual and national corruption. It is this which unites the long opening series of allusions leading up to the apostrophe to Blunt, and this which, in a symmetry both formal and meaningful, has its destructive energies finally displayed in the tale of Sir Balaam, that perfectly unified and frighteningly comprehensive short story, in which the narrative momentum, become one with the speed of corruption, hurries the poem to its end. One of the dominant contrasts of the epistle is, then, that between the metropolitan setting of the dark opening and closing sequences and the rural/urban setting of the central picture of the life of Kyrle. This contrast is, however, mediated by others, heightening the expressive symmetries of a long, potentially shapeless, poem. Thus the balancing and contrasting portraits of Old and Young Cotta, introducing the theme of the country house society whose values are to be seen fulfilled in Kyrle, mediate between the opening sequence and the centre of the work, with the more admirable Young Cotta significantly closer to that centre. The later pair of contrasting portraits, Villiers and Cutler, reversing the miser-spendthrift sequence of the Cottas with spendthrift-miser, places the more sympathetic figure closer to Kyrle, and that which conveys the most bleak spiritual sterility (Cutler) closer to Sir Balaam. This artistry of placing and contrasting provides moral gradations for the reader as he proceeds through the poem, and lends to its copious detail, and conversational and rhetorical verve, a series of crucial human focuses, an almost architectural structure ordering the dark confusion of its subject.

If the country house ideal was accommodated to modest means and a less than noble station in life in the Man of Ross portrait, in *To Bethel* (1734) it is accommodated to Pope's personal circumstances. The country house ideal is here united with Pope's poetic autobiography. *To Bethel* is at once a poem which grew out of Pope's correspondence (and doubtless his conversation) with the old friend to whom it is addressed, and an imitation of the Second

[47] *Corr.*, iii, pp. 290–1 (Pope to Tonson, 7 June 1732).

Satire of the Second Book of Horace. It praises a life of simplicity, temperance and retirement, and towards the end once more affirms the principle of Use. As early as 1723 Pope had, in a letter to Bethel, expressed the view that for most men there was little pleasure or advantage to be got from wit, learning or high birth, but 'Humanity and sociable virtues are what every creature wants every day, and still wants more the longer he lives, and most the very moment he dies. It is ill travelling either in a ditch or on a terras; we should walk in the common way, where others are continually passing on the same level . . .' (He continues, in a lighter vein, to recommend the *Odyssey* to Bethel, on his travels).[48] These humane and unassuming virtues are the qualities which Pope praises in his friend. Four years later Pope wrote to Bethel: 'I know the world too well, not to value you; who are an example of acting, living and thinking, above it, and contrary to it.'[49] Pope is here concerned with defining a humble, firm and independent attitude towards the delusions and excesses of life; pragmatically, from thinking about and writing to his friend, he finds it in 'the common way', the middle path, the Aristotelian and Horatian mean, recommended by Horace in the poem Pope was to imitate and address to Bethel. In writing to Bethel, Pope often reverted to the themes and metaphors of travelling and of being at home. During the Summer of 1726, when he was entertaining Swift and his friends, Pope wrote:

> For tho' my house is like the house of a Patriarch of old, standing by the highway side and receiving all travellers, nevertheless I seldom go to bed without the reflection, that one's chief business is to be really at home: and I agree with you in your opinion of company, amusements, and all the silly things which mankind wou'd fain make pleasures of, when in truth they are labour and sorrow.

Speaking, at the end of the same letter, of the death of a friend, Pope concluded:

> . . . a good mind rewards its own sufferings. I hope to trouble you as little as possible, if it be my fate to go before you. I am of old Ennius his mind, *Nemo me decoret lachrymis*—I am but a *Lodger* here: this is not an abiding City. I am only to stay out my lease, for what has Perpetuity and mortal man to do with each other? But I could be glad you would take up with an Inn at Twitenham, as long as I am Host of it: if not, I would take up freely with any Inn of yours.—Adieu, dear Sir . . .[50]

These themes—hospitality, being really at home, fortitude in the face of change and the certainty of death, the insignificance of ownership since in life itself one is but a lodger staying a night on a journey, and back to hospitality

---

[48] *Corr.*, vol. ii, p. 179 (Pope to Bethel, 12 July 1723). A brief discussion of Pope and Bethel will be found in Pat Rogers, 'Pope and the Social Scene', in Peter Dixon, ed. *Alexander Pope* (London, 1972), pp. 120–6.

[49] *Corr.*, ii, p. 436 (Pope to Bethel, 24 June 1727).

[50] Ibid., pp. 386–7 (Pope to Bethel, 9 Aug. 1726).

again—are also the themes of *To Bethel*. That Pope was aware of the potential link between his actual letters and the evolution of his epistles is perhaps suggested by the fact that in 1728 Pope asked Bethel if he would return the letters which have been quoted above.[51] In the same letter Pope compliments his friend through a gastronomic metaphor (and an echo of Rochester) which also anticipate the poem: 'My confidence in your good opinion ... is the chief cordial drop I taste, amidst the Insipid, the Disagreeable, the Cloying, or the Dead-sweet, which are the common draughts of life.' This brings us to the topic of food, about which much is to be said in *To Bethel*. Bethel was a great advocate of plain fare, and in this he had Pope's approval. But Pope was also a gourmet and often intemperate at table.[52] He and Bethel had too many friends in common for this to remain a secret, and a mischievous passage in a letter from William Kent to the Earl of Burlington suggests that the paradox in Pope was a source of mutual amusement:

> my service to mr Bethell and tell him his friend Pope is the greatest Glutton I know, he now talk of the many good things he can make, he told me of a soupe that must be seven hours a making he dine'd with mr Murry & Lady betty & was very drunk last sunday night he says if he [Bethel] comes to town he'll teach him how to live & leave of his rosted apples & water . . .[53]

In addressing an imitation of the Second Satire of the Second Book of Horace to Bethel Pope undoubtedly chose a poem through which a number of his and his friend's common preoccupations could be expressed. At the same time he changed Horace in a significant way. The countryman and farmer, Ofellus, who had once owned his own land but who now led the same simple life on rented acres, is the foundation of Horace's poem. The greater part is an account by Horace of this man's blunt and simple wisdom, leading to a conclusion in which Ofellus himself expresses the fortitude with which he now regards the loss of his property and the inevitable mutability of human affairs. The shift from paraphrase to direct speech gives a dramatic culmination to the poem. In substituting Hugh Bethel for Ofellus Pope put a gentleman in place of a peasant farmer. This may suggest that he thus erected a barrier between himself and the kind of experience which made up the life of *Ofellus rusticus* in Horace. In fact, however, much of Horace's poem is devoted to an attack on gastronomic luxury, and he has not used the opportunity given him by his central character to convey that rich sense of a working country life that is expressed by Virgil in the *Georgics*. Since the poem denounces the excesses of the rich with some knowledge and authority, Horace may have been observing a propriety in making this longer portion of the poem a *paraphrase* of Ofellus's views. The direct speech at the end shows no such inside knowledge of the habits of the rich. Of all who figure

[51] Ibid., p. 501 (Pope to Bethel, 17 June 1728). It is of course just possible that Pope revised these letters, unpublished until 1737, in the light of his poem; Pope is our only authority for them.
[52] T.E., iv, p. 65, n. 137.
[53] Corr., iv, p. 150 (Kent to the Earl of Burlington, 28 Nov. 1738). This was four years after the publication of *To Bethel*, which gave Kent greater opportunity for teasing.

in Pope's poems and letters, John Kyrle (had Pope been personally acquainted with him) would have been the best Ofellus to Pope's Horace. As it is, Pope does not lose much by pressing Bethel into his poetic service. And in fact this decision is consistent with the other main alteration of Horace which Pope makes: the assigning of the first and longer part of the satire to the direct speech of Bethel, who though he lived plainly was well acquainted with luxury; and the making over to himself of the impressive closing speech.

The satire is couched in a rougher style than is customary in Pope, appropriate to *Ofellus rusticus* perhaps, possibly also a reflection of the blunt speech of Bethel.

> By what *Criterion* do ye eat, d'ye think,
> If this is priz'd for *sweetness*, that for *stink*?
> When the tir'd Glutton labours thro' a Treat,
> He finds no relish in the sweetest Meat;
> He calls for something bitter, something sour,
> And the rich feast concludes extremely poor:
> Cheap eggs, and herbs, and olives still we see,
> Thus much is left of old Simplicity!   [ll. 29–36]

This is very much the characteristic manner and theme. It is the general sense of Horace, and equally the Pope and Bethel of the *Correspondence*. As in the *Correspondence* and Horace the middle way is commended: 'Between Excess and Famine lies a mean' [l. 47], Bethel declares, and:

> He knows to live, who keeps the middle state,
> And neither leans on this side, nor on that:
> Nor stops, for one bad Cork, his Butler's pay . . .   [ll. 61–3]

It must be noted that in the mouth of Bethel 'the middle state' takes on something more of a class meaning (neither nobleman, nor labourer, but landed gentleman—neither terrace, nor ditch, but the common way) than it has from Ofellus, and the last line quoted, which is more Pope's than Horace's, confirms the *ambience*. As the satire proceeds the theme of change and decay comes to the fore, and Pope picks up the echo of Rochester (from *Artemisia to Cloe*, [ll. 44–5]) which we noted in the *Correspondence*:

> For fainting Age what cordial drop remains,
> If our intemp'rate Youth the Vessel drains?   [ll. 89–90]

In all this the satire touches on the country house ideal in that it attacks ostentatious luxury and self-indulgence. Towards the end of Bethel's discourse the right use of wealth is touched on, and 'Imperial Works' ('Make Keys, build Bridges, or repair White-hall'—l. 120) commended.

There was a good practical reason why Pope chose to take the *persona* of Ofellus over from Bethel at the end of the satire. Pope might not be a peasant farmer, but like Ofellus he had once lived on his own (or at least his father's) land while now his house and land was rented and the property of

others. He was personally concerned with the relation between use and
possession, as Ofellus and Horace had been, but as Bethel was not. There
is now a change from the rough to a softer tone as Pope speaks on his own
part:

> Thus Bethel spoke, who always speaks his thought,
> And always thinks the very thing he ought:
> His equal mind I copy what I can,
> And as I love, would imitate the Man.
> In *South-sea* days not happier, when surmis'd
> The Lord of thousands, than if now *Excis'd*;
> In Forest planted by a Father's hand,
> Than in five acres now of rented land.
> Content with little, I can piddle here
> On Broccoli and mutton, round the year;
> But ancient friends, (tho' poor, or out of play)
> That touch my Bell, I cannot turn away.
> 'Tis true, no Turbots dignify my boards,
> But gudgeons, flounders, what my Thames affords.
> To Hounslow-heath I point, and Bansted-down,
> Thence comes your mutton, and these chicks my own:
> From you old wallnut-tree a show'r shall fall;
> And grapes, long-lingring on my only wall,
> And figs, from standard and Espalier join:
> The dev'l is in you if you cannot dine:
> Then chearful healths (your Mistress shall have place)
> And, what's more rare, a Poet shall say *Grace*.
> Fortune not much of humbling me can boast;
> Tho' double-tax'd, how little have I lost?
> My Life's amusements have been just the same,
> Before, and after Standing Armies came.
> My lands are sold, my Father's house is gone;
> I'll hire another's, is not that my own,
> And yours my friends? thro' whose free-opening gate
> None comes too early, none departs too late;
> (For I, who hold sage Homer's rule the best,
> Welcome the coming, speed the going guest.)   [ll. 129–60]

In the opening the balance of the lines enacts that of Bethel's and Pope's
resolution. Speaking is in equipoise with thinking, to Bethel; the line weighs
up the two with its medial pause. The unpausing forward-movement of the
next line parallels his determination; and his 'equal mind'—the 'ballance of
things' within the individual personality—causes the equation of imitation
and love in Pope, and helps sustain the strong middle-point between the
fantasies of extravagant and irresponsible gain (the South Sea Bubble) and
fears of an arbitrary and crippling tax (the Tory view of Walpole's Excise
scheme). It is the perceiving, but not indifferent, equanimity which preserves

a quality of life whether in an inherited country house or five rented acres. It is temperance in the original and best sense of the term. This virtue Pope struggles to fulfill in himself, no ideal person, and in no ideal world. The candid references to South Sea year, in which the nation including Pope had indulged itself, and to the hated contemporary measure of the man who had risen to power through South Sea year, make it plain that the scene with which poem will end is far from the 'white Town' of Kyrle, or another, future age of golden harvests. We are presented with a man inheriting from Horace, Jonson, Carew and others a long tradition concerning country living, hospitality and the right use of wealth, and attempting to live in accordance with it so far as possible in (Brower's words) 'the actual England Pope knew'. There is a very amused humility in the diction and sound of 'Content with little, I can piddle here', and a very pleasing sense of the everyday in the line following. The faint air of apology as Pope speaks of his own hospitality ('But ancient friends . . ./. . . I cannot turn away') seems to glance back at Bethel's 'opinion of company, amusements, and all the silly things which mankind wou'd fain make pleasures of' in the *Correspondence*; Pope endows this 'company' with a sense of loyalty and pleasure. In the following lines we are given that sense of a humanized nature which was found in 'To Penshvrst', and which contrasts with the distortions of nature's offerings which the luxury-hunters of the earlier part of *To Bethel* produce. It is nature seen neither in a wide landscape, nor an estate, but a garden. Here grapes, nuts and figs are cultivated; the nearby Thames supplies the homely-named gudgeons and flounders, Hounslow Heath and Banstead Down provide mutton. The success of this passage lies in the fact that these simple, everyday circumstances, the homely details and the familiar English names, are palpably as much part of the real world, 'the actual England Pope knew', as the South Sea scandal and the Excise Scheme. Here simple and balanced human needs can be met: hunger satisfied, friendships sustained—and a poet says Grace. (This last detail most delicately touches in the sense of religion; it is a less marked pointer than Kyrle's spire, but central all the same.) In a modest way, that same sense of a community recognized by hospitable acts, notable in the country house poems, is found here. It is thus very naturally that Pope can ask: 'how little have I lost?' and revert once again to the absence of those paternal acres—

> My lands are sold, my Father's house is gone—

which have traditionally been the economic and moral basis of the country house ideal. This ideal, as we have seen in Jonson, Carew and in the Epistle *To Burlington*, rested on the principle of Use. This now coincides with the Roman right of *ususfructus*, as alluded to by Ofellus:

> Nunc ager Umbreni sub nomine, nuper Ofelli
> Dictus, erit nulli proprius; sed cedet in usum
> Nunc mihi, nunc alii.   [Horace, *Satires* II. ii. 133–5]

Pope can fulfill the essential values of his life without the right of *dominium*, possession, so long as 'the Use be mine', and even honour that remote but distinct connection between domestic eighteenth-century England and the considerate hospitality of Menelaus in the *Odyssey*, who revered 'the golden Mean', and whose words he quotes.[54]

Pope's allusion to the *Odyssey* (it is not in Horace) is perhaps a bow to Bethel's interest in his translation of the poem, and also suggestively takes up the theme of travelling from his letters to Bethel.[55] In the letter of 9 Aug. 1726, quoted above, Pope had first described his own house as standing on the highway side receiving travellers. At the end of the same letter Pope himself is imaged as a traveller and his house an inn. When he writes: 'I am but a *lodger* here: this is not an abiding city . . .', a declaration which this passage of *To Bethel* surely recalls, he is quoting Thomas à Kempis ('Hic non habes manentem civitatem; extraneus es et pregrinus . . .'—we are strangers and pilgrims in this world; property is no more than an inn or lodging).[56] Spiritually and physically, life may be seen as a journey to a far country and a journey home. The quotation from Menelaus's words to Telemachus evokes the journeying homeward of both Telemachus and Odysseus in our minds, and sets the hospitality of Pope in his rented house in a suddenly longer and more spiritual perspective. Homer, Horace, and Thomas à Kempis link up here in a delicate web of classical and Christian allusion, though some of the Christian undertones are hardly divined without knowledge of the relevant letter to Bethel.[57] That they are a consistent part of Pope's thinking about landed property, however, is suggested by the fact that in a later imitation of Horace on this same theme Pope echoes quite clearly the same passage of the same letter to Bethel.[58]

Throughout this passage a kind of inner debate about use *versus* possession has been going on; twice Pope has declared how little he has lost and in this we see Pope's deployment of his *persona* to suggest an arguing down of the conventional view, to present someone in process of convincing himself and the reader at the same time. This small dramatic evolution reaches a further stage when the conventional view that possession is better than mere use is bluntly introduced through another *persona*, that of Swift:

> 'I wish to God this house had been your own . . .'   [l. 162]

This gives Pope the opportunity to rebut the view once again, this time by arguing against an external opponent, and the presumption is now clear that the speaker has at least convinced himself. Perhaps he convinces us also, as the poem returns to the theme of mutability which it has evoked several times

---

[54] Horace, *Opera*, Interpretatione, Notis & Indice illustravit Lodovicus Desprez (Amsterdam, 1695), p. 637. (Pope possessed a copy of this edition, purchased and inscribed by him in 1707, now preserved in the library of Hartelebury Castle, Worcester. *The Odyssey*, in Pope's translation, Bk. XV, ll. 75–84; T.E., x, pp. 72–3.

[55] *Corr.*, ii, p. 179 (Pope to Bethel, 12 July 1723).

[56] Thomas à Kempis, *De Imitatio Christi*, Bk. II, i, 3–4.

[57] Published in 1737.

[58] *The Second Epistle of the Second Book of Horace, Imitated*, ll. 246–9; T.E., iv, p. 183. Cf. *Corr.*, ii, p. 387 (Pope to Bethel, 9 Aug. 1726). See H. H. Erskine-Hill, ed. Pope, *Horatian Satires and Epistles* (Oxford, 1964), p. 161.

earlier, and in the *ambience* of intimate discussion that starkly simple question is asked ('What's *Property?* dear Swift! you see it alter . . .' [l. 167]) in the tone of one who has got to the bottom of his case. In rather weary melancholy the concluding lines rehearse the changes and chances of the world of affairs. The familiarly significant references to Peter Walter, 'to a Scriv'ner or a City Knight', with the contrast between a 'booby Lord' of the present and Lord Bacon from the past, sketch a dark future for men like John Caryll and William Digby, who lived on their inherited estates and tried to make their country houses the fount of benefits for the surrounding community. In the face of political change, of changes between different generations, and changes in the social ownership of land and wealth, the individual can only strive to be master of himself, and within the limits of his power hold firmly to his principles.

It may be asked at this point whether the Horatian ideal of Stoic retirement is not a different thing from the country house ideal as expressed in 'To Penshvrst' and *To Burlington?* How proper is it to include *To Bethel* in a discussion of Pope and the country house ideal? The answer, I think, is that these two traditions are not mutually exclusive. One only has to read Jonson's *The praises of a Countrie life* (Horace, Epode 2) and then his country house poem 'To Sir Robert Wroth' to see that the Horatian tradition is a powerful presence in the relevant English writings. What makes the English country house ideal partly different is the change of stress from personal hospitality to public 'housekeeping', and the underlying assumption of a neo-feudal structure of society in which the lord of the manor and his house are the centre of the local community and of a pattern of inter-dependent relationships between people of different kinds. The country house ideal is more public, the Horatian more private. What we find in practice, certainly what we find in Pope, is two overlapping concepts, with the emphasis falling now on one, now on the other. In *To Burlington*, clearly, the chief emphasis is the public one; Pope is talking about lord and tenants and the use of landed wealth for community and country. Yet 'His Father's Acres who enjoys in peace . . .' —this could be the first line of a purely Horatian poem in praise of country retirement. In *To Bethel*, on the other hand, the chief emphasis is on how the individual in a private situation should live. Yet '. . . whose free-opening gate/None comes too early, none departs too late;'—this gives a quite public feel to Pope's hospitality to his friends, and we recall the phrase to Bethel ('. . . my house . . . standing by the highway side and receiving all travellers . . .') which lies behind it. The Man of Ross portrait, in *To Bathurst*, comes mid-way between the more public and the more private emphasis; John Kyrle is presented as a man of private means, of no inherited public responsibility, yet fulfilling the country house ideal through public acts. This indicates a continuity of attitude on Pope's part, and shows that *To Bethel*, for all its difference of emphasis, is an organic part of those values and attitudes in Pope's work which we have been examining in this chapter. The order in which we have considered these three positive affirmations of an ideal—*To Burlington, To Bathurst, To Bethel*—has been chronological, and this suggests a development of a rather different kind from the one we traced in the previous chapter. There our exploration moved outwards from particular references— in some cases unchronologically—to Pope's most comprehensive poetic statements. Here, having recognized a tradition and its social continuity, we have traced a development from the statement of a widely comprehensive ideal, capable of a high degree of practical fulfilment, through an exceptional and even saintly example of how much a man can do with little, to a more modest, limited, and privately practicable ideal. In this development we find an attempt by Pope to bring a public ideal and his private practice into relation with one another. Concerned in many ways with the projection of himself, through *personae*, into his poetry, Pope is in this instance anxious to show that, within his limited means, he practises what he preaches. He lacked the wealth and power of a Burlington and a Bathurst, and he lacked the simple, early Christian virtue of Kyrle, though like Kyrle's his whole life might be seen as an attempt to bring the great out of the small. With the ideal as exemplified by Ofellus, however, Pope could without pride or incongruity profess some degree of identification; the Horatian poem represented the extent to which he personally could fulfill the country house ethic which he admired.

X. Imperial Works

1. ROMAN WORK

'ROMAN-WORK; for few such things have been made since', was William Digby's comment on the two aquaducts he saw in 1683 near Blois.[1] The casual remark is widely representative. It expresses a Renaissance sense of the architectural achievement of Rome, and bears witness to the constant impressiveness of its visible relics. Thus Palladio had written, in the Preface to *I Quattro Libri dell' Architettura* (1570), that since 'the antient *Romans*, had not only greatly surpassed those who are to come after them in the several *Arts*, but also in *Building*, I took *Vitruvius* as my Master . . .' and '. . . sought out for all such *Ruins* of antient *Edifices*, as have resisted the waste of Time . . .'[2]

This note is not heard in the expression of the country house ideal, whether we are thinking of poems or letters. The creativeness of the country house tradition was felt to reside within continuity rather than restoration, and to comprise the satisfaction of natural and social needs through a daily and seasonal pattern. The poems treat building as a major theme, but their characteristic stress, excepting Appleton House only, is on the virtue of a house long-built—sufficiently long-built that it has become assimilated into the 'use' of its way of life, and may be contrasted with the 'enuious show' of the newly built. The country house poem participates in that backward-idealizing habit which, as Raymond Williams points out, seems a perennial characteristic of writing about the country; the poems in effect idealize the origins of the houses by being able to ignore the circumstances of their building.[3] Many houses, after all, must once have been regarded as 'enuious show' and been raised by some man's groan; but, in the idealizing view of the poems at least, good use has through long continuity naturalized and domesticated them. It is entirely in keeping with the country house tradition that Lord Caryll could write about not letting his old house in Harting drop down in his time,

---

[1] See Ch. V, n. 3 above.
[2] *Andrea Palladio's Five Orders of Architecture Translated and Revised by Colen Campbell* (London, 1729), Preface, n.p.; *I Quattro Libri Dell' Architettvra Di Andrea Palladio* (Venice, 1570), Preface, n.p.
[3] Raymond Williams, *The Country and the City* (London, 1973), see especially pp. 40–1.

for old acquaintance sake; and Pope could write with approval that Lord
Digby was 'better amus'd' than to carry out much architectural improvement
at Sherborne.

Digby's comment about the Roman aquaducts at Blois is an example of
the registering of a greater challenge than anything the country house and
landed gentry tradition could so far provide—a challenge residing in the
Roman heritage of Renaissance Europe. New building, on a Roman scale,
might be a conspicuous but not ostentatious creative assertion, and might
serve the public in different ways, also, from that of the mansion of the landed
aristocrat or gentleman. Widespread architectural renewal was a conceivable
and indeed powerfully attractive ideal in seventeenth-century England, and
while there were obvious differences between Inigo Jones's Palladianism and
Wren's Baroque, both contributed to an increasingly conspicuous and radical
transformation of English building into classical forms—a transformation
which received strong impetus from the rebuilding in London after the Great
Fire. Furthermore, architecture is never merely a matter of style. New architectural forms are new social forms, at the very least new social symbols.
Those who looked to Vitruvius found at the opening of his treatise acknowledgement of Augustus's equal concern with adding new provinces to the state and
with expressing the majesty of the empire through the dignity of new public
building. Vitruvius stressed, too, the contribution of all the humane arts
and disciplines to architecture.[4] Following Vitruvius, seventeenth-century
writers about architecture, for example Sir Henry Wotton and John Evelyn,
were much aware of architecture as a social form,[5] while the continuation of
such thinking into the earlier eighteenth century is most tellingly evidenced
by Berkeley's Essay Towards Preventing the Ruin of Great Britain. In his
Epistle To Mr. Congreve (1693) Dryden used the architectural forms of the
Doric and Corinthian columns as metaphor both for literary construction
and, through the web of association pervading that complex and important
poem, for civilization itself.[6] Thus in the new age of English building, beginning
in the eighteenth century with the work of Colen Campbell and the Earl of
Burlington, architectural renewal, albeit seen principally in villas and country
houses, constantly intimated the possibility of a radical renewal of civilization,
of 'Imperial Works'.[7]

It is unnecessary to detail the stages of this new age of building—the second
wave of Palladianism in England—nor is this the place to explore in full
Pope's imaginative involvement with it, as social critic and poet. But it is

[4] M. Vitruvii Pollionis De Architectvra, Bk. I, Ch. I; (Venice, 1567), pp. 2–3; Bk. II, Ch. I,
p. 50; Bk. I, Ch. I, pp. 3, 6.
[5] Sir Henry Wotton, The Elements of Architecture (London, 1624), n.p. Pope was familiar with
Wotton's treatise (Spence, 617). For crucial instances of Evelyn's view, see Roland Freart, A
Parallel of the Antient Architecture with the Modern . . . [Translated]. By John Evelyn (London,
1664), n.p. I am indebted to Mr. R. G. Knowles for this reference.
[6] For Berkeley's Essay, see Ch. VI, n. 117 above; Dryden, To my Dear Friend Mr. Congreve,
ll. 1–19.
[7] John Summerson, Architecture in Britain 1530–1830 (Harmondsworth, 1953; 4th. revised
and enlarged edn. 1963), p. 197.

worth noting that Pope, writing to Robert Digby on 1 Sept. 1724, could talk of the columns of 'the Fabrick of Friendship';[8] and that for Pope the connections which Berkeley had already suggested between public probity and the activity of building had a peculiar imaginative force. It is then interesting to look back at the six lives presented in this book, and to reflect that neither Walter nor Blunt showed interest in building. But as early as 1700 Kyrle, 'passionately fond of Architecture', had completed the building of his 'Prospect' in remote Ross-on-Wye, and by 1730 Pope, probably through Bathurst or Oxford, themselves enthusiastic builders, had heard of his public works. Digby subscribed to *Vitruvius Britannicus* and Leoni's translation of Palladio's *I Quattro Libri* in 1715, and though he might be 'better amus'd' than to execute the portico for his house at Sherborne which the poet sketched, still he was responsible for the 'beautiful Altar-piece of Architecture' in the abbey, and designed the 'neat Chappel for the use of the Towns-people', both of which Pope praised. But of all these men, Allen is the figure of real importance in the new wave of architectural enterprize. Palladian taste reached him early, through his friend and patron General Wade, and in his consistent support of John Wood he supported an architect of great skill and enormous ambition. Wood not only built a great Palladian country house, as Campbell and others had done, but conceived the re-shaping of a whole city in unified architectural sequences of breathtaking scale and beauty: Queen Square, the 'Forum' of the Parades, and the Circus whose use of a plan deriving from the Colosseum to bring a series of town-houses into a formal yet subtle relationship perhaps epitomizes the Augustan ideal in eighteenth-century England. The Circus by Wood the Elder, and the Crescent by his son, were the high-water mark of the new age of building; the transmutation of Bath was far enough advanced in Pope's lifetime for him to appreciate what was being done, though neither he nor Allen lived to see its completion.

Ralph Allen's Bath shows, in terms of actual achievement, the take-off point of the country house ideal for the Roman ideal of 'Imperial Works' and a public civilization. This is one way of saying that lives of public probity and benevolence, lives like those of Kyrle, Caryll, Digby and Allen, were the columns of such a fabric, and that the social reality of the country house concept, imperfect and declining though it might be, was the necessary experiential basis from which Pope could feel his way into a wider idealism. We have already compared *To Burlington* with the earlier *To Addison*. If the prospect of a 'happy Britain' at the end of the later poem were to possess a greater inner vitality than the end of the earlier poem, be further removed from bookish hyperbole, then Roman and country house values had to be imperceptibly intertwined in the earlier sequences of the epistle, and the ascent from the ideal within present practice ('His Father's Acres who enjoys in peace . . .') to a greater ideal within a future prospect ('You too proceed . . .') had to be made a convincing evolution. The energy which the epistle has already generated through an immediacy of presented experience and a dramatic dialectic of procedure is ready to be released in the final paragraph.

[8] *Corr.*, ii, p. 253.

2. RESTORATION

When Pope brings his Epistle *To Burlington* to a conclusion by extending the country house ideal into the Roman ideal of great public works, architecture has for him the comprehensive meaning which Dryden gave it in the Epistle *To Congreve*, and the excitement which Pope experienced through involvement in a new age of building:[9]

> You too proceed! make falling Arts your care,
> Erect new wonders, and the old repair,
> Jones and Palladio to themselves restore,
> And be whate'er Vitruvius was before:
> Till Kings call forth th'Ideas of your mind,
> Proud to accomplish what such hands design'd,
> Bid Harbors open, public Ways extend,
> Bid Temples, worthier of the God, ascend;
> Bid the broad Arch the dang'rous Flood contain,
> The Mole projected break the roaring Main;
> Back to his bounds their subject Sea command,
> And roll obedient Rivers thro' the Land;
> These Honours, Peace to happy Britain brings,
> These are Imperial Works, and worthy Kings.　　[ll. 191–204]

From the end of the description of Timon's villa the epistle has evolved into a series of movements from the present to the future, from statement to prophecy. 'Yet hence the Poor are cloath'd . . .' proceeds to 'Another age . . .' and 'His Father's Acres who enjoys in peace' turns naturally to 'future Buildings, future Navies . . .'. So in the final passage the strong imperatives stretch into the future: 'proceed', 'erect', 'repair', 'restore', 'be', 'Bid' (three times repeated) and '. . . command'. The whole passage is orientated imperiously to the future, and yet pays honour to the paradox at the heart of the concept of the Renaissance, in active reverence for the past. To care for the past is to care for the future; hence the poised and balanced antitheses of the first two lines:

> . . . Erect new wonders, and the old repair.

The imperative 'Erect' gains drama, and means rather more than 'build', by contrast with 'falling Arts' in the previous line, since falling arts, and buildings in decay, are marks of a civilization in decline. At the same time what is so satisfying about this line is the sense of practical power which it conveys; 'new wonders' defy experience and understanding, but the phrase, with all its suggestiveness, is symmetrically flanked by the two commanding verbs which begin and end the line, and which retain the full force of their literal and practical meaning: build and repair, something that a skilful man can do. The next two lines give the genealogy of the English Palladian movement:

---

[9] See, eg. *Corr.*, ii, pp. 23–4 (Pope to Jervas, 12 Dec. ?1720), p. 44 (Pope to Robert Digby, 1 May 1720).

the two Renaissance figures with the Roman Vitruvius behind them, the three
bridging the Dark Ages, the periodic possibility of which has already been
hinted at in the phrase 'falling arts'. '. . . *to themselves* restore' (my Italics)
conveys the necessary selfless effort of historical imagination, and with the
verb we encounter a key-word in Renaissance consciousness. The full force
of 'restore' in the context of a discussion of Palladio may be gathered from
Campbell's Preface to his *Vitruvius Britannicus*:

> We must, in Justice, acknowledge very great Obligations to those
> Restorers of *Architecture*, which the Fifteenth and Sixteenth *Centuries*,
> produced in Italy. Bramante, *Barbaro, Sansovino, Sangallo, Michael
> Angelo, Raphael Urbin, Julio Romano, Serglio, Labaco, Scamozzi*, and
> many others, who have greatly help'd to raise this Noble Art from the
> Ruins of Barbarity. But above all, the great *Palladio*, who has exceeded all
> that were gone before him, and surpass'd his Cotemporaries, whose in-
> ingenious Labours will eclipse many and rival most of the Ancients. And
> indeed, this excellent Architect seems to have arrived at a *Ne plus ultra*
> of his Art . . . With him the great Manner and exquisite Taste of Building
> is lost; for the *Italians* can no more relish the Antique Simplicity, but are
> entirely employed in capricious Ornaments, which must at last end in the
> *Gothick*.[10]

Pope is praising Burlington for his re-affirming and re-enacting of the Renaissance programme; as the architects of fifteenth and sixteenth-century Italy
had been 'Restorers' of ancient architecture, so now the restorers Palladio
and Jones must be restored by Burlington. In addition, Campbell makes
explicit the consequences of failure which Pope touches on when he speaks
of 'falling arts'. There could not be a clearer statement than this from Campbell
of the cyclical view of the arts, and of civilization, widely held in the eighteenth
century as in earlier times. In the same way Vasari, in the Preface to his
Le Vite De Piu Eccelenti Pittori . . . (1550), had written how 'a small beginning leads to the highest elevation, and how from so noble a situation it
is possible to fall to utterest ruin', drawing the analogy of the youth, maturity
and age of the human body.[11] Once the peak of maturity and perfection has
been recognized, according to such a view, man can only resist a new barbarism
by repeatedly drawing back to that standard. For Campbell, and undoubtedly
for Burlington and Pope, this standard is Palladio, and it is to resist the decline
into a new dark age that Pope bids Burlington

> Jones and Palladio to themselves restore,
> And be whate'er Vitruvius was before: [ll. 193-4]

The naming of Vitruvius, as we have seen, places the standard of Palladio by
that of the architecture of the Roman Augustan Age. With this in mind, it

[10] Colen Campbell, *Vitruvius Britannicus, Or The British Architect* . . . (London, 1715), i, n.p.

[11] Georgio Vasari, *The Lives of the Painters, Sculptors and Architects*, tr. A. B. Hinds, ed. William
Gaunt (London, 1963), i, p. 18; *Le Vite De Piu Eccellenti Architetti, Pittori, et Sculptori Italiani*
. . . (Florence, 1550), p. 124.

may be right to see the latinism with which the passage opens: 'You too proceed!' as a deliberate echo of the 'tuque dum procedis . . .' of the Second Ode
of Horace's Fourth Book, for that ode is an invitation to celebrate the return
to Rome of the Emperor Augustus.

Where then is the new Augustus? Vitruvius and Horace had their man;
Dryden and Evelyn thought they had theirs in Charles II. For Dryden architecture expressed civilization itself, including an harmonious polity. Pope
recognizes present failure in the same line as he expresses hope for the future:

> *Till* Kings call forth th'Idea's of your mind . . . (my Italics)

and Burlington is set, as a man of lofty imperial vision, above the contemporary
Hanoverian monarchy. Pope's note confirms the point, for after observing
that he turns now to the 'proper objects of Magnificence . . . those great and
public works which become a Prince', he launches into a long list of contemporary architectural abuses and failures, starting with the subsequent
fate of what might be termed the final 'fixt intention for Magnificence' of a
British monarch, the act of Queen Anne for fifty new churches. And for
almost every positive command in the remainder of the poem there is a negative
equivalent in the note. In the verse Pope only criticises by implication, abstains
from satire, and with a forward-looking strength creates the poetic embodiment
of his ideal. The line in which Pope speaks of kings is now splendidly completed by the next; it is notable how they convey the complete nature of
Burlington's creative activity, how 'th'Ideas of your mind' is carried forward
into 'what such hands design'd', where once again the sense of real practical
skill balances and fulfills the concepts of the imagination. Burlington was not
just a nobleman 'with a Taste' but an architect.[12] And now Pope displays
architecture in its most fundamental role. As he does so we notice a change
in the relation between nature and the works of man from what Pope has
been saying earlier in the epistle. Hitherto he has advocated a sensitive co-
operation with the effects of nature—'Consult the Genius of the Place . . .'
and his advice has been in keeping with a precept in Wotton's *Elements of
Architecture*: 'For as Fabriques should be *regular*, so Gardens should be
irregular, or at least cast into a very wilde *Regularitie*.'[13] In the last lines of
the poem, however, nature appears not as a creative force to be consulted, or
as 'a modest fair' to be decently dressed, not over-dressed, but as a destructive
force which man must tame. This is because the poem now deals not merely
with the building of gentlemanly or aristocratic villas, which presupposes an
existing social order, but of works which make social orders possible through
releasing man from the dominion of nature. Pope is harking back to the
original Vitruvian contrast between men living in woods and caves in savage
state, and *humanitas*, a state of civilization. This is perhaps the point which
Warburton made on Pope's behalf about these lines: '. . . the wonders of
Architecture ought first to be bestowed on the public . . . and when the

---

[12] Summerson, *Architecture in Britain*, ed. cit., pp. 198, 368.
[13] Wotton, op. cit., p. 109.

public has been properly accommodated and adorned, then, and not till then, the works of private *Magnificence* may take place. This was the order observed by those two great Empires, from whom we received all we have of this polite art.'[14] Pope, no less than Evelyn and Dryden, sensed a precariousness in such civilization that Britain enjoyed; his descriptions of broken columns, deserted temples, desecrated graves and obscured memorials, in *Windsor Forest* and *To Addison*, were not mere gestures, and some of the contemporary details which he kept out of his poem but put in his note: new churches sinking in marshland, crooked deals leading to incompetent construction, the Dagenham Breach, which caused the flooding of thousands of acres, the failure to open public roads and build necessary bridges, though small things in themselves, all spoke to Pope of corruption, of fundamental fears. Against these fears stands the strength of the lines of his own poetry:

> Bid the broad Arch the dang'rous Flood contain,
> The Mole projected break the roaring Main;
> Back to his bounds their subject Sea command,
> And roll obedient Rivers thro' the Land;   [ll. 199–202]

There is a kind of creative resolution in the lines. The order which they celebrate, and which they evince, is not mechanical but a strenuous mastery, a meeting of force with force. Nothing expresses this better than Pope's various placing of the verbs; no less than Dryden in his Epistle *To Congreve* does he make his verse enact the thing he describes. The 'dang'rous Flood' is placed in the centre of the first line while the verbal force of the syntax— 'Bid . . . contain'—reaches across it; the focus of the second line follows the mole out into the sea, and the verb is placed centrally at the point where artifice and nature encounter. The pushing of the verb to the end of the third line, and opening the fourth line with a verb, has in itself a symmetry in variety, and, it may be felt, expresses ease after the difficulty of control.

Pope concludes with an unmistakable allusion to Dryden's version of the *Aeneid*, Book VI, in which Anchises foretells to Aeneas the destiny of Rome:

> Let others better mold the running Mass
> Of Mettals, and inform the breathing Brass;
> And soften into Flesh a Marble Face:
> Plead better at the Bar; describe the Skies,
> And when the Stars descend, and when they rise.
> But, *Rome*, 'tis thine alone, with awful sway,   ⎫
> To rule Mankind; and make the World obey;   ⎬
> Disposing Peace and War, thy own Majestick Way.   ⎭
> To tame the Proud, the fetter'd Slave to free;
> These are Imperial Arts, and worthy thee.   [ll. 1168–77]

Pope's line: 'These are Imperial Works, and worthy Kings' joins with 'You

---

[14] *The Works of Alexander Pope Esq.*, ed. William Warburton (London, 1751), iii, p. 291 (commentary on ll. 179–200).

too proceed !', and the naming of Vitruvius, to confirm the specifically Augustan associations of the ideal which are here expressed. If the echo of the Second Ode of Horace's Fourth Book is deliberate, as seems likely, the work of Burlington is associated with a *poem* to welcome the true Augustan ruler; while the allusion in the last line associates it with the *political* achievement of empire. Architecture thus remains a metaphor for civilization itself, and only with the final line, which expands the metaphor to encompass a political order of many nations, is that steady expansion of viewpoint, which we have seen evolving through the epistle, completed. Its completion effects, among other things, the final moral 'placing' of contemporary monarchy, confirming the critical implication of 'Till Kings call forth . . .' with an added irony of understatement, since the imperial is surely more than just worthy of the royal.

In the most successful poems of Pope, it may be seen that the shaping of individual couplets, and of those sequences of couplets forming larger syntactical or rhetorical patterns, is related to the total design of the work. There is a sense in which Pope's labour with words was towards the formation of 'Imperial Works' and to trace the architectural analogy is to display not only how in all probability he often thought about his art, but also how his larger literary structures have as much expressive form as his smaller ones. The line we have noted: 'Erect new wonders, and the old repair' has, as shown, an expressive symmetry, but this is not just a local effect, since awareness of ancient achievement and sense of present possibility together form, in the most fundamental sense, the situation of the poem, and pervade every part of it. The line is indeed highly articulated, but its particular union of theme and form harmonizes with the whole. When we consider the Epistle *To Burlington*, as a whole, this twofold balance is present in its design, for, as we saw in the last chapter, the characteristic procedure and form of the epistle is an alternating swing of the attention from negative to positive precept and example, in which each turn is more deliberate and sustained, and through which our sense of engaged seriousness deepens as the viewpoint upon human life widens. The procedure is surely a triumph in the way it takes the easy, colloquial turn of the Horatian middle style and gradually structures it so that the long, lively and dramatic account of Timon's Villa (too often the prey of the anthologist) is formally balanced, and in the vision of the poem superseded, by the powerfully stated prophetic idealism of the end. Both these two parts of the whole, highly articulated, statement and counter-statement, are necessary to one another and to the total design. The ordering of parts in the whole is not easily or mechanically done; they 'stand out' and are just compelled into that final symmetry so expressive of man's consciousness, divided between the certain present imperfection and the possible future ideal.

To read through the poetry and correspondence of Pope is to recognize that for him, more than for the generality of men, it was necessary to be able to admire—in the modern sense of this word. He had an enthusiastic moral nature, an unusually intense moral sensibility, which led him to find around him, if he could, examples of kindness, integrity, public spirit and resolution. It was by such examples that he plotted the moral map of his world, which became, through the shaping spirit of his imagination, the world of his social poems. In his need to admire lies the origin both of his satiric art and his art of praise. The society in which he lived, despite radical limitations and the disappointments it had in store even for a traditional idealist, yielded him the examples he needed, even in the last years of his life when he, in common with many others, felt a darkness gathering over the life of the land. The possibility of thinking about society in a comprehensive moral way offered itself only in terms of a slowly disappearing paternalistic social structure, yet from this Pope was able to derive values and viewpoint capable of serious poetic expansion. When Pope singled out the Man of Ross 'to distinguish real and solid worth from showish and plausible expense', when he called Caryll 'the best man in England' and, years later, Allen 'the Most Noble Man of England', and when he praised Lord Digby for preserving the 'Integrity of ancient Nobility', he was recognizing examples in the social reality of his time, deriving positive values from those good though of course mixed and imperfect lives, which formed and fed the moral energy of his verse. It is this moral energy which informs the quiet but firm harmonies of the end of *To Bethel*, Pope's accommodation of his own life to his social values, and this which powers the comprehensive ideal prospect of a future Britain with which the Epistle *To Burlington* concludes.

Bibliography of Primary Sources

1. MANUSCRIPT SOURCES
(Separate references have been divided from each other by semicolons. Where necessary a proper name has been added in square brackets after a reference, or series of references, to indicate the relevance of the source.)

Allen, Michael, Esq.
Ralph Allen to Mrs. Buckeridge, 29 Nov. 1735
William Pitt to Ralph Allen, June 1757
(both included among MSS. in the Bicentenary Exhibition, *Ralph Allen and His Circle*, Bath Art Gallery, 27 June to 18 July 1964)

Bath Reference Library
'The Friendship of Pope the Poet and Allen the Postmaster . . .' (compilation of documents made by A. M. Broadley in 1910); BB (B 827.55)
MS. A.L. 385
MS. 1103 Class No. 927.36 (Allen's Will and Codicils)
'The Life of Richard Jones' (*c.* 1776); B 926
MS. A.L. 1502 (photocopy of Allen's Letterbook of Instructions to Surveyors, 1729–40, in the G.P.O. Archives)
(Photocopies of Contracts and Reports concerning Allen, in the G.P.O. Archives)

Birmingham Reference Library
Digby 'B' Collection: 78–82; 83c; 137; 146–7; 153/1; 153/3–5; 153/8; 153/30; 159; 161–3; 173.

Bodleian Library
MS. Smith. 49 [Digby]

British Museum
Add. MSS. 8880 [Walter]
Add. MSS. 9828, f. 8 [Kyrle]
Add. MSS. 15936, f. 258 Add. MSS. 25494, f. 4 [Blunt]

Add. MSS. 28224; 28226–31; 28237; 28240–1; 28244; 28250–3; 28618; 34635; 36125   [Caryll]
Add. MSS. 32695; 33064–5   [Walter]
Add. MSS. 32729, f. 291; 32732; 32875; 32900   [Allen]
Add. Charters 13610   [Kyrle]
Egerton MSS. 1950 (Pope's *Brutus* MS.)
Egerton MSS. 1952   [Allen]
Egerton MSS. 2540   [Digby]
Stowe MSS. 186   [Caryll]

Buckinghamshire Record Office
D/MH 35; 35/3; 39; 39/3; 39/6   [Walter]

City of London, Guildhall Library
MS. 4069/2 (Wardmote Inquest Book for Cornhill)   [Blunt]

Digby, Miss Fiona
Letters of John, Robert and Edward Digby to Lord Digby, *c.* 1710–25.

Dorset Record Office
796   [Walter]
KG 2732–4; 2746A; 2752   [Digby and Walter]
KG 1475; 2624; 2690; 2709; 2721; 2726; 2728; 2739; 2749   [Digby]

General Post Office Archives
General Accounts, vol. i (1701–10); vol. ii (1711–20)   [Allen]
(See also items in Bath Reference Library cited above)

Greater London Record Office (Middlesex Records)
ACC. 446/M20; 446/EF/8/2–8; 446/ED/363; 634/70; MJ/SBB. 819/45; MJ/OC 2/107d   [Walter]

Hereford City Library
L.C. (Deeds), 908; 929.2 (Rudhall and Westfaling Papers), item 34; 1020; 4164; 7071; 7465; 7498–9 10,718
Hopton Collection (Deeds), 77
The Parish Register of Ross   [Kyrle]

Hertfordshire Record Office
Gorhambury MSS. IX. C. 4; IX. C. 9a–b; IX. C. 136 [Walter's personal account book]; XI. C. 38   [Walter]

St. Bartholomew's Hospital Archives
Ha 1/11 [St. Bartholomew's Hospital Journal, 1734–8]
Ha 19/7/29; 19/10; 19/29/6; 19/29/9; 19/29/12; 19/29/14; 19/29/19; 19/30/7; 19/31/19; 19/31/21   [Allen]

Somerset House, Principal Probate Registry: Literary Department
The Will of Sir John Blunt

Somerset Record Office
Walker Heneage MSS. DD/WH h 550   [Walter]

Staffordshire Record Office
D(W) 1734/2/5/1s; 1734/3/1/16   [Walter]
D 603 (Chiefly correspondence between Walter and the Earl of Uxbridge, 1714–40, and associated letters)

Victoria and Albert Museum
48.g.4/19#446 (Forster) [Pope to Caryll the younger, 1 March 1712/13]

Warwickshire Record Office
MI 167/7 (microfilm of Warwickshire portions of the Muniments of the Compton Family, item 1091 in the *Catalogue of the Muniments of the Compton Family preserved at Castle Ashby* by I. H. Jeyes, 1921.
H2/152a (Account Book of Coleshill Free School, 1693–1836)   [Digby]

2. PRINTED SOURCES

Allen, Ralph, *Ralph Allen's Own Narrative*, ed. A. E. Hopkins (London, 1961)

Alumni Oxonienses, Early Series, 1550–1714, ed. Joseph Foster (Oxford, 1891–2)

Anon., *The Compleat English Copyholder: Or, A Guide to Lords of Manors . . . By a Gentleman of the Inner Temple* (London, 1735)

Anon., *The Particular and Inventory of Sir John Blunt*, in *The Case of the South Sea Directors* (London, 1721)

Anon., *A True Account of the Payments made by Mr. John Blunt into the Exchequer on his Receipt of the Class Lottery* (London, 1712)

Anon., *Publick Spirit Illustrated in the Life and Designs of Thomas Bray* (London, 1746)

Berkeley, George, Bishop of Cloyne, *Works*, ed. A. A. Luce and T. E. Jessop (London, 1948–57)

Blunt, Sir John, Bt., *The True State of the South Sea Scheme* (London, 1722)

Boyer, Abel, *The Political State* (London, 1713–40)

Bray, Thomas, *A Brief Account of the Life of the Reverend Mr. John Rawlet* (London, 1728)

Bunyan, John, *The Pilgrim's Progress*, ed. J. B. Wharey, 2nd. edn. revised by Roger Sharrock (Oxford, 1960)

Burn, Richard, *The Justice of the Peace and Parish Officer* (London, 1755)

Burnet, Gilbert, Bishop of Salisbury, *History of His Own Time*, ed. M. J. Routh, 2nd. edn. (London, 1833)

Burrows, Montagu, ed., *Oxford Historical Society Collectanea*, 2nd. Series (Oxford, 1890)

Calendar of Treasury Papers, 1702–7

Campbell, Colen, *Vitruvius Britannicus, Or The British Architect* (London, 1715–25)

Carew, Thomas, *Poems*, ed. Rhodes Dunlap (Oxford, 1949)

Caryll, John, first Baron Caryll, *The English Princess; Or, The Death of Richard III* (London, 1666)

——, *Sir Salamon Single: or The Cautious Coxcombe* (London, 1671)

——, 'The Hypocrite' (1678), first published in Dryden's *Miscellany Poems* (Fourth Part); *Poems on Affairs of State*, vol. ii, ed. E. F. Mengel, Jr. (New Haven, 1965)

——, *Naboth's Vineyard: Or, The Innocent Traytor* . . . (London, 1679)

——, 'Briseis to Achilles', published in *Ovid's Epistles Translated by Several Hands* (London, 1680)

——, 'Eclogue I' [of Virgil] published in Dryden's *Miscellany Poems* (First Part) (London, 1684)

Chandler, Mary, *Poems on Several Occasions* (London, 1734)

Clarke, J. S., ed., *The Life of King James II . . . Collected Out of the Memoirs Writ of His Own Hand* (London, 1816)

Cobbett, James, *Parliamentary History of England* . . . (London, 1806–20)

Journals of the House of Commons, vol. ix (1667–87)

House of Commons: *Private Acts*, 1–5 George I, 1714–19

——, 32 George II, 1758–9

Dalton, J. N., ed., *The Manuscripts of St. George's·Chapel, Windsor Castle* (Windsor, 1957)

D'Anvers, Caleb [ie. Nicholas Amhurst and others], *The Craftsman* (London, 1726–36)

De F. Lord, G. general ed., *Poems on Affairs of State*, vol. ii, ed., E. F. Mengel, Jr. (New Haven, 1965)

Defoe, Daniel, *The Anatomy of Exchange Alley: Or, A System of Stock-Jobbing* . . . (London, 1719)

——, *An Essay on Projects* (London, 1697)

——, *A Tour Thro' the Whole Island of Great Britain*, 4th. edn. (London, 1748)

Desaguliers, J. T., *A Course of Experimental Philosophy* (London, 1736)

Donne, John, *The Pseudo-Martyr* (London, 1610)

Dryden, John, *Poems*, ed. James Kinsley (Oxford, 1958)

——, *Works*, ed. Walter Scott (London, 1808)

——, *Letters*, ed. C. E. Ward (Durham, North Carolina, 1942)

Ellis, G. A., ed., *The Ellis Correspondence* (London, 1829)

Evelyn, John, *The Diary of John Evelyn*, ed. E. S. de Beer (Oxford, 1955)

Evelyn, John, tr., Roland Freart, *A Parallel of The Antient Architecture with the Modern* . . . (London, 1664) [Evelyn's dedications]

Fielding, Henry, *The History of Joseph Andrews*, ed. M. C. Battestin (Oxford, 1967)

——, *Works* . . ., ed. Arthur Murphy (London, 1762)

——, *The Complete Works*, ed. W. E. Henley (London, 1903; reprinted 1967)

Freart, Roland, *A Parallel of the Antient Architecture with the Modern* . . ., tr. John Evelyn (London, 1664)

Gay, John, *The Beggar's Opera*, ed. E. V. Roberts (London, 1969)

The General Account of all Monies and Effects Received and Expended By the Trustees for . . . *Georgia* (London, 1733)

The Gentleman's Magazine . . . (London, 1732–1921)

Graves, Richard, *The Triflers* (London, 1806)

Hall, Joseph, *Poems*, ed. Arnold Davenport (Liverpool, 1949; reprinted 1969)

Hanbury Williams, Sir Charles, *Works* (London, 1832)

Hearne, Thomas, *Reliquiae Hearniae*, ed. Philip Bliss (London, 1869)

Herrick, Robert, *Poetical Works*, ed. L. C. Martin (Oxford, 1956)

Historical Manuscripts Commission, 19 (Towneshend)

——, 29 (Portland), vols. ii, v, vii

——, 56 (Stuart), vols. i–ii, vi

Horace (Quintus Horatius Flaccus), *Opera*, Interpretatione, Notis & Indice illustravit Ludovicus Desprez (Amsterdam, 1695). This was one of the editions of Horace in Pope's library.

Johnson, Samuel, *Lives of the English Poets*, ed. G. Birkbeck Hill (Oxford, 1905)

Johnson, Samuel, ed., *The Works of the English Poets* (London, 1779–81)

Jonson, Ben, *Ben Jonson*, ed. C. H. Herford and Percy and Evelyn Simpson (Oxford, 1925–52)

Kennett, White, Bishop of Peterborough, *The Case of Impropriations* . . . (London, 1704)

Kettlewell, John, *A Compleat Collection of the Works* . . . [including a life of the author] (London, 1719)

King, Gregory, 'Natural and Political Observations and Conclusions on the State and Condition of England' (1697); *Two Tracts*, ed. G. E. Barnett (Baltimore, 1936)

Journals of the House of Lords, vol. xxii (1722–6)

Luttrell, Narcissus, *A Brief Historical Relation of State Affairs* . . . (Oxford, 1957)

Macpherson, James, ed., *Original Papers Containing the Secret History of Great Britain* (London, 1775)

Marvell, Andrew, *The Poems and Letters*, ed. H. M. Margoliouth, 2nd. edn. (Oxford, 1952)

Murphy, Arthur, ed., *The Works of Henry Fielding, Esq.* (London, 1762) [his 'Essay on the Life and Genius of Henry Fielding, Esq.' in vol. i]

Ogilvie, A. M., ed., *Ralph Allen's Posts* (London, 1897)

Palladio, Andrea, *Andrea Palladio's Five Orders of Architecture Translated and Revised by Colen Campbell* (London, 1729)

——, *I Quatro Libri Dell' Architettvra* . . . (Venice, 1570)

Pope, Alexander, *The Works of Alexander Pope*, ed. William Warburton

(London, 1751)

——, *The Works of Alexander Pope*, ed. Joseph Warton (London, 1797)

——, *The Twickenham Edition of the Poems of Alexander Pope*, general ed. John Butt (London, 1939–67)

——, *Pope's Epistle to Bathurst: A Critical Reading with an Edition of the Manuscripts*, ed. E. R. Wasserman (Baltimore, 1960)

——, *Horatian Satires and Epistles*, ed. Howard Erskine-Hill (Oxford, 1964)

——, *Poetical Works*, ed. Herbert Davis (London, 1966)

——, *Letters of Mr. Pope, and Several Eminent Persons* . . . (London, 1735)

——, *The Correspondence of Alexander Pope*, ed. George Sherburn (Oxford, 1956)

Russell, Lady Rachel, *The Letters* . . ., ed. T. Sellwood (London, 1773)

St. John, Henry, first Viscount Bolingbroke, *Works* (London, 1754)

Sheridan, Thomas, 'An Historical Account of Some Remarkable Matters . . .' (*c.* 1702), HMC 56 (Stuart), vol. vi

Smallbroke, R., *Some Account of* . . . *Dr. Hough* (London, 1743)

Spence, Joseph, *Observations, Anecdotes, and Characters of Books and Men*, ed. J. M. Osborn (Oxford, 1966)

——, *Anecdotes, Observations and Characters of Books and Men*, ed. S. W. Singer (London, 1820)

Swift, Jonathan, *Prose Works*, ed. Herbert Davis (Oxford, 1939–62)

——, *The Poems of Jonathan Swift*, ed. Sir Harold Williams (Oxford, 1937)

——, *The Correspondence of Jonathan Swift*, ed. Sir Harold Williams (Oxford, 1963–5)

Toland, John, *A Collection of Several Pieces* . . . (London, 1726) [containing 'The Secret History of the South Sea Scheme']

Vanbrugh, Sir John, *The Complete Works*, ed. Bonamy Dobrée and Geoffrey Webb (London, 1927–8)

Vasari, Georgio, *The Lives of the Painters, Sculptors and Architects*, tr. A. B. Hinds, intro. William Gaunt, revised edn. (London, 1963)

——, *Vite De Piu Eccellenti Architetti, Pittori et Sculptori Italiani* . . . (Florence, 1550)

Vitruvius, M. Pollio, *De Architectvra* (Venice, 1567)

Warburton, William, *A Critical and Philosophical Commentary on Mr. Pope's Essay on Man* (London, 1740)

Warton, Joseph, *An Essay on the Genius and Writings of Pope* (London, 1756–82)

Whiston, William, *Memoirs of His Life and Writings* (London, 1749–50)

——, *An Historical Preface to Primitive Christianity Reviv'd* . . . (London, 1711)

Wood, John, *An Essay Towards a Description of Bath*, 2nd. edn. (London, 1749)

Wotton, Sir Henry, *The Elements of Architecture* (London, 1624)

INDEX